Spirit Possession
and Popular Religion

Spirit Possession and Popular Religion

From the Camisards to the Shakers

CLARKE GARRETT

The Johns Hopkins University Press
Baltimore and London

TO HENRY J. YOUNG

© 1987 The Johns Hopkins University Press
All rights reserved
Printed in the United States of America

The Johns Hopkins University Press
701 West 40th Street
Baltimore, Maryland 21211
The Johns Hopkins Press Ltd., London

LIBRARY OF CONGRESS CATALOGING-IN-PUBLICATION DATA

Garrett, Clarke, 1935–
  Spirit possession and popular religion.
  Bibliography: p.
  Includes index.
  1. Enthusiasm—Religious aspects—Christianity.
2. Spirit possession. 3. Camisards. 4. Shakers. I. Title.
BR112.G37 1987   248.2   86-46284
ISBN 0-8018-3486-4 (alk. paper)

Contents

Preface

This book had two separate origins. An interest in the Shakers was first stimulated, quite a few years ago, by an independent study project that Suzanne Fost Green carried out under my direction. Then, in the 1970s, I incorporated the Shakers into a course on the history of communal societies from the eighteenth century to the present. I was able to try out my ideas on the students in those classes, and to receive in return their insights and perceptions, which helped to sharpen my own.

Meanwhile, a research interest in popular religion that originated in George Mosse's courses at the University of Wisconsin had resulted first in a book on millenarians and the French Revolution, then in a series of articles on European witchcraft. Since witch prosecutions were often triggered by outbreaks of "demonic possession," especially in France, I was led to consider more broadly the question of the relationship between possession and European popular religion. A sabbatical leave in 1976–77 enabled me to pursue the topic into the eighteenth century.

The project finally came into focus in the summer of 1977, thanks to a fellowship at the Huntington Library. Because of the range of their collections, I was able to supplement my work on England and Scotland with an examination of developments on this side of the Atlantic. Above all, I was able to go through the published materials on the eighteenth-century Shakers in a reasonably systematic fashion. The testimonies recorded by dozens of Shakers and former Shakers are an exceptionally rich and varied source for the student of popular religion. They provide fascinating and sometimes deeply moving insights into the religious experience of ordinary people.

The book is about the origins of the Shakers, though only the final four chapters deal specifically with them. This emphasis on the Shakers is justified, I think, by their intrinsic importance both as a religious sect and as the most successful communal society in history.

A grant from the American Philosophical Society made possible a summer's research in London and Manchester. Finally, a fellowship from the American Council on Learned Societies, funded by the National Endowment for the Humanities, together with a sabbatical leave from Dickinson College, made it possible to spend a full year in 1984–85 working on the book.

Among the many libraries that have extended their hospitality over the years, I owe special debts of gratitude to the staffs of the Trask Library at Andover Newton Seminary, the Winterthur Library, in Wilmington, Delaware, the Shaker archives at Canterbury and Sabbathday Lake, the Moravian Archives in London, and the John Rylands Library in Manchester. The help of Karen Dyson, formerly interlibrary loan librarian at Dickinson, was indispensable.

An earlier version of portions of the introduction and first chapter was published in *Popular Traditions and Learned Culture in France from the Sixteenth to the Twentieth Century* (Saratoga, Calif.: Anma Libri, 1985). I am grateful to the editor, Marc Bertrand, for permission to use it here.

Among colleagues in the field of popular religion, I have benefited from the comments and suggestions of Robert Glen, Jim Hopkins, the late Theodore Johnson, Steve Marini, Bruce Lincoln, and especially Jon Butler and Mike Zuckerman. Rosemary Ciccarelli, Amy G. McCoy, and O. F. Davenport read the entire manuscript, and I am grateful for their continued encouragement. Like everyone who studies popular religion, I owe a special debt to Natalie Z. Davis. Her own writings are models of style and perception. In addition, for more than ten years, she has been generous with ideas and assistance on many occasions.

At Dickinson, I thank Noel Potter, Bob Winston, Sharon O'Brien, Kim Rogers, Martha Slotten, and Gladys Cashman for their help and advice. I have dedicated the book to my friend and colleague Henry J. Young, who first encouraged me to work in American history. For those of us who treasure the special environment of the liberal arts college, he embodies the ideal of the teacher-scholar.

Once again, I owe special thanks to Peg, my best friend and traveling companion.

Spirit Possession
and Popular Religion

Introduction: Anthropology and History

A long time ago, the great French historian Marc Bloch said that history was retrospective anthropology. Bloch did not live long enough to see his insight taken as seriously as it deserved to be, but in the last decade an increasing number of historians have come to recognize that the theoretical frameworks and methodological approaches of anthropology can provide many perceptions and conceptions that can inform historical materials.

Anthropologists would be quick to point out that they have the great advantage of being able to live with their subjects in the field and to observe them directly, whereas historians are limited to whatever bits and pieces of evidence have happened to be preserved from the past. On the other hand, as anthropologists themselves are coming to recognize, historians have the advantage of being able to use this scattered evidence to discern the processes of change within societies over long periods of time. And since one of the most influential contemporary anthropologists, Victor Turner, has taught that life consists essentially of process, the historians' insight into "the process of process" is good anthropology as well. Shortly before his death, Turner wrote: "I am convinced that social anthropology should intertwine with history, like the snakes on Hermes's staff." Perhaps the day is not very distant when we will say that history and anthropology have converged into a single discipline that takes for its subject the entire course of human social and cultural evolution.[1]

There is a second tendency in contemporary historical and anthropological studies that Marc Bloch would have approved as well. The scholarly study of popular religion, the analysis of the belief systems of ordinary people, is coming to be accepted as a legitimate and autonomous field of historical inquiry, closely related to social and intellectual history but not subordinated to them.

Although the present study traces a single facet of popular religion in the Atlantic civilization of the eighteenth century, its topic is, from an anthropological perspective, universal. Every human society believes that it is possible to reach levels of consciousness that differ from everyday reality. Sometimes the experience of transcendence comes in dreams; sometimes there are rituals of prayer, singing, and dancing that take the participants to a different realm. Sometimes altered consciousness is achieved with the assistance of the ingestion of substances as arcane as sacred mushrooms or as banal as beer. Sometimes the experience of transcending the ordinary world is available to everybody, but often it is limited to the chosen few—priests, shamans, or gurus.

Most cultures also believe that sometimes supernatural spirits take possession of people on earth. The phenomenon is especially dramatic among the adepts of *vodu* in Haiti and *condomblé* and *macumba* in Brazil, and in the phenomena of spirit baptism and speaking in tongues, or glossolalia, it is equally central to the worldwide pentecostal movement and the charismatic movements within the established Christian churches. The remarkable expansion of Pentecostalism within Christianity demonstrates that even today the idea of the immanence of a divine presence that can be sensorily experienced is enormously attractive.[2]

In ancient Greece, when someone was possessed by a god it was called enthusiasm. That would be a satisfactory title for this book; however, since the eighteenth century the term has carried unnecessarily negative connotations of unbridled emotionalism. It is also the title of a brilliant, tendentious, fascinating, and wrongheaded book written by Ronald Knox some thirty years ago. While the book is still worth reading, the author's insistence that religious enthusiasm represents a persistent irrational deviation from the path of orthodoxy is not very useful for a historical understanding of religious developments.

For the past decade or so, anthropologists, psychologists, and some historians have been interested in the varied phenomena that they call spirit possession: an ungainly but useful term that incorporates a wide variety of beliefs and behaviors. When spirit possession takes place during sleep or an ecstatic trance, we call it a vision. When a god (or God) speaks through the mouth of an entranced individual, we call it prophecy. When a god, an ancestor, or a bad spirit takes control of the body of a person, producing behavior that can be bizarre, dramatic, or both, we have a variety of names, one of which is hysteria.

Many observers and critics in seventeenth- and eighteenth-century Europe contended that there was something physically wrong with those who claimed to be possessed by evil spirits or by God (and sometimes by both), but it was only in the late nineteenth century that J. M. Charcot's famous demonstrations in the Salpêtrière Hospital led to the contention that they had all been victims of the ancient malady called hysteria or, as he preferred to call it, neurosis. Late in his career, Charcot himself recognized that hysteria was not a disease in any conventional sense, writing that it was "less a disease than a peculiarly constituted mode of feeling and reaction."[3] Nevertheless, since Charcot the tendency of historians has been to regard those who claimed to be possessed by spirits as hysterics coping with unresolved psychological and psychosexual conflicts.[4]

Similarly, some anthropologists have spent a lot of time asking whether or not the behavior of those people in primitive societies who become ritually possessed is "normal." Are the inspired shamans of Siberian and native American cultures neurotic or marginally deranged individuals whose behavior while in communication with spirits is the closest they can come to reality? On the other hand, are they perfectly sane individuals who perform roles crucial to the social health and ritual of their societies? Further, when entire communities exhibit behavior that they interpret as spirit possession, does it not make nonsense of the term to contend that they are all hysterics?

Other anthropologists have tended to discount psychological explanations entirely, insisting that possession phenomena must be understood solely in a society's own cultural terms, nearly always manifested in some sort of ritualized public performance. The behavior of the possessed, however alien and uncontrolled it may seem to the outside observer, is a form of dramatized communication that can transmit cultural understandings as readily as speech. Mary Douglas has written that "the physical experience of the body . . . sustains a particular view of society." There is "a continual exchange of meanings" between ordinary experience and that which is expressed in possessed behavior, "so that each reinforces the categories of the other."[5]

John A. Grim argued in a recent study that the possessed shamans of Siberia enact in a symbolic and gestural form "a revelatory experience of transcendent reality." While the experience is shaped by the social and psychological facts of existence, the perceptions of mundane reality are shaped in their turn by the messages brought by the shaman or seer. In the form of a ritual performance or religious drama, they embody the culture's conception of the sacred.[6]

Thus an anthropological as against a psychiatric explanation of the phenomena of spirit possession would concentrate on the specific social and cultural contexts in which they took place and on what messages they communicated. Since whatever a culture interprets as spirit possession implies certain assumptions about the ways the divine acts in that culture, the ways in which it is manifested "change with the opinions of the times"; spirit possession "has a history of its own."[7]

It should be added that the psychiatric concept of hysteria has changed substantially since the time of Freud and Janet. Recent studies interpret hysteria in a manner that corresponds closely to the sociocultural interpretations of possession proposed by anthropologists. For some contemporary psychiatrists, hysterical behavior is an act of communication, intended for an audience whose shared values and expectations enable it to interpret the behavior in culturally normative terms. The "language" of possession or hysteria is no longer considered to be limited to private desires and frustrations, as it was for Freud and Janet. It can include all sorts of shared human concerns relating to life, death, and eternity.[8] Thus spirit possession and hysteria become two names for the same thing—a kind of spectacular body language for expressing convictions or emotions too profound, too painful, or too dangerous to be expressed verbally. They differ only in the explanation the specific culture employs to explain the behavior.

It would be fruitful for historians to follow the example of anthropologists and psychiatrists and to consider outbreaks of spirit possession in the past as a kind of theater. All of those possessed individuals whom we have mentioned in passing—visionaries, prophets, shamans, the demon- or spirit-possessed—are "performing roles" in public situations. Their behavior is socially sanctioned. If they did not conduct themselves in culturally expected ways, their claims to have been visited by alien or supernatural beings would not be believed.

When spirit possession spread through the mountains of southeastern France at the end of the seventeenth century, a published account called it "the sacred theater of the Cévennes." In a very real sense all of the possession phenomena that will be examined in this book can likewise be considered as sacred theater: *sacred* because all of them presupposed the descent of divinity into humans as a fulfillment of the biblical scenario of personal salvation and universal regeneration; *theater* because they entailed a cultural interaction between "performers" and "audience." And that is why spirit possession, interpreted as sacred theater, can provide such a priceless resource for historians of popular religion. One can examine and describe the "performance," try to ascertain how it was understood by its audience, and ask what kinds of cultural and theological expectations the performance and its interpretation by the audience implied. All of these facets not only elicit the contexts in which the phenomena of spirit possession occur but also help to recapture the lost world of popular belief.

To say that the possessed are performing culturally determined roles is not to say that they are faking—at least not often. There are too many accounts from too many cultures which insist that the *experience* of divine possession is real, overwhelming, and unforgettable for those who undergo it. Richard Schechner argues that any theatrical performance transports the actor into a realm in which he is "not himself," yet at the same time is "not not himself." It cannot really be described; it can only be experienced.[9]

Belief in spirit possession presupposes, first of all, that there *are* "spirits," inhabitants of some timeless realm, who want and are able to communicate with humankind. The anthropologist Erika Bourguignon argues that if one believes that spirits of this kind exist, then the notion that they can take over the consciousness and behavior of chosen individuals is one of a limited number of possible ways that they might make their presence and their wishes known. It is also the most efficient, because it is the most direct.[10]

For spirit possession to take root in a culture, there are three preconditions. The culture must believe, first, that there are higher spirits who want to communicate with humans; second, that these spirits can bridge the chasm between the finite world and the infinite by means of taking control of the senses, speech, and actions of individuals; and, finally, that a person possessed by a spirit would behave as the people who claim to be possessed behave. I. M. Lewis has written that people "are only 'possessed' when they consider they are, and when other members of their society endorse this claim."[11]

While the behaviors of spirit possession and their interpretation are necessarily shaped to an important degree by the expectations and preconceptions of their social and historical setting, they do have the potential to initiate religious, social, and even political innovation. Any call for innovation that is articulated by those possessed or inspired by spirits would be presumed to have been not simply approved but demanded by divinity.

Moreover, the occasions in which spirit possession take place are those that Victor Turner called "liminal," thresholds to another kind of experience in which the usual conventions and structures break down, if only for an instant. Structure is momentarily overcome by antistructure, and community in all its ordinariness becomes the social and cosmic oneness of *communitas*. Whether the occasion is solemn or joyous, it is a moment of celebration, when "a transcendent ecstasy rooted in deep physiological passions" brings a flash of insight into "the meaning inherent in self and society."[12]

In the Old Testament, God communicates continually with his chosen people by means of possessed prophets. Sometimes, the dramatic access of divinity does generate just this kind of collective transcendence of ordinary experience. During the flight from Egypt, for example, after many of the Jews had begun to question the wisdom of the terrifying adventure that they had undertaken, God commanded Moses to gather seventy of the elders. Then (Numbers 11:25) "the Lord came down in the cloud and spoke to him, and took some of the spirit that was upon him and put it upon the seventy elders; and when the spirit rested upon them, they prophesied."

In the Jewish kingdom, ecstatic possession, ritually induced, was common and accepted. On one occasion (I Samuel 10:5–6), God sent Samuel to go and meet a "band of prophets" who were coming down from the mountains "with harp, tambourine, flute, and lyre before them prophesying." God told Samuel that he too would be overcome "with the spirit of the Lord . . . and be turned into another man."

The prophets whose pronouncements are recorded in the Old

Testament were often constrained by God to declare terrible retributions upon the wayward people of Israel, but they also provided assurance to the Jews that by sending his spirit into them and speaking through them, God demonstrated that he still considered the Jews his special people. For example, he declared through the mouth of Joel: "You shall know that I am in the midst of Israel, and that I, the LORD, am your God and there is none else. And my people shall never again be put to shame." God then proceeded to promise a future time in which his spirit would enter the world even more abundantly: "And it shall come to pass afterward, that I will pour out my spirit on all flesh; your sons and your daughters shall prophesy, your old men shall dream dreams, and your young men shall see visions. Even upon the menservants and maidservants in those days, I will pour out my spirit."

Potentially, the passage could justify a radical restructuring of spiritual priorities. When God "poured out" his spirit, the prophecy implied, the principal agents of his will would not be the established leadership but rather the humblest and most powerless members of the society. From the early Christian church to the present, those who believed themselves to be possessed by the spirit of God have frequently interpreted the experience as the fulfillment of Joel's prophecy.

In most cultures that believe in the possibility of spirit possession, if the spirits are not considered divine, they are morally neutral. In the Judeo-Christian tradition, on the other hand, the latter is a theological impossibility. If the spirits are not God's and good, they must be evil. Jesus on several occasions encountered people possessed by spirits, and he proceeded to confirm the general opinion as to their origin. Once (Mark 5:1–20), when Jesus encountered a possessed man in a cemetery, he functioned as an exorcist, getting the spirits to tell him their name ("Legion"), bargaining with them, and sending them into a herd of unclean swine. From an anthropological perspective, the story illustrates the way in which possession always implies a kind of theatrical interaction between actors and audience who share a repertory of cultural meanings for the behavior.[13]

The New Testament also contains two accounts of spirit possession that introduce important new elements unknown to the Jewish prophetic tradition. On Pentecost, the fiftieth day after the day of Jesus' resurrection, "a sound came from heaven like the rush of a mighty wind" and filled the room in Jerusalem in which the apostles were assembled. Then "they were all filled with the Holy Spirit and began to speak in other tongues, as the Spirit gave them utterance." Peter declared that it was the fulfillment of Joel's prophecy. As Joel had also predicted, he declared, a time in which the "wonders in the heaven above and signs on the earth beneath" would soon commence. It would precede the "day of the Lord," which the early Christians interpreted as the return of Jesus and the end of the world.

New "gifts" of the spirit, of several kinds, spread to other places. The new gifts included not only the power to speak in other tongues and to interpret them but also to heal, to prophesy, and to work miracles.

In his first letter to the Greek converts in Corinth (I Corinthians 12), Paul expressed some reservations about the new phenomena. Like all the early Christians, he rejoiced in these manifestations of divine power, especially that of prophecy. He predicted, however, that all of these gifts would soon "pass away." The Christians of Corinth should therefore not let any of these wonders divert them from their real calling: to build up the structures of the church and to live in love and charity with one another. While Paul could hardly repudiate the general belief that Jesus' return and Christianity's triumph was imminent, he thus encouraged the faithful to concentrate instead on the building of structures and the careful ordering of religion and society. The possibility remained, however, that God would initiate a time like that of Pentecost or Joel's prophecy, when the guidance of the Holy Spirit might sanction the renovation, even the transformation of church and society.[14]

We hear nothing further concerning spirit possession in the early church for another century, but then there occurred a remarkable outbreak in the remote province of Phrygia, in Asia Minor. It was a period of enormous difficulty for the Christians, because after several decades of tacit toleration, the Roman government had resumed the active persecution.

Phrygia had long been a center of the Greek mystery cults, notably the ecstatic cult of the mother goddess Cybele. In about the year 170, a recent convert named Montanus, who (according to the historian Eusebius) had been a priest of Cybele, began to go into convulsions. Then, in a trance, he made pronouncements that his followers believed came directly from the Holy Spirit. In one of his prophetic utterances that has been preserved, the Holy Spirit described the experience of possession in strikingly poetic terms: "Behold, the human is as a lyre, and I rush on him as a plectrum. The human sleeps and I keep awake. Behold the one who is ecstatically changing the hearts of humans and giving to humans [new] hearts is the Lord."[15]

Montanus and his chief associates, two women named Priscilla and Maximilla, declared that the promised Second Coming was at hand. Priscilla announced that Jesus had come to her in a vision and told her that the New Jerusalem was about to descend near the village of Pepuza. Thousands of people are said to have gathered there to await the event.

Despite the failure of that prediction to come true, the Montanists' revelations and their practices of spirit possession spread through much of Asia and into North Africa. They also began to record, copy, and circulate the prophetic utterances of their members, which they believed augmented or even superseded the Scriptures. Like many groups that appeared in later centuries, they saw themselves as a divinely chosen elite, called to restore Christianity to the simplicity and purity of its first years. Also like many later groups, they tended to question the legitimacy of ordinary social institutions such as marriage and to live lives of rigorous austerity.[16]

The Catholic hierarchy quickly repudiated the Montanists, condemning especially the fact that they called on all Christians to seek martyrdom (and thus hasten the Second Coming) by going to the Roman authorities and publicly confessing their faith. The sect survived nonetheless for several centuries, creating its own priesthood and prophetic hierarchy. Since nearly all of their writings were destroyed, most of what we know about them comes from what their opponents said about them. Roman Catholics have tended to see them as heretical or schismatic deviants who were led by the belief that the Holy Spirit resided in and spoke through them into fanaticism and indiscipline. On the other hand, some Protestants, including John Wesley and many present-day Pentecostals, have instead considered them to be the last charismatic remnant of primitive Christianity before it was overwhelmed by the cold ritualism of Catholic orthodoxy. In any case, the Montanists' encounters with the Holy Spirit and their incorporation of spirit possession into a broader message of divine immanence, millenarianism, and the reordering of moral and social priorities represents the first appearance of a pattern that was to appear with some frequency over the centuries.

It would be misleading to trace the course of spirit possession in Christianity any further. There is really no evidence that Montanism established a persistent tradition of spirit possession or irrationalism in Christendom. Instead, later similar movements can better be understood anthropologically, as a recurring phenomenon, a capacity or potential that is humanly universal. Whenever and wherever it occurs, the cultural and psychological origins of spirit possession are rooted in specific social and historical contexts. Among Christians, the earlier occurrences, especially those recorded in Acts and the Epistles, provided an explanatory framework and legitimizing precedents. Moreover, since spirit possession is a kind of theater, communicating the experience of the sacred through culturally comprehensible words and gestures to the believing community, it is in one sense a "learned" behavior that can be transmitted from one group to another, just as the phenomena of prophecy and ecstatic trance spread through the churches in the first century of Christianity.

In the seventeenth century, the rivalry of Protestants and Catholics generated profound religious excitement and anxiety in many parts of Europe. In an era of continual warfare in which all the wars were religious wars and the Millennium seemed to be at hand, spirit possession manifested itself in many forms, some of which we shall encounter in later chapters. In some places, possession by demons occasionally reached epidemic proportions, and the testimony of the possessed was taken to be evidence that God and Satan were manifesting themselves in a climactic time in the world's history. Others—saints, mystics, God-possessed sectarians of the radical fringe—declared instead that history had been transcended in the revelations accessible to those to whom God had chosen to reveal himself. In the decades after 1650, as Europe sorted itself out religiously and politically, these phenomena faded or disappeared, but they were not forgotten.

For reasons that will be explored in the chapters that follow, the eighteenth century witnessed possibly the greatest extent and diversity of episodes of spirit possession since the early Church. Prophecy, visions, and ecstatic trances visited the Jews and Moslems of southeastern Europe, and among the French Jansenists the ecstatics known as the Convulsionaries introduced a remarkable and bizarre repertory of behaviors which, despite persecution, persisted through most of the century.

These movements were part of a general religious awakening that spread through much of continental Europe north of the Alps between the late seventeenth century and the 1740s. It affected all of the British Isles and England's American colonies as well. Most of the time, the clergy were able to control the phenomena of spirit possession by defining what did and did not constitute suitable religious behavior, but sometimes the intensity of religious experience persuaded some that God was inaugurating the promised time of cultural innovation in which the instructions of the Holy Spirit had superseded the institutions and structures of formal religion.

One catalyst for renewed religious excitement was an outbreak of spirit possession among Protestant peasants and artisans living in the remote valleys of the Cévennes Mountains of southeastern France at the end of the seventeenth century. For nearly a decade, trance, miracles, and prophecy spread through an entire population, climaxing in a doomed rebellion by Protestant militants who called themselves Camisards against the forces of Louis XIV. The Camisard Revolt aroused considerable sympathetic interest among Protestants elsewhere, who saw in it the affirmation of the zeal that they believed their own ancestors had once embodied. After the Camisards' defeat, many of the rebels, together with their prophets, joined the thousands of Huguenot exiles living in Protestant territories on the continent and in England. Despite general indifference and occasional persecution, the prophetic message and possessed practices persisted, especially in England and Germany. Finally, in a form that the Huguenots themselves would probably not have recognized, a dozen English ecstatics who in their native Manchester had been known as Shakers brought Huguenot spirit possession to America in 1774.

In New England, the peculiar practices and cosmic pretensions that had been received with contempt in England won for the Shakers a large body of converts, New Light Puritans who had broken away from the settled Congregational and Presbyterian churches in order to be led more immediately by the Holy Spirit. By the end of the century, under American leadership, Shakerism had been transformed into a remarkable network of self-sufficient communities, always at the instigation of the Holy Spirit.

By concentrating on the religious "underside" of the sacred

theater of trance and possession, I hope to be able to come closer to comprehending, to a greater degree than would otherwise be possible, how the several eighteenth-century religious awakenings touched the lives of ordinary people. Much of the excitement and urgency of the popular movements that span the century derived from the conviction that God had come among them visibly and immediately, demonstrating the power of divinity and legitimizing new practices and structures as nothing else could have done. Thus trance and possession were not extraneous bits of deviance; they were the very stuff of religious experience.

{1}

Your Sons and Daughters
Shall Prophesy

In 1699, a German mystic named Johannes Kelpius wrote to an inquirer concerning "this late Revolution in Europe . . . which in the Roman Church goes under the Name of Quietism, in the Protestant Church under the Name of Pietism, Chiliasm, and Philadelphianism." Throughout Europe there were "miracles" taking place, he wrote, "by Ecstasies, Revelations, Apparitions, Changings of Minds" and "Paradysical Representations by Voices, Melodies, and Sensations." Something momentous was occurring.[1]

Kelpius was the leader of a small group of religious seekers who were variously known as the Contented of the God-Loving Soul, the Woman in the Wilderness, and the Chapter of Perfection. Part of the remarkably diverse movement of German religious renewal known as Pietism, Kelpius and his associates had crossed the Atlantic and settled along the banks of Wissahickon Creek north of Philadelphia in order to await the Millennium. However eccentric the religious convictions of the Chapter of Perfection may have been, they were representative of a widespread belief among Protestants of their era that God was bringing about a second reformation.

Some of the developments of the later seventeenth century might well have discouraged any such belief. The Thirty Years' War had destroyed, along with a great deal else, any hopes that Protestantism would dominate central Europe. The Peace of Westphalia of 1648, moreover, had confirmed the political and military predominance of Catholic France on the Continent. In the next decades, the German Protestant states were primarily concerned with repairing the devastation and extending their civil authority—there would be no more religious crusades. In England likewise, the Puritans' dream of building a godly "city upon the hill," a new Jerusalem, had ended abruptly with the restoration of the monarchy in 1660. In the profusion of sects that were tolerated under the Commonwealth, individuals had been encouraged to rely entirely on Scripture and the guidance of the Holy Spirit, even when it led them in some odd directions. Now Seekers and Levellers, Grindletonians and Muggletonians, Ranters and Fifth Monarchy Men all faded into obscurity. Only the Quakers persisted, preserving the tradition of the Inner Light.[2]

The Quakers had aided Kelpius's Chapter of Perfection in their voyage to Pennsylvania. So had the most influential of the Pietist groups, led at the University of Halle by Philipp Spener.[3] So had the members of a shadowy international movement known as the Philadelphians.

Like the Quakers, the Philadelphians cultivated a mystical piety based on individual spiritual experience. They too had originated in the gaudy English religious flowering of the 1650s, but like the Chapter of Perfection they were essentially a small circle of intellectuals, not a popular religious movement. After an Anglican clergyman, John Pordage, and his wife received a series of mystical illuminations, a group gathered around them "to wait together and Exercise the Gifts of Prayer, Exhortation, Singing and under a Living Power and Operation of the Holy Spirit." They lived together as a celibate community and awaited a spiritual "new birth" and the advent of the universal mystical church that transcended sects and creeds.[4]

The group's fortunes changed when it was joined in 1674 by a middle-aged widow, Jane Lead. Upon Pordage's death, she became their leader. She began to publish her visions, which combined mystical illuminations with increasingly urgent announcements of an imminent Millennium. The notion of a "philadelphian" religious society derived from her interpretation of Revelation 3:7-13, which predicted that only the church at Philadelphia would survive "the hour of trial which is coming on the whole world before Christ arrived again on earth." When the group began to hold public meetings in London in 1697, they announced that "the *Society* is not a *Church*, but *Preparatory* to the Church of *Philadelphia;* consisting of those who have *Associated* to wait in the Unity of the Spirit for its Glorious Appearance and Manifestation." They wrote a constitution, which among other things declared that in their meetings women were as free as men to declare their own "Experience, Sensation, or Manifestation in the Divine Matters," provided they did so "with all Sobriety and Modesty."[5]

Despite their peculiarities, Jane Lead's visions had some kinship with the ideas concerning religious renewal that were circulating on the Continent, and in the 1690s her writings were translated into both Dutch and German. In Germany, a number of "philadelphian" societies were formed on the model of the one in London. The movement had the support of the noted scholar Johann Wilhelm Petersen and his wife, Johanna von Merlau. In Germany as in England, its aim was to create, in the world's last days, "the spiritual church of re-born Christians, which will spread its message of love to all peoples." It had been a momentous political event in France that had led Petersen and von Merlau to study the book of Revelation and to adopt the Philadelphians' interpretation of it. In 1685, after twenty years of increasing harassment of the Protestant minority, Louis XIV had revoked the Edict of Nantes which had granted them religious toleration. By decree, a proud and vigorous religious culture was abolished after one hundred fifty years.[6]

Considering the Huguenots' militancy during the sixteenth-century Wars of Religion and their willingness in the early seventeenth century to resort to arms in defense of the religious and political rights that Henry IV had granted them in 1598, it is remarkable how docilely they accepted Louis XIV's decision that their religion should cease to exist. At least in their strongholds in the Midi, they had seemed to be expanding their power after 1650. On several occasions when some local dispute divided the Protestants and Catholics of Nîmes, for example, the Protestant consistory was able to call in a crowd of peasants and artisans from the surrounding villages in order to force the Catholics to back down.[7]

These apparent successes were deceptive. In 1660 the Protestants still numbered over 5 percent of the French population, including larger percentages of the social, political, and commercial elites, but even in former strongholds like La Rochelle and Montauban their power and independence had been slowly eroding for two generations, ever since Richelieu had managed to bring about their military defeat and to force substantial modifications of the privileges guaranteed them by the Edict of Nantes. Despite their sporadic continued militancy, the Protestants henceforth were loyal to the government in the last resort, seeing in the crown their sole protection against a hostile Catholic majority.

The Protestants lived dispersed in a broad arc from Normandy to Paris to Burgundy, then south to the Rhône valley and across the south to the Atlantic. Only in the scattered towns and villages of the Cévennes Mountains and in some places on the Languedocian plain were Protestants in the majority. Their dispersion in local and regional pockets across France helps to explain their inability to develop a coherent national response to the crown's increasing pressure. Even before their national synod was abolished in 1659, the Huguenots had tended to be absorbed in their local and provincial interests. They had also lost almost all contact with Protestants outside France. For most seventeenth-century French Protestants, religion was no longer the matter of urgency it had been a century earlier when their ancestors had been struggling for their survival. Not even the fact that on France's eastern and northern borders Roman Catholics and Protestants were engaged in the bitter struggles of the Thirty Years' War seems to have generated much of a response among the Huguenots.

Calvinist doctrine taught submission to earthly authority in all but the most exceptional circumstances, and for Louis XIV's Protestant as for his Catholic subjects, the king was God's earthly representative. Docile, leaderless, absorbed in their local and private concerns, the Protestants were thus utterly at a loss how to respond as it became progressively clear in the 1670s that the king intended to destroy their religion.

The government moved relentlessly against them. They lost the special judicial bodies they had possessed in Guienne, Dauphiny, and Languedoc. They were forbidden to enter the professions or to be masters in most trades. In 1681, the crown began the *dragonnades*. Troops quartered in Protestant homes were officially encouraged to harass and terrorize their hosts. On the flimsiest of excuses, Huguenot schools and temples were closed. Protestants began to leave the country; by the end of the century, over one hundred fifty thousand, perhaps one-fifth of all the Protestants in France, had gone into exile.[8]

The rest were ordered by the government to abjure their faith and become Catholics. While there were some Protestants who contemplated resistance to the royal command, the Huguenot notables and the clergy were nearly unanimous in their insistence that the king's will must be obeyed. Even before Louis formally revoked the Edict of Nantes in October 1685, the overwhelming majority of Protestants had at least nominally accepted Roman Catholicism. Even in the southeast, in towns and villages long dominated by the Huguenots, they yielded without resistance. At Pont-de-Montvert, a village entirely Protestant, 25 people left France and the other 975 became Catholics. In the mainly Protestant village of Lourmarin in Provence, 887 people abjured their faith in three days. In the remote province of Béarn in the Pyrenees, which boasted some of the oldest and proudest Huguenot communities in France, the royal intendant reported that twenty-one thousand of the twenty-two thousand Protestants there had accepted conversion. There were mass abjurations even in bastions of zealous Protestantism like Anduze, Ganges, and St.-Hippolite in the Cévennes. All pastors who did not convert were to leave the kingdom within two weeks. They too obeyed.

The crown had shown a mastery of the judicious use of force and terror that contemporary dictators might well emulate. The presence of regular troops and armed bands of Catholic volunteers plus the memory of the *dragonnades* usually sufficed to compel obedience. The government believed that Protestantism, deprived of its clergy and with its institutional structures destroyed, could not survive. The great majority of Protestant notables agreed, but many Huguenots persuaded themselves that the king had prohibited only the public practice of their faith and not the maintenance of its traditions in private.[9] Calvinism had always encouraged families to gather for services of worship, and these continued in many places.

There were scattered reports of clandestine assemblies that met to hear sermons and sing psalms. Between 1685 and 1689, the government broke up several dozen of them in the southeast and southwest and made numerous arrests. There were also loose networks of lay preachers who risked their lives by meeting secretly with small groups of Protestants and conducting worship services for them. Otherwise, from the point of view of the bureaucrats and Catholic clergy charged with supervising the conduct of the so-called New Converts, Protestantism had all but disappeared in France by 1686.

Yet even as they submitted, there were some among the faithful Protestant remnant who believed that God had already sent them the first signs that theirs was the true faith and that it was destined to triumph. In the summer of 1685, in Béarn, many people heard the singing of psalms coming from the sky. They were the same psalms that had been sung at their services, but the voices were not human. In December, the same miraculous voices were heard in the Cévennes. As in Béarn, the specific psalm tune could occasionally be recognized, and sometimes even the words. One of the psalms that the mysterious voices sang, the fifth, must have seemed especially appropriate: "Hear my cries, my king and my God!"

One woman in the Cévennes wrote to a friend that she was sure that the heavenly singers were "Troops of Angels," sent "for our consolation, to assure us that God has not completely abandoned us, and our deliverance approaches." Another woman recalled hearing those psalms some twenty times, along with many other people. The fact that not everyone heard them proved that the psalms were a message miraculously sent by God. She specifically remembered hearing the Commandments, in the rhymed form that was part of the Huguenot liturgy. She also had recognized Psalm 91, which includes this line: "For he will give his angels charge of you to guard you in all your ways."

An exiled minister wrote to Pierre Jurieu, a Huguenot theologian and propagandist living in Rotterdam, that before he left Languedoc he had heard the psalms in many places. Sometimes he had heard a trumpet as well. "The Trumpet sounds always as if an Army were going to Charge," he wrote. He believed that the trumpet was "a sign of a Cruel War, that will be made in a little time; and that the Harmony comes from the Mouths of Angels, who . . . Thunder out the Praises of God, at a time when these Wretched Men forbid it to Reformed Christians."

Sometimes, when the Protestants assembled at night to await the sound of the angelic voices, they heard nothing. Yet as one judge in the Cévennes noted, even when they were thus disappointed their belief that the wondrous thing had happened before and might happen again was "retarding" the efforts of Catholic missionaries to turn these forced converts into genuine Catholics.[10]

The psalms heard in the air in 1685 are of considerable significance for understanding the subsequent development of Huguenot prophetism. The singing of psalms had always been a central experience of Calvinist worship. In the seventeenth century, services always included at least three. Congregations were supposed to sing through all 150 in order, completing two cycles annually.[11] When they heard those same psalms in the sky, the sound conveyed to the Protestants, in the musical form that belonged to them alone, the assurance that theirs was still the only true faith.

The heavenly psalms also established the precedent for direct divine intervention that was to be manifested again a few years later in the prophetic movement and later still in the armed bands of the Camisards. Throughout the period, visions of angels were to be a continuing feature of ecstatic experience for the Huguenots of the Midi. "The angels are all around me," one prophet cried in 1701, and that same year, just before the entire village of Vallérargues rose up, expelled the priest, and destroyed the Catholic church, an entranced shepherd was heard to cry "that he had seen the angels and the open Heavens." Jacques Dubois of Montpellier recalled having often seen inspired young men and women who, "in the time of their Trances, have their Eyes open, and commonly lifted up to Heaven, who said, that then they saw Armies of Angels, sometimes those of Angels engaged against Armies of Men." Even if God punished them for their sins by permitting the destruction of their temples and tested their faith by letting them be tempted into abjuring it, the faithful few still believed, as a refugee wrote later in London, that "he did send unto them Thousands of Angels to declare unto them the song of their Deliverance."[12]

So they awaited the next demonstration of the divine presence, which like the angelic choirs would affirm the continuity of their faith. It came in the person of the first of the prophets, the fifteen-year-old Isabeau Vincent. For four months in 1688, until she was arrested and placed in a Catholic convent, she in effect conducted Protestant services while lying apparently asleep on a bed in a small mountain cottage. Crowds gathered to hear her recite scriptural passages and prayers from the Psalter, sing psalms, and preach sermons that called for repentance and a return to the Protestant faith. In all of her trances, she assured her hearers that if they persevered, they would be rewarded by the restoration of their religious communities and their own eternal salvation. She cited Joel's prophecy, saying that "it is not at all I who speaks, [it] is the Spirit that is in me[;] these last days your young people will prophesy and your old men will dream dreams."

People wrote down her words, and manuscript copies of them circulated among the Huguenots for many years. It is clear from these reports that her entranced pronouncements were quite orthodox in content and showed considerable familiarity with the Bible and the Huguenot liturgy. Occasional passages indicate that she also knew of Jurieu's writings, which circulated clandestinely throughout France. Jurieu placed the Protestants' sufferings within a millenarian chronology that promised divine intervention when the mystical three and one-half years [Revelation 15:9] had elapsed. Vincent made similar predictions, but they were peripheral to her central message that called on the Protestants to repent their apostasy from the true faith and promised God's blessing if they returned to it.[13]

Throughout the era of Huguenot prophetism, contemporaries were struck by the youth of the spirit-possessed. The fact was especially surprising during the Camisard Revolt, since many of the prophets who presided at worship services and preached the words of the spirit at large outdoor assemblies were too young ever to have attended Protestant services before the Revocation. As with Isabeau Vincent, their familiarity with the traditional texts seemed in itself miraculous.

Often, the prophets condemned the apostasy of their parents' generation. Isabeau Vincent had again set the pattern. She had frequently criticized her father for his cowardice and greed in conforming to Catholicism and for trying to force her to conform as well. In general, however, since the prophets' ceremonies followed the liturgy as prescribed for families, we can assume that it was in family situations that the traditions had been preserved, and in the family services children had always been active participants. Natalie Davis has suggested that the Protestants' own rejection of the shared culture of popular Catholicism and their increasingly precarious situation in seventeenth-century France would have made young Huguenots "less removed from their parents, more alone with their memories, more vulnerable to the prick of the past, more open to the family's future."[14] Their entranced behavior was not simply an adolescent rejection of the authority of their elders, although it was partly that. It was also a way of offering supernatural affirmation of the authority of the elders, despite the elders' own hesitations.

Vincent's influence was considerable. Other young people emulated her, and their pronouncements were often delivered in large outdoor assemblies. Some, like Vincent, preached while "asleep"; they too preached repentance and promised deliverance. One account described an assembly attended by several hundred people, at which two twelve-year-old girls preached and sang psalms. Both claimed that they had had visions of angels who promised "heavenly gifts." The account complained that "they always said the same thing, in a limited range of terms," but it may be that this repetition of a few themes explains prophetism's effectiveness in evoking the essence of Protestant piety for over twenty years. The refugees whose testimonies were collected and published in London in 1707 reported similar messages calling for repentance and promising divine consolation. One refugee said of the prophets he had heard that "their Exhortations to Repentance were urgent, and they assured that God would shortly destroy Babylon and reestablish his Church." Another described assemblies attended by several hundred people in 1701 at which "the common Subjects of the inspired were, to urge Repentance and to predict the ruins of Antichrist, and the Delivrance of the Church."[15]

Not surprisingly, trance preaching has been a distinctively Protestant form of spirit possession. Moreover, since the Reformation, wherever trance preachers appeared they were almost always women. Apparently the early Church at Corinth allowed women to preach, because Saint Paul specifically attacked the practice in his letter of warning against their ecstatic excesses. Since that time, with the exception of the Quakers and a few other sects, whenever women did preach they generally did so in trance or "asleep." They appeared occasionally in sixteenth-century Germany, and then more frequently during the chaos and religious upheavals of the Thirty Years' War. In the eighteenth century, a few English Methodist women preached in trance. They have been a feature of popular religion in Finland and Sweden since a revival in the 1760s brought trances, visions, and possessed behavior to whole villages. Like Isabeau Vincent, a few of the Finnish "sleeping preachers" had their pronouncements recorded and circulated among the faithful.

Like the spirit possessed in any culture, the trance preachers conformed in every case to the patterns and conventions of preaching, whether Huguenot, Methodist, Lutheran, or Mennonite. Equally importantly, in every case the sleeping preachers' entranced performances conformed to the religious presuppositions of their culture. Without in any way suggesting that they were frauds or that they were not absolutely convinced of the genuineness of their "gift," at the same time we can say that they were actors, performing the principal role in a distinctive kind of religious drama. Only as passive instruments of a higher power could they circumvent their own and their communities' reluctance to sanction their trespassing on the male role of preacher.[16]

For the Huguenot peasants of Dauphiny, the experience of having participated in the performances of sacred theater in which Isabeau Vincent or the other young prophets spoke the familiar words of scripture and liturgy while "asleep" was qualitatively different from reading them in private. To those who gathered around the prophets, their performances were deeply affecting because they were both miraculous and expected.

In any analysis of the popular religion of the Protestants of the Midi at the end of the seventeenth century, convenient distinctions between written and oral culture break down. Their written culture was based primarily on two books, the Bible and the Psalter. Some copies of both texts survived the government's efforts at their suppression, and in addition an extensive pious literature, either reprinted from sixteenth-century works or written for the present situation by exiled pastors and teachers like Pierre Jurieu, circulated clandestinely. The letters and sermons of the lay preacher Claude Brousson also circulated. Although he never participated in the prophetic movement, Brousson's writings were similar in their emotional calls for repentance and their insistence that the Protestants must repudiate the "modern Babylon" of Catholicism if they and the world were to experience spiritual regeneration. There is much evidence, however, that in the decades after the Revocation the traditions and doctrines of the faith were preserved primarily by memory and transmitted orally in sermons delivered by laymen, in the singing of the psalms, and in the teaching of the catechism at home.[17]

Books were more important in the mental world of Protestants than of Catholics in the seventeenth century, but a recent study found that in three dioceses in Languedoc there was no difference in the rate of literacy between Catholics and Protestants. In both groups, about half of the male artisans were literate. The percentage of literate agricultural laborers was much lower, and the percentage of literate women in all social classes, Protestant and Catholic alike, was lower still. Only in the eighteenth century, when prophetism was at an end, did Protestant literacy begin to rise dramatically. It rose in part as a result of Languedoc's remarkable industrial development, especially in the manufacture of textiles; it also rose, ironically, because of the crown's intensive effort to turn the Huguenots into good Catholics through enforced schooling.

In much of Languedoc and the Cévennes, Huguenots were still mainly peasants making a bare living or artisans who worked in textile and leather trades. They were the descendants of the peasants and artisans who had given the Protestantism of the region its distinctive character since the sixteenth century. It may well be that these Huguenots were indifferent to literacy, however central the divine word might be to their worship, because they saw no practical advantages in knowing how to read and write. It may indeed have been precisely because their cultural environment was still oral and their popular religious traditions comparatively flexible and informal that the Huguenot faith could persist in the villages and agro-towns of Languedoc and the Cévennes as it did nowhere else.[18]

Among the Protestants of southeastern France, the preaching, psalm singing, and Bible reading that the little prophets now performed in trance were not the only facets of Huguenot religious experience. The flexible, emotional, and sensory world of popular religion had been transformed by their conversion to Calvinism, but it had not disappeared. The Huguenot peasants and artisans needed daily ceremonies of identity and assurance and rituals of communal solidarity as much as did their Catholic neighbors. Robert Kreiser's description of the character of popular Catholicism in the same era fits the Protestants as well. Both communities needed "to maintain their religion of symbols, gestures and actions—a religion of tactile, visual, and aural experiences and sensations."

Protestant worship is more word-centered than is Catholic and orthodox worship, but there are comparatively few restrictions on how those words are to be presented. With the Reformation, sacred space lost its specificity, since the word might be read, heard, sung, or experienced inwardly anywhere. Preaching and the singing of psalms could take place as readily outdoors as in. In every case, it was a kind of performance, which had the potential of embodying "gesture, dance, patterned movement through space," as Daniel W. Patterson has written. As a kind of Protestant sacred theater, the clandestine outdoor meetings of the Huguenots resembled the great outdoor revival assemblies of eighteenth- and nineteenth-century America. One back-country preacher wrote of the setting of a camp meeting that "it was like a theater. It was a theater in the open air, on the green sward, beneath the starry blue, incomparably more picturesque than any stage scenery."[19]

The power of words lies in part in their repetition, and a kind of magical efficacy could be associated just as readily with the naive and familiar promises communicated by the prophets as with the equally naive and familiar prayers of the rural Catholic world, derived from similar scriptural and liturgical materials. The popular culture of peasants and artisans in the Midi, both Catholics and Protestants, was a culture primarily oral, in which (as Walter J. Ong has written) language is "'really' sound" and "texts must be recycled back through sound to have meaning." Oral communiation is more "an invitation to participation" than a "transfer of knowledge." It is *necessarily* stereotyped. Conceptions must be presented as formulas and commonplaces in order to be remembered.[20]

The speech that Protestant peasants of the Midi used in their daily life was the same local dialect that their Catholic neighbors used. But the fact that the language of their sermons, prayers, and psalms was French gave to all of their sacred occasions, wherever they might take place, a distinction that set them apart. Huguenot self-identity also rested on their rejection of the symbols and practices of Catholic culture. They had denounced as popish superstitions the image of the cross, the practice of abstaining from eating meat on Fridays, and the ceremony of the Mass and the objects associated with it. This became a constant theme in the pronouncements of the young prophets from 1688 onwards. Isabeau Vincent declared that going to Mass was "a great sin, and a mortal sin." One of the London refugees testified that after he had heard the young prophets he "found a perfect Abhorrence of the Train of Publick Worship among the Papists, and all the Pageantry of the Mass which delighted me before; I could hardly look upon their Churches without shivering." Yet attendance at Mass was clearly expected of the New Converts, and from 1685 onwards, the French Catholic church made a great effort to inculcate its doctrines and usages through preaching, establishing schools, and publishing and circulating tens of thousands of missals and catechisms in the formerly Protestant regions.[21]

Certainly the most distinctive feature of the Huguenots' popular religion as against that of their Roman Catholic neighbors was its concentration upon the word—the spoken word—as the means of communication of spiritual matters. In his preface to the 1543 Psalter, Calvin had contended that while other music was unsuitable for worship services, the singing of the psalms was divinely ordained. They had been dictated to David by the Holy Spirit, and singing their words engaged not only "the heart and the affection" but "the intelligence" as well. He also insisted that the words must be sung clearly and in a language that was comprehensible to the worshipers. In his views on language, Calvin was following the teaching of Saint Paul, who had told the Corinthians that when they spoke in tongues their minds were left "unfruitful" (I Corinthians 12:14). Isabeau Vincent was within the same tradition when she told her hearers that when the Catholics prayed in an alien language they were going against God's command.[22]

Huguenot prophetism demonstrated the persistence of Huguenot popular religiosity, transformed and ritualized into a sacred theater that enacted God's direct intervention in the lives of his oppressed people. Like all spirit possession, it was essentially a public phenomenon, performed for an audience. Whether there were a few gathered in a private home or hundreds assembled in a field or on a mountain top, prophetism provided the occasion, in a flexible and informal fashion, for the preservation of the rites, doctrines, and religious structures of earlier times.

From their first manifestation in Dauphiny and the Vivarais in 1688, the expressive and ritualistic core of the ceremonies conducted by the young prophets corresponded closely to the traditions of Huguenot worship. In a very real sense, prophetism represented a return to the early days of Calvinism, when armed crowds assembled to pray, to hear a sermon by someone who presented himself as a preacher, and to sing the psalms. Phyllis Crews's description of an assembly in the Netherlands in the 1560s would fit the prophetic assemblies just as well. It was "essentially a socializing experience. . . . The general atmosphere was informal, even festive." Although time, prosperity, and the increasing dominance of the pastors had obscured the fact, Calvinism had always permitted wide variations in services of worship. The presence of ordained clergy had never been deemed essential for some combination of prayer, preaching, and singing to take place. Throughout the seventeenth century, synods had encouraged informal services conducted by laymen, especially in the home.[23]

When the prophetic movement spread across the Rhône into the Vivarais at the beginning of 1689, there began the phenomena of shaking, falling, and convulsive gasping that would henceforth accompany the pronouncements of the spirit. There really is no satisfactory explanation for their introduction. Hillel Schwartz may be correct in suggesting that the physically more dramatic possessions were associated with the hopes aroused by the circulation of Jurieu's writings contending that both the prophetic book of Daniel and the Revelation of Saint John the Divine indicated that God was going to bring about the restoration of French Protestantism in that year.

It should be borne in mind that such spectacular behavior is typical of spirit possession worldwide. Similar behavior appeared equally unexpectedly among the Jansenist faithful in the cemetery of Saint Médard in 1731. Among those Parisian Catholics, the convulsions had been preceded not by entranced preaching but by miracles of healing at the tomb of the saintly François de Pâris. Just as convulsions and contortions henceforth preceded and sometimes accompanied the preaching of the Huguenot prophets, violent bodily agitations accompanied the miraculous cures that continued to take place at Saint Médard.[24]

Thus the body language of spirit possession began to supplement entranced speech. Preaching continued to be central, but as prophetism spread from village to village, it tended to consist more frequently of emotional calls for repentance, together with predictions of further divine interventions in human affairs. Sometimes the prophecies named a human deliverer whom God would send to their aid. Some insisted that Louis XIV himself would repudiate his wicked advisers and restore their religion, but the person most frequently mentioned was Jurieu's political patron, William of Orange, now King of England. One female prophet saw him in a vision, transported through the sky to France by an angel, accompanied by one hundred thousand soldiers. Another prophet predicted that a bloody battle would soon be fought near Lausanne in Switzerland and that "deliverance is coming, and . . . at Easter we will be able to take [Protestant] communion."[25]

The first of the new type of prophet was a young man named Gabriel Astier, who traveled through the mountains and valleys of the Vivarais in January and February of 1689. At a typical assembly, after beginning to speak, Astier would fall to the ground and be carried to a bed. After he had experienced some convulsions, he would start to preach, with his audience gathered around him on their knees. According to Bishop Fléchier of Nîmes, his sermons were "always the same in substance." He called on the assembly to do penitence and to "cry for God's mercy." He announced that "the Judgment of God" was going to come in three months. Like Isabeau Vincent, he urged his hearers not to attend the Catholic Mass, which was "abominable before God." At the conclusion, he would be helped to rise from the bed. After singing some psalms, he embraced each person, breathing upon them and saying, "Go, my brother, go my sister, I give to you the Holy Spirit."[26] He was emulating the conduct of Jesus, as described in the gospel of John (20:22–23): "He breathed on them, and said to them, 'Receive the Holy Spirit. If you forgive the sins of any, they are forgiven; if you retain the sins of any, they are retained.'"

As Astier moved from village to village, the prophetic assemblies spread through the region. At a meeting at Bressac, a young girl beat her hands against her head and cried loudly: "Mercy, do penitence, the Judgment of God will come in three months." When the village priest, who had attended the assembly, told her that she had sinned and was damned, she went into convulsions and insisted that she had received the Holy Spirit "as big as a grain of wheat." At another gathering, when a local seigneur tried to persuade the people to disperse, the young prophets instead embraced him and attempted to give him the gift of the Holy Spirit. After singing some psalms, two of the prophets suddenly fell to the ground. After being helped to their feet, one of them cried, in ecstasy, "I see the Heavens opened. O, how lovely the Angels are." Two other prophets described similar visions, and then the entire assembly (according to Fléchier) "fell . . . on their backs and remained as if dead without action & without movement." After they revived, there were prayers, more psalms, and then a joyous procession. Then one of the female prophets fell to the ground, beating her breast, and said that "the Holy Spirit tormented her" because a woman from a nearby village had gone to Mass. Another girl said the Holy Spirit was at the end of her finger, and a third predicted that before Easter a "blue, red & black fire" would descend from the sky. The culmination of these assemblies was always a general feeling of emotional catharsis, often accompanied by the announcement that the angels were all around them.

The mood of confidence in their imminent deliverance from oppression that the ecstasies of the prophets encouraged led the Protestants of the Vivarais to abandon all caution. They began holding large meetings during the day, preceded and followed by festive processions. On one occasion, when troops tried to break up an assembly, the crowd drove them off, killing a captain and nine of his soldiers with rocks.

The angels did not in fact protect the faithful. Instead, the culmination of the government's savage repression of the prophetic movement came on 19 February 1689, when troops confronted a large assembly at a place called le Serre de la Palle. The crowd was told to disperse, but they refused. One of the prophets assured the faithful that they would be protected from harm by a multitude of angels "white as snow and tiny as a finger." The troops opened fire, killing some three hundred people. The disaster did not discredit the prophets, but there were no more revelations of miraculous divine intervention. Instead, when the Huguenots of the Midi again resisted royal authority, they did so with the realization that they might well suffer martyrdom for the holy cause.[27]

For a decade, the prophetic movement went underground. Several of the London refugees testified that they had attended clandestine assemblies in the 1690s led by entranced prophets, and the most famous of the lay preachers who traversed the countryside, Claude Brousson, recorded several meetings with them. After visiting one of their assemblies in 1697, he wrote to his wife that he had witnessed "great marvels, which will be the subject of admiration of all the earth." In responding to one correspondent's criticisms of the prophets, Brousson contended instead that "the manner in which these people prophesy is miraculous."[28]

Then prophetism reemerged in the open, this time in Lower Languedoc and the Cévennes. In much of Languedoc, the mountains and the lowlands are like two different worlds, but here the presence of numerous valleys running down into the lowlands meant that populations and ideas circulated readily. There had been assemblies to the north in the Vivarais the previous summer at which both prophets and lay preachers took part. Then the prophets began to move south. By the beginning of 1701, entire communities had caught the spirit of the prophets.

Some of the young men and women who brought the gift of the

Holy Spirit to the lowlands were agricultural laborers from the mountains, who had come down to work in the fields as they did every year. They arrived at an especially opportune time. The intendant, Nicolas Bâville, had succeeded in capturing or forcing into exile all the lay preachers. He had also begun a campaign, in close cooperation with the Catholic clergy, to force the New Converts to conform fully to the usages and discipline of Roman Catholicism. Meanwhile, the Protestant military coalition led by William of Orange had made peace with France without even raising the question of the Huguenots. The older generation feared that time and the more rigorous royal efforts to enforce conformity would mean that their children would grow up with no memory of the true faith. Once again, it seemed that only God himself could save their religion, and the prophets brought the message that he still cared enough about them to send his angels and his Holy Spirit.

The movement spread with astonishing swiftness, generally among adolescents who could have had only the dimmest memories of the public celebration of the Protestant faith. An example was a young man named David Arnaud, who was seized by the spirit while sitting with several others. Asked what was wrong, he replied that he had received "what came from the living God." When the Catholic prior came and chastized him, Arnaud declared that he spoke "with the voice of the Eternal," and therefore he feared nothing at all. Bâville condemned him to death, hoping that by making an example of him, others would be made wary of listening to the prophets, but in the new atmosphere of desperation, martyrdom was beginning to have a certain attraction.[29]

In June 1701, the prophets for the first time incited a crowd to acts of violence against the hated symbols of Catholicism. The site was the village of Vallérargues, where for more than a week boys and girls had been assembling to pray for the descent of the Holy Spirit. The local prior raided one farmhouse and found a dozen girls gathered around the bed of a young woman who was exhorting them to repent, while upstairs a second group was listening to another prophet. A few days later, the priest encountered a crowd of women in the street, gathered around a young shepherd who, while "making grimaces and contortions," declared "that he had seen the angels and the open Heavens" and had received the Holy Spirit. Several priests grabbed him and tied him to a tree, but he escaped.

The local authorities decided that they needed to report all of this, but when they went to the notary's son, a man named Jacques Bouton, in order to get some official paper, Bouton too became possessed, crying God's judgments upon them. When they and the priests tried to seize him, a crowd of women and boys began pelting them with stones. They released their prisoner, who then proceeded to lead the crowd to the Catholic church. They broke down the doors, demolished the altar, broke the crucifix, and threw the ornaments used in the Mass into a sewer. They then entered the prior's house and destroyed books and statuary.[30]

As prophetism spread through Lower Languedoc and into the Cévennes, the violence on both sides increased rapidly, turning in 1702 into full-scale rebellion. We also hear more stories of miraculous occurrences—infants preaching from their cribs, prophets weeping tears of blood or walking on fire—but in all the accounts the ritualized ceremonies of repentance, the promises of God's redemption of his people, and the prayers and psalms continued to be within the tradition of Huguenot worship.

The pattern of violence that accompanied the Camisard Revolt had existed for several centuries before the prophets first appeared, and it would recur long after they had faded away. The Protestants could be savage, but theirs were generally the "rites of violence" that continued to have religious resonances, like the crowd actions of their ancestors during the Wars of Religion.[31] Much of the Protestants' violence had always been directed against the physical manifestations of the Catholic worship they deplored. During their abortive revolt in 1621–22, for example, Protestants at Margueritttes had staged a sacrilegious procession, saying mock litanies and chanting obscene songs, before they sacked the town. As recently as 1683, even as the Huguenot leadership counseled full obedience to the crown, crowds in both Nîmes and St.-Hippolite had attacked Catholic processions and desecrated the sacrament.[32]

During the Camisard Revolt, iconoclasm was another kind of sacred theater that preserved the memory of the Wars of Religion. The people of Vallérargues had systematically destroyed all vestiges of Catholicism in their village, and now similar rituals became regular occurrences. In 1702, the bishop of Alais reported that Protestants had pillaged four churches, breaking the images. They also had burned the rectory next door, "without however any violence to the person of the priests." When in 1703 "Colonel" Jean Cavalier's army occupied Aubais, most of the Catholics fled to the mountains. The Protestants proceeded to burn the church and sack the presbytery, rendering the sacramental vessels "broken and profaned." Then they went into the countryside and tore down ten rural crosses.[33]

Possessed prophets were involved in all of these episodes, providing a divine sanction for vengeance against the enemies of God which was a continuing theme of the Old Testament prophecies and psalms from which they drew their inspiration. People were murdered by the Camisards, sometimes horribly, but in the light of the region's history and the government's savage repression, it is difficult to sustain the premise that prophetism was its cause. A broadsheet that circulated among the Camisards suggests the wider biblical context in which their rebellion should be interpreted. It called on the Protestants to "imitate the piety of the faithful Hebrews," assuring them that "God has pardoned your sins because you have regained your zeal." One of the London refugees recalled hearing a young prophet say that "it will not be by the Power of Arms, that the Deliverance of my Church shall come, but by the Prevalence of their Prayers."[34]

There was no abrupt shift from passivity to aggression after 1700. Resistance had been a possible implication of the prophets' message from the beginning, and it was certainly a theme of the psalms and the Old Testament passages that were so important in their worship services. Until 1700, a continuing theme had been the imminent deliverance of the Protestants by God through a human agent who might be Louis XIV himself. The failure of the Peace of Ryswick to address their situation, together with the government's increasing severity, surely made many doubt that the king would save them, but the belief persisted. A handwritten prophecy found in the pocket of a slain Camisard rebel promised that "the king will give the edict that will revoke whatever is contrary to the Holy Gospel." Then France would have only one religion, "God would conserve France by a special grace," and peace would be restored in Europe.[35]

For the next several years, however, the hope in a divinely imposed peace jostled with the conviction that for the time being holy war must be fought against the oppressors. As rebel bands formed throughout Lower Languedoc and the Cévennes, they were often joined by inspired prophets—both men and women—who conducted religious services, provided God's assurance and guidance, and sometimes fought in company with the rest. One of the most remarkable of the Camisard prophets, Elie Marion, declared that it had been "by Inspiration that we forsook our Parents and Relations, and whatever was dearest to us in the World, to follow Jesus Christ, and to make War against the Devil and his Followers . . . ; this was the Source of that Union, Charity, and Brotherly Love, which reign'd among us."

In several of the guerrilla bands the commanders themselves were prophets who believed that they received divine inspiration to guide their military decisions. All of the Camisards incorporated the traditional Protestant usages of prayer, psalm singing, and preaching into the daily regimen. Their conviction that they were fighting "the Fight of Faith" was reinforced by God's continual manifestation of his presence in the bodies of their prophets.[36]

The fact that the Camisard prophets never strayed from the premises and presuppositions of Huguenot piety is especially well illustrated in the story of the famous assault on the tower at Pont-de-Montvert that launched full-scale rebellion in 1702. An itinerant band of prophets had been roaming the upper Cévennes for several months. Several of them received inspirations that called on the Protestants to move to armed rebellion. It was a divine command that could hardly have been unexpected, given the region's tradition of Protestant militancy, based firmly on the warlike history of the other Israel, and the increasing ruthlessness of the government's policy. One of the wandering prophets was Abraham Mazel, twenty-four years old. He wrote later that he had recceived a vision and several inspirations that told him that he "would carry iron and fire against the priests of the Roman Church and . . . would burn their altars." Mazel and the other prophets told some fifty young men from the area to accompany them into the forest. In that theatrical setting, they awaited God's commands. At last the Holy Spirit descended upon Mazel. The event was accompanied by such spectacular bodily contortions that everyone present knew that "something extraordinary was going to be declared" to them. Mazel wrote that God then opened his mouth and commanded the men to go home and get weapons. That evening, they were to reassemble and then march on Pont-de-Montvert and free the Protestants being held prisoner there.

Before they set out, they had a service of worship with a sermon. Then they marched down from the mountains, singing psalms. It is significant that the psalm that one of the prophets specifically remembered their having sung was not one of militancy or one promising God's destruction of the ungodly. It was instead the penitential Psalm 51: "Have mercy upon me, O God. . . . Wash me thoroughly from my iniquity." A later verse must have had enormous resonance for them as they launched their holy war: "Then I will teach transgressors thy ways, and sinners will return to thee. Deliver me from bloodguiltiness, O God, thou God of my salvation, and my tongue will sing aloud of thy deliverance."[37]

The Camisard Revolt was doomed from the outset, but it was to have continuing reverberations not only for the French Huguenots but for Protestants in other countries as well. As we shall see in the next chapters, after the Camisards' defeat some of the prophets made their way to England, and from there the gifts of divine inspiration that had first appeared in Dauphiny in 1688 spread to Germany, where their most enthusiastic disciples proved to be not the large communities of exiled Huguenots but rather Pietists and sectarians, who despite the fact that they spoke no French and shared none of the prophets' cultural and spiritual history, found in them a living manifestation of God's imminent regeneration of the whole world.

In Languedoc, the prophets did not disappear with the final defeat of the Camisard rebels in 1710, but they gradually ceased to embody the unity of a cause and a tradition. Everywhere that they persisted, the prophets tended no longer to call for immediate action as the prophets of 1688–89 and the era of the Camisard Revolt had done. Instead of the demands for repentance and the repudiation of Catholic conformity or for cleansing violence against the enemies of God that had characterized the divine messages of their predecessors, the later prophets tended instead to withdraw more and more into private worlds of vague expectancy, expressed in language that owed less and less to Huguenot biblical and liturgical traditions. They still promised God's coming to punish his enemies and reward the faithful remnant, but their speeches lacked the plainness and the immediacy that had had so much to do with the prophets' effectiveness earlier.[38]

With a few exceptions like Pierre Jurieu, the exiled Huguenot clergy had always looked with disfavor on the prophets, and even within the region more worldly Protestants had questioned whether the mood of ecstatic defiance that they encouraged was indeed in the best interests of their faith. Led by a new generation of lay preachers, the most notable of whom was Antoine Court, the Protestants of the Midi now set out to rebuild the institutional structures of the church.

Court and his associates were convinced that prophetism and the rebellion of the Camisards had brought only suffering and had failed utterly to achieve the restoration of Protestantism in France. Instead, the Huguenots should reorganize their institutional structures clandestinely, using the traditional authority of clergy and synods to maintain the faith and prevent the excesses of popular zeal that had led to disaster. Although Court had grown up among the female prophets of the Vivarais, he insisted that their activities must cease. Like the Catholics, he called them "fanatics." Like Saint Paul, he held that preaching must be reserved for men within a hierarchical power structure.[39]

As the newly reconstituted churches repudiated prophetism, the shared sense of participation in the cosmic struggle, expressed in the context of the dramatically reworked expression of Calvinist tradition in the form of sacred theater that had been prophetism's dynamic for thirty years, gradually disappeared. Only in the twentieth century have Huguenots come to accept that part of their heritage as something other than a tragic aberration. But as Henri Bosc, the dean of Huguenot historians told a recent Protestant assembly, "If there had not been prophets, there would not have been Camisards, and if there had not been Camisards . . . you and I would not be here today."[40]

{2}

The Prophetic Diaspora

Although some of the Camisard bands kept up guerrilla warfare until 1710, it had been clear for several years that their struggle was hopeless. In 1704, following a decisive defeat of the army led by "Colonel" Jean Cavalier, the Holy Spirit that had been its guide fell silent. When the new royal commander, the Duc de Villars, offered a general amnesty, many in the Camisard bands, including their prophets, accepted. Many prophets went into exile, to await further divine guidance.[1]

As refugees from the Camisard Revolt made their way into Switzerland and Germany, they encountered Huguenot populations who had shared neither the sufferings nor the elations of the revolt. Though the earlier immigrants might be sympathetic to the newcomers, and they would have known from Brousson's and Jurieu's writings of the miraculous messages that God had sent to his beleaguered remnant in Languedoc and the Cévennes, their own experience had been quite different.

If the Huguenot prophets and the Camisard Revolt failed to arouse in the French refugees any real sense of spiritual kinship, they had a more pervasive influence on general Protestant sensibilities throughout Europe. For many German, Dutch, Swiss, and English Protestants, the drama in the Cévennes was part of a greater cosmic struggle against the forces of Catholic darkness, embodied for thirty years in the marauding armies of Louis XIV. In all of these countries, the Catholic menace of the French armies intensified a widespread feeling that Protestantism had lost much of its vitality since the Reformation. Especially in Germany, there was a sense that the divine guidance of the Bible was being supplanted by the intricacies of theology and the rote instruction of catechism. As a result, the spiritual purity and sense of God's presence that the early Church had known and the sixteenth-century reformers had recaptured was being lost. All of these factors contributed to the emergence of a movement of "awakening" (to use one of its favorite terms) that was to transform popular religion in the next century.

While the movement was always too diverse to have a single name or center, it is convenient to call it Pietism, the name its German detractors gave to the efforts of Philipp Spener (1635–1705), August Hermann Francke (1663–1727), and their associates to revive the spiritual potential of Lutheranism. The name may have derived from Spener's enormously influential program for religious renewal, the *Pia Desideria*, published in 1675. It may also have been suggested by his proposal that Christians supplement liturgical worship, private prayer, and Bible study by meeting in small groups for the purposes of shared religious experience and moral guidance. He called them *collegiae pietatis*, conventicles of piety. Similar gatherings had been part of English Puritan religious practice, and they were encouraged in the United Provinces by the Dutch Reformed church.

The quite remarkable international character of the Pietist movement is demonstrated by the emergence of religious societies whose form and purpose paralleled the Dutch and German conventicles even within the religiously tepid Church of England. The first one had been formed in 1678 as the result of the work of Dr. Anthony Horneck (1641–97), a German Reformed minister who had emigrated from the Palatinate in 1661. In Spener, Horneck had been profoundly influenced by the life and teachings of Jean de Labadie (1610–74), who after a decade as a Jesuit had converted to Calvinism and preached and taught in France, Geneva, and Holland. Moving increasingly toward an internalized mystical piety, Labadie and some disciples separated themselves from all churches, organized themselves as a communal society, and moved to Germany to seek a haven where they could perfect their spirituality. In a sense, Labadie's career demonstrates the renewed circulation of ideas within Protestant Europe that had been interrupted by the twin crises of the Thirty Years' War and the English Civil War.

Whereas the English religious societies had much more modest aims, they had considerable impact on devout young men of the generation who came to maturity after the Glorious Revolution of 1688.

Often, a quest for "practical holiness" that Spener and Francke would have found congenial merged uneasily with a desire for divine illumination more characteristic of the Labadists and the mystical strain in Puritanism that had been preserved by latter-day Puritans like the Quakers.[2] The variety of influences that had shaped the Pietist movement in Germany was similarly international and eclectic, including the writings of English Puritans and German mystics and the examples of Anabaptist and reformed churches in several countries. Above all, however, Pietism derived from the thought of Martin Luther, liberated from a century of learned obscurantism and political compromise.

Despite the opposition of many in the clerical establishment, the movement won valuable political support, notably among the Protestant nobility in Wurttemberg, some of the small states in the southwest, and Brandenburg-Prussia. Spener had settled in Berlin in 1691, and through his influence Francke was appointed to the faculty of Brandenburg's newly founded university at Halle. Halle quickly became Pietism's intellectual center as well as the base for Francke's prodigious energies and organizing ability. Halle's schools and welfare institutions, its publishing house for religious literature, and the missionaries sent to other parts of the world touched Protestant communities everywhere in the next decades, providing a model for "evangelical" Christianity that has persisted to this day. In distant Boston, Cotton Mather wrote of Francke's achievement: "The World begins to feel a Warmth from the *Fire of God,* which thus flames in the heart of *Germany,* beginning to extend into many Regions; the whole world will ere long be sensible of it."[3]

Cotton Mather believed that the world was approaching a new Pentecost, when God would pour out his blessings as a preparation for the Millennium. So did Francke and many Pietists on the continent. In England as well, the millenarian excitement that had characterized the period of the Commonwealth was revived with the accession of William and Mary in 1688 and their launching of a crusade against the forces of Catholic France.

Spener wrote in the *Pia Desideria* that "our whole Christian religion consists of the inner man or the new man, whose soul is faith and whose expressions are the fruits of life." In hearing the word of Scripture, it was essential that it should "penetrate to our heart, so that we may hear the Holy Spirit speak there, that is, with vibrant emotion and comfort feel the sealing of the Spirit." Both ideas could readily be traced to Luther and Saint Paul, but as they were rediscovered and disseminated in the international religious awakenings of the eighteenth century, they had the potential for suggesting that spiritual perfection and purity of life could be attained only by withdrawing into groupings of the faithful, under the continuous and immediate guidance of the Holy Spirit.

Francke and Spener considered themselves orthodox Lutherans who simply wanted to regenerate the church from within, but there was always the possibility that their insistence that the Bible must be the sole guide to life and worship and their conviction that the action of the Holy Spirit set the awakened Christians spiritually apart might lead some people to the conclusion that they must separate themselves from the world and its churches in order to attain spiritual purity. Similar convictions had led the Anabaptists and the more radical of the English Puritans to withdraw into their own religious communities.

Especially in Germany and England, the separatist implications of Pietism received added impetus from the obscure but pervasive influence of the writings of the seventeenth-century mystic Jacob Boehme, who had taught that the true church was the church of the spiritually awakened faithful, living and dead. They were united with God's mystical presence, which they felt immediately and permanently in their lives.[4]

The Huguenot prophets of Languedoc and the Cévennes might have provided similar examples of Christian zeal through reliance on God's tangible presence, but their situation had isolated them from the excitements generated by Pietism and its sister movements of religious renovation. With the defeat of the Camisard Revolt, many who believed that they had experienced or witnessed the Spirit in France now went into exile in territories already aroused by Pietism. Jon Butler has estimated that between 1680 and 1700, Holland had received some fifty thousand, mainly from the north and west of France, and England had received another twenty thousand.[5] The refugees from the Midi, however, were much more likely to take the shorter and less dangerous route eastward to Germany (where some thirty thousand Huguenots settled, half of them in the territories of Brandenburg-Prussia), the small city-state of Geneva, the French-speaking Protestant Swiss canton of Neuchatel, or the Vaud region around Lausanne, ruled autocratically by the distant city of Bern.

When Louis XIV's intensified persecution and the Peace of Rijswyk's failure to address the Huguenots' situation triggered a wave of migration out of the south of France in the last years of the seventeenth century, eight thousand sought refuge in the Vaud alone. With the Camisards' defeat, thousands more made their way to the Swiss cantons. The Swiss were willing to provide temporary asylum and economic aid, but they could not absorb a refugee population of this size permanently. They therefore contacted other Protestant states on their behalf. German states devastated by the Thirty Years' War, notably Hessen-Kassel and the western territories of Brandenburg-Prussia, again welcomed the Huguenots as settlers. They settled in dozens of "colonies" scattered through much of western and central Germany.[6] As reformed Protestants, they received full religious liberty and quickly established their own local economic, political, and cultural structures. In general, they assimilated remarkably rapidly in their new homelands.

The same cannot be said for those refugees who still believed that the Camisard prophets would soon be God's instruments once again to announce the resumption of the holy war against the Catholics. Through the mouth of the prophet Abraham Mazel, for example, God had said: "My children, do not be sad. I am permitting you to cede something to the Devil. Do not fear that I am abandoning my work. I shall reassemble my children soon."[7] The prophets' Old Testament piety with its activism, its military imagery, and its willingness to accept martyrdom for the sake of the Protestant cause represented a religious style quite unlike the Pietists' concern for the spiritual new birth and one that the political and religious authorities in the Swiss and German states feared would be socially disruptive. When the first reports of the little prophets reached Switzerland in 1689, there had been enormous popular interest in them, but subsequent developments had made many people more wary. Soon after the first reports began to circulate in Lausanne, the pastor Elie Merlat had delivered and published a sermon that contended that even if most people cried "miracle, miracle" and believed that these wonders presaged the triumph of the Protestants, the children's alleged inspiration was in fact "manifestly false, and Diabolical." Isabeau Vincent preached against Merlat in trance, and Claude Brousson attacked his contentions in his pamphlets, but the minister's efforts were endorsed by the theological faculty in Lausanne and had the tacit support of the civil authorities.

Spirit possession continued to be a subject of controversy between Protestant and Catholic theologians and polemicists. In Geneva, the majority of witchcraft cases throughout the seventeenth century had involved demonic possession. In France, on several occasions entire convents were possessed, and the nuns' prolonged exorcism became a kind of sacred theater that attracted international attention. Sometimes, as in the case of the famous Jeanne des Anges, prioress of Loudon, demonic could be transformed into divine possession, but overwhelmingly possession was considered by both Protestants and Catholics to be a demonstration of the existence of a terrible conspiracy between religious heresy and the Devil. It is therefore not surprising that Merlat rejected the official position of the Roman Catholic hierarchy that the Huguenot prophets were frauds and the claim of some physicians and intellectuals that they were the victims of some mental or physical malady. Instead, like many who would reject or turn away from the spiritual claims of the prophets' eighteenth-century heirs in England and America, he contended that their possession was indeed supernatural, but it was sent by the Devil.[8]

Some prophets who arrived in Switzerland found that the gift of inspiration had left them. Others retained it, but the dramatic body language of convulsions and gasping that accompanied their entranced preaching and prophesying, which audiences in the Cévennes had found so powerfully evocative, was considered here to be simply bizarre. Finding themselves greeted with either indifference or hostility, some prophets and their followers joined the refugee migration to Germany, where presumably they were absorbed into the Huguenot exile communities. In any event, nothing more is heard of them. According to one Huguenot minister in London, "*Geneva, Switzerland, Germany* and *Holland* have extinguish'd these pretended Spirits, and laid their Oracles silent."[9]

Three of the Camisard prophets did manage to win a sympathetic audience for their heavenly messages, not in Switzerland or Germany but in London. They were an unlikely trio. By far the most impressive was Elie Marion, a one-time law clerk in Toulouse who had first been inspired in 1703. He had been a captain in Cavalier's army and had followed him into exile. After a brief stay in Switzerland in 1704, he had participated in a short-lived incursion into the Midi organized but barely supported by the English and Dutch. After a second defeat and surrender, he was back in Lausanne. After trying for some months to find employment, he received what he later described as "a warning from the Spirit of God" to prepare for a voyage. Marion assumed that this meant that he was to return to France to fight once more. He received a good offer of employment in Lausanne, but then he "was stopped by the Spirit of God which changed in an instant the dispositions" of his heart. On 22 July 1706, in the presence of his sister and father, God spoke through his mouth. Marion was to "quit worldly establishments" and go to England. He was then twenty-eight. Until his premature death in 1713, he dedicated his life to serving the Holy Spirit as a prophet.

When he arrived at The Hague in mid-August, he learned that two other Camisard prophets, Durand Fage and Jean Cavalier, had arrived in London and had begun to deliver divinely inspired pronouncements before groups that consisted primarily of wealthy and influential Huguenot exiles.[10]

Like Marion, Durand Fage had fought with the Camisards and had then made his way to Switzerland. Marion had met him but did not know him well. Like several others in Cavalier's army, Fage was from the town of Aubais in Languedoc, where he had worked as a weaver. He had first been inspired in 1702, when he was twenty-one. After witnessing the spirit possession of an eleven-year-old girl, he was "surprized with a *Shivering* all over . . . and some Agitation." Then his "Tongue and Lips were of a sudden forced to pronounce Words with Vehemence" that he was "amazed to hear, having forethought nothing, and no ways intending to speak."[11]

Nothing is known of Fage's career as soldier and prophet; he gained none of the fame of Abraham Mazel or Elie Marion. Not long after his arrival in Switzerland, he was expelled for some reason from Bernese territory. He went first to Basel and then in May 1706 rejoined Cavalier, his old commander, in Holland. Within a month, however, he had crossed the Channel to England, where he began to prophesy in London about the Millennium. His words, like those of Isabeau Vincent nearly twenty years earlier, were taken down by scribes. Although the simple but sincere Fage was rapidly overshadowed by other prophets, it was to him that God delivered the command that would crucially affect the transition of prophetism to England: "My Child, you have but to speak openly. You must openly announce my wonders."[12]

The third member of the trio that the London press soon began to call the French Prophets was only twenty years old when he arrived there a month after Durand Fage. Fage had met him in Geneva, but Marion had not even heard of him. Jean Cavalier, from Sauve in the Cévennes, claimed kinship with the famous Camisard leader of the same name. The colonel denied it. In any case, the claim was just one of many things about Jean Cavalier that made people uneasy. He had first been inspired in 1701, after he had attended a meeting at which several young prophets had preached in trance. For nine months thereafter, he experienced "Hiccop and Agitation without Speech." After being in ecstasy continuously for two days, without eating or drinking, he began to speak. Like all of the prophets, he insisted that he was only God's passive instrument: "I am in no wise the Framer of those bodily Agitations I suffer in my Exstasies, I do not move my own self, but am moved by a Power independently that overrules me."[13]

Unlike Marion and Fage, he had never fought with the Camisards. Instead, after an internment in his home town, in 1705 he had gone to Montpellier, where he was employed as a "merchant companion." Arrested again and quickly released, he was widely suspected by the Protestants of having betrayed their places of worship to the police. His father therefore enrolled him in the royal army. After four months, however, his gift of inspiration returned, so he left for Geneva, where he met Fage. He too went to Holland to join Cavalier's army, but after a few months he was divinely led to go to London, where his cousin, a carpenter named Jean Allut, lived. He arrived in August 1706 and immediately began to deliver divine warnings and pronouncements.[14]

In London, the three French Prophets enjoyed a freedom of movement and expression far greater than they had ever known in France or Switzerland, but they encountered among the refugee ministry the same suspicion and hostility they had met in Lausanne and Geneva.

There were twenty-four French Protestant churches in London in 1706. Most of them were either in the City or the Spitalfields district to the east, where thousands of Huguenot textile workers had settled with their families. Most of these churches had retained the Huguenot liturgy. The rest of the churches were concentrated in Soho in the West End, where the wealthier refugees—skilled artisans, merchants, and members of the professions—had settled. During the Stuart Restoration, most of these churches had succumbed to royal pressure, conformed to the Church of England, and begun to employ a French translation of the Book of Common Prayer in their liturgy. All the Huguenot churches were under the nominal supervision of the bishop of London.[15]

Only four days after Marion's arrival in London, the three prophets had the first of a series of interviews with representatives of the leadership of London's Huguenot churches. According to Marion, the initial interviews were friendly, as the trio told of what they had seen and experienced in Languedoc and the Cévennes. The meetings quickly became more heated, however, as the consistory and ministers of the Huguenots' Threadneedle Street Church in Spitalfields and the Savoy Church in Soho Square questioned the orthodoxy of the prophets' claims and the way in which their prophetic function infringed on the clergy's own role. The prophets replied (under inspiration) with denunciations of "unbelieving" ministers who had "abandoned their troops" in France. At first, they had insisted that they would soon be called back to the Midi to fight again, but gradually these pronouncements were supplanted by "warnings" of divine wrath against those who doubted God's word and their predictions of an imminent Millennium.

The climax came in January 1707, when the ministers of three of the churches in Soho declared from their pulpits, in the name of the consistory of the Savoy Church, that the three prophets' trances were in fact feigned. As to their prophecies, the ministers declared that "they have nothing new but the grimaces." They chided those who took the French Prophets seriously for "not being content with the Writers which the Holy Spirit has truly inspired." The prophets responded that they were "servants of God, sent to this city to do his will." They denied the authority of the consistory to act against them in this manner, but throughout London Huguenot opinion was turning against them.

At the end of March, at the suggestion of the bishop of London, the Savoy consistory ruled that they should be denied communion in any of the Huguenot churches. One minister defied the order and admitted them to the sacrament, but he was quickly suspended. The French Prophets now found themselves isolated from their own community. In effect, their followers in Soho and Spitalfields now had to choose between the refugee churches and the prophets.[16]

Just at the time that the clerical establishment's opposition to the French Prophets was destroying whatever hopes the prophets might have had that their divinely appointed embassy would be heard and believed by their fellow Huguenots, some of their followers were encouraging them to expand their missionary horizons to include all of England and ultimately, perhaps, the whole world.

Late in 1706, one of the wealthy Huguenot followers, François Misson, had begun to collect the testimonies of Huguenot refugees concerning the prophetic movement in the Midi. In March 1707 they were published under the title *Le Théâtre sacré des Cévennes*. Some of the testimonies were also published in English translation under the title *A Cry from the Desart*. In both French and English, Misson's collection seems to have been widely read and to have attracted considerable attention. One writer complained that since the book was "dispersed with an artificial Liberality, every one had Copies that would."[17]

Inevitably, the very different social and religious environment in London was having an impact on the style and substance of Camisard prophetism. Sacred theater as a cultural phenomenon entails a process of interaction between the actors, who figuratively or literally represent the divine, and their "audience." Actors and audience must have at least similar convictions as to how those under the power of the divine might perform their "roles" and what messages the divine might send. In London, the messages of the inspired gradually changed. The warnings against Catholic subversion of true religion were supplanted by pronouncements of divine wrath against those who failed to heed the prophets. The call for a military crusade to liberate France from the oppressor was no longer heard. Instead, the Huguenots' redemption was absorbed into promises of the universal Millennium. The bodily agitations remained essentially as they had been in the Midi, but there developed in addition a range of rituals and performances quite unlike anything seen in France. Gradually, the French Prophets and their followers turned into a sect.

A central factor in their transformation was the increasing importance of English followers. A core of Huguenot disciples, rich and poor, remained loyal. Some of them, including Cavalier's cousin, Jean Allut, became prophets themselves. It was however to be the English converts who came to dominate the movement, in the process introducing ideas and practices derived from English popular religious tradition and better adapted to reaching an English audience.

One of the most dedicated of the new followers was John Lacy, a prosperous justice of the peace and a leading member of the Presbyterian Westminster chapel. After hearing the three prophets and talking to some of the refugees about the prophetic movement in the Cévennes, Lacy was convinced that it all embodied "the Truth of Divine Inspiration." In his preface to *A Cry from the Desart,* he asserted that the contortions and agitations that accompanied the prophets' performances proved their authenticity, for many prophets in the Old Testament had also displayed "divers strange Gestures of Body." Like them, the three French Prophets insisted that they were only passive instruments of a higher power. Their words and "bodily Emotions" were produced by "a superior Agent, Angel or Spirit." Lacy acknowledged that the fact that some of the "new Inspired" were women was distressing to some people, but "Womens Preaching as ordinary Ministers is one thing, and God speaking in his own Name through their Organs is another."

He concluded his preface by suggesting that the miracles in the Cévennes had been but the first stage of a new Pentecostal outpouring of the Holy Spirit: "The wonderful Works of God ought to be own'd, and if there has been a Diffusion of the Holy Ghost in the *Cévennes,* it may be the first Fruits and Dawn of the first Resurrection; and the Dispersion of Persons inspired, into other Countries, may raise up Harbingers and Forerunners of the same elsewhere." He added that "the first Manifestation of Gifts and Judgments is to be in *England,* and accordingly are speedily expected."[18] Lacy believed that their arrival in London constituted a renewed demonstration that England had a special role to play in God's plan for the world's regeneration, just as Puritans had believed since the age of Elizabeth.

In June, Lacy became the first of the English converts to receive the "gift" of prophetic utterance. In a pamphlet he published in 1708, he described his experiences in detail. Sometimes, his fingers would contract of their own accord, and his hand would write out divine warnings. At other times, "the Respiration of my Breath hath, for sundry days, beat various Tunes of the Drum sometimes six hours in a day." His possessed behavior was similar to that of the Camisard prophets and the newly inspired among the London Huguenot community. The onset of the spirit's descent was marked by heaving of the chest, gasping, and a weird humming. Lacy wrote that the agitations and convulsions that accompanied his prophetic warnings "sensibly refresh the Body" and "do not waste the Spirits, but exhilarate."[19] As is the case today among Pentecostals and possession cults, the emotional catharsis that followed the spirit's departure was for Lacy yet another demonstration of his possession's divine origin.

Despite official displeasure and occasional mob violence against them, the French Prophets persisted throughout the spring and summer of 1707 in their determination to present their message to the people of London. Many who came to hear them were Dissenters like John Lacy; others were Anglicans who had been involved in movements of moral reform and spiritual renewal like the religious societies, the Society for the Propagation of the Christian Gospel, and the Society for the Reformation of Manners. Important clusters of new members came to the French Prophets from the Quakers and the Philadelphians. Dissimilar as they were, Quakers and Philadelphians had preserved the tradition of the religious radicalism of the English Revolution, and those who now joined the French Prophets represented a sort of cultural bridge between that tradition and the prophetism of the Cévennes.

The time was long past when Quakers in fact trembled as they awaited the descent of the Holy Spirit, nor did they any longer fall to the ground, "froathing at the mouth, and scrieching with a horrible noise." Nevertheless, their doctrine of the Inner Light preserved the same Pentecostal tradition that the French Prophets embodied, and they too had willingly risked persecution and martyrdom in order to do as they believed the Spirit commanded. They had even permitted women to preach, contending that it was not the woman's voice that spoke, but God's. For over a decade, women and men had traveled the length and breadth of Great Britain as the Lord commanded, preaching that all should live in purity and simplicity under the immediate guidance of the Holy Spirit. Others had visited Holland, Germany, and the American colonies as missionaries in order to achieve the world's spiritual reformation.

Puritans had always held that the Holy Spirit was received by the believer through the hearing and reading of Scripture, but the

Quakers had preserved as well the more radical notion that the Spirit operated emotionally and tangibly within those who had been truly converted. In their repudiation of any guides except the Bible and the spirit of God and their insistence that the individual believer must undergo an inner change or conversion before it was possible truly to live as God intended, the Quakers clearly foreshadowed the Pietist awakening that swept Europe in the eighteenth century. In their early years, the violence with which they sometimes experienced the Inner Light's manifestation and their public performance of "signs" to warn a godless world had constituted a striking form of sacred theater during the Commonwealth.[20]

Gradually, the policy of toleration which the Quakers' own example had done so much to bring about had led to a dampening of their zeal and their taste for extravagant demonstrations like "going naked for a sign" and interrupting religious services in "steeple-houses." Material prosperity had also contributed to their preferring the quiet cultivation of religious inwardness and the gentle discipline of the Quaker meetings. The Quakers did not repudiate their earlier conduct after they became respectable. They still affirmed the absolute primacy of the Holy Spirit, and they continued to insist that not even scripture could overrule the Inner Light. In the eighteenth century, people in search of a more vital and personal religious experience than was available in the Church of England or the congregations of Old Dissent might still seek a temporary or permanent haven among the Quakers.[21]

It is therefore not surprising that some Quakers considered the French Prophets to be kindred spirits. They attended their assemblies, and a few were possessed by the spirit. A woman named Ann Steed, who had for years been announcing in Quaker meetings that Christ was going to appear in England, now declared that the event had taken place "by Christ's glorious appearance in and upon the *French* Prophets." The Friends' belief in toleration had its limits, and a few who supported the French Prophets were disowned by their meetings. They nevertheless continued to consider themselves Quakers, dressing in Quaker fashion and regularly attending worship services. Throughout the eighteenth century, the French Prophets were to be an inconvenient and occasionally divisive reminder of the Quakers' radical beginnings.[22]

The mystical sect known as the Philadelphians had tried for

several years to reach a wider public, but with little success. When the aged Jane Lead died in 1704, they ceased to hold public meetings and drifted into dissension and passive waiting. When the three prophets appeared in London two years later, many Philadelphians considered them to be a new demonstration of the outpouring of God's spirit in the world's last days. In the spring and summer of 1707, at least ten of the earliest English converts were former Philadelphians, including their leading spokesman, the Reverend Richard Roach. Like John Lacy and many others, the Philadelphians brought with them, as part of their spiritual baggage, the traditions of Puritan millenarianism, notably the conviction that in these latter days England would become the Protestant New Jerusalem.

Meanwhile, the French Prophets' determination to spread their message made them a source of continued controversy within the Huguenot refugee community. A severe military defeat in Spain and some economic dislocation may have made the English public—not especially fond of foreigners in the best of times—even less happy about the Huguenots in their midst. The controversy came to a head on 4 July 1707, when Elie Marion and two of his scribes were put on trial for blasphemy and sedition for having published, in French and English, a collection of his "prophetical warnings," many of which predicted the descent of divine wrath in one form or another upon unhearing England.[23]

John Lacy had also published a collection of divine warnings. He proceeded to rent a former Presbyterian chapel in the City for the Prophets' assemblies and to register it under the Act of Toleration as a dissenting chapel. Large crowds came to see and hear. Many came simply out of curiosity, and sometimes the crowds were hostile. Marion wrote in his memoirs that sometimes the Prophets were pelted with "a hail of excrement, dogs, dead cats, . . . and often of stones." Nevertheless, they persisted in their efforts, encouraged by the fact that "God had spread his Spirit on a quantity of persons of the English nation of every age, sex, condition, and almost every sect" by infusing them with the gift of prophecy.[24] In their chapel and at the meetings that continued to be held in private home and rented rooms in taverns, they evolved into a millenarian sect, dedicated to the conversion of the world and absorbed meanwhile in the elaboration of an array of rituals and possessed performances, all of them divinely ordained by prophets "under inspiration." It became increasingly apparent, however, that as sacred theater the Prophets' performances were less and less effective at communicating shared meanings to those who witnessed them. Instead, in elaborating new ceremonies, some of which were self-consciously "theatrical," the Prophets were turning in upon themselves, staging dramas that had meaning only for those who already believed.

One ritual that at least had recognizable roots in the Camisard tradition was a ceremony of blessing that was often performed at the conclusion of meetings. Sometimes the blessing closely resembled the promises of forgiveness that had been among the pronouncements of the young prophets in the Cévennes. Similarly, in London God promised protection and forgiveness of sins to the congregation, addressing each person as "my child." The ever-present scribes provided written copies of the blessings, including English translations when necessary. When a young English printer's apprentice named Samuel Keimer received his blessing through the agency of Elie Marion at one meeting, it was one that might as easily have come out of his own Puritan tradition: "My child, till now, thou hast been rebellious to my Will. . . . I come to make thee a New Creature."[25]

A young Huguenot silk worker described a more elaborate ceremony of blessing that took place at an assembly he attended in a private home near Hatton Gardens. After Marion had made "some contorsions and shakings of the head," nearly everyone in the room gathered before him on their knees. Taking each person's head between his hands, he pronounced God's specific blessing on him or her. One blessing declared that the person was to be "established on the twelve Thrones judging the twelve Tribes of Israel." Another was told: "My child, don't be afraid because of your youth; the Spirit is going to arrive within you."

Like the prophets in the Cévennes, the London prophets occasionally passed on the "gift" of possession to others, sometimes in conjunction with the ritual of blessing. One of the English converts explained that when this happened, it constituted "the Visit of GOD's holy Spirit, to dwell in their Bodies (which he has made his Temples)."[26]

Henry Nicholson, an Anglican who left the French Prophets after he decided they were actually guided by evil spirits, was himself first possessed after he had received an elaborate blessing from one of the Prophets. "I fell into violent Convulsions," he wrote, "very differing from any I had seen of theirs; inasmuch that I cryed out with a shrill voice like one affrighted, and beat my Breast and Knees after the manner of those who are in Epilepsies." For the next six weeks, he "could neither see any of the Motions of the Prophets, or even think on them, without some irregular Motions." Instead of receiving the gift of prophecy, he became obsessed with his own sins. After he ceased working and supporting his family, his friends placed him in a madhouse. Upon his release, his convulsions returned, as violently as before.[27]

The sacred dramas in which Elie Marion was the principal performer had changed little since the Camisard Revolt, but in London as in Lausanne the violent convulsions that accompanied his pronouncements were often witnessed with incomprehension or amusement. No longer were they interpreted essentially as rituals of comfort and celebration in which God spoke to his beleaguered people in speech and in gesture. Instead, Londoners went to be entertained. One man wrote of Marion that "the poor *French Man* almost thresh'd himself to Death in his Agitations." He said of his prophetic discourse that it was "so broken and incoherent," accompanied continually by "a Gulp, or a Hiccup, and violent Agitations of the Head and Body" that he could "scarce understand, much less bear in Mind the Particulars he discoursed."[28]

John Lacy's prophetic utterances were more varied, and his possessed behavior was more overtly theatrical. At one assembly, soon after the trial of Marion and his two scribes opened, he went into a trance and then began to whistle. Then he mimed the playing of a trumpet. He announced: "My Heralds are arrived. The sound of their Voice shall go out thro' all Nations." At an assembly two days later, he imitated a man threshing and then declared: "The Harvest is at Hand. The Sickle is already put in, to gather it: and I will thresh all Nations."[29]

Sometimes the Prophets were inspired to perform roles in entranced theatrical performances that they believed were "signs" of the cosmic struggle in which they were engaged. Their behavior may have been influenced by the Quaker tradition, still an occasional if unwelcome feature of Quaker meetings, of individuals' manifesting God's displeasure by dramatic acts like going naked or pouring ashes on themselves. The Prophets' conduct was even more bizarre. Always acting "under inspiration," they introduced a form of sacred theater quite unlike the liturgies of hope and repentance that had been one of the continuities of the Huguenot prophetic movement.

Samuel Keimer described one such occasion, at which four prophets portrayed God, the angel Gabriel, the Devil, and the Church. At the climax, "the Church" was tossed back and forth "much like a Football." At another meeting, Jean Cavalier portrayed the Antichrist. First Fage and Lacy stamped on him; then they threw him down the stairs. He crawled back up, declaring that he was "still not dead." Betty Gray "kick'd him with her Feet, and threw him down Stairs again headlong to the bottom, at which all their Inspirations ceased."[30] That the Antichrist should have been portrayed by the erratic and unstable Cavalier, who left the Prophets a few years later, was a final cosmic irony.

One of the most valuable sources of information on the French Prophets' evolution in the next years is the strange and delightful memoir Samuel Keimer wrote and published in 1718, after he had left them to become a self-appointed Quaker, a vegetarian who sported a full beard in that clean-shaven era. He soon crossed the Atlantic and settled in Philadelphia, where he had the misfortune to employ in his printing shop a young man named Benjamin Franklin, who pilloried Keimer mercilessly in his own autobiography.

Keimer's story was surely typical of many young seekers after religious assurance who found temporary or permanent comfort in witnessing or experiencing God's tangible presence in the descent of the divine upon the French Prophets. He had been initially repelled by the Prophets' behavior, and even after his mother was converted and his sister Mary received the prophetic gift, "having at Times the Agitations upon her very violent and Surprising," he was unsure whether the voice that came from the Prophets was from God or the Devil. He began to be persuaded that it was God's when he heard a prosperous lawyer named Thomas Dutton ask while in a trance: "Can it be a Delusion to bid you repent? Will the Devil preach repentance?" Keimer is vague as to his reasons for deciding to join them, but one suspects that his own concerns for salvation and the examples of his family and acquaintances were reinforced by discovering an immediacy of religious experience he had not found among the Baptists and Presbyterians.[31]

By December 1707, the English followers of the French Prophets outnumbered the Huguenots. That month, the group underwent two tests of its faith which were to have significant repercussions. On the first of the month, having been found guilty by a jury of falsely claiming to be a prophet, Marion and his two scribes were condemned to spend two days on public display in the pillory. Once again, they faced hostile crowds throwing stones and excrement at them. They endured the humiliation bravely, and the rest of the group was assured by means of divine messages received by some of the other prophets that the three men's ordeal was really a sign of the ultimate triumph of their cause.

Three days later, one of the leading English converts, Dr. Thomas Emes, fell seriously ill. Just before Christmas, he died. His death was a crisis for the believers, because they had expected to serve in Christ's kingdom, which, according to all their prophecies, was coming soon. Also, they believed that they had received the Pentecostal gift of healing, which John Lacy in his writings argued was an important additional proof of the authenticity of the Prophets' claims. During Emes's illness, Lacy and other prophets had issued divine pronouncements while in convulsions that promised that he would recover.[32] Yet he died. God's answer was the promise of a greater miracle: Emes would be raised from the dead. There followed several weeks of possessed theatrics in which the principal actors were a former Baptist named John Potter, Jean Cavalier, and the twelve-year-old Anna Maria King. Significantly, Marion was not involved, and Lacy insisted that he had received no specific promises from God concerning Emes's resurrection.

The forms of sacred theater that the Prophets introduced to prepare the faithful for the miracle became increasingly elaborate and contrived. Samuel Keimer described an especially peculiar session he attended with his mother and sister at an inn, shortly after Emes's burial. John Potter "was carried violently by the Spirit" into another room. He soon returned, "under the most violent Agitations . . . his Arms extended to the utmost, in each of his Hands holding and shaking a piece of Paper, and crying out with a thundering Voice, GRACE, GRACE, GRACE." The paper promised the forgiveness of all sins. At the bottom was God's own signature: "I AM." As Keimer commented: "What could possibly be more affecting, than to believe, that GOD Himself was speaking to us, telling us, that all our Sins were Pardon'd as it were, *Face to Face?*"

Potter announced that Emes's resurrection would take place on 25

May 1708, five months after his burial. When he asked those present to raise their hands if they believed it, nearly everyone present did so, "some crying, some jumping, some leaping, one lying all along the Ground." Some time later, Cavalier came downstairs from the room in which the French were meeting separately. He declared that God had told him that the son of one of the French believers was to be resurrected as well. Then he jumped on a table, "and with his Foot, Stamp'd distinctly many times thereon, and spoke somewhat in *French*."[33]

The elaboration of means by which God communicated with his people in the two years and a few months since the three prophets had first arrived in London was altogether remarkable. Only Elie Marion continued to perform essentially in the tradition of the biblical prophets. His pronouncements dealt now with the English situation, not the French, and they consisted more often of warnings of destruction and less often of promises of comfort. Nevertheless, they still preserved the culture of divinized speech that the Huguenots had derived from their identification of the Jews of the Old Testament with themselves. For Marion as for all the prophets of Languedoc and the Cévennes, French, the language of the Huguenot liturgy and Bible, was God's language. But in London, prophets were at least as likely to speak English as French. When possessed, John Lacy might speak English or French or even Latin. Even Durand Fage had attempted to speak in an unknown tongue, but all he produced was "Tring, Trang, Swing, Swang, Hing, Hang."[34]

To speech there had now been added mimed actions and the cosmic playlets. For the French Prophets, blessed with an ever more abundant outpouring of an ever greater variety of manifestations of God's presence, at the same time confronted by hostile crowds and perhaps doubting some of their own prophets' pronouncements, the notion that God would provide his remnant with a written certificate of salvation was comprehensible.

Potter's great announcement had taken place in a private meeting, but Emes's promised resurrection now became part of their public witness, a further demonstration that they were the true heralds of the world's last days. Several prophets declared that God was going to destroy the unbelievers of London on 25 March, and Cavalier predicted that "a Boat shou'd sail in the Streets, in the Blood of the Slain." Some members of the group stopped working, and all of them were supposed to collect a six months' supply of food in preparation for the famine that would be part of God's cleansing of the earth before the Millennium. Their sense of impending doom may have been intensified by the fact that the Roman Catholic Stuart pretender was about to make his first attempt at seizing the British throne.

The divine command that Marion, Fage, and Cavalier were to return to France and resume the Camisards' struggle never came. Instead, in the exhilaration that accompanied the prophecies concerning Emes and the end of the world, the English converts began sending missionaries to other English towns. Like the Quakers two generations earlier, they traveled in pairs, preaching, prophesying, interrupting religious services. They had some success, especially in Birmingham and Bristol.[35]

May 25 came. Dr. Emes did not rise from his grave. A huge crowd was there to watch and jeer, but only one of the Prophets was present. Had God's messages ceased after the "disconfirmation" of 25 May, some of the faithful might have fallen away. Instead, some of the Prophets announced that the faithful were about to receive new gifts of the spirit, so that the group could carry an even more zealous witness to the world. For example, the membership was commanded to wear green ribbons, a yard long, "as a Mark for the destroying Angel to know us by," Keimer wrote. The ribbons served as well to set the faithful apart from the ungodly. Several received the gift of healing, which John Lacy had received the previous year.

It may be that Emes's failed resurrection led the Prophets to worry more about the possibility that evil spirits surrounded them and not God's alone. A pamphlet described a meeting at an inn during which twenty or thirty of those present began "howling like Dogs, in all Manner of Disorder." Then one of the women approached another, struck her with both hands, and said, "Come out of her, thou Devil, come out of her, thou Devil." The second woman denied that she was possessed by a devil, but John Lacy declared that she must be cast out. She was therefore expelled from the room.

According to Keimer, possessions became more violent. At one meeting, he saw "a Prophet tear a Prophetess by the Hair of the Head, leading her up and down in a very frightful manner, both being under violent Agitations." At another meeting, he heard Rebecca Cuff cry "The D-A-V-I-L, The D-A-V-I-L, The D-A-V-I-L" so horribly "that it terrified the Believers themselves." On another occasion, he saw his sister, "a lusty young woman," perform a "sign" of the fall of the whore of Babylon by throwing another woman to the floor and then treading on her with her feet.[36]

The shared experience of awaiting Emes's resurrection and then coping with its failure had helped to bind the Prophets together. Now the proliferation of divinely communicated warnings, signs, and ceremonies continued the process by which, as Keimer put it, the Prophets "were pretty well moddel'd, as a Body of People." Like the Shakers a century later, the French Prophets set about creating new social structures for themselves to supplant those of the world. In August, they were ordered to assemble for worship in groups of seven, each with its own prophet. In size, they resembled natural families; effectively and as nuclei for worship and the transmission of religious culture, they had the potential to supplant them.

At almost the same time, Marion and one of the French women prophets received a divine command that the group (which numbered roughly two hundred) was to organize into tribes, corresponding to the twelve tribes named in the book of Revelation (7:4–9) and ultimately constituting the 144,000 faithful who would be saved at the time of the Millennium. The order served to link the movement more explicitly with the biblical and Huguenot context from which it had been drifting. It also achieved a symbolic reunion of the nationalities, since all the tribes mixed French and English, men and women, prophets and followers. Each person then received a new, biblical name which was to be inscribed on a piece of parchment and sewed onto the green ribbon.[37]

At the end of 1707, the French Prophets introduced their own sacraments. While some of the members continued to attend their former churches, it must have been more and more difficult to operate in two religious environments at once. The heterogeneity of the group encouraged this new development, and so did the recent restructuring into "families" and tribes. On Christmas Day, they for the first time performed their own sacrament of communion. At this "Love-Feast," a "select company" dined together, and then when the Holy Spirit commanded it, several of the prophets administered the bread and wine to the assembly.[38]

The introduction of the ceremony of the love feast was a reaffirmation of Huguenot liturgical tradition, even among the increasingly bizarre forms of sacred theater that the group had introduced.

Yet neither it nor the creation of tribes on a biblical model succeeded in producing any really lasting cohesion within the London membership. The diffusion of the gifts of the spirit had gone too far, and its products were too diverse and eccentric. Instead, the Prophets were faced with a succession of schisms, as prophet challenged prophet and God's word in one mouth was contradicted by God's word in another.

The most serious separation was that of Abraham Whitrow. The only prophet to have gone to the cemetery on 25 May to await Emes's resurrection, he believed that only he among the sect's prophets had been entirely faithful to the divine command. He began to declare that the rich must become poor if they were to enter the kingdom of heaven. Lacy (under inspiration) declared that "God wou'd break him with a Rod of Iron." Whitrow replied (under inspiration) that Lacy's was "a lying Spirit."[39] Most of the members decided that Whitrow was one of the false prophets who were to appear on earth before the Millennium, but Sir Richard Bulkeley, one of the most prominent English converts, sided with Whitrow and accompanied him on prophetic tours of England and Ireland, contributing most of his wealth to finance Whitrow's various schemes for aiding the poor.

During the next several years, several female members were also denounced as false prophets and excluded from the group. Keimer said that five women among the French Prophets claimed to be the "woman clothed with the sun" whose appearance on the earth was to be one of the "great portents" that the Millennium was at hand. The most bizarre of them was an old woman named Dorothy Harling, who called herself "The Permanent Spring." After her exclusion, some French and English members continued to believe in her divine pretensions. According to Keimer, after each of her followers confessed his or her sins, she would whip the person and then urinate on the "several Parts that had offended."

Within the group, women continued to be prominent as prophets, although they did not administer the new sacraments or function as scribes. They too published collections of their divine warnings. As had been the case with the Quakers in the 1650s, in the eyes of the English public the presence of women as preachers and prophets was one of the great scandals of the French Prophets.[40]

Meanwhile, two of the leaders of the movement, each in association with a female prophet, began to draw away from the increasingly contentious and self-contained London group. Richard Roach and the former Quaker Sarah Wiltshire attempted to reassert the Philadelphian conception of a mystical infusion of divine love as the prelude to the Millennium. They were confronted by prophets like Thomas Dutton and the formidable Mary Keimer, who at one meeting declared to Roach, in God's voice: "Who art thou O man that Exaltest thyself? . . . How durst thou presume to speak unto me? I can this moment strike thee dead."[41] By 1712, overwhelmed by their opponents' greater prophetic firepower, Roach and Wiltshire had drawn away, although they remained in contact with some of the French Prophets.

In the summer of 1711, the Holy Spirit ordered John Lacy to leave his wife and to unite with the prophet Elizabeth Gray. He had long been fascinated with her elaborate repertory of inspired "signs" and performances. On one occasion, after watching her gyrating on the floor and rolling her eyes, Lacy had said, "when that Girl has Visions, I partake of the Joy of them." The rest of the group was scandalized at first, but then they decided that this might be a special instance of the inscrutability of God. Finally, the Spirit gave its approval, through the mouth of Mary Keimer. The pair moved to Lancashire, remaining at a discreet distance from the London core.[42]

In the five years since the three prophets had first arrived in London, the religious movement they initiated had taken some peculiar turns. Of the original trio, Fage had quickly faded into the background, and Cavalier publicly renounced his prophetic career in 1708. Only Marion had maintained a position of prominence, but God was at last calling him to return to the Continent. The French Prophets had been a source of great interest and amusement for the English press in their first years, but they no longer attracted much attention, despite the continuing stream of divine warnings that they published and circulated. They renewed their missionary tours of Great Britain in 1709, achieving some success in Scotland, where they recruited a dozen new prophets from among people predisposed to believe in the new dispensation by their reading of Boehme and the French quietist mystics Antoinette Bourignon and Mme. Guyon. Hillel Schwartz has shown that they also retained small circles of believers in some English towns, including Manchester, Birmingham, and Bristol, but information about them in the next decades is fragmentary. In 1737, Thomas Dutton wrote a friend that "the Spirit in its public Manifestations has gradually withdrawn."[43]

The French Prophets' influence on English popular religion had not ended. Only two years after Dutton wrote, the appearance of French Prophets among the new Moravian and Methodist societies in Bristol and London caused considerable consternation. Eight years after that, in 1747, they inspired, in an obscure fashion, the formation of the group of ecstatic worshipers at Bolton, near Manchester, that became the Shakers.

These developments lay in the future. For the present, the thrust of the prophetic movement was directed not to Great Britain but to the European continent. The French Prophets' first attempts at carrying their divine messages and warnings back across the Channel had not been encouraging. Late in 1708, Cavalier and his wife had made a disastrous journey to Holland, despite divine pronouncements from other prophets against the voyage. After its failure, he had publicly abandoned the group. The next spring, a mission by three English prophets and a scribe was treated with indifference in both London and Holland. In July 1710, a third mission to Holland led by Jean Allut did manage to generate some interest, but two months later Allut and the others were arrested and then expelled from the country.[44]

Despite these failures, the Holy Spirit again commanded the prophets to go to the Continent. This time Marion, Allut, and two scribes were to be the divine emissaries. And this time God was sending his prophets to Germany, Pietism's heartland, where millenarian and mystical ideas were at least as general as they were in England. More specifically, they were to journey to Brandenburg, where tens of thousands of Huguenot refugees from the south of France had settled.

{3}

The Community
of True Inspiration

The manner in which the Holy Spirit declared that the French Prophets were to extend their mission to Germany was sufficiently dramatic to assure the group, if they needed assurance, that they were still specially called and chosen to carry on the work of the Lord, despite all the disappointments, frustrations, and dissensions of the past several years. The most basic of the divisions within the group remained, however, for God spoke not to a general assembly but to "the French Brethren & Friends."

On 3 June 1711, Jean Allut issued the divine command that a basin of water be brought. He then performed several actions that signified the importance of what was to follow, "such as Terrible Agitations, Sighs, Groans, Cries, Quakings of ye Whole Body, such Faintings as made him fall backward, &c." God then spoke: "My will is . . . in Three Weeks . . . 4 of you go out of this City, out of this Kingdom, to carry my Word & my Message into another[;] I mean in Brandenburg."[1] God then declared that the chosen four were to be Allut, Marion, and two scribes, Charles Portales and Nicolas Fatio de Duillier.

They went first to Holland, where two years earlier the Cavaliers had embarrassed the prophetic movement and the English delegation and had met with general indifference. The mission in which Allut and his wife had participated in 1710 had been more successful, despite the hostility of most of the exiled Huguenot clergy, and it had resulted in two volumes of published divine warnings. The several prophets had also made some very useful friends for the movement. One of them was Benjamin Furly (1636–1714), an English merchant long resident in Rotterdam. He was from Colchester, just across the English Channel from Holland, and his family had long been prominent in the Quaker community. In 1677 and 1686, he had accompanied George Fox, William Penn, and George Keith on their tours of Holland and Germany and had served as their interpreter. He was Penn's principal agent on the Continent for the latter's project for settling Mennonites, separatist Pietists, and others persecuted for their religion in the "German Township" northwest of Philadelphia.

Both Furly's religious sympathies and his work for Penn had generated an extensive correspondence with the leading German Pietists and with the Petersens, the leaders of the German Philadelphians. He had been interested in the French Prophets since their arrival in London. One of the first English converts, Sir Richard Bulkeley, was a longtime friend, and his native town of Colchester was one of the towns on the eastern coast that had a circle of their adherents. Since the French Prophets' first visit to Holland, he had supported them financially, written in their defense, and intervened for them before the civil authorities.[2]

The French Prophets remained in Holland only briefly in 1711, and they almost always restricted their meetings to people who had already "made Profession to acknowledge this a Divine Manifestation," as Portales wrote in his memoir of the journey. Almost certainly, Furly would have been among those whom they visited in Rotterdam.

So would Pierre Jurieu. The indefatigable advocate of the Huguenot cause and propagandist of the miraculous events in the Cévennes in 1689 had never lost his faith in the world's millenarian redemption through the joint agency of the Protestant remnant and the British crown. He had zealously defended the Camisard Revolt and the prophetic manfestations that accompanied it as signs of the Millennium's near approach. After Marion, Fage, and Cavalier made their way to London, he quickly became their advocate as well. Two months before the French Prophets arrived in Holland in 1711, Daniel de Superville, the leading Huguenot minister in Rotterdam, wrote the chief minister at the Savoy church in London that his old friend Jurieu had changed considerably over the past four years, "and all because of the pretended inspired."[3] Thus Jurieu and his wife, an equally devoted supporter of the French Prophets, were certainly among those whom the four missionaries visited that summer. Like Furly, the Jurieus kept up an active correspondence with Francke and other leaders of the Pietist movement. Presumably they now wrote them about the prophets' arrival.

After Marion, Allut, and their scribes left Holland, they traveled across northern Germany to Berlin. The trip was uneventful, and only once were they visited by the Holy Spirit. They arrived in Berlin in late July and remained three weeks.

The diverse conglomeration of territories ruled by the Hohenzollerns had been elevated to the status of a kingdom only a decade before. Their capital of Berlin, a rare haven of toleration in central Europe, was also the home of an exceptionally large population of Huguenot refugees. As Calvinists governing a population that was mainly Lutheran and Reformed but included Anabaptists, Jews, Labadists, mystics, and separatists as well, the rulers were led both by state policy and religious sympathies to look sympathetically on Pietism as a means of promoting unity among their religiously diverse subjects.

Soon after the four missionaries' arrival, the Pietists' chief representative in Berlin, Carl Hildebrand von Canstein, reported to Francke in Halle on the arrival of "two prophets from the Cévennes, who have caused such a sensation in England." They held public meetings attended by sizable crowds of Germans and French. Once again, however, the Huguenot clergy was united against them; as in London and Holland they complained to the civil authorities. The four were called before the minister of state and ordered to leave Berlin immediately and the kingdom within three days.[4] That same night, the spirit descended on Marion. "Do not rebel against ye Will of ye Lord," it declared, "for he has spoken [when] he sent you hither. He at this time speaks in his withdrawing you from it. . . . You shall have my Will in a few days. Direct your way towards Halle."[5]

When the Hohenzollerns had acquired Halle in 1680 together with the rest of the Duchy of Magdeburg, it was a poky little place that had not yet recovered from the devastation of the Thirty Years' War. In 1685, the Elector began inviting Huguenot refugees to settle there. Merchants and artisans, they quickly became a dominant force in the town's reviving economy. After the founding of the university in 1694, some of them had become associated with the Pietist movement and with the *Stift*, Francke's religious foundation at the university.

While in Halle, the four missionaries met with Francke himself and his principal associates, but since Halle was in Prussian territory, they dared remain there only briefly. Francke's own religious eclecticism included a strong interest in divine manifestations of all kinds. A decade earlier, while serving as a preacher at Erfurt, he had publicly endorsed the ecstasies of several young female visionaries in the town. Even after he had been expelled from Erfurt and come to Halle, he had continued to be interested in possession phenomena, notably those of Anna Maria Schuchart, who recited verses while in a trance and exuded blood from her hands and forehead.[6]

According to Portales's memoir, the Halle Pietists had been very interested in the first reports that they received of the French Prophets' first pronouncements in London, but after Dr. Emes's failed resurrection they had been "very much stagger'd, if not totally estrang'd from this Dispensation." Apparently Marion and his companions managed to explain the episode satisfactorily, because after they had arrived at Leipzig, the capital of Saxony, Francke sent several of his associates to have further conversations with them. They also attracted the interest of a number of people in Leipzig, including many students at the university. Once again, their presence aroused controversy, so they moved on.

They visited several other towns, seeking out either Pietist enclaves or Huguenot colonies. At Coburg, they were "visited by ye Spirit, in ye presence of some Germans, Pietists whom we were recommended to." At Nuremberg, they received an elaborate announcement from God ("preceeded by expressive Signs of Wrath & fury") that their final destination on this trip was to be Vienna. They were then to return to Holland and arrange for the publication of all the warnings that they had received in Germany.

They stayed in Nuremberg for two weeks without incident. They held no public meetings, but they were visited by "several Persons of Quality very sober & Judicious."[7] From Nuremberg they traveled to Schwabach and Erlangen, both of which had large Huguenot colonies. There they encountered some people from "our *Cévennes*" who "in ye time of ye Grand Effusion of ye Spirit of ye Lord" had been "Eye Witnesses to a great many Miracles." At Ratisbon, the Holy Spirit commanded them go to Vienna "the sooner ye better," for "Babylon" was about to battle "the Lamb." Then, the Spirit declared, "Christ is coming in his Glory to re-enter into his Kingdom."

During their stay in the militantly Roman Catholic capital of the Habsburg Empire, they saw no one and delivered no divine warnings. Instead, they performed a silent "Sign unto it" that "within a Few, a few, a few, a few years" God was going to destroy Vienna. After receiving a divine command to depart, the four men returned to Holland, revisiting Ratisbon and Nuremberg on the way. In Rotterdam, they wrote out all the warnings, prayers, and "Prophetic Hymns" that the prophets had received during their journey and arranged for their publication in both French and Dutch. They arrived back in London on 15 December 1711.[8]

They did not remain in London very long. On 3 April, God declared through Elie Marion: "March, march, march toward the North, so that the Levant may hear my Voice." On 22 May, on the eve of the fourth anniversary of the Emes debacle, the same four missionaries met with four other prophets (two of them French, one Scottish, and one English) for a special sacrament of communion. The cup was placed between the Old and New Testaments, symbolizing the new dispensation that the French Prophets were about to proclaim.[9]

From Holland, they traveled to Sweden, whose Protestant warrior-king, Charles XII, was engaged in a confused struggle against the Russians, Poles, and Turks. In Stockholm, the Spirit descended on the prophets, but since the warnings were in French and the scribes were unable to translate them into Swedish, they were not comprehended by those who came to see the four missionaries. Bewildered, the prophets awaited further instructions.

God declared that they were to journey to the east, and thence to Rome. But in September, while on their way through Poland, they were arrested as Swedish spies. They were shifted from place to place under close guard for eight months. Imprisoned under miserable and unhealthy conditions, Marion contracted a fever from which he never recovered. Finally they were released on the orders of the king of Poland in May 1713. They had no money and no passports. They did manage to write a letter to their supporters in Holland which was then circulated in Germany and Switzerland, telling what had happened to "the four brothers of the Great Mission."[10]

Although the Treaty of Utrecht had at last ended the War of the Spanish Succession between France and her enemies, the political situation in central Europe was still very uncertain. In Danzig, the Holy

Spirit uttered a command through the mouth of Jean Allut that must have been welcomed by all four of the weary missionaries: "I call you to [go and] rejoice with your Brothers who are at Halle." They arrived there on 25 May.[11]

The French Prophets' second visit to Halle was by far the most important episode in the four years they spent wandering across Europe at the command of the Holy Spirit. Having this time received royal permission to reside there, they stayed for four weeks at the home of Allut's uncle, a French teacher, holding public meetings and conferring with Francke and other local dignitaries. As had been their practice since the prophets first arrived in London, their pronouncements were recorded by the scribes and copies distributed to those who attended. Francke cautiously declared that the prophets were not frauds; his young associate, the Reformed preacher Knauth, went further and publicly stated that their messages were divinely inspired.[12]

In his illness, Marion had ceased to prophesy, but Allut was visited by the Holy Spirit almost daily. His messages were full of the usual imagery of warfare and the destruction of the ungodly in preparation for the return of Christ, the "Captain of the Heavens," but the Pietists who heard him may have been more drawn to his prediction of the emergence of a regenerated and purified universal church, which would be "the Israel of God" and "the Land of Spiritual Canaan."[13]

Halle was almost the only place they had visited where they met with no public hostility. Instead, for a full month, they were able to deliver their messages and demonstrate the divine gift of spirit possession to crowds that included not only members of the authorized Protestant congregations but also people whose search for a "spiritual Canaan" had led them to separate themselves from all the world's churches.

Before their departure, the prophets introduced the sacrament of the love feast to an assembly that included Lutherans and members of German Reformed churches. The ceremony embodied the transcending of confessional divisions in a higher form of Christianity that French Prophets, Pietists, and Philadelphians all sought. In describing the occasion, Knauth emphasized the "experience of the greatest harmony" that all felt on that occasion. The group sang German hymns and then psalms "with French melody." There followed a rite of confession and then the Huguenot communion service.[14]

The French Prophets set out for the east, as God had commanded. They never returned to Halle, but their influence was to persist for a long time, not as a unifying but as a divisive force.

The quartet made their way across eastern Europe without incident, but without winning any converts either. They arrived in Constantinople in late August 1713. As in Vienna on their previous tour of the Continent, they saw no one and held no public meetings.

After continuing their journey to Smyrna, they boarded a ship and sailed to Italy. At Livorno in Tuscany, God declared that the dying Marion's mission was completed; he was to remain there while the others continued the voyage to Rome. He died on 29 November. He had been a prophet of the Lord continuously for more than a decade. With him died the tradition of liturgical and biblical prophetism that had first burst forth in the Midi in 1689.

The other three remained in Rome for a week. Again they issued no public warnings. Instead, God commanded that they perform a symbolic representation of the coming spiritualization of the world. They were to cut small pieces from their clothing and burn them. This was a sign that at the "Last Day," God was going to destroy the world's spiritual and ceremonial clothing "in order to clothe [his] People in Truth, Enlightenment, the Spirit of Life."

They returned to England in March 1714, having arranged in Holland for the publication of two final volumes of divine warnings and messages concerning their continental messages. They were accompanied by Madame Hélène Jurieu, who since her husband's death had been traveling the countryside with several Dutch prophets who had been inspired with the Holy Spirit as a result of the French Prophets' visits.[15]

French Prophets made no more tours of the Continent. A few Swiss and Dutch prophets joined the London circles, but there was no attempt to maintain regular contact with their followers in Halle and elsewhere. Instead, the various bands of prophets in England went their several ways. The next twenty-five years was a period that Hillel Schwartz has described as one of "personal, social and theological retrenchment." The French Prophets had not disappeared in England, although many people assumed that they had.

Meanwhile, the prophetic sparks that they had kindled in Germany began to blaze on their own. Soon after the four missionaries from London left Halle, several people who had seen and heard them there were themselves possessed by the Holy Spirit. The first was a young woman named Maria Elizabeth Matthes, who had been a servant in the home of Allut's uncle when the four had lived there. Like many of the Camisard prophets, she experienced convulsions for a time, and then in January 1714 she began to prophesy. The next to be affected were three brothers, students from Halberstadt named Pott, who in the next years were to be the principal agents for the dissemination of the pentecostal gift of spirit possession in Germany.

In Halle, the newly inspired gathered a circle of followers around them. Their most zealous advocates included Matthes's father, who was the secretary at Francke's orphanage; a man named Giezendammer who taught at his charity school; and the preacher Knauth. The learned and clerical establishment of Pietist Halle was appalled at the violence of the possessions and the theological implications of the pretensions of these new prophets, who in Germany usually called themselves the *Werkzeuge* or instruments of the Lord. Francke dismissed the three men from their positions.[16]

As in England, the clerical establishment's initial interest in prophetism gradually turned into hostility. Francke and his associates preached and wrote against the prophets and their claims, but they allowed them to continue their meetings. By the beginning of 1715, the circle numbered some forty people. They had also been joined by four prophets from Holland.

In the summer of 1714, the Halle "Inspiration Society" decided to send a delegation to Berlin in order to disseminate the divine message there. Matthes, the Pott brothers, another student, and the Potts' mother therefore traveled to the capital, where they held meetings in private homes day and night. They caused enough of a sensation to lead Johann Porst, one of the leading preachers in Berlin, to go and see them. Religiously awakened by Spener himself, Porst had warmly supported the efforts of the Halle Pietists to revitalize Lutheranism. He was also quite familiar with the Huguenot prophetic movement, having read Brousson's sermons and the *Théâtre sacré* in German translations. He now preached against the entire phenomenon, dismissing the testimonies of miracles in the Cévennes as "twaddle."

After questioning the Potts and their followers, he sent an unfavorable report on them to the king. The rest of the Berlin clergy shared his disapproval. They declared that one of the brothers was "a great ignoramus" and that their mother was "forward and filled with evil principles." In September, the king ordered the Inspired out of Berlin. At first, they intended to go to Holland, but instead they decided to ignore the royal decree and returned to Berlin. Porst interrogated them again, but they were released and allowed to resume their assemblies.

They now began to pass on the gift of inspiration to some of their Berlin followers. One of the first to be possessed was a tailor named Johann Michael Bolich, who some years earlier had undergone a Pietist conversion experience. He went into convulsions for four hours, and then "the Spirit . . . in him and through him sang a long poem." Bolich's possessions became increasingly violent, and his pronouncements more peculiar. He declared on one occasion that he was the Lord Jesus. On another, he predicted that the reign of God was going to begin on 27 September. Unfortunately, it was already November. Finally, after his possessions ceased, he told the rest of the group that he in fact had been seized by "the evil spirit."[17]

The Inspired Society of Berlin persisted for a few more years, but then it faded into oblivion. The Potts, meanwhile, sought a place more sympathetic to their message than Halle and Berlin had proved to be. They were scorned in Leipzig, but they received a more favorable reception in the Imperial Free City of Frankfort, where Pietism had flourished since the time that Spener himself had lived and worked there. One of the leading Pietists in the city, Andreas Gross, became their warm advocate. In general, however, Frankfort was no more sympathetic than Halle and Berlin had been.

The Inspired then traveled into the region north and west of Frankfort called the Wetterau, where in several small states there existed a policy of full religious toleration unknown anywhere else in Germany. As a result, especially in the four little states near Frankfort ruled by branches of the house of Ysenburg and in the counties of Sayn-Wittgenstein-Wittgenstein and Sayn-Wittgenstein-Berleburg between Hessen-Kassel and the Rhine River, there existed a diversity of religious belief and practice that rivaled the English Puritan Commonwealth at its height.

The region had been devastated by the Thirty Years' War and again by French armies in the 1680s. In order to attract colonists into their depopulated territories, the counts of Ysenburg and Wittgenstein welcomed all kinds of believers who had experienced persecution elsewhere, including Anabaptists, Philadelphians, Waldensians, mystics, and Huguenots. They also welcomed many people who (like the Seekers in Puritan England) had been led to separate themselves from the state churches, awaiting the advent of the purified and spiritualized church that Christianity had not seen since the earliest days. Many of them had been awakened in Pietist conventicles and now found themselves harassed by the anti-Pietist laws that many Swiss and German states had enacted since 1698.

It was at Frankfort that the eldest of the Pott brothers had a divine revelation that the time had come for those called by God to organize themselves in societies in order to engage in "prayer in common." While at first glance this hardly seems like a momentous announcement, for those who had separated themselves from the state churches it implied that God had at last commanded them to form a church of their own, based on scriptural example and continuing divine revelation. One of the leading German separatists, Alexander Mack, had already begun to move in that direction, gathering believers and baptizing them into the religious community that became the Church of the Brethren. Other separatist leaders repudiated the conduct of Mack's "Dunkers" as premature and unsanctioned by God.[18]

Despite the diversity of their origins and convictions, these separatists shared several notions that resembled the message that the Pott brothers and the rest of the German Inspired now brought into the Wetterau. They all believed in the possibility of new revelations, unmediated by hired clergy, which God would communicate directly in some miraculous fashion. They were all familiar with the German mystical tradition preserved in the writings of Tauler, Schwenkfeld, Weigel, Boehme, and many others who testified to the existence of some kind of divinely implanted inner word or inner light. Finally, having detached themselves from collective religious experience, they awaited a sign that the time had come once again to "pray in common." The mission of the Inspired into the Wetterau brought not only the wonders of possessed speech, with its dramatic accompaniment of convulsions and body language, but also the example of a sacramental community which the Germans had learned from their Camisard mentors.[19]

Among the separatists who found in the Inspired the revived church of Christianity's earliest days, with all the gifts of Pentecost restored to it, were Eberhard Ludwig Gruber, a former Lutheran

pastor, and his friend Johann Friedrich Rock. After years of persecution in their native Wurttemberg, they had found a religious haven
near Frankfort at Himbach in Ysenburg. Gruber had himself experienced occasional visitations of the Holy Spirit, but when he first
learned of the Pott brothers, he was skeptical, suspecting that their
convulsions might be the work of the Antichrist, acting in the world
in its final days. When the Potts arrived in Ysenburg in November
1714, Gruber's twenty-year-old son, Johann Adam Gruber, attended a
meeting at a neighbor's house at which the oldest brother, Tobias
Pott, spoke. Johann Adam Gruber wrote several years later that "the
words which he spoke, powerfully penetrated me and seemed to me
to be very majestic, and otherwise, his testimony appealed to me very
much." Two days later, the Potts came to the Grubers' house. The
father decided that their possessions were authentically divine. The
next day, obeying the Inspired Society's call for "prayer in common,"
Gruber organized a "Meeting for United Prayer," which became the
nucleus of the Community of True Inspiration. In the nineteenth
century, the remnant of that community migrated to the United
States, where their descendants live today in the seven Amana colonies near Cedar Rapids, Iowa.

A few days later, Johann Adam Gruber received the Holy Spirit.
His experience closely parallelled that which the Camisard prophets
and their English converts had experienced. He wrote that the possession was "very strange at first," and he feared that it was the work of
evil spirits. At the same time, he felt "a secret joy." He had convulsions for thirty-six hours before he began to prophesy, first one word
at a time, then for two hours without interruption.[20]

The Potts had similar success elsewhere in the region of the Wetterau, with the result that there were formed seven more circles of
believers associated with the Community of True Inspiration. The
Potts soon thereafter lost the prophetic gift, but Johann Adam
Gruber, Johann Friedrich Rock, and other *Werkzeuge* traveled tirelessly, prophesying in public and declaring the new dispensation
throughout central Europe. They succeeded in establishing more
circles of believers, scattered through Alsace, southern Germany, and
Switzerland. Eberhard Gruber never became a prophet, but he
claimed to possess a divine gift to oversee the moral conduct of the
entire Community and to distinguish between true and false
prophecies.

When the Count of Ysenburg decided that the group's missionary activities violated his policy of toleration, Gruber moved to Schwarzenau in Wittgenstein, which became the informal center of the Community of True Inspiration. From Schwarzenau, the various groups were coordinated by the periodic visits of the *Werkzeuge* and their scribes and by a code of discipline, "The Twenty-Four Rules of True Godliness," revealed to J. A. Gruber in 1716. They also compiled a large collection of hymns, many of which had been communicated to the prophets under inspiration. Their central ritual practices were (and continue to be) the mutual confession of sins and the love feast.[21]

Unlike their English counterparts, the German successors to the French Prophets quickly developed an ecclesiastical structure and code of discipline that defined clearly and unequivocally what forms of sacred theater the believers would accept as authentic. The leadership—by divine command—had stated in advance how God would henceforth appear among them.

The Community of True Inspiration never forgot its Pietist origins. It also preserved the German mystical tradition and an antirational passivity that was quite unlike the world-defying militancy that the Camisard prophets had shared with their audiences. According to a collection of instructions that E. L. Gruber compiled in 1715, all members of the Community were to "obey, without reasoning, God, and through God your superiors." They were also supposed to "abandon self, with all its desires, knowledge and power" and to "bear all inner and outward sufferings in silence." When Gruber outlined his reasons for believing that the words that emanated from the prophets were those of God, he said that they brought people to "godly repentance and atonement" and restored the experience of congregational worship.[22]

Initially, however, the experience of divine presence had generated a similarly precarious emotional state to that which the French and English assemblies had experienced. The first prophetic meetings in Ysenburg were so noisy that a government official reported on them to the Count of Ysenburg. The Inspired, he wrote, "more than ever practiced an alarming tumult and disturbance in those homes where they live and were gathered together . . . with shocking leaping, raging, crying, and shouting 'Woe! Woe!' and prophesying the most alarming judgment of God on town and country."[23]

The group was also troubled by the claims of false prophets, but

E. L. Gruber was able to "detect and exorcize" them. Whenever a "false spirit" was present in the assembly, Gruber received a warning in the form of "an extraordinary shaking of the head and shivering of the mouth." The first decade of their history was continually marked by controversies over false prophets, their denunciation, and their expulsion if they refused to accede to the admonitions of the leadership.[24]

In 1715, there were five recognized *Werkzeuge* in the Community of True Inspiration who had received the gift of divine possession. Like the French Prophets of London, they now were commanded to carry their message to the rest of Europe. Their scribes recorded all of their pronouncements, which were then collected and printed in bound volumes and read aloud at assemblies of the believers.

J. A. Gruber was one of the most tireless of the missionaries in the first years. After traveling all over Germany and Switzerland accompanied by other prophets and scribes, in January 1716 he and his companions made their way to Prague. According to the official *Inspirations-Historie*, it had been "a very difficult and troublesome journey, partly because of the harsh and cold weather and also because everyone there was Catholic." In Prague, they were commanded, "to their great astonishment," to go to one of the city's synagogues. Some of the Jews who witnessed Gruber's convulsions and prophesying were at least interested in what they had seen, and the scribe, Blasius Daniel Mackinet, explained to them in detail the whole experience of spirit possession as the Community of True Inspiration understood it. Mackinet said that first the *Werkzeug* felt "a gentle and pleasant glow which gradually becomes more intense and also fills the external body." There followed either trembling or convulsions, "and in the center of this internal fire the word of the Lord is born." Throughout his possession, the prophet was simply "a passive instrument in the hands of the Lord."

While the German Inspired were never led by the Spirit into enacting the sorts of possessed theatrics that so titillated London in 1706, they were performers nonetheless, and the manner in which they delivered their pronouncement always underscored the import of their messages. When they were announcing "punishments and judgments," it was done "with great force, majestic gestures, strong *Bewegungen* [movements, emotion] and with a true voice of thunder," especially when they were delivering their pronouncements in a public place like a church. On the other hand, when they were speaking of God's glory or were promising great rewards for the children of God, "then their motions were gentle and the gestures pleasing."[25]

After a few years, the initial fire of inspiration within the Community became a soft glow. Some of the prophets fell away or died, and few new ones appeared. J. A. Gruber lost the gift of prophecy after he failed to submit to his father's spiritual authority to the latter's satisfaction. Another young *Werkzeug,* J. C. Gleim, joined J. A. Gruber in his defiance of the older leaders. The fact that some of the membership supported them precipitated a serious crisis within the Community, because (according to the official history) this minority had been "distracted" by Gruber's and Gleim's prophecies of great events in the world that presaged the Millennium. They were therefore "unable to understand that the one and only important thing was to accomplish salvation for their souls in this their allotted time of grace."

A few years later, J. A. Gruber joined other sectarians from the Wetterau in migrating to Pennsylvania. During the transatlantic religious revival known in America as the Great Awakening, he joined with Lutherans, German Reformed, Moravians, Dunkers, and other sectarians in an abortive effort to create a single evangelical union for the German settlers. He remained in touch with the Inspired in Germany, but he was never able to organize a Community of True Inspiration in his new homeland.[26]

After the elder Gruber's death in 1728, Rock was the sole leader. When Count Ludwig von Zinzendorf, the founder of the Restored Moravian church, arrived in the Wetterau two years later, he tried to absorb the Inspired into his "philadelphic" conception of a spiritual community that would transcend all churches, but without success. By the time that John Wesley visited Zinzendorf in the Wetterau in 1738, the Moravians and the Community of True Inspiration were not on good terms.

Rock continued to issue messages and warnings for another twenty years, as tireless in his missionary efforts as ever, but he won few new converts. Until new prophets appeared in 1817, the Inspired, scattered in small congregations across Germany and Switzerland, met for worship, read aloud the divine messages that God's instruments had received in earlier days, and awaited further guidance.[27]

Modern histories of the Amana Society do not even mention the

French Prophets, but their religious parentage is beyond question. The four missionaries from London embodied in their turn the mingled hope and despair that had accompanied the emergence of the prophetic movement in the mountains of southeastern France. This the quartet brought with them to Germany, together with the entranced behavior of convulsion and body language that accompanied the warnings and messages of the Lord.

If the moderate Pietists repudiated the French Prophets and their German disciples, their influence on German popular religion was considerable nevertheless. If only a scattered minority finally accepted the newly inspired as God's messengers, many more who were religiously adrift found in the prophetic movement a repertoire of conventions and convictions which had the attractions of familiarity. Like all Pietists, the Inspired called the people to repentance and moral discipline on the basis of divine imperatives that transcended the pettiness of clergy and catechisms. They argued for an immediacy of religious experience that was accessible to all. And they showed that Christians could come together, in these the world's last days, in communities of worship which re-created the time of the founding of the primitive Christian church, when the Holy Spirit had similarly descended upon his faithful.

{4}·

The Methodist
Awakening

When news of the Huguenot prophets first circulated
through Europe, many Protestants had interpreted the
fact of their appearance as one more demonstration that
the spirit of God was working to bring into being the purified church
the world had so long awaited. While they remained in France, the
prophets themselves defined their roles more locally, as the heralds of
the restoration of their own religious community, which once again
would live under the benevolent protection of God and their king.
The failure of the Camisard Revolt had shattered that belief and led
the Protestant remnant in the Midi to come to a tacit accommodation
with the political realities by repudiating the militancy and cosmic
self-confidence that prophetism had encouraged. On the other hand,
the little circles of French Prophets in England and the groups on the
Continent associated with the Community of True Inspiration preserved the millenarian rhetoric and techniques of possession of the
Huguenot prophets.

By the 1730s, it certainly seemed that their announcements of the
Antichrist's demise had been premature. With the exception of the little bands of sectarians who preserved their memory, nobody seriously considered the French Prophets to have been more than the
most recent example of the dangers of "enthusiasm." The mood of
collective fear and exaltation that the French menace had evoked
among European Protestants a generation before had given way to
one of caution and complacency. Even in Halle, Pietism's citadel, the
vision of an evangelical Christianity that sought nothing less than the
moral regeneration and spiritual rebirth of the whole world was in
danger of becoming one more orthodoxy of theological disputes and
pious platitudes.

The dream had faded; it had not been forgotten. Centuries of popular religious tradition, supported by the interpretation of the prophetic books of the Bible, held that God's spirit must manifest itself in some general fashion before the world's end. "Not yet" did not mean "never."

It had always been a paradox of Pietism that it expected the divinely induced regeneration to be collective and universal yet at the same time absolutely personal, through God's entering the heart of the individual believer. The traditional millenarian repertoire of battles, earthquakes, and angelic interventions was not repudiated, but that apocalyptic drama had far less urgency for the Pietists than the one that every Christian experienced in trying to win salvation through the conquest of sin.

Beginning in 1735, this quite different notion of the Millennium, one associated with the concept of spiritual new birth that Puritans, mystics, and Pietists had all tried to describe, took on a new urgency in some parts of the Protestant world. During the next several years, revivals of spiritual concern swept through much of England and Wales, most of the English colonies in North America, and a wide swath of lowland Scotland. The fact that they were nearly simultaneous yet had begun independently was for their advocates one sure indication that they were the heralds of the work of universal regeneration. The English, Welsh, Scottish, and American revivals shared an evangelical tradition that included the belief that salvation took place by means of the agency of God's free grace. As George Whitefield declared in one of his first sermons, genuine conversion came only when men and women were "inwardly wrought upon, and changed by the powerful Operations of the *Holy Spirit.*"[1] All of the revivals also shared the experience of the preaching of the young Whitefield, so dramatically if ephemerally effective in arousing interest in the new birth of spiritual enlightenment that alone could bring salvation.

Despite the great hopes that they awakened, the revivals did not transform the world. The time was still "not yet." Nevertheless, for those who experienced them, they seemed to demonstrate that when he chose to do so, God could act in the world through the miraculous manifestation of his spirit.

Unlike the Huguenot prophetic movement and its English and Continental successors, there was no necessary connection between the religious revivals and spirit possession. Their large public meetings, especially those held outdoors, were apt settings for sacred theater, with the potential for evoking a strong emotional response from its audiences, but the assumption was always that the conversion process would be an inward drama, a private culmination of the public ritual of the revival service. In Scotland and among Scottish Presbyterians in the American colonies, the clergy insisted upon this distinction. Elsewhere, however, when those who experienced the spiritual rebirth were possessed by the spirit in spectacular ways, sometimes their behavior was incorporated into the scenario. Two of the movement's ablest and most zealous spokesmen, John Wesley and Jonathan Edwards, were sufficiently impressed by some of the spirit possessions that they witnessed to write in their defense, arguing in effect that spirit possession was a possible but not an essential component of the process of the new birth.

It is a convenient shorthand to call the English religious resurgence the Methodist Awakening, but it should be remembered that like Pietism the movement was remarkably diverse, comprising a wide assortment of personalities and perspectives. Nevertheless, there is no question that it was John Wesley, ably seconded by his brother Charles, who has come to embody the revival and in his sermons, letters, essays, and published journals gave it structure and definition. And it was John Wesley who gave his public approval to the spectacles of noisy and emotionally charged sacred theater that were often a feature of early Methodist worship. His critics dismissed them as "enthusiasm" and saw this as an indication that Methodism did not deserve serious scrutiny as a religious movement. No historian today would agree. The Methodist Awakening profoundly and permanently influenced England, not only religious but socially and politically as well.

As John D. Walsh has expressed it, Methodism was "a potent blend of traditionalism and novelty."[2] The combination is apparent in the structure of the Methodist societies, which extended and adapted the framework of the old Church of England religious societies and the Pietist conventicles, the latter brought to England in 1738 in the form of the Moravian "bands." It was equally evident in the preaching, which combined the Puritan rhetoric of moral righteousness with a heightened emotionalism. Always, Methodism set out to obtain for every believer the experience of the touch of God's spirit that alone would bring salvation.

For some people, including George Whitefield, it was Whitefield's preaching (especially his sermon *On the Nature and Necessity of Our Regeneration or New-Birth in Christ Jesus*) that "under God began the awakening at London, Bristol, Gloucester and Gloucestershire" before he sailed to America in 1737.[3] Perhaps, but preaching alone could not possibly have launched the movement that transformed eighteenth-century England. Throughout the country, there were groups that preserved the Puritan heritage of soul-searching, their prayer and reading of scripture sometimes augmented by the study and discussion of mystical writers like Boehme. They hoped for some kind of divine assurance that they were on the right track and that it was possible to restore Christianity to its original purity.

For John Wesley, it had been his chance encounter with Moravian missionaries while on his way to Georgia in 1735 that had first suggested to him that the scriptural integrity of the early Christians could be restored without separating from the Church of England. His public mission and private quest had then been crystallized for him by a young Moravian named Peter Boehler, whom he met shortly after his return to England. The volatility of the religious scene in 1738 is suggested by the fact that Wesley met Boehler at the home of Francis Wynantz, a German-born merchant who was a sometime follower of the French Prophet Hannah Wharton.[4]

Boehler told him that the experience of conversion must be instantaneous and in a sense miraculous. Wesley reread the book of Acts; to his "utter astonishment," he found "scarce any instances . . . so slow as that of St. Paul, who was three days in the pangs of the new birth." Wesley thought that God surely did not work in the same way now, but then he talked to "several living witnesses" who told him how "in a moment" they had received "such a faith in the blood of His Son as translated them out of darkness and into light, out of sin and fear into holiness and happiness." His friends, even his brother Charles, were upset and angry with him for his new notions, until (Wesley wrote) "it did please God then to kindle a fire which I trust shall never be extinguished."[5]

Charles Wesley's objections ended when he himself underwent conversion on 21 May 1738. Three days later, John Wesley had his own experience. At the religious society in Aldergate that had been organized by Boehler and Wesley's friend, the young bookseller James Hutton, someone was reading aloud the preface to the epistle to the Romans by Martin Luther, the rediscovery of whose thought had played such an important role in the formation of German Pietism. Wesley wrote in his journal: "I felt my heart strangely warmed. I felt I did trust in Christ, Christ alone for salvation; and an assurance was given me, that He had taken away *my* sins, even *mine,* and saved *me* from the law of sin and death." The passage is curiously reminiscent of Elie Marion's description of the way his prophetic possessions began: "When the Spirit of God wants to seize me, I sense a great warmth in my heart . . . which is sometimes preceded by a shivering of all my body."[6]

Wesley and Boehler had organized a new religious society in Fetter Lane, quite near (as it happened) to the site of the French Prophets' first public place of worship in the Barbican. All of its members belonged to the Church of England, but Wesley and Boehler introduced the Moravian practices of mutual confession and dividing the society into small bands, each consisting of from five to ten people, who met regularly for prayer, singing, and discussion. After Wesley had visited the continental Moravian communities, he also instituted their practice of holding "a general love feast" on one evening each month. Thus the ceremony which the French Prophets had introduced to German Pietists in 1711 returned to London, where it had first been celebrated.[7]

Boehler went to America, and in June 1738 John Wesley made his pilgrimage to visit the Pietists and Moravians in Holland and Germany. Upon his return to London three months later, Wesley began preaching and discoursing almost daily in the seven Church of England religious societies of the metropolis and in the few churches that were open to him. Everywhere he talked about the Moravians, the examples of gospel piety he had witnessed in their communities in Holland, Saxony, and the Wetterau, and their teaching concerning the instantaneous new birth.

On the first day of January 1739, in the course of a night-long love feast at the Fetter Lane society, the spirit of God descended on the assembled congregation. Wesley wrote that "the power of God came mightily upon us, insomuch that many cried out for exceeding joy, and many fell to the ground."[8] It was the first of many such instances that would accompany Wesley's ministry during the next several years.

While Wesley was quite willing to interpret this and many similar outbreaks as evidence of the hand of God, he tried to distinguish between divine inspiration and "enthusiasm," which for him was "false, imaginary inspiration." A month earlier, responding to his brother Samuel, who had chided him for accepting as authentic the claims of some of the awakened to have received visions of bursting balls of fire or of Jesus himself, Wesley wrote that "weak minds" could "pervert" such experiences "to an idle use." He then asked rhetorically, "Does it follow that visions and dreams in general 'are bad branches of a bad root'? God forbid!"[9]

Two weeks after the encounter with what he believed to be the Lord's true spirit at the love feast in Fetter Lane, Wesley had the first of his several encounters with French Prophets when he conversed with Isaac Hollis, whom he had met soon after his return to London. Wesley decided that the Prophets "think to attain the end without the means" and that their purported revelations contradicted "the Law and the Testimony." Two weeks later, he and several companions visited a young Prophet named Mary Plewit. Some of the others were impressed with her performance, but Wesley wrote that "the motion might be either hysterical or artificial." He was similarly cautious five months later when he met French Prophets in Bristol; their reliance on dreams, visions, and inspired revelations violated "the Law and the Testimony."

In declaring that the French Prophets' revelations failed to conform to "the Law and the Testimony," Wesley meant that while such manifestations might be from God, they had no validity in and of themselves. The only legitimate test was twofold: they must conform to the "testimony" of Scripture and of awakened Christians who had passed through new birth, and they must be related to the ultimate manifestation of the divine law, which was the receipt of the Holy Spirit within the individual soul.[10] One might say that for Wesley the distinction between authentic sacred theater and its feigned or satanic counterfeits depended on the occasion. If God chose to display his power in surprising ways as individuals found their way to God, so be it.

Thus Wesley distinguished, at least to his own satisfaction, between the extravagances of the French Prophets and the superficially similar behavior that some of those who came to hear him preach now began to exhibit. In these cases, he approached the question of the nature of their possession with the same "robust and almost reckless eclecticism"[11] with which he approached everything in life.

Four days after his meeting with Hollis, while he was preaching at one of the religious societies, "a well-dressed, middle-aged woman suddenly cried out as in the agonies of death." When she came to see him the next day, she told him that she had been obsessed with her sins for three years, but that now for the first time she had some hopes of overcoming them. The same thing happened to a woman in Oxford a few weeks later, who "fell in an extreme agony, both of body and soul, and soon after cried out . . . 'Now I know I am forgiven for Christ's sake.'" A week later, the behavior of another woman convinced him that "the enemy was near." He described the episode in a letter to Whitefield. "Presently Mrs. Shrieve fell into a strange agony both of body and mind," he wrote. "Her teeth gnashed together; her knees smote each other; and her whole body trembled exceedingly. We prayed on, and within an hour the storm ceased. She now enjoys a sweet calm, having remission of sins, and knowing that her Redeemer liveth."[12]

It was to episodes such as these that Wesley referred when he prefaced his 1739 journal with the statement that "these extraordinary circumstances seem to have been designed by God for the further manifestation of His work, to cause His power to be known, and to awaken the attention of a drowsy world." Charles Wesley's journal for the same period shows that he did not share his brother's opinion. He wrote of one of Isaac Hollis's possessions that "he gobbled like a turkey-cock." When at the Fetter Lane society a man named Edward Nowers "groaned, screamed, [and] roared out," Charles wrote that he "was not offended by it,—nor edified." When Count Zinzendorf, the Moravian leader, visited London in April, Charles talked to him about "motions, visions, dreams" and was "confirmed" in his "dislike of them."[13]

John Wesley meanwhile, after much hesitation and prayerful discussion, had accepted Whitefield's invitation to come to Bristol in order to continue the work that the latter's emotional preaching had begun there. It was a crucial decision for the Methodist revival, for Wesley's organizational skills preserved within the religious societies the intensity of religious concern that Whitefield had aroused.

The same "extraordinary circumstances" of outcries and ecstasies accompanied his work in Bristol. When it first occurred, Wesley rejoiced that "signs and wonders are even now wrought by His holy child Jesus." It quickly became a regular feature of the meetings. At one meeting, "one, and another and another sunk to the earth; they dropped on every side as thunderstruck." The next day "all Newgate rang with the cries of those whom the word of God cut to the heart." A few days later, he noted that "many were offended at the cries of those on whom the power of God came." The next day, at another society, Wesley's "voice could scarce be heard amidst the groanings of some and the cries of others." As in London, physical manifestations of the process of the new birth were sometimes accompanied by dreams or visions that the individuals believed to be divine. When Wesley wrote his brother Samuel, still an outspoken critic of his brothers' activities, he defended what was happening in Bristol by contending that the experience produced in these people a complete moral transformation so that they overcame their sinfulness and felt only "a pure desire of doing the will of God." What he heard and saw in these meetings were "facts." They proved "that God now, as aforetime, gives remission of sins and the gift of the Holy Ghost, which may be called visions."[14]

Even stranger performances by some of those who underwent the process of conversion in the sacred theater of the meetings of the religious societies led Wesley to conclude that God was not the only supernatural force at work in Bristol. On 2 May a weaver named John Haydon, who had deplored the "strange fits" that were now a feature of meetings of Bristol's religious societies, was himself possessed while reading Wesley's sermon on "Salvation by Faith." Wesley noted in his journal that "in reading the last page he changed colour, fell of[f] his chair, and began screaming terribly, and beating himself against the ground."

The "cue" for Haydon's performance had been contained in Wesley's sermon, which referred to "the adversary" who always worked against those who preached salvation by faith. When Wesley and some of Haydon's neighbors came to see him, Haydon communicated to them the drama he believed to be taking place in his soul, crying out: "O thou devil! thou cursed devil! . . . Thou canst not stay. Christ will cast thee out." The group responded in their turn, praying over him, until finally "his pangs ceased, and both his body and soul were set at liberty." Two weeks later, an equally spectacular drama of satanic affliction was performed by Thomas Maxfield, who was to become a leading figure in Methodism. Maxfield "began to roar out and beat himself against the ground, so that six men could scarcely hold him." Wesley wrote that "except for John Haydon, I never saw one so torn of the Evil One."

Wesley had with some hesitation continued Whitefield's very different kind of sacred theater, preaching to large crowds in the open air. In May, episodes that Wesley interpreted as the struggle of divine and satanic spirits for the soul of the believer became a feature of these meetings as well. He wrote to his brother Samuel that God "began to make bare His arm, not in a close room, neither in private, but in the open air. . . . One and another, and another was struck to the earth, exceedingly trembling at the presence of His power. Others cried with a long and bitter cry, 'What must I do to be saved?'"[15]

A very different account of these developments was recorded by young John Cennick, who until Wesley broke with him in 1741 was one of his most trusted lay associates. According to Cennick, Wesley encouraged the possessed behavior which he and others interpreted as "the work of the Holy Ghost, the bruising of the Serpent's head, casting out the old man, etc." Sometimes people would foam at the mouth and become "violently agitated." Others would "sweat uncommonly, and their necks and tongues [would] swell and twist out of all shape. Some prophesied, and some uttered the worst blasphemies against our Savior." Other members were so distressed at the commotion, especially "when they saw Mr. Wesley encourage it," that they left the societies.

A clergyman in Bristol wrote *The Gentleman's Magazine* that several of Whitefield's friends who had attended the meetings had told him that Wesley had brought on the screams and convulsions when he prayed "*that God would visibly manifest some Token of his Favour.*" Wesley had then told the congregation that those who were afflicted could no more help it "than the sun can cease to shine."[16]

Clearly the issue is more complicated. There was a subtle dynamic at work between preacher and audience. Whitefield's effectiveness lay to a degree in the fact that he was consciously a performer, utilizing gestures and the modulation of his voice to elicit the intended emotional responses from his audience. Wesley was not at all a performer in that sense, but by some theatrical chemistry he suggested to some of his hearers that they might be acted upon by supernatural power in publicly evoking the private drama of conversion. The possessions did not occur because Wesley expected or even wanted them to happen, but when they did happen, it was consistent with his own exuberant and occasionally credulous zeal to incorporate them into a framework of sacred theater.

Why should Bristol have been so receptive to the Methodist Awakening and so susceptible to the physical manifestations of religious enthusiasm? It is true that since the days of the Commonwealth, Bristol had been a haven for religious radicals of all kinds. In 1656, the city had witnessed the period's most notorious performances of sacred theater when the Quaker leader James Nayler was persuaded by Bristol Quakers to enact the role of Jesus in a triumphal procession through the streets. The most bizarre of all the seventeenth-century religious radicals, the Ranters, were a presence there as well.[17] The French Prophets had found the city relatively sympathetic to their message, and they continued to be a disturbing presence, occasionally winning Quakers and even Baptists to their cause. Yet neither the tradition of Puritan radicalism nor the presence of the French Prophets explains the outbreaks of divine and diabolical possession that persisted sporadically among the Methodists of the Bristol area for twenty-five years. A cautiously anthropological approach might propose that they persisted because the tradition of Puritan radicalism and the tacit approval of Wesley and his converts provided a cultural context and a mutually satisfactory explanation for possession. Wesley's own explanation was simply that it was God's doing—or more precisely that God and Satan were battling for the souls of Bristol's sinners.[18]

John Wesley was not an emotional preacher, but apparently his carefully reasoned and clearly presented sermons touched religious sensibilities already aroused by Whitefield's emotional calls for the new birth. While Wesley quickly accepted the trances and convulsions as manifestations of the supernatural, Whitefield shared Cennick's and Charles Wesley's serious reservations. He may also have been piqued that Wesley was eliciting more emotion from his hearers than even Whitefield himself. He wrote Wesley that should he give similar "encouragement to those convulsions, . . . how many would cry out every night! I think it is tempting God to require such signs." Whitefield agreed that there was "something of God in it," but "the devil . . . interposes. I think it will encourage the French Prophets, take people from the written word, and make them depend on visions, convulsions, etc., more than on the promises and precepts of the gospel."[19]

In June Wesley returned to London, because the Fetter Lane society was "in great confusion" as the result of the activities of a French Prophet named Mary Lavington and her supporters. In addition to claiming the kind of prophetic inspiration that John Wesley had already rejected in his encounters with other French Prophets, Lavington promulgated a notion that was to be an issue of contention among Methodists for several decades. When at one meeting a man asked whether a person could "attain perfection here," Charles Wesley quickly responded that he could not. But Lavington "cried out vehemently, 'Look for perfection; I say absolute perfection.'"[20]

In a sense, it was the old antinomian notion once more, which as Christopher Hill has said "attended on Calvinism like a shadow." In the seventeenth century, there were some in both old and new England who believed that those whom God had chosen transcended the laws and limitations that were the lot of lesser folk. Similarly during the transatlantic awakening of the 1740s, some who underwent what they believed to be the miraculous infusion of grace at the time of their conversion were persuaded that they could sin no more. It was a dilemma that Methodists, American New Lights, and their spiritual heirs the Shakers all confronted. If conversion produced a New Being, surely that person was spiritually unlike the old creature. For both the Methodists and Shakers, sinlessness was a possibility, but one that could be achieved only within a framework of social structures, moral discipline, and spiritual hierarchy. Nevertheless, the fervor that accompanied both movements occasionally generated in their converts the conviction that sinless perfection was the necessary culmination of true conversion and the permanent state of the true Christian.[21]

Fortunately for the Wesleys, the prophet Lavington's claims to perfection clashed with the facts of her "lewd life and conversation," which Charles Wesley recorded and presented to the society. She also claimed that she could have Christ appear to her in any shape that she chose: "As a dove, an eagle, &c." When he confronted her at a society meeting and asked, "Who is on God's side? Who is for the old Prophets rather than the new?" nearly all the members accompanied him into another room. Thus when John Wesley arrived in London the next day, the crisis had been nearly resolved. He addressed the Fetter Lane society and told them "not to believe every spirit, but to try the spirits, whether they were of God." The membership agreed to "disown" the prophet Lavington.[22]

The French Prophets were active in other towns as well, notably in Bristol. After nearly thirty years of obscurity, they had resumed their public witness, sometimes reviving the theatrics that had given the early Quakers such notoriety. For example, when three Prophets appeared at the Quakers' Yearly Meeting in Bristol in 1738, one of them removed her cloak at the meeting's conclusion and "appeared in a monstrous and frightful Habit, with a Covering of Sackcloth . . . strewing *Ashes* upon her Head, and begun such a raving, with Postures so frightful, that the Meeting broke up immediately."[23] Upon Wesley's return to Bristol on 22 June, he found that French Prophets were visiting the religious societies there as well. In warning against them, he again declared that there was one "certain test—the Law and the Testimony."[24]

The French Prophets never again posed a serious challenge to Methodism, but they continued for at least another five years to appear at meetings and make their noisy witness. The Welsh evangelist Howell Harris noted in his diary in 1744 that while in London he heard "an account of the French Prophets and of the devils acting in them, and how they design on Mr. Wesley."[25] For both the Methodists and the Moravians, the French Prophets were an irritating presence, but they succeeded neither in infiltrating their religious societies nor in drawing members away. Their principal significance lay in the fact that they forced the Methodist and Moravian leaders to confront the implications of a reliance on the Holy Spirit unmediated by institutional structures and the moral guidance embodied in the Scriptures.

Throughout 1739, large crowds came to hear the Wesleys and Whitefield when they preached, both in the societies and out of doors. John Wesley divided his time between Bristol and London. In both cities, the faintings and outcries continued, although with somewhat less frequency. He may have been gratified when one of Whitefield's sermons in Bristol produced similar ecstatic behavior. Whitefield did not mention the episode in his own journal, but Wesley commented in his that "from this time, I trust, we shall all suffer God to carry on His own work in the way that pleaseth him."[26]

During the fall and winter of 1739-40, strange new episodes of possession broke out in the area called Kingswood, near Bristol. Its population lived under primitive conditions in scattered settlements, eking out a bare living from the forests and mines. According to the diarist James Jenkins, who spent his childhood there, "most of the people were exceedingly poor, and exceedingly wicked." Kingswood had never been incorporated into the parish system of the established church. When the Reverend William Morgan (who subsequently became a Quaker) and then George Whitefield preached outdoors in the clearings, they were gratified by a remarkably warm and interested response from the miners and their families. Whitefield laid the cornerstone for a school for the children, and a religious society was organized. When John Wesley took charge of ministering to the Methodists of Bristol, he too was encouraged by the apparent concern for salvation and moral improvement exhibited by many of the people of Kingswood.[27]

John Cennick, only twenty years old, was placed in charge of the Kingswood school. With Wesley's tacit approval, he also preached at various assemblies, the first layman within the Methodist movement to do so. Cennick had been disquieted by the possessed behavior that he witnessed in Bristol, which he tended to ascribe to the Devil. When even more violent exhibitions began to appear at his meetings in Kingswood, he immediately concluded, as he wrote to Wesley, that the struggle of "the Serpent" with "the Spirit of God" for the souls of the awakened had produced "a fierce combat in the inward parts, so that the weaker part of man, the Body[,] is overcome, and those Cries and Convulsions follow." He was preaching one evening at the school: "It was pitch dark; it rained much; and the Wind blew vehemently. Large Flashes of Lightning, and loud Claps of thunder, mixt with the Screams of Frightened Parents, and the Exclamations of nine distressed Souls! The Hurry and Confusion, caused thereby, cannot be expressed. . . . I never saw the like, nor even the shadow of it before."[28]

By the time that Wesley returned to Bristol from a preaching tour in Wales in October, three young women in Kingswood had claimed that they were possessed by devils. According to Cennick, they were able to predict who would be possessed next; one of them, though illiterate, was able to answer questions put to her in Greek or Latin. When Wesley asked another of them how the Devil had entered her, she replied, "By thy gospel, thou toad!" As the three women writhed and screamed, John and Charles Wesley prayed over them. After several hours, they were released from their torment.[29]

According to Cennick, "things of this kind were frequent everywhere, and all manner of fancies were preached by such means." John Wesley's journal does suggest that he had come to consider convulsions and ecstasies to be a necessary feature of the conversion experience. When a series of meetings in Bristol a few months earlier had produced no dramatic phenomena, he wrote that perhaps the Methodists had "grieved the Spirit of the jealous God by questioning His work; and that, therefore, He is withdrawn from us for a season." Thus the demonic possessions at Kingswood in the fall of 1739 may have been for him a kind of negative assurance that God's spirit was still present in Bristol.

The following spring, similar phenomena appeared in London. At society meetings, many people were afflicted with "a spirit of laughter." A former Quaker named Lucretia Smith "laughed until almost strangled" and then began cursing, blaspheming, and writhing about "with incredible strength." When two women questioned whether those thus afflicted were truly possessed, Wesley wrote in his journal, "God suffered Satan to teach them better." For two days, they laughed continually, "a spectacle to all," until the group prayed over them, then they were "delivered in a moment."[30]

Cennick's opinion was quite different. Like many of the Methodists' critics, he concluded that the themes of the Wesleys' preaching encouraged the convulsions and demonic possessions. He therefore stopped preaching on sin and damnation; nor did he describe the conversion process and the possibility of Christian perfection. Instead, he preached only on "Him and His righteousness. And so all the fits and crying out ceased wherever I came." In effect, Cennick had denied that religious services could legitimately be the setting for a sacred theater that included public displays of divine or satanic power. Once the premise that they could occur had been removed, they did not occur.

It was the beginning of a split with Wesley that would culminate in Cennick's expulsion from the Methodists early in 1741. The issue was partly one of doctrine, as Cennick moved toward the Calvinistic convictions of Whitefield and Howell Harris. His preaching, as Wesley freely admitted, attracted bigger crowds than Wesley's own, and he became increasingly outspoken in his criticisms of the Wesleys' theology. Cennick wrote Whitefield in 1741 that "no atheist can more preach against Predestination than they; and all who believe Election are counted enemies to God, and called so." He was also distressed at the ideas and behavior of some of the Bristol converts, notably Edward Nowers, who claimed to be "the sinless perfect man" and the equal of God himself. Nowers's religious eccentricities had already led both Whitefield and the German Moravians to break with him, but Wesley wrote James Hutton that he thanked God for sending Nowers to him: "He was the man I wanted. . . . I have not had full proof of any one who appeared to have more of the discernment of Spirits, and that sometimes without a word being spoken." Several others also claimed to be perfect and without sin, and a Mrs. Jones declared that God himself visited her every morning at 3 A.M.[31]

Cennick organized his own network of societies in the Bristol region. He also began preaching in association with Whitefield at the latter's Tabernacle in London. He had entirely repudiated the idea that the new birth entailed a prolonged emotional struggle, preaching instead that "no faith is without assurance" and telling Howell Harris that he himself "conversed with Christ continually, and was always happy." He was already attracted to the similar emphases of the Moravians, and in 1745 he shifted his allegiance to them. After ten years of tireless missionary work for the Moravians in England and Ireland, Cennick died, worn out, at the age of thirty-six.[32]

Gradually, the Methodists in Bristol and Kingswood settled down. Since the varieties of possessed behavior that had led to Cennick's disenchantment were exclusively associated with the process of conversion, they could not become an enduring feature of collective religious experience for the Methodists as they had for the Huguenots of Languedoc.

The Wesleys accepted the possibility that the phenomena might recur, but Charles was persuaded that sometimes the faintings and convulsions were feigned, especially by young women who wanted his brother to "take notice" of them. Henceforth, whenever people fell into convulsions or cried out during his own preaching, Charles had them gently removed from the room, and no further notice was taken of them.[33]

John Wesley modified neither his preaching nor his attitude toward those who were "torn" by sin and the Devil, but after 1740 convulsions and outcries accompanied his preaching much less frequently. On the other hand, to the end of his life his published journals and his *Arminian Magazine* were full of reports of bizarre spiritual phenomena of all kinds: demonic possessions, people who communicated with the dead, the ecstatic "Jumpers" of Wales, and female sleeping preachers.

Meanwhile, a more serious crisis was developing in London. When Wesley had returned there from Bristol in November 1739, he found that a Moravian missionary named Philip Molther had introduced the practices of Quietist mysticism the Moravians called "stillness" at the Fetter Lane society. It was the kind of religious passivity Wesley always deplored. A few weeks earlier, he had read a book on the new birth by William Law, whose earlier writings had been so influential in his own spiritual formation. He noted in his journal that Law's ideas were "philosophical, speculative, precarious; Behmenish, void, and vain!"[34] And now here was Molther, eagerly seconded by his own friends John Bray and James Hutton, promulgating an even more extreme denial of the power of the intellect and will to confront the human condition of sinfulness, let alone to prepare, through prayer, liturgical worship, and moral conduct, for the divine infusion of God's spirit.

In Wesley's opinion, the Moravian doctrine of stillness denied the ordinances divinely established in the Church of England as means to salvation. Using a phrase that was to be a continuing theme of the Shakers' message, he also deplored the fact that the Moravians rejected "self denial and the daily cross." Finally, he contended that they denied to God the power to work as He chose: sometimes quietly and gradually, but at other times with suddenness, in dramatic and visible manifestations.

Molther's view was quite different. In his opinion, Wesley had allowed "extraordinary usages" to become part of the worship at Fetter Lane. At the first meeting that Molther attended, he was "alarmed and almost terror-stricken at hearing their sighing and groaning, their whining and howling, which strange proceeding they called the demonstration of the spirit and of power." It had been the Moravians who had first convinced Wesley that faith came instantaneously, through the miraculous infusion of the Holy Spirit. Molther did not deny it; but he taught that conversion brought with it the assurance of salvation. Therefore, the kind of behavior that for Wesley was a plausible accompaniment to the conversion experience was for the advocates of "stillness" at best irrelevant and at worst false and blasphemous. One of Wesley's companions on his continental journey,

Richard Viney, wrote from the Moravians' community in Holland that "the Holy Spirit does and will guide us; but these are so seldom and extraordinary, that I would not advise any one to take every Fancy for the Dictates of the Spirit." Wesley, in contrast, believed that when they denied that these kinds of experiences could be part of Christian worship and the work of conversion, the Moravians were also rejecting the facts of "the Law and the Testimony."[35]

Molther and those who adopted his teachings might have agreed with the Exeter clergyman who told Wesley after hearing one of his sermons that while everything that he said was true, "it is not guarded. It is dangerous. It may lead people into enthusiasm or despair." Both Moravianism and Methodism attracted a diverse body of seekers, some of whom were tempted on occasion by French Prophets, perfectionists, or the voice of the Devil. For Wesley, all of the bizarre phenomena that he had witnessed in Bristol and London were explicable because the Holy Spirit was at work in saving souls. But now, as James Hutton noted in a letter to Count Zinzendorf, many of his "heroes" said they had not been truly converted after all and were still "poor sinners."[36] Some of his most trusted colleagues, including Hutton, Bray, Cennick, and even for a time his brother Charles, found in Moravian quietism an alternative understanding of the new birth that deflected and discouraged the disturbing features of behavior that Wesley's preaching and teaching had inadvertently encouraged. Neither by temperament nor by conviction could John Wesley possibly find such teachings satisfactory. They denied "the law and the testimony" and circumscribed the power of God.

The final break came in July 1740 when twenty-five of the men and nearly all the women who belonged to the Fetter Lane society joined Wesley's new society (which already had nearly three hundred members) at their meeting place, a former royal cannon foundry in Moorfields. The Foundery would henceforth be the center of Methodism.

The break was probably inevitable. Wesley was a man of strong convictions and outspoken opinions; a clash with the imperious Zinzendorf and his German emissaries was only a matter of time. The controversy convinced Wesley once again that the Holy Spirit must be allowed to operate however and wherever it chose.[37]

The Wesleyans were able to work in friendly cooperation with Calvinistic Methodists like Whitefield and Howell Harris, despite their disagreement on the question of predestination and free will. The Moravians, on the other hand, were rivals, despite Wesley's continued acknowledgment that they were mutually called to win the world for Christ. He could dismiss the French Prophets as misguided zealots, rightly considering them to be a fading remnant of earlier religious excitements. The Moravians, on the other hand, were a dynamic force, winning converts in several parts of England to their deceptively attractive notion that all that was required for salvation was to place complete and childlike trust in the love of Jesus.

Outside London, rivalry with the Moravians was most evident in the northwest, where the efforts of several individuals had launched a religious awakening. The most effective of all was Wesley's old Oxford friend Benjamin Ingham, who had accompanied him to Georgia in 1735. Since his return to his home in Yorkshire, Ingham's evangelical preaching had led to the organization of a network of fifty religious societies in Lancashire and the West Riding of Yorkshire. Zinzendorf had sent a German missionary to him in 1738 at Ingham's request, and four years later Ingham turned his societies over to the Moravians. By then, one of Wesley's most dedicated lay preachers, John Nelson, was at work in the same area, vehemently attacking Moravian teachings. The revival in the region was intensified in the early 1740s by the efforts of several men who organized societies independently of both the Wesleys and the Moravians, notably the Reverend William Grimshaw, rector of Haworth. Whitefield preached frequently in the region, on his way to or from his extended visits to Scotland in 1741 and 1742.[38]

Whitefield had returned to England in March 1741 from the triumphant tour of the American colonies that helped to launch the revival that would later come to be known as the Great Awakening. We shall consider those American developments in the next chapter, but it should be borne in mind that in the 1740s the "greatness" of the awakening lay in its transatlantic character. Whitefield's preaching was one factor that linked the revivals in England with those in Wales, Scotland, and the American colonies.

Jonathan Edwards's writings were another. His description of the wave of revivals that had swept the Connecticut Valley in 1734–35, *A Faithful Narrative of the Surprising Work of God,* was published in both Boston and London. John Wesley read it on his way to Oxford in October 1738, and it may well have provided him with an explanatory framework for the phenomena that he encountered in London and Bristol a few months later. Edwards's cautious defense of the outcries and ecstasies that by 1741 were causing deep divisions within the New England religious establishment, *The Distinguishing Marks of a Work of the Spirit of God,* was also widely read in Great Britain. Whitefield urged other ministers to read it, calling it "the best Thing of its Kind I ever saw."[39]

The leaders of the several revivals kept track of developments elsewhere through copious correspondence, some of which was published in periodicals like the Glasgow *Weekly History* and the Boston *Christian History* that were created specifically in order to report on the progress of the great transatlantic awakening. Despite theological differences, the Calvinist evangelicals reported sympathetically on the efforts of Wesleyans and Moravians. Clearly implying that they were all part of one great divinely ordained effort, one of Whitefield's associates reported to Boston that "there are few or no Counties in *England* or *Wales* where there is not a Work begun."[40]

Of all the revivals that collectively seemed to comprise a continuing "surprising work of God" whose culmination would surely be universal, one of the most remarkable was the one that spread through western Scotland in 1741–43. In his introduction to the Scottish edition of another of Edwards's sermons, a minister named John Willison wrote: "How astonishing are the Dispensations of a provoked holy God in our Day! That in the midst of Backslidings and Provocations from his Churches, he should *come suddenly into his Temple* . . . ; first in America, through the *British* Colonies there; then in Britain itself, and particularly in several Parts of the West of *Scotland,* whereby many are awakened and converted from Sin to God."[41]

Whitefield had come to Scotland at the invitation of the ministers who had formed the schismatic Secession church after their expulsion from the Church of Scotland in 1740. They broke with him after he declined to take a stand in their controversy with the state church, but he was then welcomed by Church of Scotland ministers who had refused to join the schism but agreed with the Secession that the country was in desperate need of spiritual regeneration. Whitefield's preaching was enormously effective once again. As he smugly reported to Howell Harris: "I have a constant Levee of wounded Souls, and many quite slain by the Law. God's Power attends me continuously, just as when I left *London.*[42]

Among those who heard Whitefield preach in Glasgow was the Reverend William M'Culloch, minister at the village of Cambuslang, five miles southeast of the city. Cambuslang is now part of the industrial metropolis, but it was then a typical rural Scottish parish, consisting of peasants, a few weavers and miners, and their families. M'Culloch had been preaching on conversion and the new birth for several years, but to little effect. He had also read acccounts of the revivals in New England to the congregation. In the aftermath of Whitefield's visit, several of his parishioners who had also heard the Great Itinerant began meeting informally and talking to the others. In January 1742, ninety heads of families asked M'Culloch to give weekly lectures on religious topics. M'Culloch was no Whitefield— according to one ministerial colleague, he had "a weak voice, no violent Action, and [was] far from endeavouring to stir up unreasonable Passions"—but nevertheless an atmosphere of excitement began to build within the congregation. On 18 February, after three days of fasting and prayer, the Cambuslang congregation experienced what it believed to be the effects of the spirit of God.

It came not in the form of the heightened emotion and outbursts of weeping that had accompanied Whitefield's preaching. Instead, as the Reverend William Hamilton reported to *The Christian History* in Boston, people were afflicted with the same "severe bodily Agonies, Out-crying and Faintings . . . which we hear [have] attended the same good Work in most Places in your Country." The news that the spectacular body language that had already visited the revivals in New England had now come to Scotland brought large crowds to Cambuslang. Soon, the same phenomena appeared at many other places in the region. As Hamilton explained, "God has made use of these uncommon Circumstances to make his work spread the faster." Another minister wrote that the Scottish revivals were "a special, a peculiar and extraordinary Work of God, which History can perhaps scarcely instance the Parallel of . . . since the first Ages of Christianity." James Erskine, Lord Grange, prayed: "May that blessed Work run through every place of Scotland & England, of Ireland & all the British Plantations, of Germany & the whole Earth!"[43]

Their desire to emphasize the role of Scottish Protestantism in the transatlantic revivals led the ministers to extol the dramatic scenes that accompanied the revivals, but the presence of a vociferous opposition in the person of the seceding clergy meant that they carefully avoided any interpretations that might permit the suggestion of demonic influence or suggest comparisons with the notorious "Camizars."

There is no evidence that the Scottish ministers had read Wesley's published journal or were even aware that Bristol and London had been visited by similar manifestations. Their interpretation of the physical phenomena thus probably owed nothing to the Methodists, but Jonathan Edwards's writings were certainly an influence.

The ministers who now set out to publicize the Scottish revival acknowledged that the origin and meaning of these convulsions and ecstasies were ultimately unknowable. They avoided the explanation (which Whitefield, Cennick, and the Wesleys all entertained to some degree) that the phenomena could have been caused by the Devil. The Reverend Alexander Webster wrote that "if this Affair . . . don't point out a *genuine* Work of the Holy Ghost, there seems no *Criterion* left to distinguish the *Operation* of the Spirit of God from the *Spirit* of the *Devil.*" Their reason is not difficult to discern. In their view, the awakening that had begun at Cambuslang demonstrated that God was in their churches and not in those of the Secession; the schismatic ministers replied that it was instead the Devil who was at work. James Erskine wrote James Hutton in London that "the Seceders" said that "they renounced & would allways oppose the God of Cambuslang, a place where the gracious power of our dear Lord had been manifested wonderfully."[44]

It was not the first time that religious revivals had moved through Scotland "like a spreading moor-burn."[45] A little over a century earlier, great emotion had accompanied the preaching of the Covenanters over a period of several years. The Covenanter tradition was alive in many villages around Glasgow, including Cambuslang. Furthermore, the secession crisis of 1740 was only the most recent of a long series of expressions of popular frustration with the corruptions and compromises of the Church of Scotland.

In Scotland as in other Protestant countries, there had existed since the seventeenth century the practice of assembling in small conventicles for prayer and pious discussion, but the religious radicalism of Quakers and Ranters had never established itself in Scotland. The French Prophets had made some inroads, but most of their disciples had been mystically inclined members of the upper classes.[46]

The ministers were quite content to accept the revivals as essentially miraculous, an answer to their prayers and a refutation of the contentions of the schismatic clergy. They were at the same time less willing than Wesley to propose that the convulsions and ecstasies were divine in origin. Both M'Culloch at Cambuslang and James Robe at Kilsyth carefully recorded the testimonies of their parishioners' experiences at the time of their conversion, and both concluded that the explanation was natural rather than supernatural.

Robe wrote that while the French Prophets "had their bodily agitations from a supernatural power," in the present revival "the distresses upon the Bodies of our People proceed in a natural Way from their great Fear of God's Wrath." None of the people claimed divine inspiration or pretended to have visions. Instead, "they give us a rational Account of themselves, know and remember what they say and do." He contended that "the Distress of their Minds" was so intense that "they could not but naturally have such Effects upon their Bodies." He asked them "What they apprehended and felt in their Minds before they fell a Trembling, cryed out or fainted." Often, they could cite a biblical text or a specific point in a sermon that had brought on the hysterical symptoms. Another minister wrote Robe that the converts' ability to give "rational and distinct Accounts of the Grounds and Methods of their Awakenings" proved that the phenomena were not "the Result of *Mechanism* or *diabolical* Influence."

As always, the preconceptions of the cultural leadership served to shape and define the character of spirit possession. While the Scottish ministers never questioned the sincerity of those who fell in convulsions or cried out in agony, their assumption that there was a natural and rational explanation (one, it must be said, not very different from that put forward by contemporary Deists and religious skeptics) surely had the effect of greatly limiting their incidence and their significance. By 1743, Robe could report that "Convulsive Motions, or Hystericisms of any Sort" were now unknown.[47]

Although Robe and his associates did not yet realize it, the Scottish Awakening was already fading by 1743. Its climax had come at two great outdoor communion services held at Cambuslang the previous summer. According to all accounts, they both provided the sacred theater of solemn celebration, the ephemeral moment of liminality, that Victor Turner has described.

The first was held in July. M'Culloch wrote to *The Christian History* in Boston that Whitefield's preaching produced "a very great

Weeping and Mourning among the *Auditory*," whose numbers he placed at twenty thousand. When the second assembly met a month later, the crowd reached thirty or perhaps forty thousand. Again the preaching, by Whitefield and a dozen Scottish ministers, went on for several days. A few cried out, and there was "a very great but decent Weeping and Mourning." Whitefield himself seemed to be "in a kind of Extasy or Transport" as he administered communion Sunday evening, but nothing similar, apparently, occurred among the congregation.[48]

Then the revival disappeared as rapidly and mysteriously as it had begun. Although M'Culloch remained at Cambuslang for several more decades, nothing like it ever took place again.[49] Spirit possession never really established itself in the Scottish Awakening. The clergy was too orthodox for that, and the tone of the attacks of their rivals in the Secession would have prevented their countenancing any conduct that might recall the Camisards or other "enthusiasts." John Wesley was probably correct in believing that the Jacobite Rebellion that broke out in 1745 had been a crucial factor in the precipitous collapse of the Scottish Awakening. It had torn "it all up by the roots and left scarce any trace of it behind."[50]

John Wesley spent most of 1742 in London and Bristol. Friendship overcame theological differences when he and Whitefield were reconciled during one of the latter's visits to London. Despite the rivalry of the Moravians in London and Cennick's adherents in Bristol and Kingswood, Wesley's societies thrived in all three places. He elaborated the rules of discipline to which their members must adhere, and he initiated two institutions that would henceforth be central to Methodism when he established class-meetings within the societies and began to use lay preachers on a regular basis.[51]

The Methodists began to establish themselves in other parts of England, including the southwest, the northeast, and the Midlands. In the northeast, Newcastle-upon-Tyne rapidly emerged as Methodism's third major center. In Staffordshire in the Midlands, on the other hand, the Methodists encountered vigorous and sometimes violent persecution.

John Wesley first visited Newcastle in May 1742, having preached en route at several places in Yorkshire in association with John Nelson. He went in part at the urging of the Countess of Huntingdon, the pious patroness of Whitefield and Howell Harris. Newcastle was then a rough, raw town. Its poorer citizens, especially the miners and their families, were barely conversant with the rudiments of Christianity or civilized behavior. Wesley wrote in his journal that he had never seen "so much drunkenness, cursing, and swearing (even from the mouths of little children)." As at Kingswood, his outdoor preaching met with astonishing success. He and his associates began to teach the doctrines of the new birth and to organize religious societies.

When he returned in November, he began to encounter the scenes that were by then familiar. Wesley believed there was "a deeper work in many souls" than he had seen before when "many trembled exceedingly; six or seven (both men and women) dropped down as dead; some cried unto God out of the deep." Wesley was delighted. He wrote that he had never seen "a work of God, in any other place, so evenly and gradually carried on."

In a village Wesley called "the very Kingswood of the North," people described for him symptoms that in the south of Italy would have brought an immediate diagnosis that the Evil Eye was at work. Some felt "as if a sword were running through them." Others felt oppressed by "a great weight," or choked so that they could scarcely breath. Finally, there were those for whom "it was as if their heart, as if their inside, as if their whole body, was tearing all to pieces." Wesley's interpretation was initially more cautious than it had been in London and Bristol. He wrote: "These symptoms I can no more impute to natural cause than to the Spirit of God." But then he added: "I can make no doubt but it was Satan tearing them as they were coming to Christ."[52]

Meanwhile, in Staffordshire, the Methodists' efforts met with riotous opposition. When the Wesleys first visited there, they were courteously received by the vicar at Wednesbury, but unfortunately the lay preachers they then sent from London rashly criticized the Church of England and the morals and piety of the local clergy. According to one contemporary account, the preachers taught that "every Person must receive the Holy Ghost in a sensible Manner." When people began to "fall down in Fits, under violent Agitations of Body, and made Strange hideous noises," the preachers declared that the work of conviction had begun. Some people, when the new birth was attained, were "raised into strange unaccountable Extasies."

One class leader anticipated the claims the Shakers would make for themselves when he told his class: "If you will now tell me your sins, you will be pardon'd, and then you will be fit to die."

All of this conduct served to antagonize public opinion and to foster the formation of mobs, publicly encouraged by the local gentry and clergy. According to one contemporary diary, the incident that triggered the first riots took place at a parish worship service in Darlaston when several people went into convulsions, making strange noises, and claimed that they had received the Holy Ghost.[53]

The villages of the Staffordshire Black Country may have been an exception, but the behavior of the first converts there does suggest that without the restraints of Methodist organization and discipline, its style of preaching and worship had the potential to encourage the kinds of excesses that had made the radical Puritans so notorious in the seventeenth century.

The persecution of the Methodists in Staffordshire and elsewhere persisted for a few years and then completely died away. With one exception, so did the collective sacred theater of public conversion that had characterized Methodism's early years. Looking back on that era twenty years later, Wesley wrote: "The danger *was* to regard extraordinary circumstances too much, such as outcries, convulsions, visions, trances. . . . Perhaps the danger *is* to regard them too little, to condemn them altogether."[54]

Wesley's reflection was occasioned by an episode that in bizarre theatricality rivaled even the scenes at Kingswood. In 1758, a revival broke out in the village of Everton, near Cambridge. The vicar of the parish, the Reverend John Berridge, was not a Methodist; indeed, he was not altogether sure that he approved of the conduct of Wesley and Whitefield. There was nothing to distinguish Everton from hundreds of other agricultural villages.

Berridge's career had been competent but hardly distinguished before 1758. He had been preaching on the need for conversion for some years, but without much success. Only in 1758 had he begun to preach, extemporaneously, that one must "only believe" in order to be saved. He was not an impassioned preacher, but like Edwards and Wesley he held that one must be brought to a conviction of one's sinfulness and an awareness of the terrors of damnation before conversion was possible. He wrote that "a heart cannot be broken where there is a sense of merit; it is only broken down by a dread of sin, or by a loathing of it." The process of sanctification could begin only if first "we are taught to loathe ourselves."[55]

After the revival broke out, Berridge began a correspondence with Wesley and invited him to come to Everton. During the two years that the revival lasted, Wesley came to the area three times, preaching in the churches and carefully recording his observations. He also included in his own journal the "Journal of an Eyewitness," in fact a composite of five separate accounts kept by participants in the revival.

What is unusual about the Everton Revival is that spectacular manifestations of physical contortions and emotional catharsis occurred not in small society meetings or in all-night prayer sessions but during regular services in the parish churches. The liturgy of the Book of Common Prayer certainly provides the framework for a kind of sacred theater, but hardly for the kind of possessed and entranced behavior that now became a regular feature of worship in Everton.

On one Sunday in May 1759, for example, during the service of morning prayer, many cried out, especially "children, whose agonies were amazing." During the afternoon service that same day, "when the power of religion began to be spoke of, the presence of God really filled the place." One heard "a mixture of various sounds, some shrieking, some roaring aloud. The most general was a loud breathing, like that of people half strangled and gasping for life." Many fell to the floor, some of them in convulsions. Most of those "on whom God laid his hand turned either very red or almost black."[56]

The revival also affected the nearby village of Wrestlingworth under the ministry of the Reverend William Hicks, despite the fact that Hicks, like Berridge, had little "eloquence" and was "rather weak in speech." People came to both churches from great distances. Sometimes the crowds would break pews or windows in their excitement. When the services ended, people continued to roll in agony or cry out in joy on the lawn outside. Sometimes the most distressed cases were taken to the vicarage to be prayed over.

Berridge and Hicks began to itinerate, preaching outdoors to crowds that numbered in the thousands. They also began to use laymen as preachers. When one of them, a domestic servant named Caleb Price, addressed a group of about two hundred, "several fell to the ground, some of whom seemed dead, others in the agonies of death, the violence of their bodily convulsions exceeding all description."

In several parishes, people began to claim to have visions, and these too became part of the repertory of the revival. One seven year old astonished everyone "with her innocent, awful manner" of describing her visions. Another child was examined by a physician who declared that her entranced behavior was "no distemper of mind, but the hand of God." A young man would go into a trance, "stiff and motionless as a statue," and then begin to pray aloud, "with a melodious voice." Wesley interviewed several of those who "went away, as they termed it" and experienced entranced visions of eternity. He was persuaded that their experiences were genuine.[57]

Gradually, all of these manifestations faded. When Wesley came to Everton in November 1759 to preach, "none were in trances, none cried out, none fell down or were convulsed; only some trembled exceedingly." It was then that he reflected on the place of such "extraordinary circumstances" in the divine scheme. He observed that it had also been the case in New England and Scotland that after the revivals' dramatic beginnings, "the work goes on more quietly and silently." Therefore "those whom it pleases God to employ in His work ought to be quite passive in this respect; they should choose nothing, but leave entirely to Him all the circumstances of His own work."[58]

When Wesley returned to Everton in 1762, he was distressed to find that those who had been so wondrously affected now doubted that it had been the work of God after all. Whereas formerly many had insisted that "none can have true faith but those that have trances or visions, they were now ready to think that whoever had anything of this kind had no true faith." He was glad to find that at least people in the area still responded visibly and emotionally to the Word. In one parish, he had only named the text for his sermon when "a murmur ran through the whole people, and many of them were in tears." In fact, even if nothing on the scale of the Everton revival occurred again, it had marked the opening of a revival of religious excitement among the Methodists that spread through much of England during the next several years.[59]

In the same year that brought the varieties of godly possession to the Methodist Awakening for the last time in the excitement and commotion of the Everton revival, 1758, a young woman in Manchester named Ann Lee joined an obscure sect whose mode of worship consisted of tremblings, convulsions, trances, and noisy outbursts of pious joy. The Shakers themselves claim no connection with Methodism, but as we shall see in the sixth chapter, there were points of contact, some of them direct and some tangential.

It would be tempting to claim that one of those points of contact was the "tradition" of revival that occasionally produced those possessed phenomena that John Wesley always insisted were supernatural in origin. That is unfortunately not possible. There is no evidence that Ann Lee and the Shakers of Manchester even knew what had occurred in Bristol and Kingswood and Everton. Yet it was to be the case that after they had come to the United States, for fifty years the great majority of those who joined the Shakers came to them by way of religious revivals.

The most important influence of Methodism upon the English Shakers was rather what might be called their "style" of conversion. Even if the setting was likelier to be a private home than a public meeting, conversion was still sacred theater in the sense that it was a drama that unfolded over time, in which human emotions from grief to elation found expression in a repertory of culturally validated words and gestures. Even if the drama had no human audience, the fact that the convert was encouraged to describe his or her experiences to the class meeting encouraged others to expect divine grace to work upon them in a similar fashion.

To a degree, the conversion process that Methodists experienced and then described to others resembled what seventeenth-century Puritans had elaborated in theological tracts or testimonies like John Bunyan's *Grace Abounding*, some of which were still being reprinted in the eighteenth century. Wesley printed some of them, as well as many Methodist conversion testimonies, in his *Arminian Magazine*. If Methodists only occasionally gave public display to the warfare of God and Satan for their souls after 1742, they believed that the warfare went on. The new birth would occur in a moment, but its gestation might take months or even years. Perhaps Wesley's teaching that assurance, when it came, would be absolute and that sinless perfection was possible for true Christians made the inner struggles that accompanied conversion even more intense. As a former Methodist noted, even those who claimed that they had had a "foretaste of heaven, and their full assurance of sins forgiven" said that they were "miserable for the greatest part of their time, having doubts, fears, horrors of mind, &c. continually haunting them wherever they are."

The contrast with Moravian doctrine could not have been more profound. The Moravians held that "one must become a sinner, then one is given grace, and with that everything is accomplished." Wesley's quite uncharacteristic bitterness against his former associates like James Hutton and John Cennick who were won over by the Moravians' doctrine can be understood only if we realize that for Wesley that could *not* be the way that conversion took place.[60]

Sarah Ryan was a seventeen-year-old domestic servant in London when she was converted by Whitefield and Wesley in 1741. Listening to Wesley at the Foundery, she had a vision of Jesus "in the eye of [her] mind." When she received communion in the former Huguenot church in Spitalfields, she was "overwhelmed with the power of God" and was "utterly regardless of outward things." A few weeks later, when she received assurance that her sins were forgiven, she received another vision of Jesus. Despite these experiences, she then began to doubt, "in great distress and anguish," whether she had truly been saved. She had some respite after Wesley persuaded her to remain in London and "save souls" rather than join her husband in migrating to New England, but then the doubts returned. When she sweated and trembled all over, she "knew it to be the power of God." She experienced another vision of Jesus, but meanwhile her body "was in such an agony, as it is not possible to repeat." At last, she felt "the Spirit of God" go through her. The next Sunday, in church, she had a final vision, of Jesus standing with a child dressed in white. She realized that the child was like herself, and that Jesus was showing her that she would "grow up to the measure of his full stature" of sinless perfection.[61]

A young tailor named Richard Moss was similarly drawn to the Methodists after hearing John Wesley at the Foundery. He followed all the procedures Wesley recommended for those seeking salvation. He prayed often, took communion regularly, and fasted, but still he felt he "was under condemnation, and had no rest." Then, one night, he saw Jesus "by faith," and his "fears and doubts and sense of guilt vanished away." His sense of comfort lasted only three days. On the fourth morning, "all was dark. My comfort and my GOD were gone. I had no fear of death or of hell, and I had continual power over all outward sin. . . . But I could not see GOD; I could not see CHRIST; and therefore I was in sorrow and heaviness." He continued his regimen of spiritual discipline. He fasted continuously, until he was so weak that he could barely walk. Instead of regaining his earlier peace, he instead "felt a strange horror" that the Devil was constantly beside him. Then, during one of Wesley's sermons, he again had a divine vision. For a time he "saw nothing but heaven and GOD. He had at last received assurance; from that moment, he never "lost for a moment the Light of GOD's countenance."[62]

For John Varton, who first associated himself with the Methodists in 1764, the process of conversion was even more protracted. He would lie groaning on the floor for entire nights, praying "with great violence." Visions of God would bring peace, but then his "misery" would return. "Hell rose up" against him. He "felt hatred to God and longed to curse him." Like Richard Moss, he prayed, read his Bible, and fasted constantly, but nothing seemed to help. Then the spirit of God entered him again, and he was "transported to the third heavens, and had a most glorious display of that celestial place." On another occasion, the thought of Jesus so agitated his body that he thought "the vessel must break to set the soul at large." He cried out: "The Love of God will kill me! It is too much. I cannot contain myself!" For brief periods, he would be at peace, but then doubt and satanic temptation would return, and he "cried, screamed, roared, and tore" himself until he "in an agony of prayer concluded the day." One would have thought that Varton was emotionally prostrated by these experiences, but he managed to earn his living as a clerk while preaching in the Methodist society and teaching children to read and write in an evening school. When he recorded his experiences in 1780, he was still oscillating between hope and despair, but he did report that one recent morning he had had "the most gracious visit from heaven" that he had received in years.[63]

Anyone reading Varton's testimony today is surely put off by the self-righteous enumeration of his own sufferings and the clearly sexual undertone to his ecstatic experiences. It was probably a story that Varton told many times in society and class meetings. Varton's experience was not typical, but there were many other Methodists for whom the process of conversion was similarly protracted, and who described it in similarly lurid and dramatic terms. Moreover, as Wesley recognized, the account recalled the spiritual experiences of many Catholic saints. Yet he chose to print Varton's story over several issues of the official Methodist magazine.

Ann Lee's experience, as recounted after her death by her earliest disciples, was remarkably similar to John Varton's. For nine years after joining the obscure religious society in Manchester, she oscillated between hope and despair. She suffered "violent temptations of the enemy." For entire nights, "her cries, screeches and groans were such as to fill every soul around her with fear and trembling." She fasted until she grew so weak that others had to feed her. Through all her tribulations, there were "intervals of releasement," culminating in a vision of divinity. For Ann Lee, though, the vision brought with it a revelation that announced a new age of the spirit and provided a new way to salvation and sinless perfection.[64]

Even if Methodism was never the wild and unrestrained movement that its enemies claimed, there was within its culture a willingness to accept as religiously legitimate a profusion of ideas and behaviors that were unthinkable in most of the other churches and religious groups of eighteenth-century England. Like Quakerism in the preceding century, "methodism" was as much a style of spirituality and an affirmation of the possibility of the immediate experience of divinity as it was an organized religious body. It was the most visible sector of a broad movement of popular piety that affirmed that the age of miracles was not past and that Christianity would regain the purity and vitality of its beginnings.

{5}

The Transatlantic Awakening

B y 1745, the first dramatic phase of the religious awakenings in Great Britain was at an end. Whitefield continued to draw large crowds until his premature death, but bouts of ill health incapacitated him more and more frequently. For the Wesleys, the spectacular early successes were followed by the less spectacular but more lasting achievement of the creation of a network of Methodist societies in hundreds of towns and villages in England, Ireland, and Wales, ministered to by a corps of itinerant preachers. The Calvinistic Methodists under the patronage of the Countesss of Huntingdon were similarly successful on a more restricted scale. So were the Moravians. Meanwhile a growing body of clergy within the Church of England had also begun to press their parishioners to seek conversion and to live lives of Christian purity. Despite their continued differences, all of the evangelical groups believed that together they were working toward the fulfillment of a divine plan, by which the whole world would at last be brought to true Christianity.

In March 1745, John Wesley wrote James Erskine, the Scottish lord who corresponded with all the leaders of the revivals, to thank him for sending a copy of a letter from James Robe, the chief propagandist of the Scottish Awakening. Robe had proposed the establishment of a "concert of prayer and praise, for the revival of real Christianity." Wesley, who had always contended that the theological disagreements among the various groups were mere "points of opinion," warmly agreed with the letter, but he believed that Robe had not gone far enough. "Might it not be practicable," he wrote, "to have the concurrence of Mr. Edwards in New England, if not of Mr. Tennant also, herein? It is evidently one work with what we have seen here. Why should we not all praise God with one heart?"[1]

Wesley was not alone in his interest in the revivals in the American colonies that seemed to parallel so closely those in the British Isles. Jonthan Edwards's narrative of the Connecticut Valley revivals of 1734–35 had been published in England before it was published in America, and his description of the emotion and "agitations" that the revivals generated may have made the similar manifestations in England and Scotland comprehensible. William M'Culloch at Cambuslang saw in the fact that the awakening had come first to New England a confirmation of the prophecy of Isaiah (59:19): "So they shall fear the name of the Lord from the west, and his glory from the rising of the sun." Mc'Culloch wrote to Edwards that *this Prophecy* eminently points to *our Times*." It meant that "the glorious Revival of Religion, and the wide and diffusive Spread of vital Christianity in the latter times of the Gospel, should begin in the more *westerly* Parts, and proceed to these more *easterly*."[2]

The study of the Great Awakening—the American aspect of the transatlantic awakening of the 1740s—has been a sizable cottage industry for historians for two generations. Despite (or perhaps because of) all this effort, they have been unable to agree on many major questions, notably the Great Awakening's significance for American religious history and its influence, if any, on the American Revolution. There is very little agreement even on its dates, its geographic extent, and the relative importance of its principal actors. As Jon Butler pointed out in a controversial and challenging essay, even the name is in question. It was only at the end of the nineteenth century that the wave of revivals that started in about 1740 began to be called the Great Awakening.[3]

One of the most recent analyses of the Great Awakening contends that "religion itself was different in America."[4] The statement is too simple. Religious belief and practice was too diverse, even in the comparatively homogeneous New England colonies the contours of whose "mind" have been lovingly traced by intellectual historians. Moreover, as Jon Butler wrote in another important essay, there is "an astonishing vacuum in our knowledge of lay religious behavior." Only now, thanks to his work and that of a few other historians, notably David D. Hall, is the study of American popular religion even approaching in precision and sophistication the kinds of studies that have distinguished English and French history for a generation.[5]

The religious diversity of the American colonies in the early eighteenth century was in part a reflection of their economic and ethnic diversity. In the southern and middle colonies, increasing numbers of settlers were not English but Scotch-Irish or German, not Anglicans but Presbyterians, Quakers, Lutherans, Mennonites, or separating Pietists. For some, like the Quakers and German sectarians, religion was a pervasive influence on their lives, but many of the other immigrants lived without religious institutions of any kind.

New England was a special case. Among the factors that united the region religiously were the Puritan heritage, the organization of the towns according to the congregational system of the "church-state," and the educational monopoly of Harvard and Yale. On the other hand, the patterns of settlement, the distrust of any kind of overpowerful human authority, and the continued possibility of migration into the forested back country meant that, potentially, New England's minds could be as diffuse as her communities.

To a greater extent than in any of the other colonies, New England's clergy dominated intellectual life. In the absence of evidence to the contrary, we assume that the laity—at least those who attended church—accepted the theological and liturgical premises of their ministers. On the other hand, the ministers themselves in the first part of the eighteenth century continually deplored their people's falling away from the faith of their fathers, some even abandoning the churches of Christ for those of the Baptists and Anglicans.

In sanctioning lay initiatives in religious behavior and expressions of emotionalism and mysticism that had seldom surfaced before, the revivals of the 1740s undermined the spiritual hegemony of New England's Puritan establishment. Equally significantly, the revivals suggested to a growing minority that the true church of Christianity's culminating era had not yet been revealed. After the Great Awakening, there persisted both the memory of the millenarian urgency of those revivals and the belief that they had been marked by immediate and visible descent of the Holy Spirit.

The same pattern developed in the other colonies as well. In New Jersey, New York, and Pennsylvania, young ministers sponsored by the *Stift* at Halle, the Dutch Calvinist classis in Amsterdam, or the Moravian communities brought to the new settlements the Pietists' conception of the new birth, their emotional preaching, and the practice of forming conventicles for prayer and Bible study. In New Jersey and Pennsylvania's Delaware Valley, these ideas were absorbed by

Presbyterian ministers already committed to the Scottish tradition of evangelical revival. In some places, an "awakening" had begun in the 1730s. After the revivals had swept through the northern and middle colonies, Moravians and New Light preachers from New England brought the message of spiritual revival to the remote settlements of the inland South. Everywhere the effect of the Great Awakening upon religious institutions and experience was permanent, but nowhere was it as profound as in New England.[6]

Perhaps because the intentions of their founders had been so lofty, the failure of the New England colonies to build the scriptural city upon the hill was especially painful to their successors in the early eighteenth century. It had therefore been a welcome indication of religious vitality when a wave of revivals swept the churches of the Connecticut Valley in 1734–35. The awakening became a matter of general interest in both New England and Great Britain when the minister at Northampton, Massachusetts, Jonathan Edwards, wrote a narrative of the event that was published on both sides of the Atlantic. He called the revivals a "late wonderful work of God," the most recent of the "harvests" that from time to time brought New Englanders to spiritual awareness. Not even Edwards imagined when he wrote the narrative in 1736 that within five years nearly all the American colonies would experience an awakening that in geographical extent and theological implications overwhelmed anything the region had seen before.[7]

When revival spread through Bristol and Cambuslang and Everton, it had been a divine mystery what had at last brought people to readiness to receive the infusion of divine grace. In the revival of 1734, Edwards believed that it had been the sudden deaths of a young man and a young woman in his parish that had led other young people to agree to Edwards' suggestion that they meet in the evenings for what he called "social religion"–the conventicles and religious societies of Europe by another name. In his sermons, Edwards began to attack what he and many others called Arminianism, declaring that it was blasphemous and spiritually dangerous to suggest, as many ministers did, that human effort and good behavior could lead to salvation. In a voice that his pupil Samuel Hopkins described as "a little too languid" though "much relieved and advantaged by a proper emphasis," Edwards insisted that one was justified by faith alone, having first been brought to a recognition of one's own spiritual worthlessness. Only then, instantaneously and miraculously, might saving faith be received.[8]

Edwards wrote in his narrative that there had always been "a great deal of talk about conversion and spiritual experiences" in Northampton, but only when they were really touched by the spirit of God in 1734 did they find out what it was to be genuinely converted. When the divine spirit did begin to move among them, they had been spiritually prepared for awakening by sermons, evening meetings, and private conferences with the minister. Sometimes the conversion process was quiet and gradual, but often it was accompanied by the kinds of behavior with which we are by now familiar. Sometimes fears of damnation produced noisy expressions of mental distress "in which Satan probably ha[d] a great hand." At last, the drama of conversion reached its climax, as sinners received divine grace. Sometimes individuals gave vocal expression to the experience. "Sometimes they han't been able to forbear crying out with a loud voice, expressing their great admiration."[9]

Puritan worship had always been comparatively free of formal liturgical constraints, accepting a holy spontaneity, especially during prayers and psalm singing. But this was something new; the meetinghouse had become the setting for a sacred theater of word and gesture, open to wide variations of individual and collective improvisation, whereby the divine mystery of conversion received its metaphorical expression in word and gesture. The scene resembled that which the English Methodists would witness a few years later, but in New England this sacred theater of spiritual "awakening" was to be more intense, more extensive, and much more lasting.

By the summer of 1735, Edwards wrote, "there were remarkable tokens of God's presence" throughout Northampton. News of what had happened there helped to produce similar revivals in thirty-two other towns in Massachusetts and Connecticut, from Northfield near the New Hampshire border through Springfield and Enfield to Groton and Old Lyme on Long Island Sound.[10]

The *Faithful Narrative* is a remarkable document, not least because it is written in a clear and vigorous prose style that few writers in the eighteenth century could equal. Edwards was a careful participant-historian, candid about his own successes and mistakes. He made no apologies for placing so much emphasis upon arousing the emotions (the "religious affections") of his congregation. At the same time, he was cautious (more cautious than John Wesley would be a few years later) when he encountered the more bizarre forms of spirit possession. Edwards avoided saying that any of the converts had heavenly visions, commenting only that while some "indeed had a great sense of the spiritual excellency of divine things," he was not sure "whether their imaginary ideas have been more than could naturally arise from their spiritual sense of things." In describing the "strange enthusiastic delusions" that afflicted three men in other towns, he may have been especially concerned because one of them claimed for himself functions that belonged only to the ordained ministry. Even more distressing was the case of Edwards's own uncle, who grew so obsessed with his own sinfulness that he cut his throat. As news of the suicide spread through the valley, "multitudes in this and other towns seemed to have it strongly suggested to 'em, and pressed upon 'em, to do as this person had done."

The revivals quickly faded. Edwards wrote that "after these things the instances of conversion were rare here in comparison of what they had before been." The spirit of God "appeared very sensibly withdrawing" from all the Massachusetts communities that had been affected, although it persisted somewhat longer in Connecticut.[11]

As C. C. Goen has pointed out, the revivals of 1734–35 "set a pattern of conversion" unlike anything New England had known before, one that depended to a great extent on bringing people to a pitch of emotional distress and even terror that would compel their recognition of their utter sinfulness and open their minds for the mysterious experience of faith. Several of the ministers whose congregations had revivals in 1735, for example Eleazar Wheelock, Benjamin Pomeroy, Jonathan Parsons, and Andrew Croswell, would be in the forefront of the "New Lights" of 1741. The Connecticut Valley was not the only place where religious revivals preceded and paved the way for the general awakening of the 1740s. In several communities in Pennsylvania and New Jersey, preaching in the "new way" produced a wave of conversions, carefully supervised by the clergy. Like the young Connecticut ministers, these evangelical Presbyterians, notably Gilbert Tennent, were to play important roles in subsequent events.[12]

However remarkable the revivals of the 1730s had been, they were soon overshadowed by the much more general religious awakening that began in 1740. As in England and Scotland, the catalyst was the preaching of George Whitefield; and in New England his impact derived not from his words but from his mastery of vocal inflection, timing, and gesture. Dedicated to his mission and absolutely sincere, he was also the consummate performer. He arrived in America in late 1739, fresh from his triumphs in London and Bristol. As had been his practice in England, he moved rapidly from place to place, preaching primarily in cities. After spending eight months in Pennsylvania, New Jersey, and the southern colonies, Whitefield traveled to New England in September 1740. He had been invited by some of Boston's leading ministers, who had been trying for nearly twenty years to bring their parishioners to a pitch of religious concern that would prepare them for conversion.

Whitefield spent barely six weeks in New England. He traveled from Newport to Boston, where he spent two weeks. He made his way from there up the coast into New Hampshire, often preaching several times a day. After returning to Boston, he went to Northampton at the invitation of Edwards. He then crossed Connecticut, preaching nearly every day. After two more months of continuous itinerancy in the Middle Atlantic and southern colonies, he returned to England, where, as we saw in the last chapter, he resumed his efforts in Bristol and London before moving on to his Scottish triumphs.

He was unquestionably the greatest celebrity that the American colonies had ever seen. He was a master at organizing his own publicity, and he had the enthusiastic support of the Puritan ministers along his route. Still young and slender, with the resonant voice whose sound (if not the words) carried great distances, he brought his audiences one step closer to the spiritual concern that their ministers had been trying to arouse for years. Edwards's wife Sarah recalled that she had seen "upwards of a thousand people hang on his words with breathless silence, broken only by an occasional half-suppressed sob."[13]

The most moving description of Whitefield's effect on audiences was recorded by Nathan Cole, a farmer in Kensington, Connecticut, in an account of his "spiritual travels" that he wrote twenty years later. Cole is also virtually the only layman who wrote about his experience of the Great Awakening. It was primarily the clergy who described its effects on themselves and their congregation.

When Cole learned that Whitefield was to preach at Middletown, on his way from Northampton to New York, he left his fields and with his wife went to hear him. They "heard a noise something like a low rumbling thunder and presently found it was the noise of Horses feet coming down the Road and this Cloud was a Cloud of dust made by the Horses feet; it rose some Rods into the air over the tops of Hills and trees." Three or four thousand people assembled beside the Connecticut River. Cole thought that Whitefield looked "almost angelical; a young, slim, slender, youth before thousands of people with a bold undaunted Countenance, and my hearing how God was with him everywhere as he came along Solemnized my mind; and put me in a trembling fear before he began to preach." Whitefield's sermon gave him a "Heart wound"; he realized that his "Foundation was broken up" and his own righteous behavior would not save him.[14]

With the exception of the Church of England missionaries, the clerical response to Whitefield's preaching in New England was overwhelmingly favorable. A tour by Gilbert Tennent, one of the principal organizers and evangelists of the awakening among the Presbyterians of the Middle Colonies, was similarly successful, although Tennent caused some disquiet by demanding that the clergy give evidence of their own saving conversion. Throughout the following year, as revivals touched churches in towns and villages across Connecticut and Massachusetts, God seemed to be restoring New England to the saintliness that its founders had intended.

In many places in Connecticut, Whitefield and Tennent simply intensified religious feelings that had never completely faded after the Connecticut Valley revivals. A group of dedicated ministers, most of them relatively young, labored tirelessly for conversions, not only in their own congregations but also in other towns and villages, sometimes in the churches, sometimes in the open air. According to Benjamin Trumbull's sympathetic history, they preached "the doctrines of the reformation: —the doctrine of original sin, the regeneration by the supernatural influence of the divine Spirit, and of the absolute necessity of it."[15]

In East Lyme, for example, the religious stirrings of 1735 had recommenced by April 1741. Jonathan Parsons's preaching produced the familiar repertory of outcries, terrors, and occasional ecstasies. Tennent's visit had prepared them, and now East Lyme had become, one inhabitant wrote Tennent, a "mere heaven upon earth." Parsons wrote the Reverend Benjamin Colman in Boston that at one communion service, "near one hundred persons were melted down . . . ; many whole Pews were almost overwhelm'd."

The revivals were beginning to change Puritan worship in important ways. Whether the sacred space was the meetinghouse, a private home, a field, or a village green, a configuration that was based on lines and perpendiculars that represented and acknowledged the community's moral hierarchy of values was replaced by one of flow and circularity, as ministers and converted laymen moved through the space, alternately exhorting or comforting the assembly. It was a patterning of sacred space that was to become a permanent feature of Protestant evangelical revivals.[16]

Three months later, an even more spectacular awakening swept through a congregation gathered to hear Jonathan Edwards preach at Enfield, north of Hartford. The famous "Enfield sermon" was the climax of a cooperative effort by a number of ministers in the Connecticut Valley to rekindle the religious excitement of 1735. At a meeting the preceding night in nearby Suffield led by the Reverend Stephen Williams of Longmeadow, Massachusetts, and two other ministers, there had been (as Williams recorded in his diary) "considerable crying out . . . yea, and a screeching in the streets." The next day, the ministers, together with many people from Suffield and other towns, went to Enfield to hear "dear Mr. Edwards of Northampton."

The text for his sermon was one from which Edwards had preached at least three times before. This time, his words produced an astonishing response. Williams wrote that "there was a great moaning & crying out through ye whole House" until Edwards "was obliged to desist—ye shrieks & cry^S were piercing & Amazing." The ministers moved among the congregation, talking with and praying over those who were visibly affected. Finally they returned to the pulpit; they "sung an hymn & pray^d & dismiss^d ye Assembly." Nor was that the end of it. For the next several days, there were more religious services and informal meetings, with the efforts of the ministers supplemented by newly awakened converts, exhorting their fellows to come to Christ.[17]

In his Enfield sermon, Edwards had indeed presented to his hearers the fate that awaited them "as sinners in the hands of an angry God." But it should be noted that he also stated that many *would* find salvation. It was, he declared, God's last great spiritual harvest before the Millennium: "God seems now to be hastily gathering in his elect in all parts of the land; and probably the greater part of adult persons that ever shall be saved, will be brought in now in a little time." Of all the regions that were affected by the transatlantic awakening, it was in New England that the belief was most prevalent that the conversions were part of the cosmic drama that was to culminate in the end of the world. No one expressed more clearly than Edwards the mixture of dread and exaltation that that idea evoked.[18] Forty years later, the Shakers would make the same declaration to their New England audiences.

One of the most zealous advocates of the revivals was Andrew Croswell, who since 1736 had been the minister at the second church in Groton, Connecticut. His conviction that the revival there in 1741 was the work of God may have been connected to the inroads that Church of England missionaries had made in his church. In his sermons, Croswell declared that those who attended Anglican services were "going straight to hell" because they believed that good works could bring salvation.

Having brought his congregation to a pitch of excitement described by a hostile witness as "the most amazing screechings, screamings, faintings, convulsions and visions," Croswell early in 1742 made a preaching tour into southeastern Massachusetts. In his efforts to win converts, he went well beyond what Whitefield or Edwards would have countenanced. He would work himself and his audience into a frenzy until, while many cried out in ecstasy or distress, he declared "that the Spirit of the living God was come or coming down amongst them." He would then descend from the pulpit and go through the meeting house crying "mercy, mercy, mercy." According to Josiah Cotton's memoirs, at Plymouth the meetings lasted as long as twenty-four hours, with lay exhorters (including "boys & Negroes") assisting him.[19]

When he conducted himself similarly at Charlestown, across the river from Boston, he was attacked in the press and by some ministers. In a reply that was endorsed by several of the other Connecticut itinerants, Croswell condemned the "old way" of preaching that "turn'd out Pharisees instead of true Christians." Instead, "the awakened Sinner must have the *Way hedg'd up:* He must be *lost* in a *Wilderness* before he is *found* of Christ." Croswell believed that his methods were simply those that had already been effective in bringing religious revival to Europe. His "new way" of preaching was one that the great Pietist "Dr. Frank" in Germany had recommended.

The aim of Croswell's preaching may have been essentially the same as Edwards's or Whitefield's, but there was a crucial difference. Croswell believed that the outcries, visions, and convulsions that his preaching induced were an essential part of the conversion process. Only those who had had "divine Manifestations . . . know what true Holiness means." He contended that "God never works powerfully, but men cry out disorder; for God's order differs vastly from their nice and delicate apprehension from him."[20]

Like nearly all of the clergy who had been itinerant revivalists during the Great Awakening, Croswell modified his views later, after laymen had begun to carry on the work of revival on their own, unrestrained by anything but the guidance of the Holy Spirit. It is therefore not surprising that Croswell especially regretted his use of lay exhorters. He had realized "(too late) that the Tendency of their Ways is, to drive Learning out of the World."[21]

Many clergy described the awakenings in their communities in letters to the Reverend Thomas Prince in Boston, who published them in his *Christian History.* Prince sought not only to place the American revivals within the wider context of the similar developments across the Atlantic but also to defend them against the increasing number of opponents who deplored the emotional excesses and "enthusiasm" that often accompanied them. Like their Scottish counterparts, the ministers were careful in their letters to play down the kinds of phenomena that would provide ammunition for their critics. Nevertheless, despite this clerical "filter," the accounts provide indispensable insights into religious behavior during the Great Awakening.

In the Scottish Presbyterian settlements in New England and the Middle Colonies, the ministers controlled the revivals as thoroughly as their counterparts had done at Cambuslang. The Reverend David McGregor wrote from Londonderry, New Hampshire, that nothing "visionary or enthusiastick" had accompanied the revival. From New Londonderry, Pennsylvania, the Reverend Samuel Blair wrote that while there had been some "mourning" and "strange unusual bodily Motions" during his services, he had insisted that those who exhibited such behavior tell him what points of doctrine or which scriptural passages had produced them.[22] Many Congregational ministers similarly discouraged any behavior they considered unsuitable and severely restricted the role of lay persons in exhorting or counseling prospective converts.

In some areas, however, the ministers were unable or unwilling to restrain their congregations. This was the case in many communities along the Atlantic coast north of Boston, for example. At Gloucester, after the Reverend John White had read aloud from Edwards's narrative of the 1735 revivals, the congregation had its own day of Pentecost, in which many people, even children as young as five years old, were able to "pray to Admiration." None of the people claimed to have seen visions after White in a sermon had declared his "Sentiments concerning them," but despite his disapproval, the services continued to be "disturbed and interrupted by Outcries."[23]

Elsewhere, religious excitement was allowed to reach a much higher pitch. At Salem, Marblehead, and Ipswich, laymen who had experienced conversion were active as exhorters, encouraging the kinds of spectacular behavior ministers like White deplored. According to a hostile witness, with their own "groans, cries, screams, & agonies" they worked audiences into a frenzy of excitement until there were "some leaping, some laughing, some singing, some clapping one another on the back" as they experienced "the pangs of ye New Birth."

At Ipswich, the Reverend Nathaniel Rogers was a zealous supporter of the revivals, and his brother Daniel was one of the most indefatigable itinerants in the Great Awakening. In a printed rejoinder to the criticisms made by the minister of Ipswich's Second Church, they declared that it was their belief that the Holy Spirit had descended "upon many Places in this Land as elsewhere," to a greater degree than at any time "since the primitive Ages of Christianity."[24]

For four years, Daniel Rogers toured the towns and villages of northeastern Massachusetts and the nearby settlements in coastal New Hampshire and Maine. After his graduation from Harvard in 1725, he had remained in Cambridge, serving as a tutor at the college for most of the next fifteen years. When he finally received a ministerial appointment to Boston's New North church, he rejected it in order to accompany Whitefield on his tour. He declared that "the blessed Spirit of God has led me out; and how far I shall proceed He only knows."[25] He accompanied Eleazar Wheelock on a preaching tour of Connecticut and then returned home and began itinerating on his own. During a visit to Kittery, Maine, his brother and the local minister took the entirely unprecedented step of ordaining Rogers as an itinerant, without a settled church.

His methods, like Croswell's, were emotional to the extreme. At Ipswich on one occasion, after another minister had delivered a "rousing" sermon for two hours, Daniel Rogers went from pew to pew "like a mad man," crying "Come to Christ, with out intermission." The service went on for several hours, as laymen joined Rogers in exhorting the congregation to repent. "Ipswich & Newbury," the witness concluded, "are to be pitied by all sober Christians."[26]

Even after the revivals had faded elsewhere, Essex County, Massachusetts, and the adjoining settlements in New Hampshire and Maine continued to exhibit the sorts of behavior that were coming more and more to be deplored as religious enthusiasm. Rogers, Croswell, and others encouraged scenes of tumult and confusion in their meetings that turned some New England clergy entirely against the awakening. One of its bitterest critics, the Reverend Charles Chauncy, printed a description of such a revival service that "a friend" had sent him. Some were "*screaming* out in Distress and Anguish, some *praying;* others singing; some again *jumping up and down* the House, while others were *exhorting;* some *lying along* on the Floor, and others *walking and talking.*" Meanwhile others would "shout into a *great Laughter, laughing and singing, jumping up and down,* and *clapping their Hands* together."[27]

Chauncy implied that such behavior was general in New England during the Great Awakening. Emphatically it was not. On the other hand, there were towns and even a few regions like coastal Massachusetts and New Hampshire where ministers either condoned conduct most pro-revival ministers repudiated or else were unable to control the activities of the most zealous converts. In a few communities, the search for spiritual perfection and the true scriptural church of Christ even led some people into the same byways of antinomian heresy that had always appeared in religious reformations. But in much of New England, the clergy remained in control, and the conduct of their parishioners remained securely within the conventions approved by the Puritan tradition.

As the Great Awakening progressed, most of the ministers who supported the revivals tried to find a middle ground between rejecting any emotional and ecstatic behavior as "enthusiasm"—as the critics of the Great Awakening did—and uncritically accepting any and all outcries and possessions as divinely produced—as the most zealous advocates of the revivals in New England did. As J. M. Bumsted has written, the Great Awakening was in reality "the sum total of all the local revivals." There was no individual and no collective authority anywhere within the congregational polity that could restrain the conduct of zealots as the English Methodists, the Moravians and other German sectarians, and the Scottish and American Presbyterians were all able to do. The problem was exacerbated by the activities of the itinerant preachers and lay exhorters who roamed the countryside. Too often they tended, like Croswell and Rogers, to accept as divinely sanctioned any behavior their efforts produced in their hearers.[28]

Not surprisingly, the most searching and candid examination of the ministers' dilemma came from the pen of Jonathan Edwards. As early as September 1741, when he preached at Yale's commencement, he had confronted the dangers of uncritically accepting as divine the physical manifestations of trance, possession, and ecstasy. His text (John 4:1) was one that John Wesley had cited during several of his confrontations with French Prophets: "Beloved, believe not every spirit, but try the spirits, whether they are of God, because many false prophets are gone out into the world." Published in an expanded version under the title *The Distinguishing Marks of a Work of the Spirit of God*, the sermon's arguments were quickly adopted by those ministers who like Edwards wanted to defend the Great Awakening against its critics without accepting the excesses of zeal and emotionalism that had accompanied it in some places.

Edwards's approach resembled Wesley's reliance on "the law and the testimony," but Edwards was more willing to allow the outbreaks of noise, convulsions, and ecstatic joy to remain unexplained. Such phenomena should never be taken as proof that its subjects were under the power of God, he said, because "Scripture gives us no such rule." On the other hand, there was no rule of Scripture that might "either expressly or indirectly, exclude such effects on the body; nor does reason exclude them."[29]

Edwards's sermon was a remarkable performance. Employing what Edmund Morgan has described as "that incredible simplicity of language which no one else could quite approach," he justified the

Great Awakening by reconciling the Puritan tradition of conversion experience with the outbreaks of the kinds of behavior that the revivals' critics insisted were proof either of satanic influence or of Quaker and antinomian madness.[30]

That Edwards delivered the sermon at Yale's commencement was especially significant because so many of the Great Awakening's most fervent advocates were, like Edwards himself, Yale graduates. His effort to effect some kind of reconciliation within the New England clerical establishment was made especially difficult by the presence in New Haven that same week of another Yale graduate—the most zealous of all the itinerant ministers, the Reverend James Davenport of Southold, Long Island.

Both supporters and critics of the Great Awakening found it convenient afterwards to claim that Davenport had been peculiarly responsible for the excesses of religious zeal that brought schism and dissension in the wake of revival. While it is certainly not true that he was the only minister who believed that everything that accompanied the sacred theater of the revival service was God's handiwork, Davenport's conduct did prove to be more divisive and controversial than any of the others', because he was extraordinarily effective at arousing his audiences and entirely unrestrained in publicly denouncing those of his fellow ministers whom he judged to be unconverted.

In the tight little clerical world of New England, both Davenport's name and his reputation had preceded his arrival in Connecticut. He was the descendant of the founder of the New Haven colony and the son of the respected minister at Stamford, Connecticut. His early letters reveal a deep and restless piety. When he wrote to tell his brother-in-law of his father's death, he added a prayer that God would "thrust forth a labourer into this his harvest even an Elisha" who would "make a stop to the flood of iniquity coming in on us & turn away his anger."[31]

With his Connecticut connections, it may seem surprising that he should have settled in eastern Long Island, but the region was in fact an outpost of Connecticut, linked to New London by boats that plied Long Island Sound. Ordained there in 1738, Davenport quickly began working with another recent Yale graduate, Jonathan Barber, minister at Oyster Ponds, to bring to the people of Long Island the blessings of conversion. Having read of the success of Whitefield's preaching in London and Bristol, Barber and Davenport resolved to attempt something similar. They began holding extended meetings, preaching the "new way" that led from terror to conversion.[32]

Davenport went to New York to meet Whitefield and then accompanied him to Philadelphia, where Davenport joined Tennent and other ministers in evangelizing the city and the surrounding area. After he returned to Southold, he wrote Wheelock that his preaching had produced "very surprizing effects." Never had he seen "the word come with such power (or people so hungry after it)."[33]

Thus Davenport had considerable experience as an evangelist when he launched his first preaching tour of New England in July 1741. Wherever he went in eastern Connecticut, he was heard by large and excited crowds. According to Joshua Hempstead's diary, nearly a thousand people heard one of his sermons at Groton. After the service, many remained "under the oak tree & in the meeting house" until late at night. At Stonington, "mighty works followed[; hun]dreds Cryed out." Davenport then moved on to the adjacent town of Westerly, Rhode Island, where he was equally effective.

As Davenport continued his tour, he was led into increasingly disturbing practices. He began to employ a strange singsong tone of voice and exaggerated gestures during his preaching. The Reverend Joseph Fish of Stonington wrote later that while Davenport was "a wonderful, strange good man . . . of undoubted, real piety," in religious services he encouraged both "*noise* and *outcry* . . . by extending his own voice to the highest pitch, together with the most violent agitations of the body." As a result, his preaching produced "a marvellous mixture of, almost, everything *good* and *bad*."[34]

Other ministers who traversed Connecticut produced spectacular effects from their preaching in that impassioned summer of 1741, but only Davenport tended to equate the bodily effects that his preaching induced with the experience of conversion. Since Davenport's mentor as preacher and performer had been George Whitefield, it is ironic that the sacred theater of his own revival services should have differed so dramatically in form and content from those of the Great Itinerant. His voice and actions struck hostile observers as strange and uncontrolled, but to those who shared Davenport's convictions, his preaching was a remarkably effective theatrical evocation of the emotional intensity of the conversion experience. While he never claimed to be directly possessed by the Holy Spirit, he was similarly in "trance," in the sense that he was caught up in a collective performance in which preacher and audience raised each other to emotional catharsis.[35]

As Davenport moved from town to town, accompanied by his converts, he would interrogate the ministers he met in order to assure himself of their spiritual state. If their answers did not satisfy him, he denounced them by name in his sermons. He urged his hearers not to listen to unconverted ministers and instead to conduct their own private meetings. By the time he arrived at New Haven in September, he was decidedly the most controversial figure in New England.

The Yale commencement, the immediate occasion for Jonathan Edwards's sermon, was dwarfed by the revival that Davenport had ignited in New Haven. For several days, he attracted large crowds for highly impassioned religious services, in which he was assisted by other preachers and exhorters. Once again, as one witness noted, Davenport seemed "to lay too much stress upon inward feelings, and immediate dictates of ye Spirit." While Edwards had refrained from naming him, it was clearly Davenport who most dangerously encouraged the tendencies that he warned against in his sermon. Edwards later wrote the Reverend Aaron Burr that he thought that Davenport did more "towards giving Satan and other opposers an advantage against the work than any other person."[36]

For the next several months, New Haven was virtually inundated with itinerant preachers. Some of the most zealous advocates of the awakening began to meet separately, and in West Haven, the Reverend Timothy Allen (a Yale classmate of Davenport's) was suspended from preaching after he declared that in the work of conversion the reading of the Bible, unless it was accompanied by the immediate operation of the Holy Spirit, was of no more use than reading an old almanac. Services and prayer meetings went on almost daily, with Yale students in constant attendance, until the rector dismissed classes and closed the school at the end of March.[37]

Meanwhile, Davenport had returned to his own parish on Long Island for the winter. In the spring of 1742, he was back in Connecticut. Accompanied by two ministers and several lay exhorters, he began another preaching tour, in defiance of Connecticut's recent law against itinerancy. He was taken before the General Assembly in Hartford and accused not only of invading other ministers' parishes but also of "pretending to revelations." The assembly found him guilty of disturbing the peace. They also decided that he was mentally disturbed as the result of "enthusiastical impressions and impulses." Outside the hall, a large crowd was demonstrating in support of Davenport. The sheriff had to intervene with an armed force in order to take Davenport to the boat that was to convey him back to Long Island.[38]

Three weeks later, Davenport turned up in Boston. Thomas Prince wrote later that his arrival marked the beginning of "an unhappy period" in Boston's religious life, after eighteen months of spiritual revival begun by the preaching of Whitefield and Tennent. Davenport immediately aroused the disquiet of the Boston clergy when, having attended a morning service in Charlestown, he declined to return for the afternoon service because he thought that the minister was unconverted. He then crossed the river into Boston and marched through the streets to his lodgings, accompanied by a large crowd, all of them singing hymns. For the next several days, he preached to enormous crowds on Boston Common. The Reverend Ebenezer Parkman of Westborough, Massachusetts, wrote in his diary that in one sermon Davenport declared that "he was then in the experience of the Divine Spirit's influences. Said he was ready to drop down dead for the salvation of but one soul, &c."[39]

The Boston ministers refused to allow him to preach in their churches, but he was permitted to continue to hold outdoor meetings. In the coastal towns north of Boston, he was welcomed into several churches in which Croswell, Rogers, and numerous lay exhorters were already at work in pressing the revival toward an excess of zeal beyond what Boston's moderate advocates of the revivals thought prudent. Boston was deeply divided by Davenport's conduct, which had caused dissensions and separations in several of the churches and had led some leading ministers, notably Charles Chauncy, to declare their public opposition to the revivals. Finally, at the end of August 1742, the civil authorities intervened and shipped Davenport back to Long Island. By then, as the missionary for the Society for the Propagation of the Gospel reported to London with considerable satisfaction, many people had "forsaken their stated places of Worship & their former Teachers" and instead assembled in private homes for services conducted by lay men and women.[40]

In deciding to ship Davenport back to Long Island, the Massachusetts authorities adopted the same convenient fiction that the

Connecticut General Assembly had used and declared that he was mentally unbalanced. It is indeed true that his evangelical zeal and his belief that he was peculiarly the Lord's agent had led him to the religiously and politically dangerous conviction that he and all true Christians were under the immediate guidance of the Holy Spirit, which must supersede all scriptural and customary restraints upon the conduct of the godly. Perhaps, for a Puritan minister thus to undermine the basis of the authority of his calling was indeed a kind of madness.

In October, a council of ministers met at Southold to deal with the situation that Davenport's behavior had created in his own parish. All of his actions, his critics in the congregation said, derived from his "making immediate impulses upon his mind the rule of his conduct in many cases, declaring publicly that he is herein acted by the immediate influence of the Spirit of God." Despite all this, the congregation declared it had "great affection" for Davenport and wanted him to remain their minister if he would stop these "irregularities."[41] The council therefore took no action against him. In March 1743, he again crossed the Sound to New London, where there occurred the most bizarre episode in his career.

The revival at New London had produced a schism within the settled church. The same thing had happened in a number of other places in Connecticut and Massachusetts. In emulation of their Puritan ancestors and in defiance of the law, small groups of laymen had organized congregations of converted "saints" like the churches in the earliest days of Christianity, free of the contamination of the godless world. In New London, one of their leaders was Timothy Allen, who had come to New London after his public statements concerning the absolute primacy of the Holy Spirit had led to his removal from the church at West Haven. Allen and his followers had a further purpose in New London. The town was to be the site of a new seminary, which would train young men to go out and carry on the work of evangelism as ministers and itinerants, guided by the direct inspiration of God.

Not even the most radical of the New Light clergy could conceive of the idea of churches that dispensed with an educated clergy. Instead, what was needed was a school in which young men could be trained for the ministry in the new way, free from the rationalism and Arminian errors of Harvard and Yale. During the summer of 1742, news of a plan to launch a new school in New London circulated through New England. Sympathetic clergy and laymen were approached for financial support. In Durham, New Hampshire, the Reverend Nathaniel Gilman noted in his diary that he had received a letter signed by Davenport and Nathaniel and Daniel Rogers concerning the proposed "Shepherd's Tent" in New London.[42]

The school enrolled fourteen students that fall; Harvard had thirteen freshmen that year and Yale only ten. It managed to function despite Allen's arrest and imprisonment until November, probably for unauthorized exhorting and preaching. When the Connecticut assembly passed a law banning private schools not supervised by the government, Allen and ninety others in New London successfully petitioned for the formal recognition of their separate church. Thus the Shepherd's Tent continued to operate, as an adjunct of the church.

Scattered evidence indicates that its critics were correct in claiming that the Shepherd's Tent dispensed with conventional education. It was quite unlike the "Log College" of Neshaminy, Pennsylvania, at which the four Tennents and other young men had received from William Tennent, Sr., a thorough instruction in Scripture and Presbyterian doctrine. At the Shepherd's Tent, Allen instead encouraged his students to try to attain the immediate gifts of divine inspiration. Allen wrote Wheelock in February 1743 that he himself had spent three weeks in ecstasy, "even Swallowed up in God." He added that the students were "quite overcome with the Powerfull Love of God, & even now while I am writing I hear the most passionate pleadings of several of them much overcome." His group was about to spurn worldly possessions as they set out to prepare the world for the Millennium: "The blessed Lord seems to be coming to get himself a Kingdom again."[43]

Davenport came to New London at the invitation of the Shepherd's Tent and the schismatic New Lights of New London in order to participate in the ordination of one of their number into the ministry. On 6 March, at his instigation, the congregation symbolically dissociated themselves from the ungodly community by performing a ritual of sacred theater that was intentionally shocking. They went to the waterfront, where (as Jared Ingersoll recorded in his history) they "burnt a Quantity of Books . . . all suppos'd by them to be tinctured with Arminianism & opposed to the work of God's Spirit in ye Land." The next day, again at Davenport's suggestion, they staged a second bonfire in order to burn their fancy or superfluous apparel, but this time they were restrained at the last minute by a few of the members. Davenport by this time was not only emotionally overwrought but also physically ill. He had been lame for some time and by now was bedridden. He may have begun to have doubts about the episode, for he immediately left New London and resumed his itinerant evangelism before returning to Long Island.[44]

At the end of March, the justice of the peace, Joshua Hempstead, convened a court of inquiry concerning the incident. He noted in his diary that a number of the leading clerical supporters of the awakening, including Joseph Meacham of Coventry and Solomon Williams of Lebanon as well as former itinerants like Samuel Buell and Benjamin Pomeroy, had come to New London in order "to Settle the disorders that are Subsisting among those Called New Lights." The court hearing was preceded by a sermon by Jonathan Edwards, still trying to save the awakening from the excessive zeal of some of its proponents.[45]

The Shepherd's Tent did not long survive the scandal of the bonfire and the trial of its leaders for their part in it. Allen led a remnant to Rhode Island, but it quickly expired. When three other New Light "seminaries" were founded some years later at Dartmouth, Brown, and Princeton, they specifically repudiated the Shepherd's Tent's curious attempt to let the Holy Spirit alone educate the ministry.[46]

Back in Southold, Davenport began to recover his health and his emotional balance. Several ministers who had previously defended him now publicly criticized his conduct. Several New Light leaders, including his brother-in-law, Eleazar Wheelock, wrote to try to persuade him of his errors. In August 1744, he wrote a letter of "retraction," which Thomas Prince published in the *Christian History*. It was also published as a pamphlet and in the Boston newspapers.

In essence, Davenport conceded all the points that Edwards, the ministers of Boston, and others had repeatedly made. He admitted that he had been wrong in "exposing" ministers he believed to be unconverted, in urging people to separate from their churches, and in "encouraging private Persons to a ministerial and authoritative Kind or Method of exhorting." He had not, however, rejected his belief that supernatural powers had been at work. Instead, he now believed that what he had thought to be the spirit of God had instead been that of the Devil. During that final visit to New London, he had been "under the powerful Influence of the *false Spirit* almost one whole Day together, and Part of several Days. . . . I thought in the Time of it, that 'twas the Spirit of God in an high Degree; awful indeed!"[47]

After making his retraction, he visited many of the towns in Connecticut where he had preached before, apologized to the ministers he had denounced, and tried without success to persuade those who had left their churches at his instigation to return to them. After preaching occasionally on Long Island and in New Jersey for the next several years, in 1748 he joined the New Side Presbyterian synod of New York. At the time of his premature death nine years later, he was minister of the church in Hopewell and Maidenhead, New Jersey, where John Rowland had launched a revival on the Scottish model a decade earlier. He never lost his conviction that the world must be brought to God through the efforts of an evangelical ministry. He had accompanied Samuel Davies on a successful preaching tour of Virginia, and he corresponded with Whitefield to the end of his life. In a sermon he delivered in 1775, he was surely thinking of his own early excesses when he said that ministers were tempted more than others, "as Officers in an Army are more aim'd and pointed at by the Enemy than private Soldiers." God permitted these temptations to afflict the clergy in order "to *prove* them, and bring them to know more of themselves." As a result, they become "more watchful and circumspect, more diligent in their Work, and probably more successful too."[48]

It had not been Davenport alone who had discarded all the theological restraints of the Puritan heritage in order to bring down the Holy Spirit. Even Jonathan Edwards had for a time encouraged lay participation in the clerical function of bringing sinners to salvation through exhortation, prayer, and counsel. If Edwards refused to ascribe to God the strange and powerful physical manifestations that New Light preaching produced, he encouraged them all the same. A small army of young and dedicated itinerant preachers had brought a new kind of direct emotional experience of divine presence to towns and villages throughout the colonies. In some parts of New England, they discovered that the popular excitement generated by the revivals went beyond anything they had anticipated.

By 1744, even one-time radical zealots like Davenport, Croswell, and Allen had come to recognize the danger that an unrestrained quest for spiritual immediacy posed to the religious and political structures of New England. Henceforth, very few ministers countenanced the kinds of conduct that had been tolerated or encouraged two or three years earlier. There were still itinerant preachers and exhorters traversing the countryside, but nearly all of them were laymen who believed that they had been called to separate themselves from the ministers and churches of the religious establishment.

In the Middle Colonies, ministerial authority had permitted nothing of the sort to take place. In England, John Wesley had supervised most aspects of the Methodist movement decisively and even arbitrarily, although his indifference to theological fine points and his conviction that God moved among his people in tangible and miraculous ways meant that a variety of eccentrics was able to function on the fringes of Wesleyanism throughout the eighteenth century.

In New England, on the other hand, the traditions of congregational autonomy and local self-government meant that there was really no effective way to force the most zealous of the converts of the Great Awakening to adhere to the cautions and admonitions of the ministers. Separatism had been a continuing problem since the days of Roger Williams and Anne Hutchinson. In the 1740s, what Stephen Marini has called "the logic of revival" generated a schismatic movement in which the regenerated saints once again set themselves apart from the unregenerate and worldly. In all, nearly one hundred Separatist churches were formed. Forty were in Connecticut and another thirty in Massachsuetts, concentrated in the southeast, in southern Worcester County, and in turbulent Essex County. The rest, in New Hampshire, Maine, and New York, consisted mainly of groups of Separates who had migrated there from Massachusetts and Connecticut.[49]

If—with at least one exception, as we shall see presently—the New England clergy drew back from the premises and practices that had produced possessed and ecstatic behavior in many localities, the phenomena did not disappear when the Great Awakening faded. They continued for some time to be a feature of the Separate movement, as lay men and women defied social and legal pressures and worshiped in houses, apart from the established churches. They ordained their own ministers, and they continued to encourage the arousing of the "religious affections" as a means of attaining an emotional union with God. In effect, the sacred theater that for the preachers and exhorters of the Great Awakening had been a means of preparing the individual sinner for the infusion of divine grace became part of Separate worship. It became the norm to preach in the "holy whine" that Davenport had introduced, and tears and outcries in the congregation were the accepted response. According to the Reverend Joseph Fish of Stonington, Connecicut, when a minority seceded from his church in protest against his efforts to restore godly discipline, they stated that if there were no outcries and "visible great operations" during worship services, then *there was nothing of* THE POWER."[50]

The priceless document of the odyssey into Separatism is Nathan Cole's account of his "Spiritual Travels." His encounter with the preaching of Whitefield was followed by several years of agonized reflection on his spiritual state. Like the English Methodists who described their prolonged conversions for Wesley's *Arminian Magazine*, Cole suffered extended periods in which he was convinced that he was damned, relieved by occasional visionary experiences of deity. At last, "a ray of divine light" touched Cole's soul; and "the Devil lear'd away ashamed."[51] In 1747, having decided that "the Old Standing Churches were not in a gospel order" and that "nothing was acceptable to God in worship, but what was done by the help of his spirit," Cole began to hold religious meetings in his house. When he recorded his "Spiritual Travels," he had spent seventeen years in search of the true church that belonged solely to those genuinely converted and led by God.[52]

Nathan Cole's belief that worship should be guided by the immediate promptings of the Holy Spirit was general among the separating New Lights in the 1740s. When someone complained to one of the ablest leaders of the Connecticut Separatists, Elisha Paine, that they should not claim to see into other men's hearts, which only God could do, Paine responded, "We don't judge by Men's Judgment, but by God in us." The lay pastor of the Separatists in Preston, Connecticut, declared that they had left the settled church because it "refuse[d] the members should improve there Gifts of Preaching & Exhorting Publickly &c: as also were offended at the Powerfull opperations of the Spirits of God." When eighty-three members of the First Church in Newbury, Massachusetts, separated from it, one of the seceders explained to the minister that they "lookt upon it as the natural right of every Man to enquire and judge for himself in matters of Religion & that without Check or Control of any Man."[53]

As C. C. Goen has shown in his excellent and sympathetic study, there are no easy generalizations that one can make about the Separatists. In many communities, they included many of the leading citizens. Often, the separations had their basis in part in long-standing political and social frictions or in family loyalties and rivalries. Recent studies of New London and Canterbury, indeed, contend that it was above all the existence of closely linked networks of families that generated and perpetuated the separations.[54]

That also seems to have been the case in Enfield, Connecticut. After the dramatic experience of Edwards's sermon there in 1741, the revival proceeded without incident, but in about 1747 a group seceded from the settled church. The leaders were members of two prominent local families, the Peases and the Markhams. In 1751, they reported to the Canterbury Separatists that they had organized their church and ordained a minister. All was not well, however. Joseph Markham wrote that there was dissension that threatened to "Destroy this body of Saints as a Church . . . there fore help help help for the Cause of god." Two years later, Ezekiel Pease wrote to Solomon Paine at Canterbury that the Enfield group was "under Broken Surcumstances, Divided into two Parties."[55] Despite the controversies, the Separate church persisted, and in 1770 it managed to be recognized as the Second Ecclesiastical Society of Enfield. The contentious Joseph Markham had died in 1761, bequeathing to his children property valued at nearly one thousand pounds, including land, two houses, and three mills on the river. In 1781, three of his sons were among the first converts of the Shakers, and their property became the nucleus of the Enfield community.

In Enfield as in many communities, continuing questions over the nature of the conversion experience helped lead some people to reject infant baptism as unscriptural. It is not clear how or why the issue emerged in Enfield, but at about the same time that Markham's group seceded, a second Separate congregation was also formed. Four years later, in 1757, they adopted Baptist principles. This congregation was dominated by another of Enfield's leading families, the Meachams. In 1781, they too heard and were persuaded by the message brought by Ann Lee and the English Shakers. Among the converts were the minister, Joseph Meacham, and his sons Joseph, David, and Moses.[56]

From Ipswich and Newbury through the settlements in New Hampshire and Maine, the coastal region north of Boston continued to be stirred by religious excitement for some time after it faded elsewhere. In Durham, New Hampshire, the Reverend Nicholas Gilman had since 1742 presided over a revival of exceptional intensity. After his ministerial colleagues, including even Daniel Rogers, had come to have doubts about it, Gilman persisted in his belief that God was speaking miraculously and directly to the people of Durham, through several ecstatics in his congregation and a strange itinerant exhorter named Richard Woodbury.

Although even the Gilman family history dismisses Nicholas as a victim of pious delusions, his unusual career deserves further examination, especially since in the 1780s New Hampshire was to be one of the areas in which Shaker evangelism was particularly successful. Forty years earlier, the efforts of a few ministers and some zealous lay persons had legitimized visionary and possessed behavior among the subjects of revival that would have been roundly condemned almost anywhere else. Gilman himself recorded all of it in a diary that is one of the fullest and most candid accounts that we have of the sacred theater of spirit possession during the Great Awakening.

Gilman's early career had resembled that of Daniel Rogers, whom he had known since they had been students at Harvard. He had spent fifteen years teaching and filling in occasionally as a preacher when he received a call to the church in Durham. The religious situation in the town was in considerable turmoil when Gilman arrived; the congregation had just dismissed the eccentric Hugh Adams, their minister since the church's establishment in 1718. Part of the congregation had seceded to follow Adams, who among other things declared that God would strike down his enemies.[57]

Gilman's diary shows that he read all the literature that the transatlantic awakening had generated. He read William Law's *Serious Call*, Whitefield's and Wesley's sermons, a biography of Francke, Woodward's history of the English religious societies, and Luther's commentaries on the epistles of Paul. Above all, he read Edwards. After reading the *Narrative* of the Connecticut Valley revivals, he wrote, "Oh! the Amazing depths of the Divine Counsells—how Wonderfull are his Works and his Ways Past finding Out." In the fall of 1741, he began to hold evening meetings in private homes, at which he read Edwards's sermons aloud. By January, revival was sweeping through his congregation. At an all-night service of worship, Gilman himself underwent an ecstatic experience and "was constrained to cry, with a loud voice—Glory to God on high—Glory to the Redeemer etc.—for some considerable Time." He concluded: "It seemed the Shortest and I think the Sweetest Night that I have seen."[58]

As he prepared for his ordination, Gilman continued to reflect upon his mystical experience in his diary. It had been, he wrote, like "the Blank paper in the Printers press recieving [sic] upon it a Variety of Truths at One and the Same Impression." The experience also persuaded him that those in his congregation who had claimed to see doves and angels and bright lights in the meeting house had been similarly visited by divinity. He began to record his parishioners' visions and to read them aloud at private assemblies. Not surprisingly, trances and visions became increasingly frequent. One young woman fell into a prolonged ecstasy in which she "lay Blessing and praising God in whispers, in the Language of a Soul actually in Heaven."[59]

As if the faithful of Durham needed further spiritual excitement during that summer of 1742, Daniel Rogers came there often, accompanied by his brother John (the minister at Kittery, Maine) and a lay exhorter from Portsmouth. Gilman continued to read everything he could on the awakening. The itinerant Samuel Buell gave him "a Narrative of his conversions," and he bought and read aloud to his congregation Robe's narrative of the revival at Cambuslang.[60]

What is most striking about Gilman is his unquestioning eagerness to share in all conceivable aspects of the great transatlantic outpouring of divine revelation. Except for his single mystical experience, his diary suggests that he was essentially a pious observer of the wonders that descended upon Durham, uncritically accepting them all as equally divine in inspiration. Despite his great admiration for Edwards, he ignored entirely Edwards's warnings against ascribing the outward manifestations of the psychology of conversion to God's agency. Convinced that he himself had had an insight into divinity during his visionary experience, he believed anyone who made similar claims; whatever the "religious affections" produced was necessarily the direct work of God. His credulity is nowhere more apparent than in his association, from late 1742 until his death six years later, with the lay exhorter Richard Woodbury.

Like most of the laymen who felt themselves called to preach during the Great Awakening, Woodbury is a shadowy figure. A native of Rowley, Massachusetts, just south of Newbury, he traversed the coastal region for at least a decade, preaching, exhorting, and, increasingly, claiming exalted spiritual pretensions for himself. By 1760 he was back in Rowley, a public charge of the town.[61]

Initially, Woodbury's activities were encouraged by the New Light ministers of the region, but they all—except Gilman—quickly became wary of him. Gilman noted in his diary: "Mr Woodbury spoke much to the Offence of Many." Then: "The Town in an Uproar."[62] Meanwhile, the ecstatics in Gilman's congregation had settled down; at least, there are fewer descriptions of their visions in his diary. He was in Durham less and less frequently, as he accompanied Woodbury on preaching tours of the Maine and New Hampshire settlements and Essex County, Massachusetts. Gilman believed that Woodbury had direct access to God, noting for example that "Mr. Woodbury told me this day the Lord woud [sic] take the work into his Own hands to decide the Differences" that were by now polarizing the Durham congregation.

His friend Daniel Rogers expressed his concern over Gilman's "leaving his people" for extended periods as he toured with Woodbury, but Gilman paid no attention. Rogers also questioned Woodbury's "perfection doctrine."[63] Apparently Woodbury claimed to possess the spiritual powers that accompanied sinless perfection. While he and Gilman were in Ipswich during the summer of 1744, his conduct led eleven ministers to publish a protest in a Boston newspaper. They declared that Woodbury claimed to possess the "Power to bless and curse eternally whom he pleases." When someone questioned him about his conduct, he "did with strange Emotion and violent Agitation throw himself upon and rowl upon the floor, crying out, 'You have crucified Christ in what you have said.'"[64]

Long after nearly every other minister in New England had been led to repudiate the spiritual excesses that revivals sometimes generated, Gilman continued to give them his full support. In August 1746, two other ministers, Jeremiah Wise of Berwick, Maine, and Samuel Chandler of Gloucester, Massachusetts, came to Durham to participate in a fast service at the church. During Wise's sermon, there was considerable commotion, as people talked, clapped their hands, or cried out. A few people rolled on the floor in convulsions. At the sermon's conclusions, Gilman got up from his pew and disagreed with Wise's conclusions, contending that "perfection" was "attainable in this life."

Everyone then went to Gilman's house for refreshments. Gilman came in, accompanied by his "high flyers." One of them, a woman named Hannah Huckins, declared that "she had gone through adoption, justification & sanctification & perfection & perseverance. She said she had attained perfection & yet had a bad memory." When Chandler questioned her, she "fell to dancing around the room, singing some dancing tunes, jiggs, minuets, & kept the time exactly with her feet." Others joined her, while the rest applauded. One of them danced up to Gilman and asked him if he approved. He said that he did. "The house was full of confusion," Chandler recorded in his diary, "some singing bawdy songs, others dancing to them & all under a pretense of religion. . . . Mr. Gilman justified their proceedings. They do it out of a good design, he says, and that there is no sanctity in tunes, and that the reason we cannot approve of it is because there is no light in us." The next day, the same behavior accompanied Chandler's sermon as ten or twelve people "made wry mouths & extraordinary gestures of body, often crying out aloud." At last, the group "jumpt up & out they went, crying out & railing & made a hideous noise." After the service, Gilman told Chandler that he would not "receive those that don't receive Woodbury and all those persons in all their extravagancies."[65]

A year later, the New Hampshire ministerial association sent a delegation to Durham to inquire into the situation. They found that Gilman had abandoned his clerical functions entirely and that a "considerable number" of the church members had separated and were meeting in a private house. At their services, the delegation reported that "there were very disorderly vile & absurd things practiced," including "profane singing & dancing, damning the Devil, [and] spitting in Persons Faces whom they apprehended not to be of their Society."

Gilman died of tuberculosis in 1748, at the age of forty. The church found a new minister, the nephew of Hugh Adams, whom they had dismissed in 1741. The Separates persisted for a time. Woodbury was still there in 1751, when the Baptist leader Isaac Backus preached to them, but Backus noted in his diary that after having been led for so long by the "false Spirit," the congregation was now "wonderfully subdued."[66]

After 1751, the "high flyers" of Durham disappear from the records. Twenty-five years later, when religious revival swept the New England back country, virtually identical behavior, including ecstatic singing and dancing and "damning the Devil," appeared in several frontier communities in New Hampshire and Maine.

The notion that God might again make his spirit manifest in outbreaks of possesed behavior persisted within the Separate tradition, but in general their worship services and ecclesiastical structures came to resemble those of the settled churches from which they had seceded. They did, however, continue to encourage expressions of emotion. As the chronicler Hannah Adams noted, they had "strong faith in the immediate teachings of the Spirit," which they held to be "above, though not contrary to reason." It was, after all, the conviction that God was revealing himself anew that had led their critics to give the supporters of the revivals the label of "New Lights." It had been this point of view, for example, that had led Ebenezer Parkman to inscribe in his diary a prayer that "all New Light" might be entirely extinguished so that "the Old the true Gospel Light may Shine forth."[67]

The Separates and Baptists also continued to affirm that each of the gathered saints received a "gift" from the Holy Spirit that must be "improved" and exercised. The Separates at Norton, in southeastern Massachusetts, echoed Saint Paul (I Corinthians 12:1–8) when they stated in their articles of faith that "all the gifts and graces that are bestowed upon any of the members are to be improved by them for the good of the whole."[68] In practice, the exercise of "gifts" was controlled by consulting Scripture, submitting individual promptings to the collective judgment of the church, and seeking the advice and guidance of the ministers and laity of nearby churches, but occasionally believers claimed that the promptings of the Holy Spirit superseded all of these restraints.

Separate and Baptist leaders like Isaac Backus devoted much of their time to mediating disputes that had originated in claims to spiritual gifts. Both his diary and his *History of New England* are filled with accounts of them. Usually, they were strictly local affairs, but one controversial claim was widespread and persistent. Within a number of communities in Connecticut and Massachusetts, people claimed to have received what was in effect the ultimate spiritual gift: sinlessness and immortality.

It is not clear whether the idea emerged independently in several localities, or whether it spread from a single source. The first instance that Backus recorded was in 1746. A group of men and women in Windham, Connecticut, claimed that they "were perfect and immortal; and one of them declared that he was Christ." Three years later, people in Easton and Norton, Massachusetts, similarly contended that they were "Getting into a state of perfection in this World . . . so that they Shall Never Die." They also claimed that in their perfected states they would be united in "Spiritual Union" with a partner who was not necessarily the husband or wife to whom they were civilly married.[69] In 1751, several members of the Easton Baptist church were expelled, but the ideas persisted. Similar ideas appeared in Norwich, Connecticut, Cumberland, Rhode Island, and Grafton and Upton, Massachusetts.

In 1764, Backus's church at Middleborough withdrew "fellowship" with the Easton Baptists because they persisted in condoning perfectionism, spiritual wifery, and baptism by "unordained itinerants." A number of people in Easton and Norton told Backus that "they were already perfect and immortal: or that they expected soon to pass into such a state, even with their new companions." In 1768, some members of a Baptist church in nearby Attleborough advanced similar views. The ideas also persisted in Connecticut. When Ann Lee and the English Shakers passed through there in the summer of 1782, they encountered people in Windham "who held the doctrine of a community of wives." There was a celibate perfectionist group in New London as late as 1790.[70]

One of the most active evangelists for this particular elaboration of the ancient Christian notion of perfectionism was Sarah Sartell Prentice, the wife of the Reverend Solomon Prentice. Prentice had come to the Congregational church in Easton in 1747 after being dismissed from the church at Grafton in Worcester County. In both communities, some of the Separates claimed to be perfect and immortal, and Mrs. Prentice may have been the link. Ebenezer Parkman noted in his diary in 1754 that he had heard that she had been back to Grafton and that "her Exhortings have Success." When he talked with her the next year, she was on her way to Charlestown, her birthplace. He noted that she was "very deep into Errors,; and Yet . . . exceeding Spiritual, heavenly and Purify'd." Isaac Backus also met Sarah Prentice. In 1753 she told him that she had recently undergone a tranformation by means of which "her Body would never see

Corruption, but would live here till Christs personal coming." Backus noted that she stated this as a simple fact; on other topics, her conversation "seemed very agreeable."[71]

Solomon Prentice never accepted his wife's spiritual claims and deplored the fact that she had separated from his church and been rebaptized by "a despicable layman." Yet he continued to live with her and apparently to love her as his wife, despite the fact that her conduct contributed to his being dismissed by the churches in both Grafton and Easton. They had been married in 1732, soon after Prentice was settled at Grafton, then a frontier settlement. Prentice had warmly welcomed the Great Awakening; he was moreover one of the ministers who unreservedly accepted visions and outcries as the working of God's spirit. He described in great detail the spiritual experiences of one woman in the parish, whose conversion had been triggered by the news of the death of her father. Prentice does not name the woman, but it was almost certainly his own wife. Her father, Captain Nathaniel Sartell, a wealthy merchant and shipowner with considerable property in both Groton and Charlestown, died in 1741.[72]

For nearly five weeks, Sarah Prentice went through an agonized process of conversion. She would lie silent and motionless for extended periods, but then she "did as a Wife or Mother . . . under the Head of Duty." Sometimes she was afflicted with the symptoms of hysterical possession, with "her Nerves and Sinews . . . contracted, and her Tongue Stiff in her head. Then she regained the power of speech and cried, "*Come See the Power of God on Me!*" At the moment of her conversion, she went into an ecstatic trance, crying "*its Lovely! its Lovely!*" Almost daily for the next several months, she "continued drinking of the Streams of Gods Delight."[73]

The revival continued in Grafton for nearly two years. Prentice welcomed the young itinerant ministers to his church, and he made preaching tours as well, sometimes addressing large crowds outdoors or in barns. He and other New Light ministers in the settlements in southern Worcester County held protracted meetings that lasted for three and four days. Those who attended had "but Little Sleep or other Refreshment; yet many were the Tears, and great the Manifestations of Sorrow, that the Exercises were over." Throughout the area, hundreds of people were dramatically and publicly brought to Christ. The behavior that accompanied their "great and pungent

Convictions," he wrote, was "as tho' God was purposely designed to evidence to the whole World, that it was His Work."[74]

The revivals faded in Worcester County in late 1743, but the Prentices' religious zeal continued to distress many people in Grafton. Some of the clergy in the area tried to mediate, notably their longtime friend, Ebenezer Parkman. After several years of controversy and several ministerial conferences, the crisis came to a head in 1747. A group had already separated; in their number was Mrs. Prentice. The congregation demanded Prentice's dismissal, and the ministers of the county reluctantly agreed.[75]

Grafton was not the only community in the area in which people claimed spiritual gifts that far exceeded what moderate New Lights like Backus considered scriptural and proper. Ezra Stiles noted in his *Itineraries* that in several Worcester County towns there were people who "declared themselves IMMORTALS." In Hopkinton, Nathaniel Smith declared that he was God and "wore a Cap with the Word GOD inscribed on its front." Stiles added that they were all followers of a lay exhorter in Charlestown named Shadrach Ireland and that Mrs. Prentice "used to lie with Ireland as her spiritual Husbd."[76]

Shadrach Ireland had been a pipe fitter in Charlestown when he felt called to become a preacher and itinerant exhorter during the Great Awakening. He continued in that capacity for about ten years. Then, in the spring of 1753, he "professed to have experienced such a change, both in body and mind, that he was become perfect and immortal, and a number more with him."[77] We know from Backus's diary that one of those who attained perfection at that time was Sarah Prentice, a native of Charlestown and former resident of Grafton who still visited both places.

While we know nothing further about how it came about, Ireland became the head of a "church" of perfectionists, scattered through central and southeastern Massachusetts, who believed themselves to be physically immortal. His followers were to be celibate until they attained sinlessnes, at which time they were to unite with divinely chosen partners in marriages that produced sinless children. He himself left his wife and six children and began living with a young woman named Abigail Lougee.

Eventually, Ireland's religious pretensions and his practice of spiritual wifery made him notorious in Charlestown. In about 1760, he disappeared from the town. His followers said that he had died, but in fact they had taken him to Harvard, Massachusetts, where one group of his disciples resided. They built a square house in which Ireland, his spiritual wife, and some of his followers lived quietly for the next twenty years. Irelandites from all over Massachusetts visited him secretly in Harvard and received his spiritual counsel.[78]

Sarah Prentice's part in these developments in unknown. It is worth noting, however, that Harvard was six miles from her mother's home in Groton. After her husband was dismissed by the church at Easton, they had gone from town to town as he found employment as an occasional preacher. Finally in 1768 he was chosen minister at Hull, where the church had continued to encourage religious emotion and lay exhorting since the 1740s. That did not work out either, and in 1772 the Prentices were back in Grafton. Mrs. Prentice told Parkman about "the wonderful Change in her Body—her Sanctification—that God had shewn to her His mind & Will." She told him that for over twenty years she had "not so much as Shook Hands with any Mann. . . . I could not know much about Mr. Prentice."[79]

Prentice died the next year. His wife lived another twenty years. Thus she was still in Grafton when Ann Lee came through the town on her missionary journey through New England in 1781. We know from Shaker testimonies that Ireland had maintained spiritual authority over his followers in a number of communities until his quite unexpected death in 1778 raised some questions about his doctrine of immortality. While Sarah Prentice does not seem to have been among them, many of his disciples accepted Ann Lee's claim that her own divine mandate had entirely superseded that of Shadrach Ireland.

With the Irelandites in Massachusetts and the Separates and Baptists of Enfield, Connecticut, we can trace simple and direct lines from the Great Awakening to the Shakers. The Shakers sent missionaries to one-time radical New Light centers like New London and Stonington, but these had little success, in part because so many radical New Lights had left Connecticut in search of economic opportunity and freedom from the regulation and occasional persecution that controlled religious expression in the Old Colony. As these pioneers moved into the Berkshire region of Massachusetts and New York and the hill country of northern New England, they brought with them the memory of the sacred theater that had seemed to many of their fathers and mothers in the 1740s to be the commencement of the Millennium. Their churches—Congregation and Presbyterian but above all Baptist—preserved the urgency and fervor of that hopeful time in an environment that must often have seemed lonely and frightening. It was there that they, together with their fellow religious seekers from Rhode Island and Massachusetts, encountered the Shaker missionaries who represented an odd and unexpected fulfillment of the Great Awakening.[80]

⁌6⁍

A Prophetess in
Manchester

As we have seen, the wave of new spiritual manifestations and possession phenomena that had had its unlikely beginnings in the mountains of southeastern France in the late seventeenth century washed over wide areas in the next decades, merging, as it moved through Europe, with a major current of popular religiosity that went by a variety of names. At bottom, however, German Pietists and separatists, English Moravians, Methodists, and evangelicals, the awakened Presbyterians of Scotland and the American Middle Colonies, and the New Lights, Strict Congregationalists, and Baptists of New England all shared the conviction that personal salvation was absolutely central to human experience. All of these groups were moved by a sense of urgency that told them God was moving *now* in the world, and a belief that those who had been "born again" or "awakened" by the Spirit must address themselves to creating the social and moral structures in which the Christian life might be lived.

None of these developments seems to have had the slightest effect upon the scattered remnant of French Prophets who had persisted in London and some other English towns and cities. From the scattered references to them that have survived, neither their message nor their methods seem to have changed very much since 1715. After all the diverse and peculiar expressions of sacred theater that had marked their first years, they resumed the prophetic mode that Marion, Fage, and Cavalier had brought to London in 1706. When for example the Quaker Thomas Story conversed in 1735 with Isaac Hollis, the French Prophet (and former Baptist and Philadelphian) whom John and Charles Wesley were to encounter a few years later, Hollis told him that "they expect such a dispensation from God, that all the *gifts* of the primitive times should be restored, as working miracles, prophecy, healing the sick, raising the dead, &c." Hollis lived until 1774, the year that Ann Lee and seven English Shakers sailed for America.[1]

After John Wesley visited the prophet Mary Plewit in 1738, he noted in his *Journal* that while several people who had accompanied him believed that she was divinely inspired, he was unsure: "The motion might be either hysterical or artificial." She told him ("in the person of God") of "the fulfilling of the prophecies, the coming of Christ now at hand, and the spreading of the gospel over all the earth." She said that the faithful must "wait upon God," adding, "with many enforcements, that we must watch and pray, and take up our cross, and be still before God."[2]

One of the French Prophets' bases of operations had been Manchester, and it must have been through some nameless Prophets in the Lancashire region that the spark of divine possession was passed to the little body of seekers that came to be called the Shakers. According to the Shakers' own histories, it was in 1747 that James and Jane Wardley, two tailors from Bolton, near Manchester, separated themselves from the churches and with a few followers began to worship in private homes, where, as Mary Plewit had urged John Wesley to do, they awaited God's further instructions. According to the Shaker eldress Anna White: "The members gave themselves up to be led by the spirit of God and continued to increase in numbers, although suffering much from persecution. This little band became the matrix for a new influx of Deity."[3]

Two of the most informative of the "apostate" histories provide more particulars, based on oral traditions within the American Shaker communities. William Haskett was told that although most of the French Prophets had died by 1747, their example had preserved "a spark of the same, or similar spirit" that "was active in bringing itself forward. Many persons, some of whom were Quakers, received this spirit, and . . . formed themselves into the society of which Ann Lee became a member." The Shakers told Thomas Brown that in its first years the little group had no creed or distinct worship, "as they professed to be only beginning to learn the new and living way of complete salvation." Therefore "they professed to be resigned, to be led and governed, from time to time, as the spirit of God might dictate." It was Jane Wardley, called "Mother" by the group, who was the leader. It was she who introduced the distinctive practice of hearing the members' confessions of sin, and it was she who led the meetings at which the believers, like the Quakers a century earlier, would "shake and make signs and speak out against sin."[4]

That is really all we know about the first decade of the Shakers' existence. If the Wardleys were indeed Quakers before contact with French Prophets and visions of the Millennium led them to separate, the Quaker archives do not confirm it; and such an omission would be surprising, given the meticulousness of Quaker record keeping. Moreover, neither of the earliest of the Shakers' own accounts of their origins makes any mention of the Quakers.[5]

It should be remembered that in the eighteenth century as in the seventeenth, "quakerism" was as much an attitude toward the inwardness of the divine and a style of protest against the conventions of church and society as it was a formal ecclesiastical structure. People on the fringes of eighteenth-century English religious culture might for a time grow beards, dress simply, and call themselves Quakers. Besides, even though the Friends no longer evangelized actively, they still welcomed inquiring "strangers" to their meetings.[6]

It is quite true that when it was articulated in America several decades later, there were aspects of Shaker doctrine that may have derived from the Quakers. The Shakers were pacifists, for example, and it was this above all that led to their persecution in their early years in the United States. They also rejected the sacraments, relying instead on the immanent and continuous leading of the Holy Spirit. Finally, they placed women in an equal or at least parallel status with men. We must remember, however, that all three traits were typical of the broad currents of prophetism (frequently female prophetism) and mystical piety in eighteenth-century popular religion. We know even less about the adherents of Jane Lead's millenarian Philadelphia Society after 1715 than we do of their old rivals the French Prophets, but their ideas may also have continued to permeate English popular religion.[7]

Quakerism was only one of a number of influences on the little band in Manchester that in the 1750s was quietly awaiting the Holy Spirit's final glorious manifestation in the world. When the Shakers ultimately made their way to the wilderness of upstate New York in 1774, they brought with them, as their spiritual baggage, the rich heritage of English popular religion. They were heirs not only to Quakers and French Prophets and Philadelphians but also to the religious radicalism of the English Revolution, which surfaced again in the eighteenth century not only in the Methodist Awakening but also in an obscure but widely diffused resurgence of mystical ideas.

Popular religion in eighteenth-century Lancashire was exceptionally dynamic, with a bewildering array of currents and crosscurrents. In the 1750s, Methodist and Moravian evangelists regularly traversed the area, and Manchester was a regular stop on Whitefield's tours of the north of England. Ann Lee later declared that she had been one of Whitefield's "hearers," but after his return from America he had taken "protection under the King; by which means he lost the power of God, and became formal, like other professors."[8]

The Shaker histories are fairly casual about dates, but Ann Lee's disenchantment with Whitefield probably came after the evangelist's return from America in 1755, before she encountered James and Jane Wardley's group. During the next several years, Whitefield made several tours of northern England and Scotland. Meanwhile in London, the continuing problem of mobs that harassed him, sometimes breaking the windows in his chapel in the West End, did indeed lead Whitefield to seek the king's "protection" by initiating proceedings against them at the King's Bench. When the Seven Years' War broke out in 1756, Whitefield published an address proclaiming his own unswerving loyalty to the crown and calling on English people of all denominations to give their patriotic support to the war effort. As his already poor health steadily worsened meanwhile, his preaching became progressively less fiery and dramatic. One can imagine the young Ann Lee, aroused earlier by the passionate sermons of Whitefield, turning now to the far more radical religious vision of the Wardleys.[9] Yet certainly Whitefield's conception of the new birth—the Holy Spirit's entering the soul of the believer who turned away from sin—was congenial to the young Ann Lee. Moreover, one can discern in matured Shaker doctrine a working out of Whitefield's evangelical proclamation of a life for the regenerate that "imparts new principles, a new understanding, a new will, and new affections . . . , nay, a renewed body."[10]

Bolton and Manchester were also early centers of Wesleyan Methodism. In both towns, Methodist societies were first organized in 1747, the same year that the Shakers began their meetings. Popular religion in Bolton was especially effervescent. Methodism thrived there, but its society was subjected to schism and dissension, as individuals and groups sought degrees of revelation and spiritual certainty beyond those sanctioned by Wesleyan caution.[11] Manchester's society was in similar trouble. In 1756, Charles Wesley spent nearly two weeks there trying to persuade the members to reject the notions being disseminated by preachers who called themselves Methodists. One who had gained a wide following was the notorious antinomian Roger Ball, whom John Wesley declared was "no more a Methodist than a Turk." Despite his efforts to counteract the influence of Ball and the others, Charles Wesley wrote to his friend William Grimshaw that of all the Methodist societies, Manchester's was "in the greatest danger, because the most unsettled and unadvisable. . . . Nothing but grace can keep our children, after our departure, from running into a thousand sects, a thousand errors."[12]

In the tense political climate of the 1750s, even Methodists like Grimshaw and Charles Wesley were persuaded that all the signs portended some kind of cosmic crisis. Grimshaw wrote Wesley in 1756: "Surely we now live in the very Eve of the World, in the very Dregs of Time. . . . Is not this the General Day approaching?"[13] This sense of millenarian expectancy became especially intense in 1763, when a recent Methodist convert named George Bell began to predict the imminent end of the world. Despite the fact that John Wesley quickly repudiated Bell's statements, news of them spread through England, disquieting the faithful in societies as far away as Staffordshire and Yorkshire.[14]

Two factors made combatting Bell's influence difficult for the Methodist leadership. In the first place, his spiritual pretensions had the full support of Thomas Maxfield, who two decades after his spectacular conversion in Bristol remained one of Wesley's most trusted lieutenants. In the second place, Bell and Maxfield had for several years been the core of a small circle of London Methodists who claimed to have reached sinless perfection. While Wesley had expressed privately his concern at their reliance on "dreams, visions, or impressions, as they thought from God," he did nothing further until it became painfully clear that Bell was at least half mad. Wesley explained afterward that he believed part of what Bell said "was from God . . . , part from an heated imagination; but as he did not scream, and there was nothing dangerously wrong, I did not yet see cause to hinder him."According to an anonymous memoir published later in the *Arminian Magazine*, the perfectionist doctrines promulgated by

Maxfield and Bell "spread through the three kingdoms" of England, Scotland, and Ireland after 1760.[15] Once again our sources offer no solid proof, but surely it is more than coincidental that an especially exalted form of perfectionism spread through English Methodist societies in precisely the years that the Shakers of Manchester were moving toward very similar notions.

In time Bell's influence evaporated, after his prediction of Jesus' return on a specific day proved false. Maxfield led a small schism among the London faithful, but elsewhere the Methodist leadership quickly restored their authority. Still, though the circulation of Bell and Maxfield's perfectionist doctrines in Lancashire can be only conjectured, we can say with certainty that mystical ideas were widely diffused in its popular religious culture. One useful source of information is a list of "spiritual persons" that a renegade Methodist named Ralph Mather compiled at the request of the Irish writer Henry Brooke, a devoted student of the mystical and occult. Mather's own spiritual odyssey had already taken him from Methodism through self-professed Quakerism into an obscure private spiritual exaltation. He would end his days as an ordained Swendenborgian minister. At the time he made his list Mather was living in Bolton, and included the names of many poor Lancashire artisans who, he said, possessed mystical understanding and a sensitivity to the signs and omens that marked the age as one of enormous spiritual urgency.[16]

Interest in the mystics was sufficiently great in Manchester to encourage a local newspaper to propose the publication in serial form of Jakob Boehme's *The Way of Christ Discovered*. If the response was sufficient, the publisher promised to publish the rest of Boehme's works.[17] Some of the people who joined the Methodists in Lancashire had belonged to little circles that met in many towns and villages to read and discuss the mystical writings of the seventeenth-century German shoemaker, whose works had first been translated into English in the middle of the seventeenth century. The pervasive influence of Boehme is apparent in Mather's list of "spiritual persons" as well. It is also evident in the sketches William Holland wrote on the origins of the Moravians' societies in the North, several of which had evolved from groups of artisans and laborers who initially met to read and discuss the writings of the German mystic. At the end of the eighteenth century, a Wesleyan preacher recalled that a generation earlier in Lancashire, many of the Methodist leaders had "imbibed the notions peculiar to the Mystics." In 1761 John Wesley had expelled six men from the Manchester society for attempting to promulgate Boehme's ideas.[18]

In England as in Germany, Boehme's influence had been slow in developing, perhaps because his language was so often obscure and the implications of his radical rejection of all the established churches were so profound. Like all mystics, Boehme claimed to have received divine illumination through the intervention of the Holy Spirit. He wrote: "The entire Bible lies in me if I have Christ's Spirit in me. What do I need of more books?"[19] To English seekers after religious enlightenment, heirs to a Puritan tradition of religious inwardness that was alive and well in Lancashire, for whom the cautious and bookish religion of the Church of England offered little comfort, the cosmic certainties of the shoemaker-theosopher held great attraction.

According to a Shaker oral tradition, in 1747 "many terrible Signs and wonders appeared, in the heavens, which were very strange and mysterious to the beholders, and which caused great fear and anxiety among the people of those days."[20] The tradition fits Ralph Mather's account of Lancashire popular religion. In another of his letters to Henry Brooke, he wrote that there had been a group in Bolton in about 1748 who predicted that spirits which had "ascended into the astral Regions" were soon going to "bring upon this very world strange devastations." Whether or not Mather was referring specifically to the Shakers, the passage illustrates the openness to spiritual manifestations, however peculiar, that was part of the spiritual baggage that the Shakers brought with them to America.[21]

In the same year that a divine revelation led the Wardleys to form their little society in Bolton, a Swedish engineer underwent a very similar experience. Having received his mystical enlightenment, Emmanuel Swedenborg devoted the rest of his life to promulgating doctrines of spiritual correspondence and human perfectibility, which nineteenth-century Shakers would find quite congenial.[22] Beginning in 1772. and for the next fifty years, the Reverend John Clowes preached Swedenborgian spiritual revelations from the pulpit of St. John's Church in Manchester. He also went to nearby cotton-milling towns to tell them the good news. Several years after Ann Lee and her followers had sailed for America, a group of pious weavers invited Clowes to Bolton, where there was soon formed one of the earliest Swedenborg societies.[23]

Unalike in so many ways, Swedenborgians and Shakers were nonetheless products of the same surge of popular religiosity. The Swedenborgians believed that the Millennium had arrived, spiritually, within themselves. So did the Shakers. Many of the Reverend Clowes's hearers in Manchester and surrounding towns were visited by angels; so were the Shakers.

By John Clowes's time, the explosion of industrialization had begun that would transform the Manchester region into a smoky wasteland of factories and slums, bringing great wealth to some and insecurity and poverty to many more. Most Shaker histories have assumed that this was the world into which Ann Lee was born, but in fact Manchester was quite different earlier in the eighteenth century. Its population totaled about ten thousand in 1739; Bolton had perhaps three thousand people. During the next decades the population grew dramatically, but thirty years later a geographical dictionary could nevertheless write of Lancashire that "the air of this county in general is more serene than that of any other maritime county in England; so that the inhabitants are strong and healthy, except near the fens and sea-shore." A local history published late in the nineteenth century stated that a century earlier Manchester had been "a little, active town, with old-fashioned industries that were literally handcrafts."[24] Whereas the cotton textiles that would one day clothe the world had been manufactured in Lancashire since the sixteenth century, in the 1750s most weavers and spinners were still peasants living in villages and working in their homes. Even in a comparatively large town like Manchester, the introduction of power-driven machinery and the factory system had barely started when the Shakers left for America, and a cotton "mill" was more like a traditional workshop than an industrial plant.

Why, you ask, is this relevant to our examination of the Shakers? Because a great deal has been made of the Shakers' having somehow constituted a protest against the crushing poverty and dehumanizing labor of early industrial capitalism. It is certainly true that nineteenth-century socialists as diverse as Robert Owen and Friedrich Engels saw in the Shaker system an alternative to the social and economic disruptions of their own times, but it does not necessarily follow that those were the Shakers' motivations. Their restructuring of the family and organization of communal economies derived instead from a radical Protestant reading of Scripture that they shared with others in the eighteenth-century religious awakenings. It was to be elaborated not in Lancashire but in the economic environment of the subsistence agriculture of the New England back country.

As the various testimonies of the English Shakers made clear, the group lived dispersed in several towns and villages of Lancashire and neighboring Cheshire, a region that even today is an odd blend of urban and rural. After the Wardleys had moved to Manchester to reside at the home of John Townley, a prosperous mason, the Shakers met there, but they continued to meet in other places as well, frequently at the large farm owned by an elderly former Methodist named John Hocknell. It was to be Hocknell's sale of his farm in 1774 that made possible the migration of Ann Lee and her English disciples to America. James Whittaker, one of the eight Shakers who crossed the Atlantic, recalled that many members had had to travel twenty miles through the countryside to attend meetings, generally going at night to avoid persecution.[25]

For a decade, the Wardleys and their followers had awaited the Lord in total obscurity. They would certainly have passed away unremembered had they not been joined in 1758 by the remarkable young woman named Ann Lees, or Lee. We must agree with the Shakers' own histories that it was young Ann who transformed the society.

In his indispensable history, *The People Called Shakers*, Edward Deming Andrews recorded the few facts about Ann Lee and the original Shakers that exist outside the Shakers' own texts. Ann's private baptism is entered in 1742 in the registry of the Manchester cathedral when (given her traditional birthdate of 29 February 1736) she was eight years old. According to the Shakers, she had worked in a cotton mill and as a cutter of velvet before her marriage in 1762, four years after she had joined the Wardleys' group. The banns of marriage are also recorded in the register of the Manchester cathedral. The fact is a bit curious, since it suggests that her adherence to the Wardleys' group was not yet complete. Shakers did marry at that time, but the occasion was generally solemnized within the group by the Wardleys themselves, not in the churches of the world. According to William Haskett's informants, however, some Shakers did defer to public and family pressure and marry in church.[26]

Ann Lee's husband, Abraham Standerin, was a blacksmith, like her father, John Lees. Neither the bride nor the groom was able to sign the register. Until the Shakers' departure for America sixteen years later, the couple lived with her parents. According to Shaker tradition, they had four children who died in infancy, and Andrews found the record of the death of one of them.[27]

For practically any other information about the Shakers' years in England, we must depend on the recollections of the English Shakers themselves, set down by American converts fifty years after the fact. In its first decades, the Shaker community had almost always refused to circumscribe the Holy Spirit's guidance by committing any of their history or doctrine to print. After they reversed the original policy in 1808, they tried to make spiritual sense out of the developments that had transformed them since Ann Lee's lifetime.

The Shakers themselves recognized that they had changed enormously. The charismatic gifts of the Holy Spirit were still sought, but now they descended through the mediation and authority of a hierarchy of elders and eldresses. The Shakers were settled across New England in a network of eleven thriving communities, with new ones forming on the frontier in Ohio and Kentucky. It was a development never envisaged by Ann Lee and her English disciples. Most importantly, the person of Ann Lee had acquired aspects of godhead which she herself had never claimed.

As the Shakers developed a mystical theology in which Ann Lee became Christ's female "second appearing," the portrait of the historical person took on a varnish of stereotypical gentleness. She had indeed been persecuted in England and America, but now these trials were molded into analogues to the sufferings and martyrdom of Jesus Christ.

Many of the stories told about her years in England are clearly legendary. For example, two of the surviving English followers insisted that at one time the authorities in Manchester had imprisoned and tried to starve her, but James Whittaker managed to sneak into the prison and feed her milk and wine through the stem of a clay pipe inserted in the keyhole. On another occasion, Ann Lee confounded several Church of England clergymen who intended to condemn her for blasphemy. While possessed by the Holy Spirit, she spoke to them in seventy-two different languages. She and several followers were then supposedly taken into a valley by a mob which tried to stone them, but the stones miraculously missed their targets. Both of these stories are presented in detail and more than once in the so-called "Elders' Secret Book" of 1816, the basis for all the later accounts.[28] They are pious emulations of Gospel stories of Jesus, either completely untrue or considerably elaborated. The irony is that the historical Ann Lee is in her way quite as remarkable as the Ann Lee of Shaker legend, and considerably more human.

The only other traces that the Shakers have left in the archives of Lancashire consist of records of prosecutions. On 14 July 1772, for example, five of them were arrested for a "breach of the Sabbath," and Ann Lee and her father were imprisoned for a month. Twice that autumn, the Manchester authorities intervened, once to break up a mob that had gathered in front of John Townley's house and once "to apprehend the gang" for disturbing the peace by their noisy worship at the Lees' home in Toad Lane. The final recorded prosecution came a year later, in July of 1773. The Manchester *Mercury* reported that "John Townley, John Jackson, Betty Lees, and Ann Lees (*Shakers*)" had been fined for going to Christ Church during morning prayer and disrupting the service.[29]

This last episode recalls similar acts by French Prophets earlier in the century, but the records of the other prosecutions imply that the nature of Shaker worship was quite unlike that of the French Prophets. The Prophets' meetings were indeed dramatic, with their "agitations" and pronouncements of the possessed and the occasional dramatic vignette in which they enacted, by spiritual command, the cosmic struggle of apocalyptic destruction that they were called to announce. Shaker worship was very different, as we know from a priceless account that somehow found its way into the (Williamsburg) *Virginia Gazette*. Here is their correspondent's description of the way in which the Holy Spirit visited the Shakers of Manchester. They would sit and quietly converse about religious matters "until the moving of the spirit comes upon them, which is first perceived by their beginning leisurely to scratch upon their thigh or other parts of their bodies." As the possession of the Spirit commenced, they would begin "*trembling, shaking, and screeching* in the most dreadful manner," while at the same time moving their heads rapidly from side to side. Their possessions would climax with "singing and dancing to the pious tunes of Nancy Dawson, Bobbin Joan, Hie thee Jemmy home again, &c." Often, their meetings lasted all night, disturbing "the whole neighbourhood for some considerable distance" until the participants were exhausted, "from which uncommon mode of religious worship they have obtained the denomination of Shakers."[30]

We know from several travellers' accounts of visits to Shaker assemblies in their first years in America that these forms of ecstatic worship (except the scratching) persisted. The songs were wordless elaborations on popular songs, and several witnesses state that Ann Lee herself had a special gift for singing. One testimony said that "she would often communicate to a whole assembly by singing, not in a loud voice, and gently motioning her hands or by speaking a few words." According to Valentine Rathbun, whose 1780 pamphlet contains the earliest detailed description of their worship in America, one Shaker would start to sing "some odd tune, without words or rule." The others would begin singing one by one: "Some singing without words, and some with an unknown tongue or mutter, and some with a mixture of English." Finally, Ann Lee would join in and "strike such notes as make a concord, and so form the charm."

The first Shaker song collection contains fifty wordless songs attributed to the English Shakers. That two of them were supposed to have been "learned of the Angels by James and Jane Wardley" may indicate that the practice had begun quite early. The dancing could be anything the Spirit ordained, including remarkable prodigies of leaping or whirling, like the Sufi mystics of North Africa. Ann Lee herself does not seem to have participated much in these exercises. According to all the early American accounts of their worship, each Shaker acted individually, as the Spirit led her or him. Rathbun wrote:

One will stand with his arms extended, acting over odd postures, which they call signs; another will be dancing, and sometimes hopping on one leg about the floor; another will fall to turning around . . . ; another will be talking with somebody; and some sitting by smoaking their pipes; some groaning most dismally; some trembling extremely; . . . others swinging their arms, with all vigour, as though they were turning a wheel, &c.

In his book on *The Shaker Spiritual,* Daniel Patterson suggests that these wordless songs may be "the only surviving musical record of the tradition of Pentecostal singing among early English Dissenting sects," related also to the "mouth music" of British folk song tradition in which the voice imitates a pipe or fiddle.[31] The French Prophets had hymns divinely communicated to them. So did the German Inspired and the Philadelphians, but the first Shaker music was quite different, with a haunting beauty remarked on by several early visitors to the first American assemblies. The early Quakers had had a similar musical technique in which one or several would hum, raising the tone higher and higher and creating in their hearers "a peculiar *Emotion,* not unpleasant to them."[32]

The singing, combined with the ecstatic postures and the "screeching," must have made Shaker worship in the early decades an eerie combination of the sublime and the bizarre. As sacred theater, it differed from anything else that we have encountered not only in the profusion of its actions and sounds but also in that it was a self-contained performance that required neither preaching nor prophetic pronouncements for its completion. It was enormously moving to many of the New Englanders who encountered the English Shakers in the 1780s. One early convert wrote that Ann Lee could "make the most stubborn and stout-hearted quiver and tremble" with her re-proofs of sin and sinner, but then by "singing a melodious and heavenly song" she could "instantly fill the assembly with inexpressible joy and rejoicing." Another wrote: "My tongue cannot express the heavenly comfort I felt in their singing."[33]

According to William Haskett, the singular form of worship described by the *Virginia Gazette* in 1769 had been initiated relatively recently, and it had been Ann Lee who had introduced the "new Gifts" of "singing, dancing, shaking, shouting, leaping, speaking in an unknown tongue, and prophesying." Her ascendancy in the society culminated about a year later when she supplanted the aged Wardleys as the Shakers' leader. Significantly, she later told one of her American disciples that she "had not been in the Church more then six months, before it was made known to me, by the revelation of God, that he would support me, through all my trials, and establish me an Elder in the Church."[34]

It seems to have been at about the time of her marriage in 1762 that Ann Lee began to undergo the sort of prolonged spiritual crisis that Methodist converts so assiduously described in the early volumes of Wesley's *Arminian Magazine.* During this period of spiritual suffering, the young convert received occasional "visions and revelations of God," climaxing in about 1770 with the one in which she learned that carnal sex was the original sin of Adam and Eve and celibacy the key to sinless perfection and salvation. She told one of her New England converts that she had received a vision in which Jesus Christ revealed to her "the depth of man's loss, what it was, and the way of redemption." From that day, she had "taken up a full cross against the doleful works of the flesh."

She then gathered the group at the Townleys' house and "opened her revelations, with the most astonishing power of God." According to Haskett, the Wardleys had already intimated to several of the Shakers that Ann Lee's spiritual gifts were superior to their own. They now "resigned their office in her favour: and, by calling her Mother, placed her at the head of affairs." According to the Shaker *Testimonies*, when she announced her revelation concerning the sin of sexuality, her announcement "had such sensible effect, in giving them power over all sin, and filling them with visions, revelations and gifts of God, that she was received and acknowledged as the first spiritual Mother in Christ."[35]

Just as the Shakers in their first decades reflected the popular religious culture of Lancashire in their ideas concerning the nature of the church, the immanence of the Spirit, and the possibility of a mystical redefinition of the biblical notion of the Millennium, so Ann Lee's ascendancy within the group confirmed those same currents and elevated them to a higher pitch of intensity. In no way did she repudiate the Wardley's teachings, but she went beyond them. They had encouraged celibacy and the confessing of sins to "Mother Jane." Mother Ann required both.

When in the late eighteenth and early nineteenth centuries the Shakers sent evangelists and missionaries first to the villages and towns of upland New England and then to the new settlements of the Ohio and Kentucky territories, they emphasized three facets of Shakerism as being absolutely central. One was the continuing manifestation of God's presence among them in "gifts" that could include miracle working, ecstatic song and dance, and possession by the Holy Spirit. The second was the compulsory confession of sins to an elder, an act which assured salvation. The third was mandatory, permanent celibacy. Not only can all three be traced with confidence to Ann Lee herself, but all three derive more broadly from the currents of eighteenth-century European popular religion.

That Shaker sacred theater constituted part of a deep and powerful current in eighteenth-century popular Christianity is surely evident by now. According to one's point of view, the Camisard example had either invigorated or subverted the state churches of Protestant Europe as they transmitted their prophetic messages in an environment of action and ritual that supplanted the cautious rigorism of the established churches and demonstrated, to those who saw and believed, that God was indeed moving, now, in them. Similarly, among the Jansenist Convulsionaries of France and the Hasidic Jews of eastern Europe, God in the eighteenth century manifested his presence in direct and visible ways.

Hostile witnesses had described the disorder of early Methodist "enthusiasm" in terms that suggest a kinship of antistructure with the Shakers. For example, the Moravian James Hutton described an early meeting as proceeding "without the least order, shouting Hurra, weeping for their sins, punching each other in the ribs, laughing, flinging stones and dirt, dealing boxes on the ear, making filthtraps for the feet, now oppressed to death, now crying Hallelujah for joy; in short a mixture of the extremes of Good and Evil."[36]

Among all of the other popular movements that we have examined, such outpourings of emotion, such diverse and bewildering varieties of reception of the Holy Spirit, were of sporadic and comparatively brief duration. Even for the Camisard prophets of the Cévennes and their heirs, the French and English prophets, sacred theater occurred within a framework that derived from the liturgical practices and theological beliefs of the religious culture. It was tacitly controlled by shared preconceptions of what might be considered rationally comprehensible behavior. In contrast, among the Shakers during the period of Ann Lee's ascendancy, traditional structures and rules of behavior were often circumvented, because for the Shakers the experience of ecstatic worship was its own justification. In the American, Scottish, and English awakenings of the 1740s, episodes of spirit possession were interpreted by advocates as the working out of the larger drama of repentance and salvation. For the Camisards and their German and English descendants, the physical manifestations of possession set the seal of divine approval on the oral expression of quite conventional messages of warning or hope.

Shaker worship, on the other hand, was unrelated to the conversion process, and only rarely was it the occasion for the communication of divine instructions in the form of ordinary oral discourse. It was what it was. No group took so literally Paul's celebration of possession by the spirit in his first letter to the Corinthians: "My speech and my message were not in plausible words of wisdom, but in demonstration of the Spirit and of power. . . . No one comprehends the thoughts of God except in the Spirit of God."

Similarly, confession had been a feature of the assemblies of the Camisard prophets and their heirs. In the form of a written or oral narration of the individual's progress from sin to salvation, confession had been built into the English Puritan tradition since the sixteenth century. Quakers, Methodists, and American New Lights alike could recount their sins in stupefying and stereotyped detail. Methodist societies and especially Moravian bands used confession to leaders as a form of moral surveillance.

The Shaker practice of confession is thus part of a broader stream of popular religious practice, but once again with a significant difference. Ann Lee taught that she and those empowered by her could forgive sins. After her years of spiritual agony, having been brought to the realization that sexual intercourse was the original sin, the whole Christian drama of sin and divine redemption had been transcended. Ann Lee and those who attained her state of spiritual perfection were beyond sin, even as they suffered vicariously for the sins of others. Those who accepted the "cross" of celibacy had made the first step toward regaining their Edenic purity, and they could preserve their saved state through submission to the discipline of confession.

Celibacy had had its attractions for many of the German separatists who singly or in groups attempted to achieve the perfect Christian life. Harassed, dispersed, sometimes persecuted, they persisted in their search for the kind of religious transcendence and apprehension of the divine that had been experienced by seventeenth-century mystics like Jakob Boehme and Jane Lead. Many of them considered the main obstacle to their continued spiritual growth to be their human sexuality.[37]

The Reformation's repudiation of celibacy as a preferred type of Christian life had been one facet of the rejection of the Roman Catholic tradition, but in the eighteenth century, in both Germany and England, celibacy again attained status as a suitable life's calling for Protestants. Both Wesley and Whitefield married, but in neither case was the relationship satisfactory by any conventional standard. Wesley was the more candid on his ambivalence over human sexuality. On several occasions, he confronted the question directly. He refused to reject marriage, but he contended (in an essay written in 1765) that it was "much easier . . . wholly to conquer our natural desires, than to gratify them exactly so far as Christian temperance allows! . . . Blessed are 'they who have made themselves eunuchs for the kingdom of heaven's sake,' who abstain from things lawful in themselves in order to be more devoted to God."[38]

A queasiness about sexuality runs through many of the Methodist and Moravian testimonies and spiritual biographies in the eighteenth century, although few were as explicit as an erratic mystic, Mrs. Mary Pratt, who wrote Henry Brooke that "the body, is bestial, sensual, devilish . . . that must be cast out." She was now "delivered from it, and experience[d] the joys of the New Heaven, and the new earth."[39]

All the popular religious movements of eighteenth-century Europe and America shared a conviction that the "awakenings" of their era presaged a coming age of spiritual perfection. They all were familiar with the passage in the twentieth chapter of Luke: "And Jesus said to them, 'the sons of this age marry and are given in marriage, but those who are accounted worthy to attain to that age and to the resurrection from the dead neither marry nor are given in marriage, for they cannot die any more, because they are equal to angels and are sons of God, being sons of the resurrection.'" No one knew this text better than the Shakers. A visitor to their wilderness settlement in upstate New York wrote that they called their house "the *Gate of Heaven* and they call themselves *the Sons of God Schoharie*."[40]

There is an entire section of the *Testimonies* that recounts Ann Lee's pronouncements on sexuality. She told one group: "I see, in vision, a large black cloud rising as black as a thunder cloud, and it is occasioned by the men sleeping with their wives." Another time, she declared that "the marriage of the flesh is a convenant with death, and an agreement with hell." She was also obsessed with the sin of bestiality. She said that she was "constrained to roar out of Zion against the sins of man with beasts. . . . If you commit sin with beasts your spirits will be transformed into the shape of beasts, in the spirit world."[41]

There is no question that Ann Lee had the charismatic power to persuade others to accept her own revelations of the supernatural, even her proclamation of absolute celibacy, but she did not act like the possessed prophets earlier in the century. She did not preach, nor did she deliver God's warnings in her own voice. She described her visions, she sang and gestured with a beauty and power that compelled belief, and, most importantly, she showed considerable psychological astuteness in maintaining her position of spiritual leadership. Like the shamans in many cultures, she often brought individuals messages from their own dead relatives, messages always intended to affirm the exclusive truth of Shakerism as revealed through her. When some people in Enfield, Connecticut, asked her when she had been converted, she replied, "Converted! . . . I converse with God face to face, every day."[42]

Ann Lee presented her visions and divine messages in a manner that was dramatic yet at the same time had an earthy literalness. Abijah Wooster, one of the first converts in Harvard, Massachusetts, recalled that he had gone through a period of spiritual doubt, and at one meeting he was "tossing-tumbling-rolling-throwing [himself] against the wall." Ann Lee came along and said, "'Why Abijah, there is some of the worst looking spirits on your shoulders I ever saw in my life.'" She raised him up, made passes over him with her hands, and he was "relieved at once" and never doubted again.[43]

Elizabeth Wood described a meeting at Enfield, Connecticut, at which she received "a gift to turn." As she whirled, she heard Ann Lee say to her brother, William Lee, "see the bright angels turning her now." She described Ann Lee's charismatic power especially charmingly when she recalled another meeting: "[Ann Lee] came in & raised her hands & shouted & the sisters gathered round her & hug[g]ed & kissed her. I got down to her feet & kissed them for I love her so well that it seemed like a privilege to touch her garments."[44]

Ann Lee also had "a swift gift against sin," as many early converts expressed it. Her dealings with the recalcitrant could be intensely personal and brutally frank. A revealing example can be seen in the story, repeated in all the Shaker histories, of the conversion of her younger brother, William. He was a blacksmith like his father and brother-in-law, a big, outgoing man whose ebullience and innocence are evident in the various memories of him recorded by early Shakers. Like his sister and father and some other members of the Lee clan, he had joined the society of James and Jane Wardley. When he told them "his trials and feeings . . . they encouraged and built him up so that he felt his mind released. But then he would go to his sister, who instead "would often spoil his comfort . . . and again plunge him deeper into tribulation than before." At last he submitted to her authority by confessing his sins to her and thus "gained releasement for himself through obedience to her counsel." Abijah Wooster said that on one occasion, after William Lee had been separated from his sister for a time, he cried out, "I want to go to my Mother; I am Sick to see my Mother; I had no God till I had a Mother."[45]

Ann Lee's domination of the Wardley's society after 1770 transformed the group by introducing a new level of spiritual experience through the night-long ceremonies of ecstatic worship and a new assurance of salvation through the dual discipline of celibacy and confession as divinely revealed to Ann Lee. Most of the Shakers who accompanied her to America, including William Lee, John Hocknell, and young James Whittaker, experienced with particular intensity the new spiritual "gifts" which Ann Lee had initiated. William Lee readily fell into ecstasies of dancing or weeping; John Hocknell (who was over seventy years old) had visions, spoke in tongues, and sometimes had the power of healing when he was possessed by the Holy Spirit. James Whittaker claimed to be absolutely free of sexuality. As he expressed it, he had "no more lust than an infant; . . . no more than a child unborn."[46]

The price of Ann Lee's innovations, however, was dissension and schism within the society. Not even her charismatic gifts could persuade some members, who perhaps preferred the milder domination of the Wardleys, to accept the double discipline of celibacy and confession. The noisy and protracted meetings for ecstatic worship and the practice of public testimony to the new faith on the streets and in the churches of Manchester brought notoriety, angry mobs, and prosecutions to a group that had managed to avoid all three for the first twenty years of its existence. By 1773 over half of the approximately sixty members had seceded. Among those who left were the society's Manchester patrons, the Townleys, with whom the Wardleys lived.[47]

It was then that a new revelation came: Go to America. One night, James Whittaker was resting by the side of the road while on his way to a meeting in Cheshire. He then had a vision of America in the form of a large tree on which "every leaf . . . shone with such brightness, as made it appear like a burning torch, representing the Church of Christ." Revelations through Ann Lee confirmed the vision, and then those divinely chosen to accompany her and Whittaker received special gifts: "They were greatly wrought upon by the power of God, and spake with new tongues and prophesied."[48]

Or so the Shaker histories claim. Yet one of the nine who sailed for America was Ann Lee's husband, whose commitment to the group was doubtful. Two others left the Shakers in order to get married, and two more seceded after Ann Lee's death. It is highly probable that some members of the Manchester group were too poor to be able to go, despite John Hocknell's generosity. Others, including James Whittaker's family, found their worldly ties in England too strong.[49]

The divine command to go to America offered Ann Lee and her most devoted followers an alternative to the apparently hopeless task of extending their influence in Lancashire and Cheshire. Persecution did not drive them to America, but conceivably the indifference of other Englishmen to their odd blend of popular mysticism, millenarianism, and ecstatic practice did.

As we shall see in the next chapter, the Shakers had no clear idea what God intended for them in the New World. Nonetheless, the American colonies offered a range of possibilities and prospects not open to them in Europe. In 1774, the resistance in the New England colonies to the crown was a subject of intense interest in the mother country, and there was sizable popular support for the colonists' cause among the popular classes. Public interest may have been especially strong in Manchester, which exported three-fourths of its production to the American colonies.[50]

John Hocknell secured passage for the nine on a ship bound from Liverpool to New York. They sailed on 10 May 1774.

{7}

The Woman in
the Wilderness

A s is so often the case with Shaker history, the various testimonies collected in the nineteenth century are full of fascinating anecdotes and details, but they are silent on many larger questions. We are told that the eight Shakers (and Abraham Standerin) disembarked at New York harbor on Sunday, 6 August 1774, after a three months' voyage full of danger and marked by divine intervention. It is not at all clear, however, whether the group had any idea what they would do in America. It would have been quite consistent with the character of their faith if they simply assumed that God would instruct them at the proper time.

In any case, once they reached New York they seem to have made two decisions. Ann Lee and her husband found employment with a family residing on what is today Pearl Street in lower Manhattan, she as a domestic and her husband as a journeyman in the family's blacksmith shop. Meanwhile, the others began making inquiries as to where land could be acquired cheaply. Some Quakers in New York City told them that one could lease land on very reasonable terms from the Van Renssalaer family, whose enormous manor of Renssalaerwyck surrounded the bustling little river town of Albany, some 150 miles up the Hudson River from New York.

John Hocknell, possibly accompanied by James Whittaker and William Lee, therefore went to the manor and arranged for the lease of 200 acres of swamp and forest in the wilderness about eight miles north of Albany, at a place called Niskeyuna by the Indians and Watervliet by the Dutch settlers. He also made arrangements, for himself and the Shakers' other wealthy patron, John Partington, to take over the leases of two adjoining farms which had already been cleared and settled by former tenants. Hocknell then recrossed the

Atlantic to collect the rest of his family and Partington and his wife and bring them with him to America. The rest of the group (according to the *Testimonies* of 1888) "scattered, seeking their livelihood . . . wherever they could find employment." Lee, Whittaker, and James Shepherd found work in Albany, in their old trades of blacksmith, weaver, and shoemaker respectively.

Ann Lee's husband is said to have deserted her, after she had nursed him through a dangerous illness. Having lost her position as a domestic servant, she went through a period of serious economic hardship, yet she managed occasionally to visit her followers in Albany, a trip that would have taken from three to five days' travel each way.[1]

On 25 December 1775, the Hocknells and Partingtons disembarked at Philadelphia and then rejoined Ann Lee in New York. In the spring, they all traveled to their lands above Albany. Few of the Shakers had ever farmed before, but they managed to clear and plant fields and build a log house on their wilderness acres. Hocknell continued to support the group financially, and Shepherd and William Lee continued to work in Albany and contributed their earnings.

John Hocknell later declared that he had been divinely led to the place the Shakers would come to call Wisdom's Valley. As he had left Albany, his hand had been forcibly raised and pointed in that direction, dropping to his side when he reached the predestined spot.[2] However that may be, the chosen land had the advantage of being accessible to travel routes (such as they were) both from the south and from New England. The rent was very reasonable (eight bushels of wheat for each hundred acres), and Albany was nearby. The Shakers' timing, however, was unfortunate. As Ann Lee and her companions were establishing themselves at Niskeyuna, George Washington was preparing to confront the British at New York. The recent failure of General Benedict Arnold's expedition had opened the way for another British army to move down from Canada via Lake Champlain. To the west of Albany, British agents were at work mobilizing the Indians for raids on the frontier settlements along the Mohawk River. For the next seven years, the upper Hudson valley would be a cockpit in the struggles of the American Revolution.[3]

The Shakers managed meanwhile to eke out a living on their farms. They assembled regularly for services of ecstatic worship at their log house. They built a large frame building to accommodate the throngs of inquirers they expected at any time, but it burned down. On one occasion, even Ann Lee was brought close to despair, but then she "received a great gift of rejoicing, attended with much trembling and shaking, and great prophesies of God."[4] The Shakers were comforted as well by the biblical parallels to their experience. Here they were, twelve of them, living in the wilderness, awaiting the world's destined conversion to their faith, the only religion for the time of the Millennium. It had all been foreshadowed in the Revelation of Saint John the Divine: "And a great portent appeared in heaven, a woman clothed with the sun, with the moon under her feet, and on her head a crown of twelve stars; . . . and the woman fled into the wilderness, where she has a place prepared by God, in which to be nourished for one thousand two hundred and sixty days."[5]

When that prophetic period had elapsed, the Shakers "opened their testimony" to the world, for God did indeed seem to send them throngs of converts in 1780, as we shall see. In the meantime, the Shakers did not go entirely unnoticed. They converted at least one of their Dutch neighbors, and they began the practice of allowing visitors to watch their services of worship. A military surgeon named James Thacher, stationed down the river at West Point, noted in his journal that he had learned of the existence of a group called "Shaking Quakers, or dancing quakers," who were led by "a female by the name of Ann Lee, niece of General Lee, of our army," who "has had the address to seduce several individuals of our country to her party." Thacher's description of their worship service, given to him by "eyewitnesses," suggests that it had changed little since crossing the Atlantic:

They spend whole nights in their revels. . . . Both sexes, nearly divested of clothing, fall to dancing in extravagant postures, and frequently whirl themselves round on one leg with inconceivable rapidity, till they fall apparently lifeless on the floor. A spectator asserts that the fantastic contortions of body in which their pretended religious exercises consist, bear the semblance of supernatural impulse.[6]

A distorted version of these visitors' accounts even reached the pages of a Boston newspaper. The occasion was an attack on the efforts of the prominent Baptist minister, Isaac Backus, to persuade the revolutionary government of Massachusetts to enact full religious toleration. The writer contended that sometimes public standards of decency might require the civil government to intervene in religious matters. He said that he had been assured "for fact" of the existence of "a sect whose conscience leads them to gross immoralities, and abominable prophaness [sic]. Every sabbath they have their meeting, when their mode of worship consists in dancing stark naked; one of them presiding whom they call their God."[7]

It must have seemed highly unlikely to anyone who read the article that any religion whose practices were so bizarre could hope to win converts among sensible and devout New England farmers. Yet during the next five years several thousand would be converted, at least temporarily, to the "abominable" sect of the Shakers.

Since the conclusion of the French and Indian War in 1763, great areas of empty land in western and northern New England had been occupied by settlers drawn by the prospect of new beginnings on better land than existed in the crowded settled sections of the colonies of Connecticut and Massachusetts. During the next thirty years, there was a continuous migration out of coastal New England toward the west and north. People from eastern Massachusetts crossed the barrier of the Berkshire Mountains and began settling the valleys to the west of them. Meanwhile, settlers from Connecticut and Rhode Island, many of them Baptists, moved into the same area from the south. In 1761, there had been three towns and 700 families in Berkshire County, Massachusetts. By 1790, there were 30,000 people and twenty-five incorporated towns.[8]

Immediately to the west, there lay a strip of land some thirty miles wide between the western border of Connecticut and Massachusetts and the Hudson River. Most of it belonged at least nominally to some of the great New York landowners, although some Indian tribes and the colony of Massachusetts disputed their claims. Much of it was virtually empty. New Englanders, contentious and independent people quite unlike the docile Dutch and Palatine German peasants among whom the Shakers had settled, began to move into that area as well. The presence of the New England squatters had led to occasional violence, but by the 1770s an accommodation had been reached. As people from Connecticut and Massachusetts continued to move in, the region east of the Hudson became a virtual extension of New England.[9]

It was in these new settlements in western Massachusetts and eastern New York that a remarkable religious revival broke out in

1779. Peter Werden, pastor of a Baptist congregation which had migrated from southeastern Massachusetts to Berkshire County, wrote to Isaac Backus that it was "a most remarkable time of the work of God in New Providence, Lanesborough, Hancock [Massachusetts], New Lebanon, Little Hoosac [New York], and some other places." Many people were asking to be baptized, while others "have declared what God has done for them. . . . O brethren help us to praise the God of Love."[10]

This "work of God" in the Berkshires was the westernmost surge of a wave of spiritual concern, sometimes called the New Light Stir, that swept through much of the New England back country during the next several years. Since the Great Awakening had petered out, several generations of New Light clergy, especially among the Separates and Baptists, had prayed for the descent of the Holy Spirit that would at last bring the whole world to Christ. There had been revivals, but none since the 1740s had been so geographically extensive or so dramatic in their spiritual and emotional manifestations.[11]

In the new settlement of New Lebanon, just across the New York line from Pittsfield, Massachusetts, the effects of the revival were especially dramatic. Presbyterians had organized a church there seven years earlier and had brought as their pastor a young Yale graduate named Samuel Johnson. After several years in New Lebanon, Johnson had obtained his dismissal and moved across the line to West Stockbridge, Massachusetts. Johnson later explained that he had left because of "the disorganized state of the society . . . occasioned by the war," but he stayed in touch with his former congregation, which continued to function without a pastor. In the fall of 1779, nightly meetings for prayer began to be held in private houses. The Baptists also had organized in New Lebanon, and they too began to participate, often meeting at George Darrow's barn.[12] The meetings could reach high emotional levels. Amos Stoner later recalled that the revival "was attended with such mighty power of God, that I have seen rugged, stout-hearted young men, who came merely as spectators, fall like men wounded in battle, and screaming so that they might be heard at a great distance."[13]

As the revival's intensity increased, some participants reached the conviction that the Millennium was at hand. And in the age of the Millennium, they believed, Christians would transcend their sinful natures and cast off the passions and impurities that kept people from

attaining the true faith of the Gospel. They therefore separated themselves from their churches and awaited further infusions of spiritual
gifts. According to one participant who later became a Shaker, they
"renounced all connexion with other denominations, together with
all creeds and ceremonies." They questioned the propriety of marriage, and most of them believed that in these last days a baptism of
the Spirit would supplant baptism in water. They had, in other words,
reached views very similar to those of the Wardleys' group in its early
years in Manchester.[14]

While a number of individuals shared the leadership of the New
Lebanon revival, one man seems to have emerged as best able to explain the spiritual phenomena the group was experiencing and to
place them in the context of the millenarian tradition. He was Joseph
Meacham, a Baptist elder originally from Enfield, Connecticut.

There had been Meachams in Enfield since the seventeenth century, where they had long been part of the town's elite. It may be
recalled that Enfield, together with other towns in the Connecticut
Valley, had been swept into the wave of revivals in 1736, even before
it attained fame as the site of Jonathan Edwards's great sermon in 1741.
In the aftermath of the Great Awakening, a Strict Congregational or
Separate church had split from the Standing Order. Soon, the anti-
pedobaptist controversy had led to the formation of a Baptist congregation as well. For some twenty-five years, Joseph's father, Joseph
Meacham, Sr., had been the elder of the Baptist congregation.[15]

At some time in the late 1760s, the younger Joseph Meacham
joined the migration from Connecticut and moved with his family
into eastern New York. By 1776, he was preaching in the new settlement of New Lebanon, where he helped to organize the congregation
of Baptists. According to Meacham's only biographer, the Shaker
elder Calvin Green, Meacham shared the conviction of some others
in the area that the chaos and violence of revolutionary warfare was
an offense to true religion. They sought "something better," and
Meacham was "verry instrumental in increasing that fervency of spirit
which had begun mostly among the people." At about that time, a
revival broke out among the Separates back in Enfield, and some of
them reached the conviction that "the second appearing of Christ &
the setting up of his kingdom was at hand." Meacham visited them
and was convinced that they were indeed "attended by divine power."
He therefore "owned the work to be of God, & blessed them, to their

great edification, and to the great confusion of their enemies." After Meacham had given his opinion, a woman who was believed to have the gift of prophecy arose and "being evidently under the operation of Divine Power" predicted great things for Meacham. Playing on the Old Testament resonances of his name, she declared that "Joseph's vine shall outstretch all other vines; & his bough shall outreach all other boughs."[16]

Meacham's experience of the Enfield revival definitely influenced his perception of the events in New Lebanon in 1779. From the few scattered fragments of Meacham's own writings that have survived, it is clear that he felt himself to have been divinely called to create a spiritual community analogous to the "church-state" of the New England Puritan tradition, but a church-state in which the experience of divine presence was permanently embodied in an ordered society of the chosen people of God.

The situation of prominent Baptists like Meacham when confronted with convulsions, visions, or entranced prophecy in the revivals of the New Light Stir—and later with the ecstatic worship of the Shakers—resembled that of John Wesley, faced with the outbreaks of possession in Bristol in 1741, or of Jonathan Edwards when he attempted in *The Distinguishing Marks of a Work of the Spirit of God* to fit the revivals of the Connecticut Valley into the divine scheme. Each of them contended that the Christian must remember the scriptural admonition in the first letter of John neither to accept nor reject the phenomena of divine possession but instead to "test the spirits to see whether they are of God."

Since the 1740s, the New Lights had preserved the conviction that God continued to manifest himself directly in the world. One reason for the fragility of the Separate movement was its reliance on the Holy Spirit's immediate presence in "gifts of the spirit." While these gifts had in fact tended more often than not to produce dissension and schism within congregations, the belief persisted that the spirit's promptings must not be resisted, however they manifested themselves, for they might announce that God was about to bring the whole world to Christ.[17]

It was probably Meacham, influenced by what he had seen at Enfield, who led the most zealous of the participants to draw apart into a body that would be the perfected church of Christ at the Millennium. By the end of 1779, however, although the revivals of the

New Light Stir continued in other communities, in New Lebanon the extraordinary spiritual manifestations had faded away. According to Calvin Green, Meacham believed that the "work" of universal regeneration had begun, but he did not know how to bring the faithful of his little community "into the kingdom."[18]

In none of the other Berkshire settlements did the revival produce a new separation, but sometimes the phenomena that accompanied the pangs of the new birth in these revivals could be as dramatic as they were at New Lebanon. Elizabeth Johnson, the wife of the former New Lebanon minister, attended many of the meetings there and also invited some of "the awakened" to come to West Stockbridge. At one meeting, she "received a good measure of the power of God" so that "for some time, days and nights seemed all alike." Her husband also received his baptism of the spirit. He wrote many years later that at a meeting in Hancock, Massachusetts, God had "struck a death blow" to his "natural powers." It was then made manifest to him "by the visions of God and the spirit of prophecy, that the coming of Christ and his Kingdom were at hand, even at the door."[19]

The American Revolution was a factor in the special intensity with which some in the Berkshire region experienced the revival of 1779 and interpreted it in millenarian terms. Calvin Green implied that it shaped Joseph Meacham's quest for a purified church. Samuel Johnson said that at the outbreak of the war he had been "inspired with an ardent zeal in the cause of liberty," but a "night vision" or spiritual dream had convinced him that "people could not be followers of Christ and live in wars and fightings." At Hancock, where Johnson first experienced the possession of the Holy Spirit, the Baptists had split in 1777 when part of the congregation defected from the local militia and rallied to Burgoyne's army, which was passing through on its way to defeat at Bennington. At Pittsfield, one of the leading Baptists in the area, Valentine Rathbun, had also abandoned his initial support for the Revolution by the time that the revivals commenced.[20]

When Meacham, Johnson, Rathbun, and many others encountered the Shakers in 1780, they found a band of believers who had not simply renounced "wars and fightings." The Shakers declared not only that they were the only true church but also that theirs was the only world that mattered. They claimed to have God's continuous guidance through the mediation of their Mother Ann and to have discovered in the notion of the mystical immanence of the spirit the secret of the Millennium as well. As they told an inquirer several years later, Jesus Christ had "now come in them the second time"; and the Last Judgment had "begun in their church."[21]

In April of 1780, two former participants in the New Lebanon revival, Talmadge Bishop and Reuben Wight, left the settlement for the west. William Haskett says they went "on business" and "fell in" with the Shakers; Calvin Green says they intended to "get some farms in that new country" when they were "providentially led" to Niskeyuna. In any event, they not only were persuaded that the Shakers represented a continuation or culmination of the revival so hopefully begun the year before at New Lebanon, but Bishop in addition received from the Shakers their "gifts" of spirit possession.[22]

When Bishop returned to New Lebanon and told of what he had experienced, the group thought it advisable to send some of the leaders of the revival to inquire. Meacham, along with a Presbyterian elder named Calvin Harlow and two other men, therefore traveled the forty-five miles through the forest and across the Hudson to the log cabin at Niskeyuna. According to Calvin Green, Meacham spent an entire day questioning James Whittaker about the Shakers' beliefs as he sought "to measure his light with theirs, to see whether they had in reality the spirit of Christ in his Second Coming or not."[23] Convinced that the Shakers were indeed the people of God, the four confessed their sins to them and returned home. The next day, they reported what they had seen and heard. According to William Haskett, one of the four spoke in tongues and in an entranced state cried, "Away old heavens and old earth, away with it."[24] Others from New Lebanon made the trip to Niskeyuna and were similarly convinced.

Those who had visited the Shakers went to other places touched by the New Light Stir and told what they had seen. After hearing Talmadge Bishop's description of the Shakers, Samuel Johnson visited New Lebanon in order to learn more about them. At a meeting at Samuel Fitch's house, Fitch "had the power of God upon him, and was exercized in divers operations." Johnson was convinced that these phenomena were sent from God, for they corresponded to the gifts of the Holy Spirit to the first apostles, the purity of whose original and primitive church would be restored in the Last Days.

Johnson then went to Niskeyuna on foot and confessed his sins to

Whittaker. While he had often confesed to God in private, open confession was different. By his public admittance of all his wicked deeds, Johnson believed, God's promise had been fulfilled, for he "felt entirely released from the burden of sin." He also received a baptism of the spirit far more powerful and lasting than he had received at Hancock. He was first "baptized with the spirit of humiliation," which led him to perform "many mortifying and humiliating signs and operations" that taught him the vanity of his education and theological training. He then received gifts of prophecy, saw heavenly visions, and (like the English Shakers) could "discern the secret state of souls." Johnson's possession lasted for a considerable time. Even after his wife had finally sent someone to New Lebanon to bring him home, he "was still under such powerful operations that the neighbors gathered in to see him." They were not convinced, but she was fully persuaded that God was the author of her husband's possession.[25]

A young woman who had recently moved to New Lebanon and who had not taken part in the revival had a similar experience. One day she saw Talmadge Bishop passing her house while he "was operated upon by the power of God." Intrigued, she then attended one of the meetings of ecstatic worship at Isaac Harlow's, where she was so overwhelmed by the might of God that she was unable to stand. Another woman recalled that she was first drawn to the Shakers when she heard one of the converts in a nearby house singing in a new and wonderful fashion. That night she was shaken "by the power of God . . . as tho' the whole earth trembled."[26]

Among people already prepared to expect some sudden and dramatic manifestation of God, who heard their preachers pray for it every week, the ecstatic practices that the new adepts brought back from Niskeyuna could be interpreted as a confirmation of the divine presence, even in the rough and remote settlements of the Berkshire valleys. They also brought some color and excitement into lives that were generally short of both. Even some who left the Shakers insisted that those experiences, while they lasted, had been strangely powerful and deeply moving. The fact that the phenomena were unfamiliar and even bizarre could be considered to be proof that they were from God, for the Bible taught that He sent forth such signs and wonders whenever events of cosmic significance were imminent.[27]

About a month after word of the Shakers began to spread among the settlements of the Berkshire region, most of New England, from Albany to Rhode Island and north into New Hampshire, experienced a different kind of marvel, the strange "Dark Day." At eleven o'clock in the morning on 19 May, the sky turned an eerie yellow. Within an hour, it was so dark that people had to dine by candlelight. In the afternoon, the clouds took on what the Boston *Gazette* described as a "higher and more *brassy*" color, with occasional flashes that resembled the Northern Lights. Throughout the night, the darkness was impenetrable. Angell Matthewson remembered that the Dark Day was not the only omen people in his community of Buckland, Massachusetts, had seen in the sky that year. On another occasion, there were red streaks in the sky that resembled blood and fire. During a display of the Northern Lights, "Some supposed they heard drums, fifes and men's voices in the air." As with the Huguenots a century earlier, the experience of war and revolution produced their resonances in heaven.[28]

We have learned from anthropologists like E. E. Evans-Pritchard and Clifford Geertz that humans devote a great deal of ingenuity to devising explanations for experiences that are threatening or unfamiliar. Not content with a single explanation, they are quite capable of developing several explanations, even mutually contradictory ones, and sometimes of employing them simultaneously.[29] So it was with the Dark Day. There was a natural explanation, and one that was immediately evident. The air smelled like burning leaves, and there was a sooty deposit on the surface of ponds and rain barrels. With the coming of fine spring weather, people in the new settlements from New York to Maine had been clearing and burning on their land, and the wind had simply blown the smoke across New England.

For us, this explanation suffices, but for people who had lived through the strangeness of the day, it might not. After all, the Revelation of Saint John had predicted that in the last days, at the time of the opening of the sixth seal, "the sun became black as sackcloth, . . . the sky vanished like a scroll that is rolled up." Throughout New England, the Dark Day led individuals to think more seriously about salvation. The revivals of the New Light Stir, which had been sinking into complacency everywhere, came back to life.[30]

At Niskeyuna, Ann Lee and her followers believed that the Dark Day was God's sign that the time had come at last for the conversion of the world to Shakerism. Three years later, they told William

Plumer that it was "the signal from Heaven" to Ann Lee "to send forth her Elders to *preach the everlasting gospel to them who dwell on the earth.*" The work of evangelism would begin in America, but soon it would be spread to Europe by preachers miraculously able to speak all languages. Within a decade, the world would be brought to recognize the truth of God's revelation to them.[31]

The first major success from the public preaching of "the testimony" came with the conversion of many of the leading Baptists in Pittsfield, Hancock, and Richmond, Massachusetts to Shakerism. Settled less than twenty years earlier, Hancock was a mostly Baptist community dominated by the numerous and prosperous Goodrich clan. In Pittsfield, the Baptists had been organized in 1772 by Valentine Rathbun, a man of little education but considerable drive and ability, who had built a fulling mill there for the manufacture of cloth.[32]

A few weeks after the Dark Day, the congregation asked Rathbun to go to Niskeyuna to find out about the Shakers. Upon his return, a large crowd of people from the three settlements gathered in a barn to hear him. He told them that the Shakers were indeed the true "people of God. . . . They sing the song of the redeemed, they sing the song of the hundred and forty four thousand [Revelation 7:4], which are redeemed from the earth; they sing the song that no man can learn." While Rathbun was speaking, a man named Walter Cook jumped onto a bench and began to cry out, "Amen, Glory, I know it is the way of God!" He shouted it over and over, bowing up and down as he did so, until his friends took him out and laid him on the grass. He continued in a distraught state for several days and then died.

Six days later, a large crowd assembled for Walter Cook's funeral. Thankful Goodrich recalled that "it was attended in the dooryard and the scene of confusion was solemn and awful." In one room, Amos Rathbun rolled on a bed in an agony of despair. In another part of the house, people were "speaking, shaking and stamping, and the house rocked as with a mighty wind." Amos Rathbun was one of many in the Pittsfield area who made his way to Niskeyuna, confessed his sins, and joined the Shakers. Some years later, he said that he had placed parents, family, and possessions on one side of the balance and his soul on the other: "I quick found out which ballanced; my soul was my all, and obedience to Mother was my salvation and promise of eternal life."[33]

Thankful Goodrich's remarkable narrative gives us some sense of the emotional intensity that the sacred theater of the collective search for salvation generated in the Berkshire settlements. Other accounts attest that many who visited the Shakers at Niskeyuna believed not only that they had now achieved it, but also that the Shakers lived in the kind of spiritual community that the New Lights had been trying to build for two generations. Daniel Rathbun recalled that there had been "the most extraordinary appearance of love and union among them" that he had ever seen.[34]

Daniel Rathbun left the Shakers five years later and wrote a scathing attack on what he regarded as their hypocritical evasions of the Christian ideals they professed. His brother, Valentine, lasted only three months as a Shaker, and after he left them he too had written a pamphlet against them. He also launched a veritable crusade to persuade the civil authorities to intervene. His bitterness against them was in part personal; his brothers, several of his children, various other relatives, and most of his congregation had remained Shakers. Even when one takes all of that into account, however, his pamphlet is an indispensable document. The only full description of the English Shakers in the crucial year of 1780 that we have, it went through ten separate printings between 1781 and 1783.[35]

Rathbun visited Niskeyuna just at the time that the Shakers had decided to begin a more public and assertive evangelism. He experienced what Stephen Marini has called their "fluid and continuous social process of religious communication that the Shaker leaders controlled by a kind of ensemble improvisation."[36] After welcoming him and giving him something to eat, they sang "odd tunes, and British marches, sometimes without words, and sometimes with a mixture of words known and unknown." After a period of "shaking their heads in a very extraordinary manner," Ann Lee prayed in an unknown tongue, which was then interpreted by one of the men. Another (presumably Whittaker) explained some of the Shakers' doctrines to him. Sinless perfection was possible; the need for the sacraments had ended; public confession was the essential first step toward salvation.

Their worship was as completely unstructured as it had been in Manchester: "Lest, as they say, they should be connected with Babylon." There was "no public prayer, no preaching, and but little reading." They told him that they must not resist the power of God when it came upon them, whether it led them to collapse to the floor, to whirl, to groan and cry out, or even when it produced periods of "great laughter and lightness." Rathbun himself experienced the power that they said came from God. His description of its onset is virtually identical with those recorded seventy years earlier by the Camisard prophets or their heirs John Lacy and Johann Adam Gruber. He first began "gaping and stretching," and then began to twitch, "as though his nerves were all in convulsion . . . ; the person believes it is the power of GOD, and therefore dare not resist, but wholly gives way to it."[37]

In the light of the later development of Shaker doctrine, Rathbun's description of Ann Lee's role is especially interesting. In no conventional sense was she the leader of the group. She had come to him, "looking very smiling," and had begun "to sing a strange tune with a mystical voice, in a mixture of words, known and unknown, which seemed a perfect charm." The other Shakers told him that she was the woman described in Revelation who was clothed with the sun. She was "the mother of all the elect." Salvation came only through her, through confession and her "being possessed of their sin."[38] Her role was thus closer to that of other female prophetesses of the century like Mrs. Buchan, Catherine Théot, and Joanna Southcott than it was to the female Christ of nineteenth-century Shaker theology.[39]

Ollive Miller first visited the Shakers at Niskeyuna when she was a girl of fourteen. Her description of it, set down seventy-three years later, is as vivid as Rathbun's and similarly illustrates the Shakers' skill at giving personal attention to every inquirer. The Millers lived at Hinsdale, just east of Pittsfield. They had been involved in the revival there, and like many others had failed to experience in preaching the sense of comfort they sought. It was early in 1781 that a group of seven or eight went through the melting snow to Niskeyuna. They stopped at John Partington's farm and had supper. In the evening, they went on to Ann Lee's cabin, accompanied by John Farrington, one of the leading converts from New Lebanon. Ollive found many people gathered in the small house "to see and hear."

She and her mother slept that night in the same room with Ann Lee and her young companion, Mary Partington. The next day, after hearing William Lee and James Whittaker speak, she confessed all her sins, resolving to forsake them entirely and to "bear a daily cross."

Her parents, who had joined the Shakers a few months earlier, remained at Niskeyuna, but Ollive joined some others in making the journey back to Massachusetts. They stopped at several converts' houses along the way, and she stayed overnight at Gideon Turner's. When her parents arrived there, they set out for Hinsdale. "We reached home the same evening," she said, "with our clothes wet and some frosen [sic], but feeling such a degree of thankfulness that we had found a way out of all sin, we did not regard our sufferings but very light."[40]

During Ann Lee's lifetime, there was a very clear distinction between the English Shakers, who alone constituted "the church," and the American converts, although a few of the latter were given duties as evangelists and even confessors. According to Valentine Rathbun, some of the converts were led by what they regarded as the power of God into excesses the English Shakers did not necessarily countenance. This seems to have been a factor in his own departure. He wrote that "the effect of this new work in many, appeared so wild, that it troubled me much." The experience of what they believed to be the power of God had led them to place all their religious faith in "their pretended visions, prophecies and signs." Sometimes, possessed by what they believed to be the Holy Spirit, converts would run through the woods "hooting and tooting like owls." While at dinner, they might decide that the spirits of deceased relatives had "come on the table and set on a pye." Sometimes they stripped off their clothes, believing themselves to be angels and invisible, or they might be led by the spirit to burst into a house and awaken the occupants.[41]

Out of the presence of "the Mother," and perhaps more importantly without the restraining influence of James Whittaker, the Shakers' belief that the Holy Spirit must be the soul's only spiritual guide could and did lead to some bizarre situations. It also contributed to their first brush with the civil authorities, only two months after the public "opening of the testimony."

The doctrine of pacifism was a logical corollary to the Shakers' belief that they inhabited a spiritual world only incidentally connected with the material one. Not even Valentine Rathbun claimed that it was central to their message, but some of their new converts, after four years of revolutionary unrest, may have seen the matter differently. As we have seen, the Reverend Samuel Johnson had turned against "wars and fightings" even before he joined the Shakers. After his conversion, he wandered from place to place while in a state of spirit possession, often declaiming against the war. Samuel Fitch, at whose house Johnson had first attended a Shaker meeting, seems to have behaved similarly.[42]

On 7 July, the Commissioners for Detecting and Defeating Conspiracies in the State of New York received a letter from a justice of the peace in the King's District that included New Lebanon. People there had complained that three farmers were preparing to drive some sheep toward the west, perhaps to the aid of the British. He had had them arrested and taken to Albany to be interrogated. They explained to the commissioners that the sheep were intended to feed the crowds that visited the Shakers at Niskeyuna. Satisfied that they were not subversives, the commissioners were preparing to release them when one of the men, David Darrow, quite unnecessarily announced that he denied "the Authority of the Board and all Civil Jurisdiction in this State," adding that because of his religious principles, he was "restrained from taking up Arms in defence of the Country." When John Hocknell and Joseph Meacham appeared before the commissioners on Darrow's behalf and declared "that it was their determined Resolution never to take up arms and to dissuade others from doing the same," all three were placed in custody.

The commissioners then learned that a notorious Tory from Connecticut had been to Niskeyuna several times "for the purpose of associating himself with a set of people who call themselves Shaking Quakers" and that a paroled prisoner of war living in Albany, an American who had served with the British army, claimed to be a Shaker and was trying to persuade people not to take up arms. The commissioners decided to call them in for interrogation as well.[43]

Having received more complaints from Niskeyuna that the Shakers were subversives, the commissioners sent their constable, Jacob Kidney, to bring in "John Partherton, William Lees, and Ann Standerren" for questioning. The zealous Kidney arrested James Whittaker, Calvin Harlow, and Mary Partington as well. All six, together with Hocknell, Meacham, Darrow, and several other recent converts, were confined in the Old Fort, Albany's temporary prison for Tories and prisoners of war. A month later, the commissioners transported Ann Lee and her companion Mary Partington to Poughkeepsie because of Ann Lee's "Influence in bringing over Persons to the

Persuasion professed by the People called Shaking Quakers." From Poughkeepsie they were to be "removed behind the Enemies Lines."

Meanwhile, at a worship service at Isaac Harlow's house in New Lebanon, the authorities arrested the notorious Samuel Johnson. He was confined separately and then released into his brother's custody because he was judged to be "at present Insane." Several others, including Samuel Fitch, were questioned and released. In October, Valentine Rathbun wrote to Albany to denounce his former mentors, but the commission no longer regarded the Shakers as any serious threat to the government. By the end of the year, they had all been released, the leaders paying hefty fines of a hundred pounds each.[44]

If the commissioners had hoped that the arrests of the Shakers would end their popularity, they were quite mistaken. News of their imprisonment at Albany had aroused popular interest, and crowds had come to the Old Fort to see them. The Shakers were allowed to proselytize through the bars and to conduct their services of ecstatic worship. One man who visited them in Albany recalled that when they sang "it really seemed . . . as if the very foundation of the prison trembled."[45]

The Shakers' five months in prison actually made them more accessible to inquirers than they had been at their cabin in the forest. Increasingly, people came from beyond the Berkshires to see them, returning with news of the message of salvation that they had heard and the marvels of spiritual power that they had witnessed. In the spring of 1781, the Shakers decided that Ann Lee, William Lee, and James Whittaker would lead an evangelical mission into New England in order to win more adherents to the faith. The political situation may have been a factor in their decision. Another convert had been stopped and questioned by the authorities, and on 30 May the commissioners in Albany received a complaint that the Shakers were buying arms and ammunition in order to aid the British.[46] The following day, Ann Lee and her companions left for Massachusetts.

{8}

Into New England

According to the Shaker tradition, Ann Lee's journey to the east was motivated by her vision of a new site for the establishment of the millennial kingdom in America. More pragmatically, the trip brought to the more settled sections of New England the experience of collective evangelism that the Shakers had employed so successfully at Niskeyuna and during their imprisonment at Albany. Despite the difficulties of travel and communication, there were now believers scattered through central and southeastern Massachusetts and in a few towns in Connecticut. In addition to wanting to extend their evangelical network, the Shakers may have hoped to escape the harassment for political subversion that had dogged them in New York. In this they were to be disappointed.

Ann Lee was accompanied throughout the journey by James Whittaker, her brother William, and her companion, Mary Partington. The rest of the English brethren remained at Niskeyuna, under the temporary direction of John Hocknell. They and many of the American converts joined Ann Lee for portions of the journey, sometimes making pilgrimages of a hundred miles and several weeks' duration to do so.

After stopping briefly at two small settlements in the Berkshires, Ann Lee and her companions traveled to Joseph Meacham's birthplace, Enfield, Connecticut. Meacham's brother David had been an early convert, and his father, Enfield's Baptist preacher, had been convinced by a visit to the Shakers during their imprisonment at Albany. Their arrival had been prepared by the evangelical team of Joseph Meacham Junior and Samuel Fitch, who had visited the area earlier in the year to tell about the Shakers.[1]

Elizabeth Wood remembered many years later that she had been picking strawberries by the side of the road when Ann Lee and her party arrived. Ann Lee got down from her wagon and asked her, "Where is the old man?" Elizabeth took them to the home of Joseph Meacham Senior. After dinner, Elizabeth confessed to Ann Lee that she had called her a witch and had "wished she was shot with a piece of silver." In Enfield and many other places, for the next several years, one popular explanation for the strange power that Ann Lee and her followers displayed would indeed be that they practiced witchcraft.[2]

Although the town of Enfield was much older than places like New Lebanon and Pittsfield where the Shakers had had their first success, life there was equally difficult. A century after the area's settlement, agriculture was at a bare subsistence level. Enfield's first historian wrote that most houses "were miserable huts built without regard [to] convenience or comfort."[3] Much of the town was forested; timber, tar, and turpentine were the only things Enfield produced that could be sold elsewhere. It was largely the lack of economic opportunity that had led Joseph Meacham and many others from Enfield to migrate elsewhere.

There is surprisingly little information on the origins of the Enfield Shaker community, which would always be a sort of island, rather remote from other settlements. It is clear from an examination of the Shakers' death lists that many of the first converts had been members of the Separate church whose 1777 revival had so impressed Joseph Meacham. The list is full of Markhams and Peases, the families that had dominated that church during its turbulent history.[4]

Ann Lee and her companions next stopped for a few days at Grafton, Massachusetts, where the Reverend Solomon Prentice had had so much trouble with the self-professed "immortals" who followed the prophet Shadrach Ireland. As the Shakers' subsequent route demonstrated, they had identified in the remnant of Ireland's disciples an important source of potential believers in the millennial kingdom that was embodied in the revelations of Ann Lee. After leaving Grafton, they traveled to Upton, where they stayed with Daniel Wood, one of Ireland's disciples. Wood had been converted to Shakerism after having visited Niskeyuna the previous winter. From Upton they traveled north to Harvard, forty miles west of Boston, where they stayed for a week at the home of Isaac Willard, a longtime disciple of Ireland's.

A week later they moved to the deceased Ireland's headquarters, the "Square House" on the outskirts of Harvard. They had arrived, according to the Shaker tradition, at the place Ann Lee had seen in a vision while in England. At New Lebanon, Pittsfield, and Enfield, the Shakers had been able to win over important segments of New Light communities already persuaded by the sacred theater of Shaker ecstatic worship that the Millennium was at hand. At Harvard, even more remarkably, Ann Lee managed to succeed to the mantle of a deceased prophet.

According to Isaac Backus's indispensable *History of New England,* Shadrach Ireland's spiritual pretensions had become so controversial that in about 1758 he had fled the Boston area in order to avoid prosecution. He had gone to Harvard, where a number of his disciples had settled. About ten years later, they built the Square House. Ireland lived quietly there with his "spiritual wife" and Samuel Cooper's family, which had moved from Grafton in order to be near him. For the next twenty years, disciples from all over central Massachusetts came to Harvard for his advice and blessing.[5]

Like others on both sides of the Atlantic who experienced spiritual awakening in the eighteenth century, Ireland held that it was possible for the regenerate to live in a spiritualized state in which sexuality had been transcended. More exceptionally, he also professed to have achieved a state of physical perfection through spiritual discipline that would make him and his disciples immortal. Then he died. According to Backus's informant, a former disciple, Ireland accepted his own unexpected demise with calm and resignation, saying to Abigail Cooper: "Sister Nabay, the Lord hath Done with me, and I have Completed all the work he sent me to do; but Don't be Scared, for I am going; but don't bury me, for the Time is very Short. God is Coming to take the Church."[6]

The faithful placed his body in lime in a corner of the basement and awaited some divine manifestation. After nearly a year, a few disciples took Ireland's remains and buried them in a cornfield. Their faith in the prophet somewhat shaken, the group drifted into dissension as they tried to comprehend what had happened. It is not clear when the Harvard Irelandites first heard about the Shakers. According to Jemima Blanchard and Beulah Cooper, two of Ireland's followers who became Shakers, an Irelandite from Upton named Daniel Wood came to Harvard after a visit to Niskeyuna and reported that the Shakers "confessed their sins and were operated on by the power of

God." His description of the Shakers' doctrine of salvation through celibacy and confession impressed some of the Irelandites, who like Wood also began to experience episodes of spiritual possession. Beulah Cooper recalled that "those who received Daniel's word were very wild and strange in their gifts but they had great power." Most of the Irelandites, however, chastened by Ireland's death and unpersuaded that these odd manifestaations were indeed divine, held aloof.[7]

According to the Shaker accounts, Ann Lee and her companions simply presented themselves at the door of the Square House and persuaded Abigail Cooper to let them in. With her customary spiritual assurance, Ann Lee announced that God had sent her to bring this lost group back to the path of salvation. She was tactful enough to declare that Ireland had "had greater light and power of God, than any before him in America," but he had fallen from grace and was now in Hell: "I have seen him in the bottomless pit bound with devils . . . and I have heard him roar louder than thunder, and I hear him now while I am speaking."[8]

Stephen Marini has shown that those in Harvard who converted to Shakerism were in every respect a social and economic cross section of the community. The former Irelandites were numerically the most important, but the Shakers drew away members from the newly established Baptist church as well. Once again, the combination of Ann Lee's prophetic presence, the riveting sacred theater of Shaker worship with its astonishing "gifts" of divine power, and the promises of salvation and sinless perfection had won them Baptist converts.[9]

One gets a nice sense of the way the Shakers worked with individual seekers in the recollections of one convert, Elizabeth Woodman, who had come to Harvard to see them:

One time Mother Ann spoke to me and said come out from that old man of sin and be like an angel and serve God. Elder William [Lee] says It is your lust that makes you afraid. Elder Whittaker says take up your cross and follow Christ in the regeneration[.] Elder Calvin [Harlow] said confess your sins turn out your works of darkness and come to the light and find everlasting happiness.[10]

When a disgruntled minority of Irelandites protested Ann Lee's assumption of the mantle of the prophet, the Shakers had no difficulty in collecting from their converts in Harvard and elsewhere the sum of nearly $1,700 to purchase the Square House from Ireland's heirs. Harvard became an important base for further evangelism in nearby towns, despite sporadic mob violence directed against the Shakers because of rumors that they were British spies. As large crowds continued to visit them, the Shakers also organized a system for feeding them, sending disciples to the Berkshires to collect food from converts there. During those first months in Harvard (Jemima Blanchard recalled many years later), it had not been unusual to feed two hundred people at a time. People ate quickly, content to use the unwashed plates, knives, and forks left by the last group at the table.[11]

Although ecstatic worship had not been part of the Irelandites' practice, the Shakers introduced it in Harvard with complete success. One of their histories describes a meeting attended by a multitude of believers and spectators at which the noise could be heard for several miles. William Plumer described scenes he witnessed at Harvard in 1782 that are virtually identical to what others had described at Niskeyuna or in the Berkshires. On one occasion, thirty people gathered in a large room, men at one end and women at the other. One young woman performed remarkable prodigies of whirling. People cried out, "*Ho, ho* or *Love, love*," and the entire company then clapped loudly for several minutes. Plumer wrote that "some were shaking & trembling, others singing in whining canting tones words out of the Psalms, but not in rhyme, & others were speaking what they called the unknown tongue.... [at] other times the whole assembly would shout as with one voice & with one accord."[12]

Plumer was surprised at the advanced age of many of the Harvard Shakers. The community's death records bear this out. Whereas in all of the other communities the first Shaker converts were most often in their late teens or early twenties, many at Harvard were past middle age, having been Ireland's disciples for decades.

Ann Lee is supposed to have denied their belief in their own immortality with her usual directness. She told them that when Ireland or one of his disciples died, they had blamed "some secret cause, or some thing which they have done," but in fact they all of them "carr[ied] about all the marks of mortality."[13] Nonetheless, the belief persisted. It even seems to have spread to places that had probably never heard of Shadrach Ireland. When Plumer visited the Shakers in Canterbury, New Hampshire, in 1783, they told him that Ann Lee and the six or seven who like her were "perfectly & wholly free from all sin & impurity" had bodies that were also "wholly pure—no seeds of death remain[ed] in them, & they [would] never be subject to death." Instead, when the Millennium came, their bodies would be transformed into pure spirit, so that "death will have no power over them, or will they need food or raiment."[14]

When Valentine Rathbun had visited the English Shakers at Niskeyuna in 1780, they had told him that at the Millennium they would be "changed in the twinkling of an eye, and go from this to the upper regions."[15] This notion, however, was a reasonably conventional interpretation of passages in the biblical Revelation of Saint John the Divine, quite different from the physical immortalism Shadrach Ireland and his disciples professed. One of the latter, Jonathan Wood, had moved from Harvard westward to Worcester County, where he built several mills on the Deerfield River near Ashfield. According to the "Reminiscences" of the former Shaker Angell Matthewson, Wood's conversion to Shakerism had not led him to change his belief in his own immortality. He praised the Shakers' teachings of "self denial & the cross" to anyone who visited his mill, insisting that they constituted "the true light of the Gospel." He then assured his hearers that as surely as they saw the sun shining, he would be there "a thousand years hence tending this mill."[16]

Meanwhile, at Harvard, the rumors persisted that the Shakers were subversives who were gathering a supply of weapons at their Square House. Finally, after seven months of missionary success and intermittent persecution, "the church" (as Ann Lee and her English companions were then designated) made their way back to Enfield. This time hostile crowds harassed them there as well. They moved on to Ashfield, Massachusetts, where several members of the Baptist church had already converted to Shakerism.

Like most of the New England towns in which the Shakers succeeded in winning converts, Ashfield was a subsistence community that had only recently emerged from the frontier stage. Nobody was rich; comparatively few were desperately poor; nearly everyone farmed. The Baptists were numerous and influential, and in 1780 they had experienced a revival during the New Light Stir that increased the number of their members to nearly one hundred.[17]

Then Israel Chauncy and his sister went to Niskeyuna. Upon their return, Chauncy told the Baptist elders and deacons that the Shakers were the true church of the Gospel. His sister-in-law, Hannah Chauncy, recalled that Israel told her that Ann Lee had seen him "thro' and thro'" and knew all his sins. His sister "did not look much like herself, and she shook till her hair was thrown everyway." Hannah decided that the Shaker religion must be "the way of God," and that she must accept it "or never find salvation."[18]

News of the Shakers' coming led the citizens of Ashfield to form a Committee of Safety which was instructed "to warn the Straglin Quaquars to Depart the town immediately."[19] Instead, the authorities not only left the Shakers alone but also prevented the vigilante mobs that followed the Shakers from entering the town.

Ann Lee and her companions stayed in the area two months, residing at Asa Bacon's in Ashfield and with Jonathan Wood and his nephew Aaron in Shelburne. Matthewson wrote that before his conversion Aaron Wood had been "one of the most slack lazy men in creation," but after visiting the Shakers at Harvard, "the power fell on him." As a result, "he most continuously either shook his head or stretched out his hand & ran after it." Wood seems to have had the same sort of gift for sacred theatrics that had made Jean Cavalier's performances such a sensation among the French Prophets. One Shaker recalled having seen Wood lying on the floor during a worship service at Harvard, performing "a sign" of the danger of damnation: "His face looked black, & his tongue was ran out of his mouth." On another occasion, he rolled across the room, crying "mercy!" as he rolled. He then tucked his knees up to his chest and rolled some more, still crying for mercy. According to Matthewson, he announced that it had been a "sign" of "the awful sins of the damned." Wood also displayed spiritual gifts at singing, dancing, and whirling. He quickly became one of Ann Lee's special favorites among the American converts.[20]

After organizing the Shaker converts of the area in "one worshipping assembly" under Jonathan Wood's direction, in May 1782 they returned to Harvard.[21] The hostility against them had not diminished in Harvard; in August, Ann Lee and "the church" traveled first to southeastern Massachusetts, where there were a few converts in Rehoboth and Norton, then across Connecticut, staying several weeks at Stonington and for shorter periods at Windham, Preston, and Stafford. Separate Congregationalists and Baptists had been active in all of these towns since the 1740s. Stonington was the place of origin of the Rathbuns of Pittsfield, who despite the defection of Valentine Rathbun were a numerous and important clan among the

Shakers in the Berkshires. In none of the towns, however, was there the conversion of church leaders that had given them footholds elsewhere. In Stonington, in fact, the hostile mobs were organized and led by the Baptists.[22]

In September, they arrived again at Enfield. A hostile crowd which had followed them from Stafford attempted to force its way into the house where Ann Lee was. In the ensuing riot, David Meacham was injured by one of the rioters, but not before he had grabbed his antagonist and (as Elizabeth Wood recalled) "spanked him about right. It sounded pretty smart since the chap had on a pair of leather briches." They visited several groups of Shakers in Berkshire County and then returned to Ashfield.[23]

Throughout the winter of 1782–83, great crowds came to see them. On one occasion, John Farrington counted sixty sleighs and 600 people. In order to accommodate them, the Shakers built a large log meeting house which functioned as a heaquarters for the area, just as the Square House did at Harvard. Matthewson described the elaborate arrangements that were made for feeding the visitors, many of whom stayed for several days. Provisions were contributed by Shakers elsewhere, and food was continuously available on a large round table in the middle of the meeting house. Throughout much of the day and night, "singing and dancing went on around the table behind the backs of those eating." When they had finished, they joined the worshipers, and others took their places at the table.[24]

The winter of 1782–83, spent in the relative safety of Ashfield, was crucial for the Shakers' development of institutional structures. Despite claims in their later histories that Ann Lee had foretold the "gathering" into "Gospel order" of the clusters of believers scattered across much of upland New England, these are no more than pious traditions. Nevertheless, even if the creation of the eighteen remarkable communities that were the Shakers' most lasting achievement was almost exclusively the work of Joseph Meacham and his chosen lieutenants, it is true that a kind of informal biblical communalism evolved at several localities including Ashfield. The organization of a system for feeding crowds that numbered in the hundreds, for an entire winter, was itself a remarkable achievement.

That the English Shakers in addition envisioned the formation of collective agricultural enterprises operated by their American disciples is indicated by a letter James Whittaker wrote to Josiah Talcott, one of the believers at Hancock in the Berkshires. Whittaker accused Talcott of being "idle and slothful" for leaving much of his land unimproved. Such conduct would bring upon Talcott "wrath and poverty as well as the wrath of God in hell." The women in Talcott's family, he continued, were "breeders of lust and abominable filthiness" who needed to be put to work in order that they might "find health in their bodies as well as their souls"—an early variant of the later Shaker motto, "hands to work and hearts to God," perhaps. Whittaker commanded Talcott to bring other Shakers to his farm, for he had "land enough to maintain three families or more, well improved."[25]

Beginning in the fall of 1782, the Shakers supplemented the missionary efforts of Ann Lee and "the church" by sending out pairs of evangelical "laborers" who itinerated, like their contemporary rivals, the Baptist and Universalist lay preachers. Three teams were sent out: Joseph Meacham and Samuel Fitch, Calvin Harlow and Joel Pratt, and Ebenezer Cooley and Israel Chauncy. They visited those who had accepted the faith, maintaining a framework of doctrine and discipline—a difficult task, given the Shakers' refusal in this period to be bound by any guide other than the immediate promptings of the Holy Spirit. They also made contact with groups of potential converts. Like Ann Lee and her English companions, they were empowered to hear confessions, forgive sins, and bring to people who might never see Ann Lee or experience her special charisma the promise of salvation and sinless perfection.[26]

Fitch, Pratt, and Chauncy are shadowy figures, early believers of no particular distinction. Meacham, Harlow, and Cooley, on the other hand, were probably the ablest of all the American converts. They all had experience as preachers and religious teachers that the English leadership now put to good use. Meacham and Harlow, as we have seen, had been the leaders of the New Lebanon revival that provided the Shakers with their first converts. It was to be Meacham above all who saved the Shakers from extinction after the deaths of Ann Lee and James Whittaker, through his creation of religious communities governed by rigid spiritual hierarchies. Until his premature death, Harlow was one of Meacham's most trusted lieutenants. Ebenezer Cooley receives less attention in Shaker histories, possibly because he was almost continuously traveling as a missionary and therefore not involved in the formation of the communities. When he joined the Shakers in 1780, after having served in the Revolutionary army, he was a middle-aged man with six children—neither his wife nor his children joined the Shakers. Until his death thirty-seven years later, Cooley traveled the roads and paths of New England and the Ohio Country as an evangelist whenever the Shaker leadership "opened the Gospel" to new converts.[27]

In September 1782, Cooley and Chauncy arrived at the remote settlement of Canaan, New Hampshire. As the town's name suggests, it had been settled in part by Connecticut people, including some members of the extensive Meacham clan. The area had been wilderness only fifteen years earlier, when Samuel Meacham of Norwich, Connecticut, brought his bride, Phebe Main of Stonington, to Canaan. Close to one hundred thousand people had swarmed into northern New England since 1763, but there were still fewer than seven thousand in all of Grafton County. The Shaker histories do not indicate why their missionaries should have detoured to a frontier outpost like Canaan. Possibly the presence of numerous Meachams in the area was a factor.[28]

The two Shakers were accompanied to Canaan by Zadock Wright, the former prisoner of war whose self-proclaimed conversion and vociferous pacifism had contributed to the Shakers' imprisonment at Albany in 1780. After his release from confinement, he had rejoined his family at Hartland, New Hampshire (now Vermont), where they had been among the first settlers.[29]

Cooley, Chauncy, and Wright had no success in Canaan, but in nearby Enfield they managed to convert several of the more prosperous settlers and their families. According to the nineteenth-century Shaker elder Henry Blinn, some of the Enfield settlers belonged to "a peculiar sect of new light doctrines." It is worth noting that the two leading families who joined the Shakers, the Jewetts and the Pattees, had migrated there from religiously turbulent Essex County, Massachusetts. In all, about eleven families in the area joined the Shakers, dispersed in several frontier communities besides Enfield. For the next several years, they would be distant outposts of believers, without very much connection with the Shakers to the south.[30]

According to the testimonies of several former Shakers in Enfield, the three missionaries presented doctrines similar to those promulgated by the Baptists, but with the important difference that they declared that Ann Lee was the woman clothed with the sun described in the twelfth chapter of the Book of Revelation, who "was in the resurrection, judging the world." The testimonies are contained in the most vehement of the anti-Shaker tracts, Mary Marshall Dyer's *A Portraiture of Shakerism,* but their descriptions of disorganization at Enfield and frequent outbursts of spiritual vagaries often at odds with the Shaker leadership are borne out by other sources as well. According to a manuscript history of the community, the Enfield Shakers "had no particular creed or form of faith, laid down as a standard, or any fixed or particular manner of worship." Blinn wrote that they understood only "imperfectly" what was expected of them as Shakers; instead, they were frequently guilty of "high sense, and self esteem." According to the Shakers' published *Testimonies,* some of the new converts decided that since the world was to end soon, they would make "a very undue use of their property, by squandering it away in a profuse manner." When some of the others therefore went to Ashfield for advice, they were told to store supplies "as though they were to live a thousand years." For the next several years, the Shakers in the Enfield area continued to be a special problem, following their own spiritual light and frequently resisting or ignoring the admonitions of the central leadership.[31]

In November or December, the Shaker missionaries arrived at Canterbury, New Hampshire, north of Concord. Many Baptists in the church at Canterbury and Loudon, including their preacher, Edward Lock, had been caught up in the evangelical movement that became the denomination of Freewill Baptists. Its founder was Benjamin Randall, who after several years as an itinerant Baptist preacher had received a call from a congregation at New Durham, near the Maine border. Like many of the Baptists who found their way to the Shakers, Randall had turned from support of the revolutionary war to a conviction that all wars were evil and that Christ's Second Coming was at hand. Following a visionary experience, he was convinced—like the Shakers—that a life of sinless perfection and an assured salvation was possible for all people who accepted Christ's promise and followed the true Christian life. The power of his personality and message won support among the members of several Maine and New Hampshire churches, including the one at Loudon and Canterbury.

Excluded from the Baptist association, Randall, Lock, and their followers began in 1781 to promulgate their doctrine of "a free gospel and unlimited atonement" by means of itinerant preaching. A Baptist preacher named Samuel Shepard wrote Isaac Backus that as soon as Lock was ordained by his congregation, "he drove . . . Through the Wilderness; Preaching & Baptizing, all he could Flatter, or fright to be Baptized. . . . He made grate Disturbance, among Some Churches in the Wilderness, for about Two years." Lock and the other "Free-willers" also launched revivals that were accompanied by dramatic scenes of emotion and ecstatic experience.[32]

According to the standard history of the Freewill Baptists, the Canterbury church quickly fell into "a distracted state, some of its members having indulged in fanatical notions of worship." John Whitcher, whose family left the church and joined the Shakers, put it differently. Many of the Canterbury Baptists received "great additional light and power," he wrote, "to discover the secret cause of their innate darkness and troubles." Some of them were even led to prophesy "that the day of redemption was at hand."

During the summer of 1782, they learned of the Shakers from an itinerant peddler who had visited New Lebanon. They therefore sent Lock and one of the church elders to Harvard to inquire further. They were both enormously impressed. After their return, they told the congregation that the Shakers possessed "far greater light and power of God than they had ever before witnessed." They had not, however, confessed their sins and joined the Shakers. Instead, they introduced some of the Shaker practices, including oral confession, into their own worship.[33]

They were in this halfway situation when Cooley and Chauncy arrived, accompanied by James Jewett and Asa Pattee of Enfield, New Hampshire. They stopped first at the home of Alice and Henry Beck. They declared that they were "the angels spoken of in the revelations of St. John, flying through the midst of heaven, having the everlasting gospel to preach to them that dwell on the earth." Within less than a month, the missionaries had succeeded in converting over twenty people, including the elders, the deacons, and the majority of the membership. Within a year, there were over two hundred Shakers in Canterbury and other settlements in the area. As at Enfield, they included many of the wealthy and influential members of their communities.[34]

The elder who had accompanied Lock soon left the Shakers. He told Samuel Shepard that he "could not hold with the Shakers, without Giveing up his Own judgment, and Reason." Lock also left the Shakers, but not before he had employed his evangelical gifts in converting the majority of members of the Freewill Baptist congregation at Crown Point, near Strafford.

Not surprisingly, the Shakers' remarkable success in winning converts in the New Hampshire back country distressed many people in the state. Jeremy Belknap wrote a friend that the general opinion in New Hampshire was that these Baptists turned Shakers were "under the power of *witchcraft*. This is the usual way (among ignorant people) of solving every uncommon appearance." He added that these Shakers believed that they were "judges of the world, and that the dead are daily rising, and coming before them to be judged." When William Plumer visited the Canterbury Shakers in February 1783, Ebenezer Cooley told him the same thing. When the Shakers spoke in unknown tongues, Cooley said, they were preaching to the dead. If the dead heard and believed and confessed their sins, they too would "become new born souls & live forever in full & open vision with God." The power to preach to and convert the dead was a power that Ann Lee herself claimed; it had now become a spiritual gift of some of the American converts as well. According to Whitcher's history of the Canterbury community, the outpouring of spiritual power that the converts received was astonishing. "Some had the gift of visions and discerning of Spirits," he wrote. "Others the gift of prophecy, expressing both by words and signs what was to take place in the progress of the work."[35]

Plumer's account of his conversation with Cooley is invaluable; it provides the only reasonably dispassionate contemporary evidence we have of Shaker theology during the sect's formative period. Cooley told him that the church comprised "7 or 8 persons only—they say no person can be a member of it untill he is perfectly & wholly free from all sin & impurity." Cooley said that "the propagation of the human specie[s] is absolutely unlawful—that it is the greatest of sins—that copulation is what is called *original sin*." The present one was to be "the last generation of men."

The Second Coming had commenced not in the person of Ann Lee (as the Shakers were to declare in the nineteenth century) but rather in "the church" collectively: "He is now come in them the second time, & . . . the judgment is begun in their church." While Plumer wrote that the Shakers "really worship[ed]" Ann Lee, her role was still, as in England, that of a prophet and visionary. The authority of the Shaker leadership, Cooley told Plumer, was absolute and infallible. "The Church knows as God knows," he declared. They were "perfectly well acquainted with the hearts & tho[ugh]ts of all men— ... their Elders communicate instruction & reproofs tho' absent from them, & that without the aid of letters— ... tho' absent in body they are present in spirit." Those who were "of the society but not of the church" were guided by the Holy Spirit, but they had not yet been born again. They must therefore "reverance the orders of the church as the command of God [and] believe what they are told, & practice what they are bidden, without murmuring or disputing."

Unlike the contentious converts in Enfield, the Canterbury Shakers rapidly developed a stable and vigorous religious community. On their own initiative, they also formed two collective agricultural enterprises in which many of the membership resided. It was an idea that was germinating before the Shakers arrived. In 1780, the Freewill Baptists in Loudon had ordained a deacon who was to assess each member's worth and determine what each must contribute to the congregation. They had also built homes for needy members.

The Shakers in Loudon and Canterbury went one step further. They invited the poorer members to come and live on the farms of two of the wealthiest of the converts. Henry Clough, a wealthy bachelor who owned 400 acres of land, took in several poor families plus a number of single young people. For ten years, some thirty people lived and farmed together. Benjamin Whitcher and his family were joined on their large farm—the site of the present Canterbury Shaker community—by nearly forty other people. According to John Whitcher, both collectives were very successful, although the land was poor. They practiced an informal communism, receiving no wages for their labor and instead sharing in the fruits of it. Their diet was varied and ample. In summer, they had "puddings, meat and sauce" for dinner and "porridge for breakfast and supper, sometimes with butter and cheese." In winter, their breakfast and supper "consisted of bean porridge, a very nutritious and wholesome diet." Plumer wrote that "several who had valuable farms have sold them & given the money to support the common cause," which included not only their own maintenance but also that of the traveling missionaries.[36]

When Plumer visited Canterbury, he attended a public worship service at Whitcher's farm. His description of it suggests that possession by the Holy Spirit was leading the New Hampshire converts into some bizarre behavior. One Shaker jumped up and down so hard that he broke through the floor. Several people ran "with great violence" from room to room. Others whirled for extended periods; a few of them grew dizzy and vomited. Their vomiting, they said, was "*putting off the old man & his deeds.*" After the meeting, some went out into the field, where they ran for several hundred yards "backwards & forwards, as fast as they could" for half an hour.

In the spring, some of the New Hampshire converts accompanied Cooley into Maine to win others to their new faith. They were once again successful among Freewill Baptists, but they also encountered small groups of sectarians whose ecstatic practices recall the behavior of Nicholas Gilman's group at Durham, New Hampshire, a generation earlier. At Gorham, they encountered a group known locally as the "New Lights" or "Come-Outers" who had drawn away from the settled Congregational church nearly a decade before in order to follow the gifts of the spirit and to hear the preaching of any member who felt called to do so. Their meetings had become more emotional during the New Light Stir, which in Maine and New Hampshire had been generated to a considerable extent by the evangelical efforts of the Freewill Baptists. According to a local historian, veterans returning to Gorham from the revolutionary war with their religious ideas "unsettled" joined the "Come-Outers" eagerly. The meetings, which went on for entire nights, were characterized by "exhortations of the most exciting nature, singing, dancing and whirling."[37]

Gorham was one of several inland Maine settlements in which Shakers and Freewill Baptists competed for converts for a decade. Elisha Pote, who became a Shaker elder, recalled that when he was converted by Freewill Baptist evangelists during the New Light Stir, their preaching convinced him and many of his friends that a true Gospel church must stand for both "a life of celibacy, or virgen purity" and "one joint interest." It soon became clear to him that the Freewill Baptist preachers tended instead to "so quallify these precious truths, so as to do them all away."

The excitement of the revival faded. Then the Shakers arrived in Gorham in 1783, preaching those same truths. Pote and others accepted their testimony. Immediately, "the gifts and power of God was displayed among us in a wonderful manner," he recalled. He and the other converts "made the wilderness ring with shouting praises to God, singing and dancing."[38]

The process was similar in the remote settlement of Alfred, Maine, where, a few years earlier, many of the families had lived in tents. Alfred had been visited by the Freewill Baptist evangelist Benjamin Randall, whose preaching helped to launch a revival there in 1781. The revival services were intensely emotional experiences, in which people were led by the Holy Spirit to sing, dance, and prophesy. Because of their religious ecstasies, their neighbors scornfully called them the Merry Dancers.

The behavior of those possessed became increasingly bizarre. They would interrupt others' religious services, becoming so rowdy that occasionally it was necessary "to take them out and fasten them with ropes to a tree." Two of the most exuberant were John Barnes and John Cotton, who began the practice of "hooting the devil." They would march around the village pond, crying loudly "woe! woe!! woe!!!" Cotton wore an untanned cow hide over his clothes; Barnes had a wig on his head with a cow's tail attached to it. Many years later, when the Shaker elder Peter Coffin asked Barnes why they hooted the Devil, got drunk, and engaged in other "indecent and immoral practices," Barnes told him that "they were a sort of carnal slough which they were doomed to pass through preparatory to spiritual regeneration" in their conversion to Shakerism.[39]

According to the Shaker histories, it was John Cotton who first brought word of the Shakers to Alfred. He and Daniel Coffin had stopped off in Enfield, New Hampshire, while on their way to visit a farm they had bought in Vermont. They stayed with James Jewett, who had recently joined the Shakers. Convinced by what Jewett told him that the Shakers' was the true faith, Coffin confessed his sins to Jewett. A few days later he was entirely possessed by the power of God. "It raised me from my chair," he wrote later, "and under its influence I turned around, swiftly, for the space of half an hour. . . . This was a seal to my faith and a baptism of the Holy Spirit."[40]

Cotton decided to return to Maine, where he told family and friends what he had experienced. Then Ebenezer Cooley came to Alfred, accompanied by Eliphalet Comstock of Hancock, Massachusetts, and Jewett. As at Canterbury, Gorham, and the other settlements, they went from house to house, preaching the Shaker's message of salvation. Among those converted was Cotton's friend

Benjamin Barnes, whose farm became their place of worship and later the nucleus of the Alfred Shaker community. Barnes and Cotton accompanied the missionaries to other settlements, in all of which (the Shaker historian tells us) there were "many of the New Light Baptists who were prepared for a higher and more progressive work."[41]

In New Hampshire and Maine as in Massachusetts and Connecticut, the Shakers were successful in their evangelism when certain preconditions existed. The most important was the memory of the experience of religious urgency and spiritual presence that in many villages and settlements had accompanied the New Light Stir. It was an experience that the Shakers could generate continuously in their sacred theater of ecstatic worship.

For those who had gone through the revival, Shaker doctrine, as presented by able evangelists like James Whittaker, Joseph Meacham, or Ebenezer Cooley, had the appearance of an intriguing blend of the familiar and the strange. The Millennium was indeed at hand, as Puritans on both sides of the Atlantic had believed intermittently for two centuries. The church of Christianity's early and uncorrupted days had been reconstituted for all time, short as that time might be. Just as the strangeness and even violence of Shaker worship could be attractive or repelling depending on what one expected of the Holy Spirit, so the absolute certitude with which the Shakers put forth their doctrines, which contemporary observers like William Plumer or Isaac Backus dismissed as fanaticism, was simply the expression of revealed truth to educated converts like Ebenezer Cooley and Daniel Rathbun. Cooley refused to debate on religious questions, calling it *"disputing with corrupt minds that are reprobate concerning the faith."* When Backus visited Daniel Rathbun in order to learn more about the Shakers and raised scriptural objections to their teachings, the people in the house immediately began to shake and to cry out. Rathbun declared that he would not permit "the speaking of any thing against that spirit in his house."[42]

The Shakers' testimony was especially welcome among groups that had cut themselves loose from the restraints of traditional ecclesiastical structures, even those as loose as the Baptist associations. This was perhaps nowhere more apparent than in Maine. Merry Dancers and Come-Outers and Freewill Baptist evangelists had all tapped a longing for religious certainty which expressed itself in phenomena of religious ecstasy. They all implied that salvation was connected with divine immanence and individual decision. Then the Shakers appeared, with their twin answers to the perpetual question. If one confessed all of one's sins and accepted the spiritual discipline that began with celibacy, salvation was assured.

The Shakers made no converts in large towns or in the long-settled seaboard areas. In the subsistence communities of the interior, they were successful only when splintered religious groups that included prominent members of the community were among the converts. And wherever they were able to establish themselves, their converts were not individuals but families, even clans. The Meachams of New Lebanon and Enfield, the Goodriches of Hancock, or the Woods of Shelburne were only the most prominent. At New Gloucester, Maine, two clans, the Briggs and the Merrills, between them provided fifty-six Shaker converts.[43]

Like the Freewill Baptists, Universalists, Christ-ians, and Methodists who traversed the back country during the next decades, the Shakers offered a religious immediacy and emotionalism generally absent from the services of Presbyterians and Congregationalists. Even those who joined the Shakers and then left them—and they were at least as numerous as those who remained in the church—remembered with wonder the visionary and ecstatic phenomena that they had witnessed or experienced while they were of the faith.

It is noteworthy that the Shakers encountered none of the mob violence in northern New England that became nearly endemic in Connecticut and Massachusetts. Its absence suggests that it was the fact that Ann Lee and her companions were English, not the nature of their religious message or even the commotion that their worship produced, that made their missionary efforts so difficult and even dangerous.

For the time being, the English Shakers were secure in their haven at Ashfield. Elsewhere, their American converts were making impressive gains for the church. Meanwhile, during that winter of 1782–83, the promptings of the Holy Spirit were taking Ann Lee and "the church" in some peculiar directions.

{9}

Spiritual Wars and
Sharp Testimonies

A ny movement of religious revival that is accompanied by phenomena of spirit possession has the potential to take its believers in new and unconventional directions. When a god comes to reside in a prophet or shaman, divinity is not simply present; it also instructs, admonishes, and directs the faithful. When a religious community incorporates spirit possession into its ritual, the potential extent of innovation is limited only by the capacity of the believers to accept the revelations as authentically divine. If the spirit orders it, what was against the law can become the law. In the last years of Ann Lee's life, this is what happened to the Shakers. In their own terminology (as Thomas Brown said in his history), whatever was said or done "in the gift" was right, even if "out of the gift" it might have been a sin.

In holding that God would choose those who should direct the faithful by implanting in them the light of inspiration, the Shakers shared with Quakers, Methodists, Pietists, and New Lights a notion that contrasted with the coldness and intellectualism that too often prevailed in the pulpits of the established churches. Other groups that we have examined were as dedicated to following the guidance of the Spirit as the Shakers were, but all of them, even the Camisard prophets and their German and English heirs, were constrained by a tacit biblicism that not even their prophets and visionaries overstepped. It is true that some of the last isolated Camisard prophets were led into some bizarre behaviors, and their English disciples were led by divine commands into wearing green ribbons and organizing themselves into the twelve tribes of Israel, but even they were attempting no more than to create an Old Testament community in London.

The Shakers, on the other hand, had from the outset believed that the messages sent by the Holy Spirit could be in any form and could entirely supersede anything that Scripture had commanded for earlier generations. The fact that their techniques of inducing ecstasy in their worship services affected everyone present meant that everyone present had access to the prophetic "gifts" that the Lord rained upon them. While it is true that a hierarchy, led by Ann and William Lee, Whittaker, Hocknell, and a few of the American converts, was already in place, the remarkably high emotional pitch that the protracted worship services invariably induced had the potential of leading to odd and unexpected behavior. After observing some of the strange "signs and operations" performed by some of the converts at Harvard, Ann Lee told young Jemima Blanchard that she had no idea what they meant. Then she paused and said: "It is of God and it is not for me to condemn it."[1] A great deal therefore depended on how the leadership responded. As in any kind of spirit possession, signals were crucial. What kinds of possessed behavior were accepted or encouraged? Were traditional cultural and social sanctions to be upheld or subverted by them?

The premise of this chapter would be entirely unacceptable to the Shakers themselves. Put simply, it is that in the period between late 1782 and Ann Lee's death two years later, Shakerism adopted practices that had they persisted might well have threatened its survival as a religious system. The innovations were the result of the leadership's total acceptance of the premise that the Holy Spirit must not be restrained. As Valentine Rathbun had pointed out in his pamphlet in 1780, the Shakers placed "their whole knowledge in their religion, on their pretended visions, prophecies and signs."[2] It was to be the achievement of Ann Lee's successors, James Whittaker and Joseph Meacham, between 1784 and 1796, to bring spirit possession under the leadership's control and direction, making it a vehicle for collective rather than individual religious experience.

There are only occasional hints in the nineteenth-century collections of Shaker testimonies that something had gone wrong. The evidence is to be found in a few contemporary diaries and memoirs, in some of the testimonies collected with great persistence and absolutely no restraint by the former Shaker Mary Marshall Dyer, in pamphlets written by Daniel and Reuben Rathbun after they had left the Shakers, and in the ex-Shaker Thomas Brown's *An Account of the People Called Shakers.*

The Shakers' own testimonies and histories fail to mention the allegations of the ex-Shakers, but they specifically deny the two charges that were the most widely rumored at the time. It was said that Ann Lee and some others had become dependent on alcohol as a means for inducing visionary experience and that the Shakers sometimes danced naked.

Only one of the several excellent recent works that deal with the early Shakers, Lawrence Foster's *Religion and Sexuality*, takes the apostate testimonies seriously and rejects the Shakers' contention that they are entirely without merit. Admittedly, some of the stories in these accounts are bizarre, but they are consistent with patterns of development present in movements of spirit possession in other cultures.[3]

I have followed the ex-Shakers' as the against the Shakers' version of what occurred in 1782–1784 mainly because I am persuaded that it is the truer one. It is important to examine their stories of religious excess, because if correct they provide an important perspective for the ultimately successful efforts to bring the phenomena of spirit possession under some kind of human control without repudiating Shakerism's belief that the Holy Spirit had always led them and continued to do so. Equally remarkably, Whittaker and Meacham accomplished their reconstruction of Shakerism without repudiating the special status of the deceased Ann Lee, whose conduct had been a principal cause of the crisis in the first place.

By all accounts, the winter of 1782–83 spent in Ashfield brought extraordinary effusions of the spirit. The size of the crowds that came to see them and the apparent success of their evangelical efforts confirmed to Ann Lee and the English Shakers (if they needed such assurance) that the conversion and purification of the world had begun. It may also have encouraged them to root out the vestiges of the old world of corruption more ruthlessly than ever. This is surely what the Shakers' printed *Testimonies* meant when they declared that at Ashfield "there were great spiritual wars . . . , and sharp testimonies against the nature of the flesh, and all manner of sin." Ann Lee told one believer that "Michael, and his angels, and the dragon and his angels, are at war, and those who have part in this war shall have part in the first resurrection."

The *Testimonies* also acknowledged that the introduction of new "gifts of God" had led to many defections. Those believers "who were honest-hearted, found a great increase of power over evil"; but "those who were rotten-hearted, and insincere, began to wither away, more and more, till they fell off, as withered branches." The adjectives are revealing. It is difficult to imagine a history by Methodists or even Mormons that dismissed all who left the faith as "rotten-hearted" and "insincere."[4]

Like many of the eighteenth-century movements of spiritual awakening, Shakerism had always been suspicious of learning. It will be recalled that during the Great Awakening Timothy Allen had been dismissed from his New Haven church for saying that the Bible was of no more use in attaining conversion than "an old almanac." He had then gone to New London to help James Davenport to establish the school for New Light preachers called the Shepherd's Tent, but it was a school that during its short life had systematically denigrated human learning in favor of inculcating saintly behavior and visionary experience. Davenport meanwhile had led the notorious burning of religious books and fancy clothing that had so seriously hindered the New Light cause.[5]

When William Plumer visited the Shakers at Canterbury, Ebenezer Cooley, himself a former Baptist preacher, told him that it was "absolutely unnecessary to write any more treatises on religion." Daniel Rathbun wrote that Joseph Meacham had told him that "the Mother and Elders are beyond all that is written," and therefore "the scriptures were good in their day, but nothing to us now."

At Ashfield, their trust in immediate inspiration, especially as it was manifested to Ann Lee and James Whittaker, led the Shakers into a crusade to emancipate the faithful from what the world called education. During one of his sermons, Whittaker told the believers that "schools among children were of no use, as he that preached Christ never would lack a tongue for a minister." Only two books were henceforth to be permitted: the Bible and a spelling book purged of pictures and "fables." One of the Enfield Shakers, Joseph Markham, told Matthewson that the two Joseph Meachams, father and son, had obeyed the command and burned their "very extensive & valuable library of books." The ex-Shaker Josiah Watson said the leadership at Canterbury forbade him to read the Bible and made him burn his religious books. Eunice Wild, who joined the Shakers in 1782 at the age of ten, recalled many years later that her greatest "trial" had been the leadership's prohibition on her attending school because of the schools' "opposition to the work of God." She however realized that "salvation could be obtained only in obedience to Mother." As late as 1803, the Shaker leader Benjamin Youngs wrote in his diary that it had been "thought best that a putting away of all unnecissary [*sic*] books be made." Youngs, one of the ablest and best educated of the Shaker leaders, commented that he was quite willing "to lt ye rubbish go & labr after ye Spirit." Eventually, the Shakers would develop a system of elementary schools that won wide praise, but during their first decades schooling was nonexistent, and the children of the first generation of converts grew up without it.[6]

The Shakers had always claimed to have the gift of healing. Their printed collections of testimonies contain a number of healing miracles, many of them by John Hocknell, who while in a trance could discern the nature of an ailment and cure it. Now the growing obsession with attaining purification through ridding themselves of all vestiges of the world's evil led them to emphasize spiritual "healing" by exorcising the demons that Satan sent against them. The *Testimonies* describe one fairly conventional exorcism. During that winter of 1782–83, a woman came to Ashfield bringing her young daughter, who was possessed by an evil spirit. Hocknell went to the child, spoke in "an unknown tongue," touched her on the head, and the evil spirit left her. Ann Lee then said: "We have the power to bind and to loose, and to cast out evil spirits."[7]

According to Matthewson's "Reminiscences," the expelling of demons now became a regular ritual. Aaron Wood emerged as the person who was the "best skilled" at casting out devils. He would begin by launching into one of his prodigies of whirling, while crying out, in a "grim and hollow" tone, "you devil you." He would then seize someone in whom he discerned an evil spirit and physically expel it by spinning and pummeling the person. On one occasion, in the presence of Ann Lee and her companions, he grabbed Isaac Chauncy by his waistband, spun him around thirty or forty times, then screamed at and pushed him. After twenty more spins, the exorcism was complete. Chauncy then knelt and gave thanks "for the gift of God administered to brother Aaron." During that winter, a hundred believers had demons exorcised in this fashion.

The twelve-year-old Matthewson was told that there were devils everywhere. It was therefore essential that "the people of God always . . . keep up a warfare against them." One day in the spring of 1783, he saw the believers, led by Aaron Wood, marching in one circle around and around the room. "The scene was astonishing," he recalled. "They had crowded & pushed till the whole body went in succession round the room like a whirl, everyone screaming, stamping, yowling, howling & fighting the devil."[8]

The Shakers introduced a form of sacred theater in which they enacted the warfare against the Devil in what they called the "warring gift." In 1783, it consisted in marking a circle in the dirt, which they then stamped out while hissing and crying out against sin. They also ritually destroyed furniture, jewelry, and fine clothing, much as James Davenport and his followers had done in New London in 1743.[9]

Since they believed that sexual intercourse had been Adam's original sin, it is not surprising that in the warfare against Satan the Shakers gave a great deal of attention to rooting out sexual desire. And while Shakers often insisted to "the world" that like Saint Paul they accepted marriage as a legitimate alternative for those not yet fully regenerate, in fact they did not and could not, given their convictions about the imminence of the Millennium and the origin of human sinfulness. When a visitor declared that marriage was legitimate for Christians, a number of the converts at Canterbury surrounded him, and one woman exclaimed, "O, that's . . . lust, I am ashamed of it!" The crowd began to shout. According to William Plumer, "Their noise was loud, resembling that of geese and bulls, & a violent stamping on the floor." Several of them repeated, over and over, "Damn his devils, damn his devils."[10]

Lust of the flesh was something of an obsession for Whittaker. The *Testimonies* declared that "his spirit was in continual opposition to the ties of carnal nature, and all natural relation." He said that he hated them as he hated "the smoke of the bottomless pit." The fact that he was young and handsome may have complicated his relations with some of the female believers. When Beulah Cooper confessed her "fears and temptations" to him, he stamped on the floor and told her never to tell him anything like that again. She also recalled that if any of the young women tried to touch him, "he would spring away from them" and say they must not touch him, but "when we get into heaven you may hug and kiss me as much as you have a mind to."[11]

Reuben Rathbun declared that the "first Ministers" taught that believers must destroy "the nature of generation, both as to the inclination of the spirit and the natural faculties of the body."[12] In

1783, the destruction of the lusts of the flesh became one of the justifications for the increasingly strenuous character of the "labor" of the dance. A few years later, as we shall see, such "mortification" became the principal purpose of Shaker dance.

According to several of the Shaker apostates, the battle against the lusts of the flesh also included rituals aimed at destroying the natural affections of husband and wife and parent and child. Daniel Rathbun wrote that he was present when Samuel Fitch brought in his own wife, son, and daughter, and solemnly renounced all ties to them. Rathbun added that "under the Mother's ministry" he had witnessed "the greatest abuse from children to parents." One day, in the presence of Ann Lee and a large group of people, he had seen a young Shaker order his father to strip. He then "hauled him about, exclaiming horrible denunciations against *his old heavens.*" Isaac Backus recorded a similar episode in his diary. In September 1783, three Shakers—William Morey, Morrell Baker, and Abigail Pitts—were fined in Taunton, Massachusetts, "for strip[p]ing Pitts's mother naked last May." Surely such scenes were exceptional, but they illustrate the way in which the absolute freedom that the Shakers ascribed to the promptings of the Holy Spirit, coupled with the leadership's obsessions with sexuality, could lead them into rituals of bizarre theatricality.

Many of the Shaker testimonies affirm Ann Lee's special interest in the young believers and her ability to win their devotion. Unlike Whittaker, she hugged them frequently and assured them that they were her favorites. "Thus," Eunice Wild said, "she weaned affections from [their] natural kindred and gathered them to her and to the work of God." It was a task that Joseph Meacham continued by different means. While he was in the process of bringing the Shakers into the "gospel order" of communal life and discipline, he wrote the elders at Hancock that for believers to serve in their new spiritual families, it was essential that they hate "that nature and relation they had by their first birth."[13]

At the end of April 1783, Ann Lee and the elders left the secure haven of Ashfield and returned once again to Harvard. The move is something of a mystery, since their previous experience there had brought continual harassment and occasional persecution. Not only was Ashfield the only place east of the Berkshires where the English Shakers had not been mobbed; it was also a more convenient location for the large number of believers in the Berkshire region of

Massachusetts and New York. On the other hand, it was a small and isolated community, less suitable than Harvard for expanding the Shakers' base into the more populated coastal areas.

At Harvard, they were left unmolested for a month, but then the violence resumed. The Shakers persisted, visiting the believers in several surrounding communities. According to the *Testimonies*, their final meeting in the area was "a very joyful meeting, attended also with sharp war against the flesh and all sin." They then headed west. Bypassing Ashfield, they stayed for a week with Joseph Bennett at Cheshire, north of Pittsfield. A week later, they arrived at the home of the faithful Samuel Fitch. They were back in the region of their first triumphs.[14]

This time, however, they met with opposition there as well. At Hancock, they were attacked by a mob organized by their old antagonist Valentine Rathbun. According to the *Testimonies*, the crowd reviled them with "the most false and scandalous accusations against Mother and the Elders." Rathbun also managed to persuade the civil authorities at Richmond to arrest Ann Lee and the English elders together with Samuel Fitch and two other local Shakers on the charge of "blasphemy and disorderly conduct." According to one Shaker who was there, after they had been taken to the home of the justice of the peace, Ann Lee "looked out of the window and sung a very melodious song and her Brethren below labored in a very lively motion for a short time." Her entire countenance, he added, "showed that her soul was filled with the power and gifts of God."

The charge of blasphemy derived from Fitch's having said that "in Mother Ann, dwells the fullness of the Godhead, bodily." Ann Lee and the English elders were fined twenty dollars and released, on the condition that they leave Massachusetts. The three Americans, having refused to pay bonds for their good behavior, were jailed at Great Barrington.[15]

The *Testimonies* are silent on the nature of the allegations of disorderly conduct, but in his pamphlet Daniel Rathbun contended that it was at this time that he saw "flagrant proof" of what he "had in part seen and so long suspected." On the day that Ann Lee appeared before the justice of the peace, "her drunkenness was manifest to all who saw her." A few days later, when she came to his house after visiting the three prisoners in the Barrington jail, Ann Lee appeared to him to be "as full of what you call the power of God, as ever, and would keep for some time hallowing out aloud, as her usual manner was." Rathbun "knew and could not but think that every one that saw her must know that she had more rum religion than any other at that time."[16]

Daniel Rathbun's pamphlet was not as widely read as his brother Valentine's had been, but it proved to be as damaging. Mary Marshall Dyer included long extracts from it in her various tirades against the Shakers, and both Thomas Brown and William Haskett relied on his allegations in their histories. After having visited Rathbun to inquire further about his charges, Brown decided that he was "a man of veracity and good moral character." Brown also visited Rathbun's son, Daniel Junior, who had left the Shakers after Ann Lee's death. The younger Rathbun supported his father's claims. He told Brown that he had seen both Ann and William Lee drunk on a number of occasions. Asked how he and his father could have continued to believe in the elders' divine mission, he told Brown that he and the other converts "were infatuated, and taught to believe that they were bearing out states, and that it was the evil nature in us imputed or transferred to them; and that they had to suffer thus on our account, and to act that evil spirit and nature out, that we might have a visible sight of that which was still secret within us."[17]

The fact that the Rathbuns were one of the leading families in the Berkshires may have made their testimony weigh more heavily with Brown and other critics of the Shakers than that of other apostates. Valentine's and Daniel's grandfather, Valentine Wightman, had been the first Baptist minister in Connecticut, having founded a church at Groton in 1743, during the Great Awakening. Daniel had been the deacon in Valentine's church in Pittsfield and occasionally preached. Their brother John (who did not join the Shakers) had organized the Baptist church in the nearby settlement of Westford. Since moving to the Berkshires from Connecticut, the Rathbuns had prospered in the clothing business and had been active in local politics. Their published pamphlets and their letters show them to have been men of some education. While they certainly approached the exposure of the Shakers as a kind of crusade, their writings contrast markedly with the scattershot attacks of people like Mary Marshall Dyer.[18]

The Shakers' own testimonies show that they believed that God was communicating with them constantly through physical manifestations of the outpouring of the Holy Spirit in a time that they believed to be the world's last days. It is therefore not surprising that practically anything could be considered to be a divine operation. Angell Matthewson wrote that while Ann Lee had been at Ashfield, people had believed "that the mother actually vomited up the sins of the people." After Ann Lee and her companions had returned to Niskeyuna, she called young Elizabeth Wood to her and said: "See how sick I am & how I have puked. I am under great sufferings for some that are coming here & they will be here soon."[19]

Daniel Rathbun had joined the Shakers together with Valentine and another brother in the spring of 1780. Valentine's quick disenchantment and subsequent zealous opposition had had no apparent effect on his own convictions. When Isaac Backus visited him in 1782, he was appalled at Rathbun's unwillingness to hear any criticism of the Shakers, but he described him as "a man of considerable capacity . . . whose whole family is in the Shaking scheme." After he began to have doubts, however, Rathbun became less zealous. On one occasion, John Partington had chastised him, "thumping" on him, for failing to deny the rumors that Ann Lee got drunk and for not insisting that people were "falsely accusing the people of God."[20]

It is clear that his brother Valentine had encouraged him to publish his allegations against the Shakers after he and his wife left them in 1785. His own pamphlet, while three times the length of Valentine's, is organized similarly, and Valentine wrote the preface. Like Valentine, Daniel Rathbun insisted that he had seen and experienced miraculous things among the Shakers which he had now decided were "lying wonders" sent by Satan. As we shall see, a third Rathbun, Valentine's son Reuben, published a pamphlet of his own in 1800. While at least two of Valentine's children remained Shakers, the rest of the "family of Rathbun" had indeed (as the *Testimonies* put it) become "bitter persecutors."[21]

Does that necessarily mean that they were liars as well? Daniel Rathbun's pamphlet is filled with detailed instances to support his allegations, and Thomas Brown wrote of his son Daniel Junior that he appeared to be "so candid and free from prejudice" that the Shakers themselves "could not have doubted the truth" of his story. Brown was further persuaded by the fact that in many respects Rathbun's account in his pamphlet fit what some of the Shakers themselves had told him "of Mother's bearing the states of the people, even the state of the drunkard."[22]

Rumors of excessive drinking among the Shakers were circulating before Daniel Rathbun's pamphlet appeared. A French traveler who visited New Lebanon a few weeks after Ann Lee's death in 1784 wrote that he was told by people in the town that "her immoderate use of liquors, undoubtedly hastened her end." The same year, Backus wrote in his *History of New-England* that the Shaker leaders "delight themselves much in feasting and drinking spiritous liquor"; and Jeremy Belknap claimed that some of the New Hampshire Shakers began a meeting "by handing round a bottle of rum; of which each taking a large draught became *inspired*." A few years later, a periodical stated that despite the Shakers' denials, it was "notorious" that the use of rum as a means of attaining spiritual experience had been "forcibly inculcated by the mother, both by precept and example, and continue[d] to be so still."[23]

It is worth noting that Valentine Rathbun had made no accusations of immoderate drinking, as he would surely have done if such rumors had been circulating in 1780. Neither does Angell Matthewson in his "Reminiscences," but he had seen Ann Lee and the English elders only on a few occasions and did not move to New Lebanon until after Ann Lee's death. This would be consistent with William Haskett's statement in his history of the Shakers that the practice of using alcohol as a means of generating visions and gifts of the spirit had developed only gradually. Thus it may have become a serious problem only after the leadership's return to the Berkshires.[24]

Cotton Mather was probably being his usual alarmist self when he noted in his diary that "love of *Rum*" was ruining many people in New England, adding that "the Consequences of the affected Bottel" in both Connecticut and Massachusetts were "beyond all imagination." There is ample evidence, though, to indicate that in the eighteenth century distilled spirits had supplanted beer and wine, especially in the inland settlements. Rum, produced in Boston and Newport distilleries from molasses brought from the West Indies, was cheap, portable, and powerful. The diary of Matthew Patten of Bedford, New Hampshire, suggests not only that drinking was the primary act of sociability in the back country, but also that rum was a medium of exchange in communities where money was a scarce commodity and of unstable value. Many of the newer settlements lacked churches; few if any lacked taverns and "tippling houses." *Ames's Almanac for* 1776 included "Sir Richard Rum's Advice" to the soldiers, which warned them that overindulgence would "knock up the heels of them that abuse me and throw them flat on their backs." Thus even if, as their opponents charged, some Shakers were led into over-indulgence in their quest for spiritual experience, the fact of their routine and liberal use of alchohol was neither shocking nor exceptional in the back country environment.[25]

There is no reason to question the Shakers' testimonies concerning their persecution after their return to the Berkshire region, although Edward Deming Andrews noted that the participants' recollections had become "exaggerated and highly colored" over the decades. As with the stories of Ann Lee's persecution in England, the version that emerged in the printed *Testimonies* owed a great deal to Gospel accounts of the life of Jesus. In the history that Eldress Anna White wrote at the end of the nineteenth century, the parallels were spelled out. In calling the Shaker elders' return to New Lebanon "a triumphal procession," White clearly intended to recall Jesus' final visit to Jerusalem. She also described one of Ann Lee's prayers as "the complement of that wonderful prayer in the upper chamber at Jerusalem."[26]

If one relies solely on the printed *Testimonies,* the fury of the opposition is surprising. The revolutionary war had ended, so rumors that the English Shakers were spies no longer made sense. The hostility of people like Valentine Rathbun had its effect, but the several clusters of converts in the Berkshires seem to have been left alone until the arrival of the English leadership in 1783. Stephen Marini has suggested that their style of evangelism, with crowds of believers following in their train and joining in noisy meetings that generally lasted well into the night, aroused opposition in a way that conventional evangelism by itinerant preachers would not have done. That was certainly a factor, but the intensity and persistence of the opposition suggests that the rumors of excesses committed in the name of religion had turned otherwise peaceful people into their violent opponents. After Ann Lee and her companions left, the harassment of the Shakers became less savage, although it persisted. If the later missionary efforts by James Whittaker and others met with anything similar, the Shaker testimonies do not mention it.

The second unanswered question is whether Ann Lee and her companions intended, when they began their missionary tour into New England, to return to Niskeyuna. The Shakers' own narratives suggest that they did. For example, Ann Lee told some of the younger believers at Harvard that they were to make regular pilgrimages to Niskeyuna. Surely if Ann Lee and her companions had intended to resettle at a more central place like Ashfield or Harvard and were then forced by persecution to abandon the project, the Shaker texts would say so.

On the other hand, it is difficult to think of any reason other than persecution for their returning, after two years and four months, to a place as remarkably inconvenient as Niskeyuna, several days' or even weeks' journey away from most of their converts. Perhaps the explanation is that the English Shakers saw themselves only incidentally as preachers and missionaries. They were God's only community of the perfect, and whatever place they happened to be was the mystical Jerusalem. Such a conception provides a useful perspective on the long letter that James Whittaker wrote to his parents from Niskeyuna in 1784. He told them of the persecutions he and the others had endured. God had now commenced "his great and strange work in this land, and is carrying it on by swift degrees; and great are the gifts which come thro' Mother to the people." His soul was now clothed with "the Divine nature." His hope was that the American converts who had been "gathered into obedience" might share "in the enjoyment of the inutterable & transcendent happiness, in beholding the unequalled beauty of Christ," as Whittaker and his companions now experienced it in the New York wilderness.[27]

Considering the richness and variety of information on Ann Lee's journey into New England, there is surprisingly little information on the period between her arrival back in New York in the fall of 1783 and her death a year later. It is clear from the manuscript testimonies that crowds continued to come to see her there, but now they were believers seeking to renew the experience of her special charisma and to receive the spiritual guidance and discipline of "the church." On one occasion, she came into a room filled with people and said: "I was an Angel before I came from England; but now, what do I here, among all these people?" Then she calmed herself, and by her "spirit" sent spiritual gifts into many of those present. She had been heard to remark when this happened that "when the great wheel turns, it sets all the little wheels a going."[28]

During the last year of Ann Lee's life, believers regularly came to see her from as far away as Petersham and Harvard. In the summer of

1784, twenty-five Shakers in New Gloucester, Maine, chartered a boat in order to go to Niskeyuna and see the Mother and her elders for themselves. They sailed down the coast to New York, then up the Hudson to Albany. Then they walked to Niskeyuna, where Ann Lee came out to welcome them, informing them that she had already known by means of visions that they were coming. When Jemima Blanchard arrived from Harvard with five other young Shakers, having traveled two hundred miles across the snow in the middle of winter, Ann Lee said to Calvin Harlow: "These are the very people I have borne in mind and soul all night." Levit Clough came from Canterbury, New Hampshire, but he described a very different reception. He testified to Mary Marshall Dyer that after his arrival, for several days he was told that Ann Lee was "under great sufferings, and could not be seen." When he finally was allowed to meet her, she seemed to be drunk and could not talk coherently.[29]

The fullest description of life at Niskeyuna was provided by Elizabeth Wood, who went there with five other Shakers from Enfield, Connecticut, in 1783. They attended an all-night worship meeting, at which James Whittaker "read and spoke a great deal." At sunrise, they all lay on the floor to rest, covered by a little straw. The room was so crowded that "if one turned over all had to turn also." During the day they worked for the English Shakers. Wood knitted "muffets" for William Lee and slippers for Mary Partington while others sewed. There was worship all night every night; they "had no sitting meetings but labored all the time." They were fed broth for breakfast and broth again for supper.

Wood wanted to remain at Niskeyuna, but Ann Lee told her to return to her family. After a week, her group set out. As they were leaving, William Lee came out of the house and "expressed great thankfulness for the way of God with tears running down his cheeks." When she recorded those experiences at Niskeyuna seventy years later, Elizabeth Wood remembered above all the enormous spiritual power that Ann Lee had exercised over those who came to see her.[30]

The apostate accounts imply that it was also during that year at Niskeyuna that Ann and William Lee introduced one last curious gift of the spirit. When Thomas Brown first joined the Shakers in 1800, he asked several people whether the rumors were true that in Ann Lee's time the believers had danced naked. They assured him that it was not true. He had a long conversation on the subject with Mary Hocknell, who had known Ann Lee since her childhood and had come to America with her in 1774. She absolutely denied it. "There were many operations by the power of God," she said, such as speaking in unknown tongues, trembling, groaning, and sometimes turning round; on account of which people would report we were drunk, as they did formerly about the apostles. . . . And because the brethren pulled of[f] their coats, or outside garments, to labour, or as the world call it, dancing; and in warm weather the sisters being lightly clothed, they would report we danced naked."

Some time later, he talked to a young Shaker named Derrick Veeder, whose family had been neighbors of Ann Lee and her companions at Niskeyuna. Veeder said that the rumors were true. It had "tried" his mind, he said, "because the Elders at first denied it, when they knew it was the truth, and had danced naked themselves." Brown then talked to the elder who had insisted the stories were untrue. This time he admitted that there had been meetings of worship when it had taken place, but to tell young believers about them and to explain that it had been "a real gift of God . . . would have been so out of their sight, they could not see it nor receive it as such."[31]

When Brown then talked to Daniel Rathbun, Jr., Rathbun told him of an episode in which he himself had been involved. One afternoon, William Lee had been drinking "very freely." He assembled about twenty Shakers and told them he "had a gift to rejoice." He ordered them to strip naked and join him. Ann Lee tried to enter the room, but William told her not to, for if women were present, they would "*have war*, that is, have to fight the rising of nature." When she persisted, brother and sister began fighting. The other Shakers intervened; and "thus ended the gift of rejoicing."[32]

Again, is the story an elaborate fabrication? Perhaps not. Even the most bizarre elements are consistent with other pieces of evidence. The testimonies of the Shakers themselves portray William Lee as emotional to the point of instability. His frequent fits of weeping were followed by periods of ecstatic rejoicing. At Harvard, Jemima Blanchard had often heard him say, "Be joyful; joy away, Joy away." Then he would add that there was no one "to say to poor William be joyful." He said of one believer who was possessed by the Holy Spirit: "His tongue praises God, and his hands praise God, and his feet praise God. His whole body is devoted to serve, praise and worship

God." He was fond of pointing out, with an irony that may have been unconscious, that his sister was now his mother as well. "Altho' she is my sister," he would say, "yet she has become my Mother, and the Lord God has made me to love her." The *Testimonies* quoted Whittaker as saying of him after his death that he was "the most violent man against sin that ever my eyes beheld."[33]

The notion that the warfare against Satan included the overcoming of all physical manifestations of sexuality, even of male believers' having erections, is certainly peculiar, but it fits the crude literalism that characterized many of the English Shakers' pronouncements on "lusts of the flesh." William Haskett also accepted Rathbun's story as true. He emphasized in *Shakerism Unmasked* that the ritual of naked dancing was the precise opposite of an orgy. Instead, it represented a celebration of the fact that the believers had transcended the bonds of sin, especially as embodied in their sexuality, and thus had regained the innocence and purity of the Garden of Eden.

Seventeenth-century Quakers and twentieth-century Russian Doukhobors similarly stripped themselves as a sign of their own purity. Matthewson wrote that one of the deacons in the Niskeyuna Shaker community had told him that the "extraordinary gift of God" of dancing naked had been introduced there by Ann Lee herself. She had declared that just as King David had "flung off his clothes & danced naked & behaved as one of the vile fellows," and the prophet Isaiah had "walked naked & barefoot three years for a sign to the people," so the Shakers, whose church had now "risen in a much more enlightened day . . . were certainly able to dance naked & not be ashamed who lived lives of strict self denial." Haskett wrote that Ann Lee berated those who resisted out of modesty, calling them "fleshly creatures" who had not yet been freed from the sense of shame that had been the first product of Adam and Eve's sins of carnality.

Haskett believed that they gradually abandoned ritual nakedness as they came to realize that they could not regain the innocence of the Garden, but the fact that there is no evidence that naked dancing was introduced anywhere except at Niskeyuna suggests that it was practiced only briefly. According to Matthewson's informant, James Whittaker was heard to say to Ann Lee, "If you ever make the people strip naked again, you shall see my face no more." As a result of his intervention, Matthewson says, the practice ended abruptly.[34]

There are a number of other indications of Whittaker's increasing importance. While he accepted the power of the spirit that operated in the night-long meetings and fully believed that Ann Lee was divinely inspired, he was also concerned with creating a framework of order and discipline in which the Spirit would operate. One day at Niskeyuna, Jemima Blanchard encountered him in a hallway with another of the English Shakers, James Shepherd, who was kneeling before him. Whittaker said he would "reprove an Old England Devil as quick as a New England Devil." Shepherd had failed to "unite with the leading gift in meeting." Unlike Ann and William Lee, both of whom urged the believers to follow their "gifts" wherever they led, Whittaker wanted to impose some structure in worship. He seems to have been the only person who addressed the meetings at Niskeyuna, generally warning against sin and damnation.

In organizing affairs at Niskeyuna, he was assisted by Lucy Wright Goodrich, who had been made "caretaker" of the females there while Whittaker and the Lees were on their New England journey. Her husband Elizur had been one of the first converts in the Berkshires. Lucy had been sympathetic to the Shakers, but she had not finally joined them until two years later. Curiously, although Lucy Wright was to lead the Shakers for over thirty years, not one of the testimonies mentions her presence at Niskeyuna. What they remembered was the experience of ecstatic worship, enhanced by the charismatic presence of Ann Lee. Lucy Wright, meanwhile, was responsible for the daily maintenance of a "household" that fluctuated in size between a dozen and fifty or more.[35]

Several former Shakers claimed that Whittaker's ascendancy led to what Reuben Rathbun called "an unhappy disunion." According to them, William Lee had been assured by his sister before they came to America that he was to be second in "the lead," but Whittaker had proven himself to be a much more effective evangelist and leader. Ann Lee was surely remarking on the contrast between Whittaker and her emotional, tearful brother when she said, with her usual directness, "James plants, and William waters."

By the time they had returned to Niskeyuna, William Lee resented his sister's favoring of Whittaker over him. According to several former Shakers, a period of "chaos and confusion" reached a climax with another fight between brother and sister. James Shepherd said that it had been like "war in heaven." As a result of the dissension, some people fell away from the faith, but in the long run Whittaker's increasing influence was decidedly beneficial for the Shakers.[36]

The issue was decided in July 1784 when William Lee died at the age of forty-four. He had been in considerable pain and had bled a great deal. According to the Shaker testimonies, he retained his "zeal and fortitude" to the end. While on his deathbed, he asked Aaron Wood to sing for him one of the wordless spiritual songs. Lee then "danced with great zeal, for a few minutes, and then laid down, and, in a short time expired."[37]

It was after William Lee's death (according to Angell Matthewson) that "visions, dreams, signs, casting out devils & working miracles ceased in the church" and "a day of more regularity & less confusion ensued."[38] It is impossible to tell from the Shaker accounts whether the daily routine that had believers at Niskeyuna working most of the day and "laboring" for gifts of the Spirit most of the night was modified. It probably was not. Descriptions of worship services after Whittaker became "Father James" indicate that they remained just as strenuous and nearly as lengthy. There was a significant difference, however. Ann Lee had always manifested in herself and elicited in others a great range of ecstatic experiences and possessed behaviors, but most of the time the prevailing mood seems to have been one of celebration, of rejoicing in the presence of the divine. Under Whittaker's leadership, the gifts of the Spirit were generally those of mortification, forcing believers to confront and overcome their own sins, especially those of sexuality.

It was a time of consolidation. There were few if any new converts. Instead, in a process typical of many religious sects, the Shakers, in their scattered communities and family groupings, drew inward, entirely caught up in the regimen of work and worship. At Canterbury, many people left the Shakers, but that may have been exceptional. Given the Shaker histories' silence about that period, it is impossible to tell.[39]

Then, quite unexpectedly, Ann Lee herself died on 8 September. According to the *Testimonies,* after her brother's death she "began to decline in bodily strength." When Ollive Miller was at Niskeyuna a few days before Ann Lee's death, the Mother was in seclusion. Two women led her onto the porch, "and walked with her back and forth; then returned to her room." Shaker tradition has ascribed her death to the violence she had endured during the tour of New England. The hostile accounts, on the other hand, claimed that excessive drinking had killed her. For at least fifteen years, day and night, she had been undergoing almost continuous ecstatic experience, ranging from visions of heaven and hell to vicarious suffering for the sins of others, living and dead. Surely such a life was exhausting, both emotionally and physically.

Her death was reported in the Albany *Gazette:* "Departed this life, at Nisqueunia, . . . Mrs. Lee, known by the appellation of the *Elect Lady* or *Mother of Zion,* and head of that people called Shakers. Her funeral is to be attended this day."[40] Many did attend the funeral, possibly the first large influx of people from "the world" to visit the Shakers at Niskeyuna in several years.

Not surprisingly, her death precipitated a new crisis among the Shakers. While Ann Lee had never claimed to be immortal, many believers apparently had decided that she was. In addition, it should be remembered that one of the most explicit Shaker doctrines concerned the imminence of the Millennium. The mystical incorporation of the entire world into the only true church was to be a matter of a few years at most. It was inconceivable that Ann Lee, who as prophet and spiritual comforter held a unique place in the Shaker plan, should not be present when the great event occurred. The leadership's explanation of her demise, that she had been chosen by God to fill a vacant place in heaven, must have sounded rather lame to many believers.[41]

Without Ann Lee, Shakerism changed. Her successors created structures of leadership and community where she had been content to follow the immediate guidance of the spirit. Neither Whittaker nor Joseph Meacham had her distinctive ability to elicit in believers a curious combination of fear, awe, and love. Among the Shakers, the gifts of the spirit did not disappear, but they would never again be so spectacular, not even in the period of spiritual visitations fifty years later that was known as "Mother Ann's Work."

Of all those in the eighteenth century who sought new revelations through direct experience of divinity, only the Shakers had placed the Pentecostal infusion of the Holy Spirit at the absolute center. For those believers whose faith could withstand the shock of Ann Lee's death, the notion that that spirit now resided most fully in her chosen successor made perfect sense.

{10}

The Gathering
into Order

About six weeks after Ann Lee's death, the Shakers at Niskeyuna had some distinguished visitors. The Marquis de Lafayette, the young hero of the revolutionary war, walked there from Albany, accompanied by one of the Virginia delegates to the Continental Congress, James Madison. They had been joined for the trip by France's principal diplomat in the new republic, the Marquis de Barbé-Marbois. Lafayette had been fascinated by the entranced behavior exhibited by the Parisian patients of Dr. Mesmer's new mental science and was curious to find out if these Shakers' possessions were similar.

Barbé-Marbois's account of their visit provides the first outsider's description of Shaker worship since the English elders' departure from Harvard. Some one hundred forty believers assembled in a large wooden "hall," men at one end and women at the other. The service began with sermons delivered by three preachers, among whom there was "no distinction of clothes or rank." Having listened to the sermons, Barbé-Marbois concluded that the Shakers' religious doctrines were "not yet well established." One of the preachers spoke against marriage, on the grounds that Jesus had had no "carnal connection" with women. Another declared that some of the Shakers were "inaccessible to sin." The speakers mentioned Ann Lee's death, stating that she had gone directly to heaven, "through some promotion."[1]

In describing the dancing that followed, Barbé-Marbois noted only that many of the participants were able to "pirouette on a single leg, with surprising rapidity." That might suggest that possession phenomena were coming under some kind of control, and that some of the bizarre gifts of the spirit that had so astonished William Plumer at Canterbury and Harvard were no longer manifesting themselves at

Niskeyuna. Barbé-Marbois also noted, however, that he saw Shakers go into convulsions at all sorts of odd times: while at work, while traveling, even during conversation. They would turn their heads back and forth, their eyes closed or turned upwards, "with an expression which proclaims ecstasy, anguish, and pain." The women would sometimes weep; the men "raised their arms, trembling; their knees gave way and knocked together." As the convulsions gradually faded, they sighed and resumed their activities.[2]

Other sources confirm the impression that while Whittaker made important changes in other facets of Shaker life, Ann Lee's belief that the power of the Holy Spirit must not be hindered in any way continued to be central to religious experience. John Farrington told young Calvin Green (whose autobiography is rich in details concerning the Whittaker and Meacham years) that once while he was traveling with Whittaker, he was visited by a strange "gift" of the spirit that surprised and embarrassed him. Whittaker told him that he must never be ashamed of a spiritual gift or he would lose it.[3]

An anonymous manuscript in the Connecticut Historical Society describing a visit to Enfield in 1785 indicates that the worship services there were quite similar to what Lafayette and Barbé-Marbois witnessed at Niskeyuna. Several preachers spoke, declaring that it was the time of Christ's second coming and that he "was manifested in the flesh" by the Shakers. After each of the sermons, solemn, wordless songs were sung, accompanied by "groaning sighing and shaking." Then, as the first preacher hummed a popular tune called "The Soldier's Joy," the group "began a violent dancing without any kind of order," with the men at one side of the room and the women at the other. Some individuals whirled for long periods. While all this was going on, the participants sweated profusely.

That phase of worship was concluded by the same loud clapping of hands that Angell Matthewson had heard when he first encountered the Shakers at Ashfield. The group then performed a ritual of solemn celebration which embodied in word and gesture the mystical union of heaven and earth that was at the core of Shaker belief. Some of the men gathered and held out their hands, as if they were supporting something. One of them declared that "this is our altar and our altar is love and none can build this altar or sacrifice upon it but the pure of heart." The rest repeated the words. As they resumed their ecstatic dancing, one of the Shakers declared: "The dead should be buried, yes we will bury the dead, but we are alive and we will sacrifice on our altar, communion, union, love, we will love one another."[4]

These two outsiders' descriptions of Shaker worship suggest that Ann Lee's death had not changed the movement in any essential way. Their services continued to be in a sense public performances, strange yet structured, mixtures of preaching, wordless singing, convulsions, and prodigies of whirling and leaping that went on for hours, always responsive to verbal and gestural cues from the leadership. The Shakers' sacred theater continued to generate a kind of collective ecstasy that was both a religious experience and an emotional release.

That Whittaker was now the Shakers' leader seems to have been accepted with little or no dispute. Matthewson said that after Ann Lee's death, "all eyes looked up to him as a teacher sent from God." He had long been acknowledged to be their ablest preacher, and his special relationship with Ann Lee had been demonstrated on many occasions. Brown wrote of him that he was "generally respected and believed to be sincere, even by those who were not members of the society." Several Shakers told him that they had "really loved Whittaker." Reuben Rathbun, who frequently accompanied him on his journeys, wrote: "I loved him as I did my own life."[5]

On the other hand, Whittaker could not and probably never intended to succeed Ann Lee in her role as prophetess. Moreover, she had been considered by believers to be the woman "clothed with the sun" who Saint John the Divine had said would appear at the commencement of the Millennium. But Ann Lee was gone; it was Whittaker's task to interpret what her absence implied for belief and practice. How were Shakers to proceed with the conversion of the world? In the two years before his sudden death at the age of thirty-six, Whittaker took several initiatives that his successors would implement in much more detail.

Because it would hinder the work of the Holy Spirit, the Shakers had always refused to write down their doctrines, but an article in the *American Magazine* in 1787 suggests that under Whittaker's leadership they were beginning to develop a theology. Their beliefs were recorded at a "public conference" which the writer unhelpfully noted was held "in Massachusetts." The so-called persons of the Trinity, the Shakers told him, were instead emanations of a single divine power. The Holy Spirit was continually present on earth, but conversions came only "from the word of the mother." Their possessed "labour" could be "any bodily work" that emanated from a spiritual "gift." Their singing, dancing, whirling, weeping, and fits of laughter were all of them "means for mortifying the body and waking up the soul." Ann Lee was described in the same apocalyptic terms that the Shakers had used during her lifetime. She was the "elect lady" mentioned in the second epistle of Saint John and the woman clothed with the sun in the book of Revelation. She was "everywhere present, as God himself is." The Scriptures were true, and their prophecies had been fulfilled "except what is now completing in the Shakers."

All of these ideas were virtually identical with those that the English Shakers had brought with them to America in 1774, but with one important addition. Believers must not only confess their sins and renounce marriage; they must also "yield up" themselves and everything they possess "to the disposal of the church."[6] That last commandment, already anticipated in the Niskeyuna, Harvard, and Canterbury communities and articulated in Whittaker's letter to a believer in Hancock, laid the foundation for the Shakers' communal gathering that Joseph Meacham was to accomplish after Whittaker's death. It should be emphasized that for Whittaker the command to give up everything to the church was also intended to initiate a determined effort to convert the entire world to Shakerism. During the next decades, the two projects proceeded together: the formation of communes steadily and gradually, the evangelization of the world by fits and starts.

The most curious project for the world's conversion involved building an ocean-going ship to transport missionaries around the world. According to Matthewson, the plan had been first proposed by Ann Lee, but Brown and Haskett both insist that it was Whittaker's idea. Calvin Green's biography of Meacham, so richly detailed on other periods of his life, says only that during the time of Whittaker's leadership Meacham was engaged "almost continually in labors and journeys." Other sources indicate that these journeys were connected with the plan to evangelize the world. Matthewson wrote in his "Reminiscences" that while the boat was being built at Rehoboth, Massachusetts, the missionary pairs led by Meacham, Cooley, and Harlow traveled through New England "preaching to the people to be ready to sail when the ship was ready to sail." Reuben Rathbun said that after Whittaker told him to sell his possessions and go out as a missionary, he traveled to Connecticut, where he was arrested at New London and jailed for four months.[7]

A final piece of evidence confirms the ex-Shakers' claims that Whittaker proposed that the Shakers make a massive effort to convert the world. Only two months after Ann Lee's death, Whittaker received a letter from Henry Van Schaack, one of Hancock's leading citizens and an outspoken defender of the Shakers. Van Schaack wrote that he had heard that they intended to "quit their present possessions and seek for an uncertain residence elsewhere." He urged Whittaker to reconsider. In all likelihood, the catalyst for Whittaker's renewal of missionary activity, after a year's hiatus, was the death of his spiritual mother and mentor. It may have been a corollary of the idea that her death must necessarily have cosmic significance. When Daniel Rathbun left the Shakers in 1785, he complained specifically of Whittaker's "new dispensation and ministration, at which the Mother is exalted above Christ, and her apostles above his."[8]

A few months before Ann Lee's death, Whittaker had written to the Shaker remnant still in England to urge them to "come over into this country for the gospels sake." Even after the plan to send a boatload of missionaries to Europe had been abandoned, Whittaker contemplated traveling to England himself. As he prepared for his departure, he wrote Meacham that "it Remaines uncertain whether I shall return or not but Love [sic] all matters with God."

Whittaker arrived in New York City after his ship had sailed. He therefore resumed his arduous journeys to the scattered settlements in New England. Two members of the original English party, John Partington and John Hocknell, did sail to England, despite Whittaker's objections. They returned a year later, but in 1788 Partington and another of the original group, James Shepherd, left the Shakers. Two other English Shakers, Richard Hocknell and Nancy Lee, had left the group after Whittaker's accession and had married. All of these developments, including the aborted project to convert the world, suggest that the English Shakers were uncomfortable with the realization that their church was turning into a sect of the American back country, less and less in tune with the odd but compelling sense of divine immanence that Ann Lee had instilled in them.[9]

Three of the ex-Shakers wrote about the boat that was to have carried missionaries back across the Atlantic. The accounts vary in details, but generally they tell the same story. After the Shaker leadership abandoned the plan (for whatever reason), two of the leading Shakers in southeastern Massachusetts, Morrell Baker and William Morey, fitted out the ship as a trading vessel and filled it with cargo, which they intended to sell in the West Indies. They made at least two trading voyages, but with little success, and they therefore returned home and sold the ship for considerably less than it had cost to build it. The Shakers of Rehoboth and Norton, who had contributed to the project at the urging of the leadership, were understandably disenchanted. There were also stories of sexual misconduct during the voyages.[10] The failure of the project may help to explain the fact that no Shaker community was established in southeastern Massachusetts, despite its volatile history of religious radicalism and perfectionism and the English Shakers' success there in 1782.

Thus Whittaker's projected evangelization of the world was a failure. If anyone at all was converted, no testimony was left of it. It was to be another ten years before the Shakers again actively sought converts. Meanwhile, Whittaker had commenced the more important of his initiatives, as he attempted to persuade the believers scattered across New England to form self-sufficient communities.

The Shakers' printed *Testimonies* are not very informative on Whittaker's activities during the period of his leadership. They consist instead of his remembered sayings, organized so as to suggest that he had anticipated the communal structures and godly discipline that became Shakerism's most remarkable features. For example, Lucy Wright, the Shakers' future leader, recalled that Whittaker said that after his death there would be a great increase in membership, but that it would be accomplished "through an increase of union, and in no other way." He was frequently quoted as expressing concern for the younger Shakers, who had joined as children. One person remembered his saying during a visit to New Lebanon that if they were "protected, the time will come, when they will be the flower of the people of God."[11]

He visited all the towns and villages in New England where Shakers were established, some of them several times. Matthewson described Whittaker's visit to the little group of believers at Shelburne, Massachusetts, near Ashfield. After they had all gathered at Jonathan Wood's house, Whittaker declared that there was "a day of immortal judgment at hand," and therefore all must confess their sins privately to him or one of the other elders. He was especially concerned to discover any "fallings out with their breathren or sisters" so that they "might be settled & brotherly love be restored." They all then "worshipped in the dance" until evening. "The church" then departed for New Lebanon, where they had a service of outdoor worship, consisting of "singing the sweet songs of Zion, doctrine, exhortation, & the dance." Whittaker declared that this was the place that God had chosen for worship at New Lebanon from then on.[12]

Clearly, Whittaker had recognized that Niskeyuna could develop no further as a Shaker settlement. New Lebanon was much more convenient, and the generosity of several of the converts meant that there was ample land on which to establish a settlement. He ordered that a meetinghouse be built at the designated site, which had been part of David Darrow's farm. Completed in the fall of 1785, the meetinghouse was the first building that the Shakers had set aside specifically for worship. Its construction must also have suggested to believers that the Millennium was not so imminent as they had believed it to be. In building the meetinghouse and urging believers to settle near it, Whittaker anticipated Meacham's designation of the New Lebanon community as the economic and spiritual center of Shakerism.[13]

In the last year of his life, Whittaker devoted most of his efforts to the formation of similar "community neighborhoods" throughout New England. In addition to New Lebanon and Niskeyuna in New York and Enfield in Connecticut, they included six in Massachusetts, not only at the future communal sites of Hancock, Tyringham, Harvard, and Shirley but also at Richmond and Pittsfield in the Berkshires. At Canterbury, New Hampshire, the formation of an economic community had already been initiated by Benjamin Whitcher and Henry Clough. After Whittaker visited the Shakers in Maine in the summer of 1785, a community was organized at Alfred. On his advice, the believers there built a large "place of worship" that contained two rooms in the attic for the use of the traveling ministers who visited there twice a year. In many other places, including Ashfield, Massachusetts, and New Gloucester (Sabbathday Lake), Maine, Shakers came together for worship but lived in their own houses as "out families," a practice which, although discouraged, continued for several decades.

The Shakers in Enfield, New Hampshire, continued on their erratic course. In his history of the community, Henry Blinn wrote that they lived widely dispersed, with their natural families and their "unbelieving husbands, or wives." Although Whittaker and other ministers visited them several times, the Enfield group refused to accept their authority.[14]

The resistance in Enfield (and probably elsewhere) to Whittaker's initiatives, together with the failure of the Shakers' efforts to win new converts, led to the decision to "withdraw the testimony" that had been "opened" in 1780. According to Reuben Rathbun, the command to sell their possessions on behalf of the missionary effort was declared to have been "a gift to try their faith." Thereafter, the traveling ministry dedicated all their efforts to bringing the believers into a communal and spiritual order.

The task had exhausted Whittaker by the time he left New Lebanon for the last time in January 1787. He rested briefly at the Meacham family home in Enfield, Connecticut, and then resumed his travels, accompanied by three of the leading American converts, Joseph Meacham, David Meacham, and Calvin Harlow. He was visiting the communities and out-families in the Harvard area when illness forced him to return to Enfield, accompanied by Harlow and David Meacham. He left Joseph Meacham in charge at Harvard. Many believers came to visit him at Enfield before he died there on 21 July, exactly three years after the death of William Lee.[15]

Since Whittaker had never claimed that he was Ann Lee's successor as seer and fulfiller of biblical prophecy, his death did not cause the same crisis of belief among Shakers that hers had. On the other hand, he had maintained that there must be a central spiritual authority, embodied in a "church," a few sinless individuals who were divinely called to hear the confessions and supervise the conduct of those who were "traveling" toward perfection. The only remaining English Shaker who might conceivably have succeeded Whittaker as head of "the church" was the aged John Hocknell, but he had never been involved in the missionary work as preacher or confessor. By default and of necessity, the new leadership would be American.

Shaker and ex-Shaker testimonies agree that the men who emerged during Whittaker's last illness as his likeliest successors were the three who had accompanied him on his last journey: Harlow and the two Meachams. A history of the New Lebanon community published in the Shaker's journal *The Manifesto* stated that before he died Whittaker had designated them jointly to continue the work.

Matthewson affirmed that upon their return to New Lebanon they declared that they were the "joint ministry."

All three had spoken at the funeral. According to Calvin Green, as Joseph Meacham spoke he "was filled with the holy spirit, and shook greatly by the mighty power of God." After their return to New Lebanon, Meacham sent his brother and Harlow to visit the other Shaker communities. He began to "discipline" the New Lebanon and Niskeyuna believers as the first step toward imposing a fully articulated religious and social order upon them. When his two colleagues returned to New Lebanon, they were so impressed with what he had accomplished that they acknowledged his leadership.[16]

In his history of the Shakers, Edward Deming Andrews wrote: "Eliminate the influence of Joseph Meacham, and the church would probably not long have survived the death of [Ann Lee], or merited more than a footnote in the social, economic, or religious history of America."[17] It was Meacham who transformed Whittaker's intentions into elaborate and coherent structures, overseen by an equally elaborate hierarchy of elders and deacons endowed with supreme power in all matters. Henceforth everything, even the gifts of the Holy Spirit, would be subject to the hierarchy's approval.

Meacham had been held in high regard by the English Shakers, but the nineteenth-century tradition that has Ann Lee naming him as the future leader is surely apocryphal. It is possible, however, that soon after his conversion he felt himself called to lead the Shakers. Calvin Green wrote that Meacham "had been a Believer a short time only, before he saw by revelation that he should be called yet to lead the people." He dedicated himself to a severe regimen of "mortification & abstinence" in order to attain sinless perfection by overcoming all sexual desire. While the Shaker theory of the dispensation of the "gifts" of entranced behavior presupposed that they were immediate and miraculous, Green implied that Meacham had taught himself to be a possessed performer. Since he had "naturally no faculty for the dance," he set out with zeal to attain that as well. As a result, "he gained perhaps the most complete, extraordinary active gift in all kinds of labor in the worship of God that ever has been gained by anyone."[18]

When Whittaker left Meacham in charge of the believers at Harvard and returned to Enfield to die, Meacham immediately began to establish a strict economic and religious order. He brought cattle from Enfield and ordered that part of the beef be "consecrated" to the use of the traveling ministry and the rest distributed among the poorer members. He gathered the Shakers together and spoke of the importance of "being joined to the lead." Just as all parts of the human body obeyed the head, so should the members of the body of Christ. "No one will ever find the kingdom of God," he said, "unless they are joined in this body of union."[19]

Meacham knew exactly what he wanted to accomplish. He neither sought nor received the boundless love and affection that Ann Lee and Whittaker had inspired in many believers, but the universally high regard in which he was held, the force and dedication with which he carried out his reforms, and the charisma he exercised over those with whom he came in contact made him a remarkably effective leader from the outset.

At New Lebanon, his first step in bringing the Shakers into what he called "church order" was to select a group of believers whom he designated as the "first order." They were to worship separately from the rest, because they were so much farther advanced in their "spiritual travel." Every day, they worshiped first, while the others stood in a ring and watched. Then the first order retired and the rest of the believers had their worship of song and dance.[20]

His next act was to name Lucy Wright as his coadjutor "in the female line." It will be remembered that Ann Lee had placed her in charge of the care and feeding of the English Shakers at Niskeyuna and the believers who came to visit them there. She had continued to carry out these functions during the three years of Whittaker's leadership. For the next ten years, Meacham worked closely and in complete harmony with her in the work of bringing the Shakers into order. In a letter he wrote to her shortly before his death in 1796, he told her that she had been "one whom I esteem my Equal in order and Lots according to thy sex." They had worked in close "union . . . for the Good of the Whole." Thus God had "Laid the foundation In & by us for the Gathering and Building of the Churches."[21]

Because of the doctrine of celibacy a separation of the sexes had always been implicit in Shakerism. It now became a basis of its theology and its communal structuring. It is tempting to theorize (but impossible to prove) that the "spiritual union" between male and female was also a conscious expression of the notion of bisexual divinity that was so important in English and German popular mysticism in the seventeenth and eighteenth centuries.

There now began the formation of the communistic societies that in the nineteenth century were to win the universal admiration of the very same "world" that they were designed to transcend. Employing the language of the New England Puritan tradition, Meacham called it the "gathering" of the faithful into "gospel order" or "church relation." Shortly after the process had begun at New Lebanon and Niskeyuna, he told the Harvard Shakers that it was the fulfilment of the prophecy of Saint John the Divine of the creation of "a New Heaven and a new Earth." Henceforth the Shakers would consecrate all their "substance to the God of the whole earth," while at the same time laboring to "gain an exceeding righteousness."[22]

From all over New England, believers were called to New Lebanon. Some were chosen because they had skills that the community would need, others because their spiritual attainments would aid others to grow toward perfection. Throughout the fall and winter of 1787, Shakers arrived, finding living quarters in whatever huts, cabins, or barns were available. On Christmas Day, they shared a communal meal. The event must have seemed strange to these former New Light Puritans, since the celebration of Christmas had been actively discouraged in New England. The leaders explained that it had been regularly kept by Ann Lee and the English Shakers in their cabin in the wilderness at Niskeyuna. When Meacham and Wright compiled the "Millenial Laws" of Shaker belief and practice, Christmas was singled out as the chief holiday, on which "believers should make perfect reconciliation, one with an other." It may have been only a coincidence, but it is worth recalling that it had been on Christmas in 1707 that the French Prophets had first introduced their ceremony of communion and reconciliation in the love feast.[23]

In the spring, the Shakers began to put up the buildings in which the community would live and work. In his autobiography, Calvin Green described what life had been like at New Lebanon in 1788. He was only eight years old. His mother was living elsewhere, and because his father was a member of the elite first order (soon to be known as the Church Family), Calvin could not live with him. He therefore boarded with various families. He worked as a "chore boy," assisting some men who were making bricks. Since there was a drought that year, food was scarce and without variety. They lived on salt meat and its broth, some fish, and potatoes, which for a time was their principal food. Green wrote: "In short, we labored hard & lived poor, & had crowded & poor accomodation [*sic*] for shelter." How could God have permitted a drought when the millenial church was being created? Green decided that it was a test of their dedication and "a sign" of the spiritual famine of the times, which had seen no religious revivals for years.[24]

At Niskeyuna, the Shakers had formed two large households, headed by David Meacham and Hezekiah Noble. Each consisted of some twenty people. At about the same time that the community began to be formed at New Lebanon, they too were gathered into order at Joseph Meacham's direction. Jonathan Clark recalled that the believers lived on a diet of rice and milk, cooked together, and occasionally sturgeon caught in the Hudson River. After spending the spring and summer in strenuous farm labor, they "looked more like skeletons than working men." Living conditions were impossibly crowded. Fifteen people slept on the floor in one room: "Some had one blanket to cover them, while others had none, and nought for a pillow . . . but a handkerchief or a chair turned down." After the harvest came in, they too lived mainly on potatoes. The drought had caused a real famine among the settlers on the frontier to the north on Lake George. The people of Albany sent them food, and they hired Clark and some other young Shakers to transport it. With the money they earned, the Niskeyuna group was able to buy flour and other food for themselves.[25]

At New Lebanon, the house for the hundred men and women of the first order was completed in November. They proceeded to form a "joint union" that was separate not only from the godless world but also from the rest of the Shaker community. They were to dedicate themselves to crafts and manufacture that could be carried out indoors and to the perfection of their own spirituality.

The rest of the believers were placed in two lesser orders, depending on their age, their economic function in the Shaker community, and the distance of their "spiritual travel." The second order consisted of young men and women who worked outside in the fields. The third order contained the most recent converts, the comparatively few aged Shakers, and those who were unwilling to commit their economic resources entirely to the community. Henceforth, any contact between the spiritual orders was forbidden. If a member of one of the lower orders addressed anyone from the first order, Matthewson said, "they would shake their heads & groan but not answer; shut their eyes and look the other way."

As the system evolved, a pair of elders was named to oversee spiritual and disciplinary matters for the men within each order, and a pair of deacons or trustees to supervise the economic activities. As the women were brought into their parallel order, eldresses and deaconesses were appointed to supervise their activities. The titles and the division of functions recalled the Congregational and Baptist polities from which nearly all the Shakers had come, but their authority was enormously extended because it derived from the continuous manifestation of the Holy Spirit, as revealed to Joseph Meacham. He and Lucy Wright fully acknowledged that their conception of order effectively superseded the unrestrained reliance on the impulses of the Holy Spirit that had been absolutely central to the English Shakers' message. When believers asked Lucy Wright why actions that were permitted "when Mother was here" were now forbidden, she answered that "such things are not allowed; we do not allow disorder."[26]

Once formed into orders, the New Lebanon Shakers made an oral covenant to be mutually bound to their joint interest as a community. In all the Shaker communities, the oral covenants were later replaced by similar written covenants signed by all the members.[27] The practice of covenanting together was yet another Puritan tradition that Meacham adapted to his vision of the pure church of the saints.

Utilizing the skills and trades that the first order's members had practiced in the world, the New Lebanon community quickly established a wide range of crafts and manufactures to complement its farming activities. For example, Joseph Bennett, who conducted the Church Family's business affairs, had been a storekeeper in Cheshire, Massachusetts. Valentine Rathbun, Jr., made cloth, as Rathbuns had done for three generations.

By 1791, the products manufactured at New Lebanon and sold on consignment by a local storekeeper included whips, felt hats, pails, tubs, shoes and boots, saddles, nails, buckles, and sheep skins. In the other communities, the same expansion from farming into manufacturing accompanied their formal gathering into gospel order. At Canterbury, the products that were produced for sale included—in addition to leather, iron, and cloth goods—clocks, candlesticks, and wagons. Nothing that was merely frivolous was produced; none of the manufactures were ever ornamented or decorated.

Thanks in part to intensive cultivation and in part to the purchase of additional land, farm production increased dramatically. In 1789, the New Lebanon community produced 3,000 bushels of potatoes as well as wheat, rye, oats, flax, barley, and corn. Early in the 1790s, the Shakers at New Lebanon and Niskeyuna (now called Watervliet) began harvesting and selling garden seeds, which quickly became their most popular product. For more than a century, Shaker seeds were sold by mail throughout the country. As with all Shaker products, they were renowned for unmatched quality.[28]

All of these enterprises were carried out by the men. The spiritual equality of women in Shakerism did not lead to their economic emancipation. A visitor to New Lebanon in 1797 noted that while the women worked just as hard as the men, their time was entirely taken up with cooking, weaving, and "above all with ceaseless laundry. Cleanliness is one of the tenets of this society."

Visitors to the communities were astonished at how much they had accomplished in such a short time. After visiting the Shakers at Shirley, Massachusetts, in 1795, the Reverend William Bentley of Salem noted in his diary that in the few years since he had last been there they had established "a settlement at their ease out of the most disorderly enthusiasm." Three hundred people lived on the 3,000 acres they had acquired or purchased. Throughout the community, walls and fences were "as straight as they can be made."[29]

The communities that Meacham and his lieutenants created were consciously designed to represent, spatially and metaphorically, the tenets of Shaker doctrine as they had been modified by him. They were, in effect, stage sets, designed to serve as perpetual reminders to believers and visitors alike that heaven had come to earth in the ordered polity of the Shakers. Meacham realized that the contrast between the severe simplicity of the Shaker communities and the haphazard arrangement of most villages in the New England back country would make a strong impression on visitors. When he visited Harvard in 1791 in order to prepare the believers for their gathering into gospel order, he told them that their fields and gardens should all be planted in straight rows because "this will be preaching to the world[,] for they admire the beautiful outward order of the people of God."

The geometric simplicity and precision that was the most striking feature of all of the communities was the visual representation of the obsessive orderliness that at Meacham's direction now permeated every part of Shaker experience. Everything, every single detail of work and worship, must correspond to the hierarchy of spirituality which for Meacham permeated the universe. He prohibited any mingling of animal species in the pastures and barns or even the grafting of a branch of one fruit tree on another species. It was also wrong to be overly "familiar" with animals because "it would corrupt the animals by raising them out of their order." Matthewson wrote that when workmen at New Lebanon built the office in which David Meacham would conduct the community's business affairs, they put a square roof on it. Joseph Meacham decreed that such a roof was not in "church order." The workmen therefore replaced it overnight with a gambrel roof.[30]

These were all external, earthly reflections of the cosmic order as Meacham conceived it. Animals and buildings were only animals and buildings, but every human being was on a spiritual pilgrimage toward salvation. The former worship practices had been suspended; no longer were the Shakers permitted to achieve the transcendence and emotional catharsis of their possessed litanies of solemn and festive celebration. Within the communities, the believers were instead performers in a very different sort of sacred theater for every moment of every day, as they worked, ate, worshiped, or lay straight in their beds at night.

Meacham told the New Lebanon Shakers that their conversion to Shakerism had been only the commencement of their spiritual new birth, which entirely obliterated the ties and obligations of the world. "For every one that hateth that nature and relation they had by their first birth," Meacham said, "is a help to the body in their own order and calling."[31]

Once the New Lebanon community was established, members of the first order were sent out to the other Shaker centers to bring them into conformity and prepare them for their own gathering into "church relation." Meacham himself traveled tirelessly throughout New England until his health began to fail. After several visits to the unruly believers in Enfield, New Hampshire, he persuaded them to accept the leaders he had designated. They were "not to look beyond their immediate lead for counsel and instruction, in any case whatsoever." Eleven families moved to Enfield from other settlements in New Hampshire. When the 1790 census was taken, fourteen people were living at Benjamin Merrill's farm and thirty-one at Zadock Wright's.[32]

The 1790 census shows that the same process of joining together in agricultural collectives was also going on elsewhere, before the Shakers were formally gathered into communal order. Twenty-eight people lived at Benjamin Pease's home in Enfield, Connecticut, where a meetinghouse had been built four years earlier. In the frontier settlement at Bakerstown Plantation, Maine, there were seventeen people living with Eliphus Ring, sixteen with Nathan Merrill, and twenty-four with Edmund Merrill. A few years later, they would comprise the nucleus of the Sabbathday Lake community. In the Berkshires there were even larger collectives that were never formed into communities, possibly because suitable and sufficient land was not available. There was one at Richmond and another at Stockbridge. There were two at Williamstown, far from any Shaker community.

In late 1790, the Shakers in Hancock, Massachusetts, followed New Lebanon into gospel order. Once again, the process was launched by holding a celebration of Christmas, as it had been observed by Ann Lee and the English Shakers. Calvin Harlow then taught them "how to keep our order as a family" through "being united with the gift of God in those sent to us from the Church." Two weeks later, Meacham himself arrived with three other leaders from New Lebanon. He told the Hancock believers that "there was not one soul upon earth could find relation to God without him." He selected twenty men and twenty women to comprise the first order at Hancock. Harlow had received the divine gift to be their leader and was to be obeyed in all things. Harlow described to them the social and economic organization of the New Lebanon community. Conforming to New Lebanon's example in everything was "the only way of saf[e]ty and protection in things both spiritual and temporal." After designating the men and women who were to oversee the organization of the Hancock community, Harlow went with his assistants to Enfield, Connecticut, where he launched the same gathering into order.[33]

In 1791, the believers at Harvard and Shirley were gathered in the same manner, again under the supervision of elders and eldresses sent from the first order at New Lebanon. During the next three years, the

New Hampshire and Maine communities were also brought into order. Most of the Shakers at Canterbury were moved to other communities, and people from New Lebanon and from Enfield, New Hampshire, were sent there in their place. The Canterbury group had been living communally for ten years; quite possibly they had their own ideas about how a community should be organized. Henceforth, they were told, they were "to follow the example of the Mother Church at New Lebanon in all things."

As the believers were brought into order, every aspect of their lives was strictly regulated. There were appointed times for meetings, for eating meals, for getting up and for going to bed. The Shakers at Canterbury were taught "to walk together in union from place to place . . . in file, two abre[a]st, each stepping right and left together." There was to be no communication with believers assigned to the other orders or families, except by their elders and deacons.

As had been the case at New Lebanon and Niskeyuna, life at Hancock was difficult and conditions crowded during the first year after the gathering into order. Everyone, including the women, helped to erect the buildings for the community. The women also cooked for the men and worked each day at "spinning, weaving, &c." At Canterbury, the men spent the winter building a meetinghouse, assisted by a few women who cooked and washed for them. The following spring, Hannah Goodrich and Anna Burdick arrived from New Lebanon to gather eight women into the communal order.[34]

The establishment of eleven thriving communal societies on the unpromising soil of the New England hill country was remarkable enough. The fact that the people who built them had been accustomed to independence and very little social and political restraint made it more remarkable still. On the other hand, Meacham was able to draw upon a Puritan tradition that had always been concerned with the ordering of society into a godly polity that reflected a hierarchy of spiritual attainments. Moreover, the American Shakers were not alone among the radical Pietists and New Lights of the late eighteenth and early nineteenth centuries in their belief that the Christian life, properly understood, implied a restructuring of society and the introduction of some kind of collective economy, modeled on the example of the primitive Christian churches of the Roman Empire.[35]

The economic success of the Shaker communities, unmatched by any other communal experiment in history, tends to obscure the fact that Meacham and his lieutenants also succeeded in reordering the Shakers' belief structures, on which everything else rested. The direct intervention of the Holy Spirit was not repudiated, yet it was now entirely controlled by Meacham's appointed leaders.

After an entire generation of Shakers had grown up under the new system, Ann Lee became the female embodiment of Christ, the divine messenger at the end of history. In the Meacham era, however, her importance was less than it had been in her own lifetime or during the period of Whittaker's leadership. When Meacham published the first statement of Shaker belief in 1790, he described the four times of dispensation, when the Holy Spirit had been made manifest on earth. The first had been to Abraham, the second to Moses, and the third to Jesus. The fourth, which had commenced in 1747 and continued to the present, represented "the second appearing of Christ to consume or destroy anti-christ, or false religion, and to make an end of the reigning power of sin." Ann Lee was never even mentioned. Five years later, when a visitor to New Lebanon asked whether Ann Lee had founded the Shakers, as was "generally believed," they denied it.[36]

The shifting of attention away from Ann Lee may have derived from a belief that the English Shakers' absolute faith in the immediate promptings of the Holy Spirit had led them into rash actions that had endangered the movement and left believers unprotected against the temptations of sin and the world. Moreover, the ecstatic, joyful aspect of Ann Lee's message had encouraged a false notion that they had overcome sin and that their salvation was assured. Meacham told Abijah Wooster that "there was no redemption of Spirit but through suffering." When a soul was "sufficiently mortified," it would be "thankful for any gift of God." During the first year after the gathering at New Lebanon, he preached every week, always on the disciplining of the church and the purging of "heresy." The young Shakers in particular were warned that it was "spiritually life to obey & death to disobey."[37]

In unpublished writings that circulated in manuscript among the Shakers, Meacham declared that the revelations of the Holy Spirit to the Shakers' "first witnesses" had compelled a new understanding of what the New Lights had considered the nature of conversion and the church of the saints. "What before had been called regeneration, or the new birth" was in reality "distant from the real work." What the

New Lights had called church order was equally "distant from a true church gospel order." No one could attain sinless perfection outside the Shaker order, because "souls must be redeemed, not only from all outward or actual sin, but from the body or nature of sin."[38]

Soon after the gathering commenced at New Lebanon, Meacham introduced an entirely new form of worship. It had come to him, he said, by divine revelation. The believers assembled in rows, the sexes separate. They all moved with slow shuffling steps backwards and forwards, precisely in step with each other, as a few men and women sang the same wordless songs that had accompanied the former worship of ecstatic whirling, leaping, and shouting. The next year, Daniel Goodrich introduced the solemn march to the believers in Enfield, Connecticut. Presumably other emissaries went out from New Lebanon to teach it to the Shakers elsewhere. At Canterbury, John Whitcher wrote, "all quick and powerful operations in worship, as well as all external or vocal warring and fighting the devil . . . ceased in the church; order being established as a substitute." For the next several years, the "slow march" was performed at the pace of a step every four seconds followed by a turn after eight steps. It was, he said, "eminently calculated to bring down the sense."[39]

In every sense, the new form of worship was a drastic change from former practices. Whereas in the past the ecstatic worship had been perhaps the Shakers' most effective method of evangelism, convincing many who came to see them that God was tangibly present in their services as nowhere else, the slow marches were intended to confront the believers with the fact that they were unworthy to receive the divine spark in their present impurity and disobedience. God had revealed them to Meacham; the other Shakers were simply taught to perform them. If we accept Victor Turner's notion that ritual performances are always acts of celebration, whether festive or solemn, then Shaker worship had ceased to be sacred theater.

A visitor to New Lebanon in 1790 recorded other details about the new dances. Men and women wore thick shoes that clattered as the believers shuffled across the floor of the meetinghouse. It was a hot August day, and everyone was perspiring: "Some of the men were wringing wet, and the sweat dropped from their faces to the floor." During the occasional intermissions in the dancing, a preacher addressed them: "Avoid carnal lusts. Labor to shake off sin; sin is hateful; I hate sin. Power of God." The services lasted for three hours in the morning and for another three hours in the afternoon.[40]

Meacham introduced variations on the basic pattern from time to time, usually in order to mortify the flesh still further. A visitor in 1794 wrote that the worshipers resembled "dancing skeletons with the dismal countenances of distress, mixed with tears." The exercise was especially laborious because everyone bent their knees nearly to the floor as they moved forward. In the next years, as the marches became even slower, Calvin Green recalled that "it was almost impossible to exercise it at all."[41]

The Shakers' own history of the New Lebanon community says simply that in the Meacham era "the religious services were of a very solemn character,"[42] but obviously something far more profound was happening. Like Ann Lee and Whittaker before him, Meacham was obsessed with sexuality: "the besetments of a carnal nature," as Green called it. In the period between Whittaker's death and the commencement of the gathering of the communities into order, the quest had led some Shakers into excesses of physical mortification that would have impressed a desert saint. It is impossible to verify the claim made by several former Shakers that exhaustion and deprivation led to many deaths from tuberculosis and other illnesses,[43] but there is no question that his obsession led the otherwise practical and sensible Meacham to encourage or at least to condone some bizarre practices for the sake of overcoming "the flesh." It is possible that one reason for Meacham's repudiation of any reception of the gifts of the spirit that did not proceed directly and specifically from the leadership had been the ill-advised call to transcend sexuality through individual practices of penance and extreme physical mortification—such as those Joseph Meacham himself had engaged in. It is not clear how widely these penitential excesses spread. They may well have taken place only in the vicinity of New Lebanon. The fact that Matthewson, who was always restricted to the lower orders, never mentions them suggests that they were confined to those who had attained sufficient spirituality to attempt them.

Reuben Rathbun described what happened when he and a dozen other young men in Hancock who had formed a collective "family" in 1789–90 attempted to overcome their sexuality through mortification. The "cross against the flesh" of compulsory celibacy had been a primary reason that Rathbun had joined the Shakers as a young man in 1780, and the "first ministers" had taught him that transcending the flesh would require the overcoming of both "the inclination of the spirit and the natural faculties of the body." Thus Rathbun believed that it was entirely appropriate when some at New Lebanon began trying to "destroy the whole order of nature" in order "to obtain the power of God, so as to wholly activate and move the human frame." When they sent ministers from New Lebanon to encourage other believers to kindle what they called the "furnace in Zion," Rathbun and his friends welcomed the challenge.

"We undertook the work cheerfully," he wrote, "and labored all manner of ways that we could conceive would have any tendency to mortify the flesh; but still the flesh lived." Some reached a point of such exhaustion that "there was not much power of erection in the parts of generation." Then, to their horror, they experienced the condition called spermatorrhea, in which semen was evacuated without orgasm. This "made some almost despair of ever being saved, as the natural seed of copulation was looked upon as the most unclean and hateful of any thing in the natural creation." Gradually, "this gift was given up." The achievement of pure spirituality must come by different means.[44]

By the time that Harlow assembled the Hancock believers in early 1791 to prepare them for the gathering into order and told them that "souls must labour to break the bands of the flesh," the word no longer had specifically sexual connotations. Green wrote that at New Lebanon the Shakers were taught that they were "almost good for nothing & never would be worth but little." They would be assured of salvation only after they had "travelled deep enough into mortification & humility."[45] Henceforth, no one received gifts directly from on high, either to worship or to mortify themselves.

The very orderliness of Shaker life in the gathered communities made unlikely the spontaneous experiences of spiritual presence that had formerly occurred, since they had always been collective experiences of entranced performance, divinely sanctioned first by the English leadership and then by the believers' own experience. Spirit possession does not just happen; it is generated in an environment that provides the emotional excitation and social cues that encourage it. Abruptly, this framework was replaced by one that discouraged—indeed made almost unthinkable—what formerly had been actively sought: the individual apprehension of deity.

Meacham's other great innovation proceeded directly from his

Puritan sense of spiritual hierarchy and his realization that the attainment of a perfected and godly society entailed vastly more human planning and social structuring than the English Shakers had anticipated. As he set out to build heaven on earth, he concentrated on the younger members, those who had joined the Shakers as children or adolescents. Only they could attain the disciplined spirituality that would enable them to go forth and convert the entire world to the truth faith. Meacham told the young people at New Lebanon that every one of them was destined to achieve his or her preordained place in "the heavenly state," so long as they were obedient in everything and never spoke out "against the way of God." When a middle-aged believer at Canterbury complained about her exclusion from the first order, she was told that her generation had lived too long in their sins and lusts: "They are all young people at the church, and are holy."[46]

The plan for the creation of a perfected generation of young men and women was initiated soon after the gathering into order had begun. A manuscript chronology kept by Jethro Turner noted that in 1790 the boys and girls at New Lebanon were housed in buildings separate from the older believers. Two years later, the "House for the Youth & Children" was completed, and fifty believers under the age of twenty-five moved in. They helped the artisans in the various shops and sometimes worked in the fields. Like the first order, they were forbidden to have any contact with people of lesser spirituality.[47]

According to Matthewson, the young people received "no kind of education except singing and dancing," yet eventually they were to travel through the entire world as preachers. Matthewson was not one of the future evangelists; he had been placed in the outer order under the supervision of the eccentric Samuel Fitch. Matthewson's account might therefore be suspect, but Elder Calvin Green, who grew up in the youth order, says essentially the same thing. He had received three months of schooling in 1788, but with Meacham's revelation that the believers must mortify themselves with discipline and the grueling worship of the solemn march, "all recreations and literary studies were suspended for a time." The only books that they were permitted were the Bible, a spelling book, and an arithmetic text. Green read when he could, but few others did.

Only in 1808 did the Shakers established a school at New Lebanon. Its purpose, Jethro Turner wrote, was to teach the young Shakers to pronounce their words "more proper and consistant [*sic*]." Perhaps the most poignant testimony to the early Shakers' neglect of education is the barely literate diary kept in the youth order by Samuel Johnson, Jr., who had joined the Shakers with the rest of his family after the conversion of his father, a former Presbyterian minister and graduate of Yale College.[48]

Green admitted that "in those times, boys were kept under restrictions & in stillness, far beyond what is now required." The result was a growing resentment that spread rapidly among the older boys. The leadership intervened, assuring the pious few like Green that they would be "crowned above all" the children who had come to the Shakers when their parents were converted. The leaders failed to halt the unrest, in part because the elder for the youth order, Benjamin Goodrich, joined the young men in their dissidence. Beginning in late 1795 and continuing for the next several years, there was a steady stream of apostasies from the Shakers, primarily among the young.

A newspaper in Stockbridge, Massachusetts, reported in 1796 that there was "a great fermentation" in the New Lebanon and Hancock communities as the young people who had been so important to the formation of the communal economies departed. New Lebanon was the worst hit; twenty left in 1796 alone. That same year, Whitcher recorded only two defections at Canterbury, and when William Bentley visited Harvard in 1795, he wrote that although he had heard that their numbers were declining "because the services are too severe," he saw no evidence of it. Elders Henry Blinn and John Lyons acknowledged that there had been defections at Enfield, New Hampshire, but they contended that those who left had been the people who persisted in claiming spiritual gifts superior to those of their designated leaders. Lyons, only fifteen at the time of the crisis, was tempted to leave but then decided to remain. He resolved henceforth to do as he was "instructed" in everything. If he "trespassed," he would always "go to the Elders and tell them of it."[49]

The Shaker leadership's response was understandable, given the nature of their theology. All those who left the communities had shown themselves too far gone in sin to accept the discipline of gospel order with humility. They were apostates, fated probably to misfortunes on this earth and surely to damnation in the next. When Meacham learned of the apostasy of Benjamin Goodrich, the youth order's elder, he said that Goodrich and the others who left had "lost their birthright," although they "were the elect, —they were all elected with me." Matthewson (who joined the apostates in 1799) was told by his elders that those who did not "obey the commands & orders of God in the church" stood "right on the brink of hell," and he was then given an elaborate description of what that hell was going to be like.[50] In 1798, the experiment of creating a selected and spiritualized legion for the conversion of the world by means of the youth order was abandoned. Those who had remained in the faith joined the first order.

The apostasies were a terrible blow to Meacham, who had been in failing health for several years. Shortly before he died in August 1796, he wrote a letter to Lucy Wright, thanking God for their collaboration and designating her as his successor. "I believe the Late . . . troubles among the young in the Church is the Chief Cause of my Present Weakness & sufferings," he wrote. "They were young and not able to Perc[e]ive that planting of faith in their understandings when gathered into the Churches." Nevertheless, all of the "Labours & Troubles with them" would prove to have been worthwhile, for they were still God's and the Shakers' great hope.[51]

Meacham's death produced no succession crisis of any kind. It is doubtful that very many believers shared Matthewson's objections to being led "by women or elders ruled by women."[52] Until her death in 1821, Lucy Wright guided the Shakers through a period that saw communities established on the New England model in Ohio, Kentucky, and Indiana, all of them acknowledging their submission in everything to the leadership at New Lebanon. According to the Shakers' own estimates, their numbers grew from approximately a thousand at Ann Lee's death to over four thousand at the time of Lucy Wright's death.[53] The communal structures that Meacham had established were preserved essentially unchanged. So was his insistence that the order that permeated their lives was the earthly manifestation of the Holy Spirit's descent upon the Shakers.

This is not to say that there were no changes. The Shakers developed and published an elaborate theology, the most significant feature of which was the claim that Ann Lee was the female manifestation of Jesus. She, not the Shakers collectively, had been Christ's second appearing. The revelation had first come in 1808, at New Lebanon. It was then promulgated by "messengers" sent out to the other communities.[54]

Most of the changes restored practices of the early years. A visitor to Niskeyuna three months after Meacham's death found that what the elders called praising God in song and dance included convulsions and speaking in tongues. The worship services retained their formal and solemn character, but a measure of joy and spontaneity returned. Once again, they had become a sacred theater of celebration, in which the elaborate repertory of steps and gestures (which were sometimes carefully rehearsed) served as a metaphor for the attainment of heaven within the disciplined Shaker communities.

After a ten years' hiatus, the Shakers' missionary efforts were resumed. When their evangelists encountered revivals among Presbyterians, Baptists, and Methodists on the frontier, they witnessed phenomena of spirit possession as dramatic and bizarre as those that the first American converts had experienced in the 1780s. They resumed the pattern of those years and sent out missionaries whenever they learned of a revival, whether it was in Kentucky, Ohio, or in some new settlement in the New England back country. At Savoy, Vermont, for example, Calvin Green found all the wonders that had accompanied the New Light Stir of 1780 or the Kentucky Revival: "Singing in the Spirit, dancing, leaping, barking, jerking &c."

In 1808, a revival spread through the Shakers' own communities. At New Lebanon, there were "powerful & strange operations, bowing, shaking, talking with tongues, & diverse gifts." Thereafter, Green wrote, there were frequent "outward manifestations of invisible Power," often preceding successful "harvests" of new converts from the world.[55]

The most spectacular phenomena of possession accompanied what the Shakers called "Mother Ann's Work." At Niskeyuna in 1837, three girls between the ages of ten and fourteen were suddenly possessed. When they recovered, they declared that they had journeyed to Heaven. After the leadership decided that these experiences were indeed the work of the Holy Spirit, similar phenomena appeared in the other communities. Some of the inspired young people brought heavenly messages from the departed "spiritual parents," Ann Lee, Joseph Meacham, and Lucy Wright. Others drew pictures of what they had seen in their visions. Lafayette visited the Shakers again, this time in spirit. So did George Washington, Napoleon, and some

Indians. There were new songs, dances, and ceremonies, all introduced by divine inspiration.[56]

Once again a new generation of believers was being incorporated into Shaker experience through the direct action of the Holy Spirit. The collective belief structures and the social cues from the communities' leadership were potent enough that none of the innovations of "Mother Ann's Work" challenged the existing order. Instead, the divine communications often affirmed that all the believers must restore the dedication, obedience, and simplicity of the first Shakers.

Mother Ann's Work demonstrated once again that the descent of the Holy Spirit had the capacity to affect profoundly a society that believed in the possibility of such a visitation, but always in ways that were determined by the society itself. One of the Shakers' most remarkable achievements had been to take several traditions of Protestant popular religion and to incorporate them into a dynamic synthesis of belief and practice. The Shaker communities were settings for sacred theater that appropriated and transformed beliefs and practices that derived variously from Puritanism, Methodist and New Light revivalism, the biblical examples of Israel and the first Christian churches, and the prophetic tradition that promised God's direct guidance in times of affliction.

As Joel had promised, at the end of the seventeenth century Huguenot "sons and daughters" were visited by the Holy Spirit, or so the Camisards believed. The sacred theater of the Cévennes was in effect a drama of the promise of collective redemption for God's faithful remnant, enacted by the Protestant communities in scenes of emotionality and possessed behavior that in their strange mixture of familiar and unfamiliar convinced their audiences that they must be authentic. Among the Camisards, the visitations of the spirit gradually faded away when they no longer communicated culturally persuasive messages to the Huguenots of the southeast.

Meanwhile, the French Prophets showed that a sacred theater in which prophecy was accompanied by a repertory of entranced performances that in diversity and literal theatricality went far beyond the biblical constraints upon Huguenot possession could find sympathetic audiences in other religious communities, provided it could be interpreted appropriately for the audiences' own presuppositions and expectations. In both England and Germany, the hostility of the larger community served to draw the believers in upon themselves. As a result, after a few years they had lost their capacity to win religious seekers to their beliefs and to respond to the challenge of other beliefs and convictions.

For the Camisards, the French Prophets, and the Community of True Inspiration, the sacred theater derived from the prophetic tradition of the Old Testament had been central to their collective religious experience. When individuals were possessed by the Holy Spirit, both they and their audiences considered the phenomena to be expressions of a shared religious reality, intended to communicate divine truths not only to the group but also the nation and the world.

The drama that the converts in the English, Scottish, and American revivals enacted was quite different. Methodists and New Lights believed that they were participating in the climactic redemption of the world, but the sacred theater that in its convulsions, visions, and entranced speech seemed to hostile observers to be virtually identical to that of the French Prophets was in fact profoundly different. In the transatlantic awakening, the collective drama of redemption was performed individually by those who were undergoing conversion, although the cultural expectations of the religious community, especially as they were mediated through the verbal and behavioral cues of the ministry, placed restraints on the nature of the individuals' behavior and experience. In England, Scotland, and New England, bitter controversies developed between those who rejected the possibility that God could possibly be the cause of such behavior and those who refused to judge how he might operate, provided it conformed to "the law and the testimony" of Scripture and theology.

However protracted the process might be, conversion could take place only once for the individual sinner. Therefore the sacred theater that was its visible and gestural expression could only sporadically be a feature of popular worship experience. Neither Methodists nor American New Lights had a cultural or religious framework to accommodate it regularly or permanently.

Nevertheless, the English Shakers did manage exactly that. Like ecstatic cults in other cultures, they were able to experience spiritual transcendence and emotional catharsis whenever they gathered in expectation of the Holy Spirit's descent. Their beliefs derived from the popular religious traditions of Lancashire, but their conduct was too bizarre and their reliance on the immediate promptings of God too extreme to attract audiences in Manchester that shared their own understanding of what their behavior meant in cosmic terms.

The same performances that in England had been scorned and reviled persuaded many people in the new settlements of the New England back country that God was present in a special and dramatic way. The Baptists and other New Light radicals who were drawn to the Shakers shared their sense of millenial urgency. Moreover, since the 1740s they had clung to the belief that at some future time of God's choosing there would be just such an outpouring of the gifts of divine power.

In the nineteenth century, revivals became a central feature of evangelical Protestant religious experience. They represented sacred theater on a grand scale, orchestrated by masters like Charles Finney with an artistry that George Whitefield might have envied. They regularly produced outbursts of emotion, but in general the kinds of phenomena that had been welcomed by the early Methodists of Bristol or the leaders of the Kentucky Revival were not encouraged, at least not until the advent of modern Pentecostalism. Other means of access to the realm of divinity persisted as well, among groups as diverse as Swedenborgians, Spiritualists, and Mesmerists.

The early Shakers' most remarkable contribution to their nineteenth-century posterity was to transform their entire communal experience into a sacred theater that included both the individual drama of redemption from sin and the cosmic story of divinity's manifestation upon the earth. Within the communities that the American Shakers created under the guidance of Joseph Meacham and Lucy Wright, the performance of this sacred theater was controlled by rules and routines, quite unlike the spiritual anarchy of the Shakers' first years. Nevertheless, it was the Shakers' possession of and by the Holy Spirit that served as the permanent guaranty that theirs alone was the church and community that Christians had sought for nearly two thousand years.

Notes

Introduction: Anthropology and History

1. Victor Turner, "Liminality and the Performance Genres," in John J. MacAloon, ed., *Rite, Drama, Festival, Spectacle: Rehearsals toward a Theory of Cultural Performance* (Philadelphia: Institute for the Study of Human Issues, 1984), 28. On the convergence of anthropology and history, see especially the essays by Bernard S. Cohn and Natalie Z. Davis in "Anthropology and History in the 1980s," *Journal of Interdisciplinary History* 12 (1981): 227–52, 267–75. Two recent examples of the convergence are Renato Rosaldo, *Ilongot Headhunting* (Stanford: Stanford Univ. Press, 1980), and Barbara Babcock, ed., *The Reversible World* (Ithaca: Cornell Univ. Press, 1978).

2. See, for example, Luther P. Gerlach, "Pentecostalism: Revolution or Counter-Revolution?" in Irving I. Zaretsky and Mark P. Leone, eds., *Religious Movements in Contemporary America* (Princeton: Princeton Univ. Press, 1974), 672–85; Felicitas D. Goodman, Jeannette H. Henney, and Esther Pressel, *Trance, Healing, and Hallucination: Three Field Studies in Religious Experience* (New York: John Wiley & Sons, 1974); and Frederick Dale Bruner, *A Theology of the Holy Spirit: The Pentecostal Experience and the New Testament Witness* (Grand Rapids, Mich.: William B. Eerdmans, 1970).

3. Quoted in A. R. G. Owen, *Hysteria, Hypnosis, and Healing: The Work of J.-M. Charcot* (New York: Garrett Publications, 1975), 63.

4. See, for example, Chadwick Hansen, *Witchcraft at Salem* (New York: G. Braziller, 1969); Emmanuel Le Roy Ladurie, *Les paysans de Languedoc,* 2d ed. (Paris: Mouton, 1966), I:614–24; and Dominique Colas, "Fanatisme, hystérie, paranoia: Le Prophètisme camisard," *Temps modernes* 35 (1980): 469–91.

5. Mary Douglas, *Natural Symbols: Explorations in Cosmology* (London: Cresset Press, 1970), 21, 65.

6. John A. Grim, *The Shaman: Patterns of Siberian and Ojibway Healing* (Norman: Univ. of Oklahoma Press, 1983), 27. See also Clifford Geertz,

"Religion as a Cultural System," in Michael Banton, ed., *Anthropological Approaches to the Study of Religion* (New York: Praeger, 1966), 40, and Victor and Edith Turner, "Religious Celebrations," in Victor Turner, ed., *Celebration: Studies in Festival and Ritual* (Washington, D.C.: Smithsonian Institution Press, 1982), 204.

7. Owsei Temkin, *The Falling Sickness: A History of Epilepsy from the Greeks to the Beginnings of Modern Neurology,* 2d ed. (Baltimore: Johns Hopkins Press, 1971), 87.

8. Paul Chodoff, "The Diagnosis of Hysteria: An Overview," *American Journal of Psychiatry* 131 (1974): 1077; Alan Krohn, *Hysteria: The Elusive Neurosis* (New York: International Univ. Press, 1978), 158–62; Carroll Smith-Rosenberg, "The Hysterical Woman: Sex Roles and Role Conflict in Nineteenth-Century America," *Social Research* 39 (1972): 678; Marc Hollender, "Conversion Hysteria: A Post-Freudian Reinterpretation of Nineteenth-Century Psychosocial Data," *Archives of General Psychiatry* 26 (1972): 311; Nicholas P. Spanos and Jack Gottlieb, "Demonic Possession, Mesmerism, and Hysteria: Social Psychological Perspective on Their Historical Inter-relationships," *Journal of Abnormal Psychology* 88 (1979): 527–46.

9. Richard Schechner, *Between Theater and Anthropology* (Philadelphia: Univ. of Pennsylvania Press, 1985), 4.

10. Erika Bourguignon, "Cross-Cultural Perspectives on the Religious Uses of Altered States of Consciousness," in Irving I. Zaretsky and Mark P. Leone, eds., *Religious Movements in Contemporary America* (Princeton: Princeton Univ. Press, 1974), 234.

11. I. M. Lewis, *Ecstatic Religion: An Anthropological Study of Spirit Possession and Shamanism* (Harmondsworth: Penguin Books, 1971), 65.

12. Turner, "Introduction," to Turner, ed., *Celebration,* 23. While these concepts informed all of Turner's work, they were presented especially persuasively in "Social Dramas and Ritual Metaphors," in his *Dramas, Fields, and Metaphors: Symbolic Action in Human Society* (Ithaca: Cornell Univ. Press, 1974), 23–59.

13. J. Duncan M. Derrett, "Spirit Possession and the Gerasene Demoniac," *Man,* n.s. 14 (1979): 287.

14. Ronald Knox, *Enthusiasm: A Chapter in the History of Religion* (Oxford: Clarendon Press, 1950), 21–24; Louis Bouyer, "Some Charismatic Movements in the History of the Church," in Edward D. O'Connor, ed., *Perspectives on Charismatic Renewal* (Notre Dame: Univ. of Notre Dame Press, 1975), 115–18.

15. Quoted in Frederick C. Klawter, "The Role of Martyrdom and Persecution in Developing the Priestly Authority of Women in Early Christianity: A Case Study of Montanism," *Church History* 49 (1980): 252.

16. Gerald Lewis Bray, *Holiness and the Will of God: Perspectives on*

the *Theology of Tertullian* (Atlanta: John Knox Press, 1979), 54–63; *New Catholic Encyclopedia*, s.v. "Montanism" by W. Le Saint. Cf. Knox, *Enthusiasm*, 25–49.

Chapter 1 Your Sons and Daughers Shall Prophesy

1. Johannes Kelpius to Steven Momfort, 11 December 1699, in Kelpius, *The Diarium of Magister Johannes Kelpius*, trans. Julius Friedrich Sachse (Lancaster, Pa.: Pennsylvania-German Society, 1917), 47; Elizabeth W. Fisher, "'Prophesies and Revelations': German Cabbalists in Early Pennsylvania," *Pennsylvania Magazine for History and Biography* 109 (1985): 319–21.

2. Christopher Hill, *The World Turned Upside Down: Radical Ideas during the English Revolution* (New York: Viking, 1972), 302–6.

3. See Chapter 4.

4. Richard Roach, quoted in Nils Thune, *The Behmenists and the Philadelphians: A Contribution to the Study of English Mysticism in the Seventeenth and Eighteenth Centuries* (Uppsala: Almqvist & Wiksells Boktrycker Ab, 1948), 51; Serge Hutin, *Les disciples anglais de Jacob Boehme aux xviie et xviiie siècles* (Paris: Editions Denoel, 1960), 81–87; Desirée Hirst, *Hidden Riches: Traditional Symbolism from the Renaissance to Blake* (New York: Barnes & Noble, 1964), 103–9.

5. *Theosophical Transactions by the Philadelphia Society*, number 2 (April 1697); constitution quoted in Thune, *The Behmenists and the Philadelphians*, 92.

6. F. Ernest Stoeffler, *German Pietism during the Eighteenth Century* (Leiden: E. J. Brill, 1973), 209–10; D. P. Walker, *The Decline of Hell: Seventeenth-Century Discussions of Eternal Torment* (Chicago: Univ. of Chicago Press, 1964), 218–22, 231–44; Fisher, "'Prophesies and Revelations,'" 313–15.

7. Robert Sauzet, *Contre-réforme et réforme catholique en Bas-Languedoc: Le diocèse de Nîmes au XVIIe siècle* (Louvain: Nauwelaerts, 1979), 257–59, 300–309.

8. Jon Butler, *The Huguenots in America: A Refugee People in New World Society* (Cambridge: Harvard Univ. Press, 1983), 20–23, 211–14; Hillel Schwartz, *The French Prophets: The History of a Millenarian Group in Eighteenth-Century England* (Berkeley and Los Angeles: Univ. of California Press, 1980), 12–14; Janine Garrison, "La reconquête catholique (17e siècle)," in Daniel Ligou, ed., *Histoire de Montauban* (Toulouse: Privat, 1984), 131–65. Any study of the Huguenot popular religious experience after the revocation owes a great debt to the works of Charles Bost: *Les prédicants protestants des Cévennes et du Bas-Languedoc, 1684–1700* (Paris: Honoré Champion, 1912); "Les 'Prophètes des Cévennes' au XVIIIe siècle," *Revue d'histoire et de philosophie religieuse* 5

(1925): 401–30; "Les 'Prophètes' du Languedoc en 1701 et 1702: Le prédicant-prophète Jean Astruc, dit Mandagout," *Revue historique* 136 (1921): 1–36, and 137 (1922): 1–31; "La première vie de Pierre Corteiz," *Revue de théologie et de philosophie*, n.s. 23 (1935): 89–121.

9. Bost, *Prédicants*, I:33–38; Philippe Joutard and Daniel Ligou, "Les déserts 1685–1800," in *Histoire des protestants en France* (Toulouse: Privat, 1977), 149; C. Cantaloube, *La réforme en France vue d'un village cévenol* (Paris: Editions du Cerf, 1949), 128–30; Thomas F. Sheppard, *Lourmarin in the Eighteenth Century: A Study of a French Village* (Baltimore: Johns Hopkins Press, 1971), 160; Patrice L.-R. Higonnet, *Pont-de-Montvert: Social Structure and Politics in a French Village 1700–1914* (Cambridge: Harvard Univ. Press, 1971), 35–36; Henri Manen and Philippe Joutard, *Une foi enracinée: La Pervenche* (Valence: Imprimeries réunies, 1972), 47–48; Samuel Mours and Daniel Robert, *Le protestantisme en France du XVIIIᵉ siècle à nos jours* (Paris: Librairie protestante, 1972), 56–61.

10. Mlle. Jeanne Des-Vignolles to Mlle. Louise Des-Vignolles, 3 January 1686, printed in Pierre Jurieu, *Lettres pastorales addressées aux fidèles de France qui gémissent sous la captivité de Babylon*, 3d ed. (Rotterdam: Abraham Acker, 1686), 55; Ami Bost, ed., *Les prophètes protestants* (Paris: Delay, [1847]), 175; Pierre Jurieu, *The Reflections of the Reverend and Learned Monsieur Jurieu . . .* (London: Richard Baldwin, 1689), 36–38; Charles Bost, *Prédicants*, 1:62. *Les prophètes protestants* was the first edition published in France of the collection of testimonies that had appeared in London over a century before (in 1707) under the title *Le théâtre sacré des Cévennes*.

11. Samuel Mours, *Le protestantisme en France au XVIIᵉ siècle* (Paris: Librairie protestante, 1967), 90–95; Roger Zuber, "Les psaumes dans l'histoire des Huguenots," *Bulletin de la société historique du protestantisme française* [hereafter *BSHPF*] 123 (1977): 353.

12. Quoted in Marcel Pin, *Chez les Camisards* (Ales: Chez l'Auteur, 1938), 20; quoted in Louis Mazoyer, "Les origines du prophètisme cévenol (1700–1702)," *Revue historique* 162 (1947): 38n; François Misson, ed., *A Cry from the Desart [sic]: or, Testimonials of Miraculous Things Lately Come to Pass in the Cévennes* [a translation of selections from *Le théâtre sacré des Cévennes*] (London: B. Bragg, 1707), 32 [hereafter *Cry from the Desart* (Bragg)]; quoted in Schwartz, *The French Prophets*, 16.

13. "Abrégé de l'histoire de la bergère de Saou," printed in Manen and Joutard, *Un foi enracinée*, 69–70.

14. Mours, *Protestantisme en France au XVIIᵉ siècle*, 124; Natalie Zemon Davis, "Ghosts, Kin, and Progeny: Some Features of Family Life in Early Modern France," *Daedalus* 106 (1977): 96.

15. "Mémoire particulier sur les assemblées tenues dans les montagnes du

Castrois. 1688," *BSHPF* 14 (1865): 163, 166; Misson, ed., *Cry from the Desart,* 20–22.

16. Aarni Voipio, *Sleeping Preachers: A Study in Ecstatic Religion* (Helsinki: Suomalisen Kirjallisuuden Seuran Kirjapainon Oy, 1951); *Arminian Magazine* 11 (1788): 91–93, 130–33, 185–88, 238–42; Don Yoder, "Trance-Preaching in the United States," *Pennsylvania Folklife* 18 (1968–69): 12–18; Alan Krohn, *Hysteria: The Elusive Neurosis* (New York: International Universities Press, 1978), 158.

17. Philippe Joutard, *Les camisards* (Paris: Editions Gallimard/Julliard, 1976), 86; Bost, *Prédicants,* 1:54–58; Joutard and Ligou, "Les déserts," 197; Bost, "La première vie de Pierre Corteiz," 11–12; Solange Deyon, "La résistance protestante et la symbolique du desert," *Revue d'histoire moderne et contemporaine* 18 (1971): 237–49.

18. Emmanuel Le Roy Ladurie, "French Peasants in the Sixteenth Century," in *The Mind and Method of the Historian,* trans. Siân Reynolds and Ben Reynolds (Chicago: Univ. of Chicago Press, 1981), 119–29; Gwynne Lewis, *The Second Vendée: The Continuity of Counter-Revolution in the Department of the Gard, 1789–1815* (Oxford: Clarendon Press, 1978), 5–7; M. M. Compère, "Ecole et alphabétisation en Languedoc aux XVIIe et XVIIIe siècles," in Francois Furet and Jacques Ozouf, eds., *Lire et écrire* (Paris: Editions de minuit, 1977), 2:44–93; Roger Chartier, Marie-Madeleine Compère, and Dominique Julia, *L'éducation en France du XVIe au XVIIIe siècle* (Paris: Societe d'édition d'enseignement superieur, 1976), 11–26; Ligou and Joutard, "Les déserts," 107, 194; David Cressy, *Literacy and the Social Order: Reading and Writing in Tudor and Stuart England* (Cambridge: Cambridge Univ. Press, 1980), chap. 5.

19. B. Robert Kreiser, *Miracles, Convulsions, and Ecclesiastical Politics in Early Eighteenth-Century Paris* (Princeton: Princeton Univ. Press, 1980), 147; Natalie Zemon Davis, "The Sacred and the Body Social in Sixteenth-Century Lyon," *Past and Present* no. 90 (1981): 53–59; Daniel W. Patterson, "Word, Song, and Motion: Instruments of Celebration among Protestant Radicals in Early Nineteenth-Century America," in Turner, ed., *Celebration,* 223; James B. Finley quoted in ibid., 222.

20. Walter J. Ong, *The Presence of the Word: Studies in the Evolution of Consciousness and Culture* (Ithaca: Cornell Univ. Press, 1977), 311. See also 103–8.

21. Jean Delumeau, "La lutte du protestantisme contre la superstition," in Delumeau, ed., *La mort du pays du Cocagne: Comportements collectifs de la Renaissance* (Paris: Publications de la Sorbonne, 1976), 109–11; Philippe Joutard, *La légende des camisards: Une sensibilité du passé* (Paris: Gallimard, 1977), 46; Kreiser, *Miracles, Convulsions, and Ecclesiastical Politics,* 147; "Relation sincère de ce qui a été prononcé par la bouche d'Isabeau Vincent en dormant

la nuit du 20 au 21 mai 1688," printed in Manen and Joutard, *Un foi enracinée*, 77; François Misson, ed., *A Cry from the Desart* [*sic*]: *or, Testimonials of Several Miraculous Things Lately Come to Pass in the Cévennes in France* (London: H. Hills, 1707), 8 [hereafter *Cry from the Desart* (Hills)]; Chartier, Compère, and Julia, *L'éducation en France*, 11–15.

22. Calvin quoted in Pierre Pidoux, *Le psautier huguenot du XVIᵉ siècle: Melodies et documents* (Basel: Edition Baerenreiter, 1962), 2:21; "Abregé" in Manen and Joutard, *Un foi enracinée*, 66.

23. Phyllis Mack Crews, *Calvinist Preaching and Iconoclasm in the Netherlands, 1544–1569* (Cambridge: Cambridge Univ. Press, 1978), 167–68; Bost, *Prédicants*, 1:447–55; Pierre Bolle, "Une paroisse réformée du Dauphiné à la veille de la révocation de l'Edit de Nantes: Mens-en-Trièves (1650–1685)," *BSHPF* 111 (1965): 222–28; Pierre Jurieu, *Pastoral Letters Directed to the Suffering Protestants of France* (London: Thomas Fautan, 1691), 77.

24. Schwartz, *The French Prophets*, 19–21; Bost, "Les 'Prophètes des Cévennes,'" 405; Kreiser, *Miracles, Convulsions, and Ecclesiastical Politics*, 173.

25. Schwartz, *The French Prophets*, 19; Charles Bost, "Le prophètisme en Dauphiné à la fin de 1688," *BSHPF* 56 (1907), 536.

26. Esprit Fléchier, "Récit fidèle de ce qui s'est passé dans les Assemblées des Fanatiques du Vivarais," in *Lettres choisies de M. Fléchier Evêque de Nismes...* (Paris: Jacques Estienne, 1715), 2:355–56; Mours and Robert, *Le protestantisme en France*, 63.

27. Pin, *Chez les Camisards*, 10–11; Schwartz, *The French Prophets*, 19; Bost, "Les 'Prophètes des Cévennes' au XVIIᵉ siècle," 405; Fléchier, "Récit fidèle," 357–59, 367–70.

28. Bost, *Prédicants*, 2:178–90; *Cry from the Desart* (Bragg), 9; *Cry from the Desart* (Hills), 2.

29. Bost, "Les 'Prophètes' du Languedoc," 136:11–12; 137:20; Bost, *Les Prédicants*, 1:1–2 and 2:300–305; Mours and Robert, *Le protestantisme en France*, 80–82; Pin, *Chez les Camisards*, 15–17.

30. Pin, *Chez les Camisards*, 18–24; Ernest Roschach, ed., *Histoire générale de Languedoc* (Toulouse: Edouard Privat, 1876–1905), 14: col. 1538; Bost, "Les 'Prophètes' du Languedoc," 136:13.

31. Natalie Zemon Davis, "The Rites of Violence: Religious Riots in Sixteenth-Century France," in *Society and Culture in Early Modern France* (Stanford: Stanford Univ. Press, 1975), 152–87; Donald R. Kelley, "Martyrs, Myths, and the Massacre: The Background of St. Bartholomew," *American Historical Review* 77 (1972): 1342.

32. Sauzet, *Contre-réforme*, 51; Cantaloube, *La réforme*, 124–25. On the persistence of violence in the Midi, see especially Colin Lucas, "The Problem of the Midi in the French Revolution," *Transactions of the Royal Historical Society*, 5th ser. 28 (1978): 1–25, and Lewis, *The Second Vendée*, 23–24, 197.

33. Bost, "Les 'Prophètes' du Languedoc," 137:12–14; Schwartz, *The French Prophets*, 29–31; Roschach, ed., *Histoire générale de Languedoc*, 14: cols. 1537–38, 1587, 1599, 1602, 1616; Robert Pic, "Les protestants d'Aubais de la Révocation à la Revolution," *BSHPF* 126 (1980): 64–65.

34. Roschach, ed., *Histoire générale de Languedoc*, 14: col. 1603; Misson, ed., *Cry from the Desart* (Bragg), 29. See also Robert Gagg, *Kirche im Feuer: Das Leben der Südfranzosischen Hugonottenkirche nach dem Todesurteil durch Ludwig XIV* (Zurich: Zwingli Verlag, 1961), 170.

35. Roschach, *Histoire générale de Languedoc*, 14: cols. 1682–83. See also Pic, "Les protestants d'Aubais," 64.

36. Misson, ed., *Cry from the Desart* (Bragg), 96; *Cry from the Desart* (Hills), 6, 13; Emile G. Léonard, *Histoire générale du protestantisme* (Paris: Presses universitaires de France, 1961–64), 3:17–19.

37. Abraham Mazel and Elie Marion, *Mémoires inédits*, ed. Charles Bost (Paris: Librairie Fischbacher, 1931), 5–7; Bost, "Les 'Prophètes' du Languedoc," 137:3–8.

38. Daniel Vidal, "La secte contre le prophétisme: Les Multipliants de Montpellier (1719–1723)," *Annales: Economies sociétés civilisations* 37 (1982): 822 n.7; Manen and Joutard, *Un foi enracinée*, 59; Pin, *Chez les camisards*, 147–50; Bost, "Les 'Prophètes des Cévennes' au XVIIIe siècle," 429.

39. Antoine Court to Mlle. Simart, 6 June 1721, printed in Alfred Dubois, *Les prophètes cévenols* (Strasbourg: G. Silbermann, 1861), 129–30; Léonard, *Histoire générale du protestantisme*, 20–23; Bost, "Les 'Prophètes des Cévennes' au XVIIIe siècle," 411–12.

40. Henri Bosc, "Les prophètes cévenols," *BSHPF* 126 (1980): 8.

Chapter 2 The Prophetic Diaspora

1. Testimony of Elie Marion in François Misson, ed., *A Cry from the Desart*... (London: B. Bragg, 1707), 98–103 [hereafter *Cry from the Desart* (Bragg)]; Elie Marion and Abraham Mazel, *Mémoires inédits*, ed. Charles Bost (Paris: Librairie Fischbacker, 1931), 61–104; Hillel Schwartz, *The French Prophets: The History of a Millenarian Group in Eighteenth-Century England* (Berkeley and Los Angeles: Univ. of California Press, 1980), 26–28.

2. Josiah Woodward, *An Account of the Rise and Progress of the Religious Societies in the City of London*... (London: J. Downing, 1712), 108; F. Ernest Stoeffler, "Pietism, the Wesleys, and Methodist Beginnings in America," in Stoeffler, ed., *Continental Pietism and Early American Christianity* (Grand Rapids: William B. Eerdmans, 1976), 185–88; Dudley W. R. Bahlman, *The Moral Revolution of 1688* (1957; reprint, New York: Archon Books, 1968), 67–70.

3. Quoted in Dale W. Brown, *Understanding Pietism* (Grand Rapids:

William B. Eerdmans, 1978), 154; Hajo Holborn, *A History of Modern Germany, 1648–1840* (New York: Alfred A. Knopf, 1964), 137–40; Peter C. Erb, introduction to *Pietists: Selected Writings* (New York: Paulist Press, 1873), 4–11.

4. Spener in *Pietists: Selected Writings*, 48; F. Ernest Stoeffler, *German Pietism during the Eighteenth Century* (Leiden: E. J. Brill, 1973), 168–70; Henri Vuilleumier, *Histoire de l'église réformée du pays de Vaud sous le régime bernois* (Lausanne: Editions La Concorde, 1930), 3:184–91.

5. Jon Butler, *The Huguenots in America: A Refugee People in New World Society* (Cambridge: Harvard Univ. Press, 1983), 210–11.

6. Franz-Antoine Kadell, *Die Huguenotten in Hessen-Kassel* (Darmstadt: Selbstverlag der Hessischen Historischen Kommission Darmstadt und der Historischen Kommission für Hessen, 1980), 22, 200–211; Jochen Dessel and Walter Mogk, eds., *Huguenotten und Waldenser in Hessen-Kassel* (Kassel: Verlag Evangelischer Presseverband Kurhessen-Waldeck, 1978), 517; Bruno Barbatti, *Das "Refuge" in Zürich: Ein Beitrag zur Geschichte der Huguenotten* (Zurich: W. Weiss, 1947), 159–60.

7. Marion and Mazel, *Mémoires*, 92.

8. Vuilleumier, *Histoire de l'église reformée*, 200–9 (Merlat quoted 204); E. William Monter, *Witchcraft in France and Switzerland: The Borderlands during the Reformation* (Ithaca: Cornell Univ. Press, 1976), 59–60, 138–41; D. P. Walker, *Unclean Spirits: Possession and Exorcism in France and England in the Late Sixteenth and Early Seventeenth Centuries* (Philadelphia: Univ. of Pennsylvania Press, 1981), 19–32; Nicholas P. Spanos and Jack Gottlieb, "Demonic Possession, Mesmerism, and Hysteria: Social Psychological Perspective on Their Historical Interrelationships," *Journal of Abnormal Psychology* 88 (1979): 527–46.

9. John Blanc, *The Anathema of the False Prophets. In a Sermon Preach'd in Several French Churches in and about London* (London: S. Bunchley, 1708), 9–10; Alfred Dubois, *Les prophètes cévenols* (Strasbourg: G. Silbermann, 1861), 96–98.

10. Marion and Mazel, *Mémoires*, 152–54.

11. François Misson, ed., *A Cry from the Desart...* (London: H. Hills, 1707), 12 [hereafter *Cry from the Desart* (Hills)]. Fage's language was almost certainly polished and "improved" either by the editor or by the translator, John Lacy.

12. Marion and Mazel, *Mémoires*, 154; Robert Pic, "Les protestants d'Aubais de la Révocation à la Revolution," *Bulletin de la société historique du protestantisme française* [hereafter *BSHPF*] 126 (1980): 65–70; Fage quoted in Schwartz, *The French Prophets*, 73.

13. Misson, ed., *Cry from the Desart* (Hills), 8–9.

14. Marion and Mazel, *Mémoires*, 154; Schwartz, *The French Prophets*, 72;

Richard Kingston, *Enthusiastick Impostors No Divinely Inspir'd Prophets* (London: J. Morphew, 1707), 9–11.

15. Schwartz, *The French Prophets*, 54–62; F. De Schickeler, "Les églises françaises de Londres après la Révocation," *Proceedings of the Huguenot Society of London* [hereafter *PHSL*] 1 (1887): 99–102; George Beeman, "Notes on the Sites and History of the French Churches in London," *PHSL* 8 (1909): 16–17.

16. *An Account of the Lives and Behaviour of the Three French Prophets . . . Part I* (London: J. Morphew, 1708), 10; Marion and Mazel, *Mémoires*, 160–62; Schwartz, *The French Prophets*, 76–80; Georges Ascoli, "L'affaire des prophètes français à Londres," *Revue du XVIIIe siècle* 3 (1916): 17–20.

17. *An Account . . . of the Three French Prophets*, 29.

18. John Lacy, preface to *Cry from the Desart* (Bragg), x, xvii, xxii, xxiv.

19. John Lacy, *A Relation of the Dealings of God to His Unworthy Servant John Lacy* (London: B. Bragg, 1708). 10–11.

20. Gerard Croese, *The General History of the Quakers* (London: John Dunton, 1696), 5; Hugh Barbour, *The Quakers in Puritan England* (New Haven: Yale Univ. Press, 1964), especially 25, 57–70, 132–33, and 255; Geoffrey F. Nuttall, *Studies in Christian Enthusiasm Illustrated from Early Quakerism* (Wallingford, Pa.: Pendle Hill, 1948), 59–61; David S. Lovejoy, *Religious Enthusiasm in the New World: Heresy to Revolution* (Cambridge: Harvard Univ. Press, 1985), 49.

21. See, for example, the records of the London and Middlesex Quarterly Meeting or the delightful manuscript memoirs of James Jenkins, both in the Friends' Reference Library, London.

22. Henry Pickworth, *A Charge of Error . . . against the Most Noted Leaders, &c. of the People called Quakers* (London: S. Noble, 1716), 143–45, 314–24, 343; Schwartz, *The French Prophets*, 52, 117n, 289; "Friends and the French Prophets," *Journal of the Friends Historical Society* 22 (1925): 2–7.

23. Schwartz, *The French Prophets*, 85–86, 93–94; D. P. Walker, *The Decline of Hell: Seventeenth-Century Discussions of Eternal Torment* (Chicago: Univ. of Chicago Press, 1964), 248; Ascoli, "Les prophètes français," 21–22, 85–87.

24. Marion and Mazel, *Mémoires*, 166.

25. Kingston, *Enthusiastick Impostors*, 34; Samuel Keimer, *A Brand Pluck'd from the Burning: Exemplified in the Unparallel'd Case of Samuel Keimer* (London: W. Boreham, 1718), 9.

26. *5 Lettre[s] d'un particulier à Monsieur Misson* (N.p.: [1708], 18–19; Sir Richard Bulkeley quoted in [Charles Chauncy?], *The Wonderful Narrative: Or, a Faithful Account of the French Prophets, Their Agitations, Exstasies, and Inspirations* (Glasgow: Robert Foulis, 1742), 29.

27. Henry Nicholson, *The Falsehood of the New Prophets Manifested with Their Corrupt Doctrines and Conversations* (London: Joseph Downing, 1708), 10–12, 28.

28. John Chamberlayne, a founder of the Society for the Promotion of Christian Knowledge, quoted in Kingston, *Enthusiastick Impostors*, 53.

29. John Lacy, *The Prophetical Warnings of John Lacy, Esq.* (London: B. Bragg, 1707), 73, 77.

30. Keimer, *A Brand*, 53; Kingston, *Enthusiastick Impostors*, 95.

31. For Keimer's biography, see C. Lennart Carlson, "Samuel Keimer: A Study in the Transition of English Culture to Colonial Pennsylvania," *Pennsylvania Magazine of History and Biography* 51 (1937): 357–86, which corrects Franklin's misstatements.

32. Schwartz, *The French Prophets*, 110–14; Lacy, *Relation*, 24–27; Keimer, *A Brand*, 11–12.

33. Keimer, *A Brand*, 22–24.

34. Kingston, *Enthusiastick Impostors*, 22.

35. Keimer, *A Brand*, 28, 31; Schwartz, *The French Prophets*, 113–16.

36. Keimer, *A Brand*, 26, 32–33, 52; *The Copy of a Letter to Mr. F– –. M– –, A Gentleman, Who Is a Follower of the Pretended Prophets* (London: J. Morphew, 1708), 7–9.

37. Schwartz, *The French Prophets*, 126–29; Keimer, *A Brand*, 29, 46; Mazel and Marion, *Mémoires*, 167 and n.

38. Schwartz, *The French Prophets*, 129–30; Keimer, *A Brand*, 29–30.

39. Keimer, *A Brand*, 34–36; Nicholson, *The Falsehood of the New Prophets*, 18–20.

40. Keimer, *A Brand*, 36, 63, 80; Schwartz, *The French Prophets*, 134–460.

41. Quoted in Walker, *The Decline of Hell*, 258.

42. Nicholson, *The Falsehood of the New Prophets*, 21–22; Keimer, *A Brand*, 57–58; Schwartz, *The French Prophets*, 144–46.

43. Schwartz, *The French Prophets*, 154–55, Dutton quoted 202.

44. Ibid., 172–74.

Chapter 3   The Community of True Inspiration

1. [Charles Portales], "A Short Historical Account of the Message of ye Spirit of ye Lord to His People in Germany in ye Year 1711," printed in Thomas S. Penny, ed., "The French Prophets of 1711," *Baptist Quarterly*, n.s. 2 (1924): 170–71.

2. Julius Friedrich Sachse, *The German Pietists of Provincial Pennsylvania, 1694–1708* (Philadelphia: Printed for the author, 1895), 433–58; William I. Hull, *William Penn and the Dutch Quaker Migration to Pennsylvania*, Swarthmore College Monographs on Quaker History, no. 2 (Philadelphia: Patterson & White, 1935), 64–74, 106; Hillel Schwartz, *The French Prophets: The History of a Millenarian Group in Eighteenth-Century England* (Berkeley and Los Angeles: Univ. of California Press, 1980), 171–75.

3. Penny, ed., "The French Prophets of 1711," 171; Daniel de Superville to C. G. de la Mothe, 18 April 1711, printed in Winifred Turner, ed., *The Aufrère Papers*, Publications of the Huguenot Society of London, vol. 40 (Frome: Butler & Tanner, 1940), 66–67.

4. F. Ernest Stoeffler, *German Pietism during the Eighteenth Century* (Leiden: E. J. Brill, 1973), 39–41; Carl Hildebrand von Canstein, *Briefwechsel . . . mit August Hermann Francke*, ed. Peter Schickentanz (Berlin: Walter de Gruyter, 1972), 449; Penny, ed., "The French Prophets of 1711," 171–73.

5. Penny, ed., "The French Prophets of 1711," 172.

6. Stoeffler, *German Pietism*, 41–42; Henri Tollin, *Geschichte der Französischen Colonie von Magdeburg* (Halle: Max Niemeyer, 1886), 2:21–26; Sachse, *German Pietists*, 304–6; Walter Delius, "Die Inspirierten-Gemeinde zu Berlin," in *Zwischenstation: Festschrift für Karl Kupisch zum 60. Geburtstag* (Munich: Chr. Kaiser Verlag, 1963), 20.

7. Penny, ed., "The French Prophets of 1711," 173–76.

8. Ibid., 176–79.

9. Elie Marion and Jean Allut, *Plan de la justice de Dieu sur la terre dans les derniers jours* (N.p., 1714), 38; Charles Bost, appendix to Elie Marion and Abraham Mazel, *Mémoires inédits*, ed. Charles Bost, Publications of the Huguenot Society of London, no. 34 (Paris: Librairie Fischbacher, 1931), 217; Schwartz, *The French Prophets*, 178.

10. Quoted in Eugene Ritter, "Magny et le piétisme romand, 1699–1730," *Société d'histoire de la Suisse romande: Mémoires et documents*, 2d ser., 3 (1891): 314–15.

11. Schwartz, *The French Prophets*, 178–79; Elie Marion and Jean Allut, *Quand vous aurez saccagés, vous serez saccagés . . .* (N.p., 1714), 9.

12. Max Goebel, "Geschichte der wahren Inspirations-Gemeinden von 1688 bis 1850," *Zeitschrift für die historische Theologie* 24 (1854): 304; F.-H. Oppenheim, "Contribution à l'histoire d'un reveil: Les 'nouveaux prophètes' allemands au début du XVIIIe siècle," *Revue d'histoire et de philosophie religieuses* 37 (1957) [part 1]: 143–48; Alfred Dubois, *Les prophètes cévenols* (Strasbourg: G. Silbermann, 1861), 110–13. Goebel's long essay, still the only full history of the French Prophets' influence on German popular religion, is also published in the third volume of his *Geschichte des christlichen Lebens in der rheinisch-westphälischen evangelischen Kirche* (Coblenz: Karl Baedeker, 1860).

13. Marion and Allut, *Quand vous aurez saccagés*, 24, 33; Schwartz, *The French Prophets*, 179.

14. Goebel, "Geschichte der wahren Inspirations-Gemeinde," 304; Delius, "Die Inspirierten-Gemeinde zu Berlin," 20; Knauth quoted in Oppenheim, "Contribution à l'histoire d'un reveil," [part 2] *Revue d'histoire et de philosophie religieuses* 40 (1960): 233.

15. Marion and Allut, *Quand vous aurez saccagés*, 117; Bost, appendix to Marion and Mazel, *Mémoires*, 217.

16. Delius, "Das Inspirierten-Gemeinde zu Berlin," 20–21; Goebel, "Geschichte der wahren Inspirations-Gemeinden," 304–5; Canstein, *Briefwechsel* [2 December 1713 and 24 February 1714], 621, 641; Gottlieb Scheuner, *Inspirations-Historie: The History of the Inspiration or Historical Account of the Founding of the Congregation or Community of Prayer . . .*, trans. Janet W. Zuber (N.p.: For the Amana Church Society, 1977–78), 1:8.

17. Delius, "Die Inspirierten-Gemeinde zu Berlin," 21–24.

18. Dubois, *Les prophètes cévenols*, 118; Oppenheim, "Contribution à l'histoire d'un reveil" [part 2], 148–49; Donald F. Durnbaugh, "The Brethren in Early American Church Life," in F. Ernest Stoeffler, ed., *Continental Pietism and Early American Christianity* (Grand Rapids: William B. Eerdmans, 1976), 225–28; *The Brethren Encyclopedia* (1983), s.v. "The Community of True Inspiration," by Donald F. Durnbaugh.

19. Goebel, "Geschichte der wahren Inspirations-Gemeinde," 307; Dubois, *Les prophètes cévenols*, 116–17; Stoeffler, *German Pietism*, 128–30, 168–71; Karl Knortz, *Die Wahre Inspirations-Gemeinde in Iowa* (Leipzig: Verlag von Otto Wigand, 1896), 8; Geoffrey Rowell, "The Marquis de Marsay: A Quietist in 'Philadelphia,'" *Church History* 41 (1972): 61–66.

20. Quoted in Donald F. Durnbaugh, "Johann Adam Gruber: Pennsylvania-German Prophet and Poet," *Pennsylvania Magazine of History and Biography* 83 (1959): 385–86; Scheuner, *Inspirations-Historie*, 1:12.

21. *Cyclopedia of Biblical, Theological, and Ecclesiastical Literature* (1873; reprint, New York: Arno Press, 1959), s.v. "Inspired"; Scheuner, *Inspirations-Historie*, 1:20.

22. Eberhard Ludwig Gruber's instructions and statements are printed in Bertha M. H. Shambaugh, *Amana That Was and Amana That Is* (1932; reprint, New York: Benajmin Blom, 1971), 198, 203, 243.

23. Quoted in Durnbaugh, "Gruber," 386.

24. Durnbaugh, "Gruber," 387; Gruber quoted in Shambaugh, *Amana*, 26.

25. Scheuner, *Inspirations-Historie*, 1:36–37; Blaise-Daniel Mackinet quoted in Durnbaugh, "Gruber," 388–89.

26. Scheuner, *Inspirations-Histoire*, 1:91–97; John B. Frantz, "The Awakening of Religion among the German Settlers in the Middle Colonies," *William and Mary Quarterly*, 3d ser. 33 (1976): 266.

27. Scheuner, *Inspirations-Historie*, 2:45–59; John Wesley, *The Journal*, ed. Nehemiah Curnock (1911; reprint, London: Epworth Press, 1938), 2:10–13; Henri Vuilleumier, *Histoire de l'église reformée du pays de Vaud sous le régime bernois* (Lausanne: Editions La Concorde, 1930), 3:219–20; Shambaugh, *Amana*, 31–33.

Chapter 4 The Methodist Awakening

1. Quoted in John Raimo, "Spiritual Harvest: The Anglo-American Revival in Boston, Massachusetts, and Bristol, England, 1739–1742" (Ph.D. diss., Univ. of Wisconsin, 1974), 20.

2. John D. Walsh, "Elie Halevy and the Birth of Methodism," *Transactions of the Royal Historical Society,* 5th ser. (London: Royal Historical Society, 1975), 25:6.

3. Quoted in Richard M. Cameron, ed., *The Rise of Methodism: A Source Book* (New York: Philosophical Library, 1954), 155.

4. Hillel Schwartz, *The French Prophets: The History of a Millenarian Group in Eighteenth-Century England* (Berkeley and Los Angeles: Univ. of California Press, 1980), 198; "Narrative of the Life of Our Departed Sister Esther Sutton West Written by Her Husband," Maudlin Street Moravian Church Archives, Bristol University.

5. John Wesley, *The Journal,* ed. Nehemiah Curnock (1911; reprint, London: Epworth Press, 1938), 1:454; Bernard Semmel, *The Methodist Revolution* (New York: Basic Books, 1973), 30–31.

6. Wesley, *Journal,* 1:465; Marion quoted in Jules Chavannes, "Les prophètes cévenols," *Bulletin de la société de l'histoire du protestantisme française* 18 (1869): 500n.

7. Wesley, *Journal,* 1:458; Frank Baker, "The People Called Methodists: 3. Polity," in Rupert Davies and Gordon Rupp, eds., *A History of the Methodist Church in Great Britain* (London: Epworth Press, 1965–83), 1:217–19.

8. Wesley, *Journal,* 2:122.

9. John Wesley to Samuel Wesley, 30 November 1738, in John Wesley, *The Letters,* ed. John Telford (London: Epworth Press, 1931), 1:275; Mrs. E. Hutton to Samuel Wesley, 6 June 1738, in John Wesley, *Original Letters, Illustrative of His Early History . . .* (Birmingham: Thomas Pearson, 1791), 67–70; "Narrative of the Life of Our Departed Sister Esther Sutton West," Maudlin Street Moravian Church Archives, Bristol University.

10. Wesley, *Journal,* 2:130, 136, 226; John Wesley to Samuel Wesley, 30 October 1738, in Wesley, *Letters,* 1:262–64; Frank Baker, *John Wesley and the Church of England* (Nashville: Abingdon Press, 1970), 60.

11. Nehemiah Curnock, in Wesley, *Journal,* 2:16n.

12. Ibid., 2:146; Wesley, *Letters,* 1:282.

13. Charles Wesley, *The Journal* (1849; reprint, Grand Rapids: Baker Book House, 1980), 1:138, 146, 148.

14. John Wesley, *Journal,* 2:179–88; John Wesley to Samuel Wesley, 4 April 1739, in Wesley, *Letters,* 1:290–91.

15. John Wesley, *Journal,* 2:190–91, 201–3.

16. John Cennick, "An Account of the Most Remarkable Occurrences in

the Awakenings at Bristol and Kingswood till the Brethren's Labours Began There in 1746," *Proceedings of the Wesleyan Historical Society* 6 (1908): 108–9; *Gentleman's Magazine* 9 (1739): 295.

17. Geoffrey F. Nuttall, *Studies in Christian Enthusiasm, Illustrated from Early Quakerism* (Wallingford, Pa.: Pendle Hill, 1948), 78–80.

18. Cennick, "An Account," 103n; Raimo, "Spiritual Harvest," 166–69; Walsh, "Elie Halevy and the Birth of Methodism," 3, 8; Luke Tyerman, *The Life and Times of the Rev. John Wesley, M.A.* (New York: Harper & Brothers, 1872), 1:260–62; Ronald Knox, *Enthusiasm: A Chapter in the History of Religion* (Oxford: Clarendon Press, 1950), 527.

19. Whitefield to Wesley, 25 June 1739, quoted in Tyerman, *Life of Wesley,* 1:258.

20. John Wesley, *Journal,* 2:216; Charles Wesley, *Journal,* 1:152.

21. Christopher Hill, "Antinomianism in Seventeenth-Century England," in *The Collected Essays of Christopher Hill* (Amherst: Univ. of Massachusetts Press, 1986), 2:177; Owen C. Watkins, *The Puritan Experience: Studies in Spiritual Autobiography* (New York: Schocken Books, 1972), 89; John Wesley, "On Christian Perfection," in Wesley, *The Works* (New York: T. Mason & G. Lane, 1840), 1:367; Semmel, *The Methodist Revolution,* 17.

22. Charles Wesley, *Journal,* 1:152–53; John Wesley, *Journal,* 2:200.

23. *The Political State of Great Britain,* 56 (1738): 145.

24. John Wesley, *Journal,* 2:226.

25. Howell Harris, *Howell Harris's Visits to London,* ed. Tom Beynon (Aberystwyth: Cambrian New Press, 1960), 47. See also Daniel Benham, *Memoirs of James Hutton* (London: Hamilton, Adams, & Co., 1856), 153.

26. John Wesley, *Journal,* 2:239, 238–39n.

27. Cameron, ed., *The Rise of Methodism,* 215–16; Cennick, "An Account," 101–4; James Jenkins, "Records and Recollections," 31 (typescript in the Friends' Reference Library, London).

28. Cennick to Wesley, 12 September 1739, printed in *Arminian Magazine* 1 (1778): 179–80.

29. Cennick, "An Account," 109–10; John Wesley, *Journal,* 2:298–99.

30. John Wesley, *Journal,* 2:246, 347.

31. Wesley to Whitefield quoted in John Wesley, *Journal,* 2:428; Cennick, "An Account," 110, 133–35; John Wesley to James Holland, 21 March 1740, in Wesley, *Letters,* 1:341.

32. William Leary, "John Cennick, 1718–55: A Bi-Centenary Appreciation," *Proceedings of the Wesley Historical Society* 30 (1955): 32–37; John Wesley, *Journal,* 2:426–34; Raimo, "Spiritual Harvest," 216–18; John Cennick, "Memorable Passages relating to the Awakening in Wiltshire . . . ," Moravian Archives, London; Harris, *Visits to London,* 59.

33. Charles Wesley, *Journal,* 247, 314.

34. John Wesley, *Journal*, 2:297.

35. Ibid., 2:312–20; Wesley quoted in Tyerman, *Life of Wesley*, 1:337; Molther quoted in Clifford Towlson, *Moravian and Methodist: Relationships and Influences in the Eighteenth Century* (London: Epworth Press, 1957), 100; Richard Viney, *Letter from an English Brother of the Moravian Persuasion in Holland to the Methodists in England, Lamenting the Irregularity of their Present Proceedings* (London: J. Roberts, 1739), 4; Cameron, ed., *The Rise of Methodism*, 256–59; Harris, *Visits to London*, 59–61; Semmel, *The Methodist Revolution*, 38–40.

36. John Wesley, *Journal*, 2:321; Hutton quoted in Tyerman, *Life of Wesley*, 1:299.

37. Towlson, *Moravian and Methodist*, 108–11; Baker, "The People Called Methodists," 1:220; John Wesley, *Journal*, 2:371; Cameron, ed., *The Rise of Methodism*, 225–28, 258.

38. David Clarke, "Another 'Son to Susanna(h): Benjamin Ingham, 1712–72," *Proceedings of the Wesley Historical Society* 38 (1972): 170–74; John Nelson, *Memoirs*, 2d ed. (Birmingham: R. Peart, 1807), 52–69; Frank Baker, *William Grimshaw, 1708–1763* (London: Epworth Press, 1963), 50–66.

39. John Wesley, *Journal*, 2:84; George Whitefield to William M'Culloch, 8 June 1742, printed in the *Weekly History* (Glasgow), no. 25, 8; C. C. Goen, introduction to Jonathan Edwards, *The Great Awakening*, ed. C. C. Goen (New Haven: Yale Univ. Press, 1972), 40–41, 53–55.

40. John Syms to "a friend in Boston," 23 December 1743, printed in *The Christian History for 1744*, ed. Thomas Prince (Boston: S. Kneeland & T. Green, 1745), 101.

41. Quoted in *The Christian History for 1743*, ed. Thomas Prince (Boston: S. Kneeland & T. Green, 1744), 82.

42. George Grub, *An Ecclesiastical History of Scotland* (Edinburgh: Edmonston & Douglas, 1861), 4:70; Whitefield to Howell, 14 August 1741, in *The Christian History for 1743*, 275; Tyerman, *Life of Wesley*, 1:336.

43. Alexander Webster, *Divine Influence the True Spring of the Extraordinary Work at Cambuslang and Other Places in the West of Scotland* (Edinburgh: T. Lumisden & J. Robertson, 1742), 15; John Hamilton to Thomas Prince, 13 September 1742, in *The Christian History for 1743*, 77; Rev. Lawson to William M'Culloch, in the *Weekly History* (Glasgow), no. 40, 6; James Erskine to unknown, 2 November 1742, Moravian Archives, London. See also Andrew L. Drummond and James Bullock, *The Scottish Church, 1688–1843: The Age of the Moderates* (Edinburgh: Saint Andrew Press, 1973), 54; John Struther, *The History of Scotland . . .* (Glasgow: Blackie, Fullarton & Co., 1828), 2:69; T. C. Smout, "Born Again at Cambuslang: New Evidence on Popular Religion and Literacy in Eighteenth-Century Scotland," *Past and Present* 97 (1982): 114–22.

44. Webster, *Divine Influence*, 19; Ralph Erskine, *Faith No Fancy...* (Edinburgh: W. & T. Ruddimans, 1745), xvii–xviii; James Erskine to James Hutton, 17 September 1742, Moravian Archives, London.

45. Robert Fleming, *The Fulfilling of Scripture* [1681] (Boston: Rogers & Fowle, 1743), 394.

46. Drummond and Bullock, *The Scottish Church, 1688–1843*, 49–54; T. C. Smout, *A History of the Scottish People, 1560–1830* (London: Collins, 1969), 234; James Robe, *A Faithful Narrative of the Extraordinary Work of the Spirit of God at Kilsyth, and Other Congregations in the Neighbourhood* (Glasgow: William Duncan, 1742), 27–28.

47. Robe, *A Faithful Narrative*, xii–xiv, 40, 45; Webster, *Divine Influence*, 19; James Young, "a preacher of the Gospel," to Robe, in *The Christian History for 1743*, 326; Robe's *Monthly Christian History* (November 1743), in *The Christian History for 1744*, 173–74.

48. Victor Turner, "Introduction," in Turner, ed., *Celebration: Studies in Festival and Ritual* (Washington: Smithsonian Institution Press, 1982), 23; *The Christian History for 1743*, 295–98.

49. Drummond and Bullock, *The Scottish Church*, 54; Smout, *History of Scotland*, 234.

50. Wesley to Thomas Rankin, 19 May 1775, in Wesley, *Letters*, 6:151.

51. Tyerman, *Life of Wesley*, 1:370–81.

52. Ibid., 1:382–85; John Wesley, *Journal*, 3:13, 60, 69. Cf. Willa Appel, "The Myth of the *Jettatura*," in Clarence Maloney, ed., *The Evil Eye* (New York: Columbia Univ. Press, 1976), 16–27.

53. *Some Papers Giving an Account of the Rise and Progress of Methodism in Staffordshire* (London: J. Roberts, 1744), 115, 20; Tyerman, *Life of Wesley*, 1:406–12; diary of Dr. Richard Wilkes, 2:172 [12 June 1743], MS no. 5006, Wellcome Library, London.

54. John Wesley, *Journal*, 4:359.

55. Berridge to John Thornton, 10 Thornton, 10 November 1773, in John Berridge, *The Whole Works...* (London: Ebenezer Palmer, 1864), 381–82.

56. "Journal of 'An Eyewitness,'" in John Wesley, *Journal*, 4:317–18.

57. Ibid., 4:320–21, 334–40, 344.

58. Ibid., 4:347, 359.

59. Ibid., 4:483–85; Robert Glen, "Visions and Ecstasies of Methodist Women in Late Eighteenth-Century Britain," unpublished paper presented at the convention of the American Historical Association, 28 December 1983.

60. J. D. Walsh, "Origins of the Evangelical Revival," in G. V. Bennett and J. D. Walsh, eds., *Essays in Modern English Church History in Memory of Norman Sykes* (New York: Oxford Univ. Press, 1966), 154–59; Zinzendorf quoted in F. Ernest Stoeffler, *German Pietism during the Eighteenth Century* (Leiden:

E. J. Brill, 1973), 154; James Lackington, *Memoirs of the First Forty-Five Years*, 7th ed. (1794; reprint, New York: Garland, 1974), 55–56.

61. *Arminian Magazine* 2(1779): 297–309.

62. *Methodist Magazine* 21 (1798): 5–8, 53–56.

63. *Arminian Magazine* 6 (1783): 461–63, 579, 636–38; 7 (1784): 14, 51, 131, 243.

64. *Testimonies of the Life, Character, Revelations, and Doctrines of Mother Ann Lee . . .* , 2d ed. (1888; reprint, New York: AMS Press, 1975), 3–5.

Chapter 5   The Transatlantic Awakening

1. John Wesley to Lord Grange (James Erskine), 16 March 1745, in John Wesley, *The Letters*, ed. John Telford (London: Epworth Press, 1931), 2:32–33; John Wesley, *The Journal*, ed. Nehemiah Curnock (1911; reprint, London: Epworth Press, 1938), 3:178.

2. James M'Culloch to Jonathan Edwards, 13 August 1743, in *The Christian History for 1743*, ed. Thomas Prince (Boston: S. Kneeland & T. Green, 1744), 361–62.

3. Jon Butler, "Enthusiasm Described and Decried: The Great Awakening as Interpretive Fiction," *Journal of American History* 69 (1982): 306. The best narrative history of the Great Awakening is Sydney Ahlstrom, *A Religious History of the American People* (New Haven: Yale Univ. Press, 1972), chap. 18.

4. David S. Lovejoy, *Religious Enthusiasm in the New World: Heresy to Revolution* (Cambridge: Harvard Univ. Press, 1985), 179.

5. Jon Butler, "The Future of American Religious History: Prospectus, Agenda, Transatlantic *Problèmatique*," *William and Mary Quarterly*, 3d ser. 42 (1985): 170; David D. Hall, "Toward a History of Popular Religion in Early New England," *William and Mary Quarterly*, 3d ser. 41 (1984): 49–55; Hall, "Religion and Society: Problems and Reconsiderations," in Jack P. Greene and J. R. Pole, eds., *Colonial British America: Essays in the New History of the Early Modern Era* (Baltimore: Johns Hopkins Univ. Press, 1984), 327–34. See also J. M. Bumsted, "The Pilgrim's Progress: The Ecclesiastical History of the Old Colony, 1620–1775" (Ph.D. diss., Brown Univ., 1965), chap. 3.

6. J. M. Bumsted and John E. Van de Wetering, *What Must I Do to Be Saved? The Great Awakening in Colonial America* (Hinsdale, Ill.: Dryden Press, 1976), 46–53, 154–55; John B. Frantz, "The Awakening of Religion among the German Settlers in the Middle Colonies," *William and Mary Quarterly*, 3d ser. 33 (1976):277–84.

7. Jonathan Edwards, *A Faithful Narrative of the Surprising Work of God . . .* , in Edwards, *The Great Awakening*, vol. 4 of *Works of Jonathan Edwards*, ed. C. C. Goen (New Haven: Yale Univ. Press, 1972), 145–46.

8. *The Christian History for 1744,* ed. Thomas Prince (Boston: S. Kneeland & T. Green, 1745), 390; Patricia J. Tracy, *Jonathan Edwards, Pastor: Religion and Society in Eighteenth-Century Northampton* (New York: Hill & Wang, 1980), 131–32; Hopkins quoted in Jonathan Edwards, *Works* (1817; reprint, New York: Burt Franklin, 1968), 2:82.

9. Edwards, *Great Awakening,* 160–62, 174.

10. Goen, introduction to ibid., 12–23; ibid., 151–57.

11. Ibid., 189, 206–7.

12. C. C. Goen, *Revivalism and Separatism in New England, 1740–1800: Strict Congregationalists and Separate Baptists in the Great Awakening* (1962; reprint, New York: Archon Books, 1969), 8, 13; Bumsted and Van de Wetering, *What Must I Do to Be Saved?* 58–70; Ned Landsman, "Revivalism and Nativism in the Middle Colonies: The Great Awakening and the Scots Community in East New Jersey," *American Quarterly* 34 (1982): 157–58.

13. *The Christian History for 1744,* 375–80; Sarah Edwards quoted in Bumsted and Van de Wetering, *What Can I Do to Be Saved?* 75; John Raimo, *Spiritual Harvest: The Anglo-American Revival in Boston, Massachusetts, and Bristol, England, 1739–42* (Ann Arbor: University Microfilms, 1974), 72–76; Lovejoy, *Religious Enthusiasm in the New World,* 184–86.

14. Nathan Cole, "The Spiritual Travels of Nathan Cole," ed. Michael J. Crawford, *William and Mary Quarterly,* 3d ser. 33 (1976): 90–93.

15. Benjamin Trumbull, *A Complete History of Connecticut, Civil and Ecclesiastical . . .* (New Haven: Maltby, Goldsmith & Co. and Samuel Wadsworth, 1818), 2:158.

16. *Weekly History* (Glasgow), no. 5, 7; Parsons to Colman, 16 December 1741, in ibid., no. 21, 2–4; Daniel W. Patterson, "Word, Song, and Motion," in Victor Turner, ed., *Celebration: Studies in Festival and Ritual* (Washington: Smithsonian Institution Press, 1982), 225.

17. William T. Youngs, *God's Messengers: Religious Leadership in Colonial New England, 1700–1750* (Baltimore: John Hopkins Press, 1976), 117–19; Stephen Williams's diary quoted in Ola E. Winslow, *Jonathan Edwards, 1703–1754* (New York: Macmillan, 1940), 192; Oliver William Means, *A Sketch of the Strict Congregational Church of Enfield, Connecticut* (Hartford: Hartford Seminary Press, 1899), 17–20.

18. Jonathan Edwards, *Works* (1817; reprint, New York: Burt Franklin, 1968), 6:455. See also Ruth H. Bloch, *Visionary Republic: Millennial Themes in American Thought, 1756–1800* (Cambridge: Cambridge Univ. Press, 1985), 13–18.

19. Ebenezer Punderson to the Secretary [of the Society for the Propagation of the Gospel], 20 December 1741, in Francis Hawks and William S. Perry, eds., *Documentary History of the Protestant Episcopal Church in Connecticut, 1704–89* (1863–64; reprint, Hartford: The Historiographer, 1959),

177–78; Kenneth Walter Cameron, *Connecticut Churchmanship: Records and Papers Concerning the Anglican Church in Connecticut in the Eighteenth and Early Nineteenth Centuries* (Hartford: Transcendental Books, 1969), 11; Josiah Cotton quoted in Clifford Shipton, *Biographical Sketches of Those Who Attended Harvard College* (Boston: Massachusetts Historical Society, 1933–75), 8:387–40; Leigh Eric Schmidt, "'A Second and Glorious Reformation': The New Light Extremism of Alexander Croswell," *William and Mary Quarterly*, 3d ser. 43 (1986): 214–44.

20. Andrew Croswell, *Mr. Croswell's Reply to a Book Lately Publish'd . . .* (Boston: Rogers & Fowle, 1742), 7–9; Croswell quoted in Bumsted and Van de Wetering, *What Must I Do to Be Saved?* 109.

21. Quoted in Shipton, *Biographical Sketches,* 8:394.

22. *The Christian History for 1743,* ed. Thomas Prince (Boston: S. Kneeland & T. Green, 1744), 195; *Christian History for 1744,* 250; Landsman, "Revivalism and Nativism," 159–60.

23. *Christian History for 1744,* 42–45.

24. Mr. Brockwell to the Secretary [of the S.P.G.], 18 February 1742, in William S. Perry, ed., *Historical Collections Relating to the American Colonial Church* (Hartford: For the Subscribers, 1873), 3:353–54; Daniel and Nathaniel Rogers, "Their Answer to Mr. Pickering's First Letter, printed in Theophilus Pickering, *Letters to the Rev. N. Rogers and Mr. D. Rogers of Ipswich . . .* (Boston: Thomas Fleet, 1742), 3; Edwin Scott Gaustad, *The Great Awakening in New England* (New York: Harper & Brothers, 1957), 46–47.

25. Quoted in Shipton, *Biographical Sketches,* 8:556.

26. Nathan Bowen's "Almanacs" quoted in William Bentley, *Diary* (Salem: Essex Institute, 1911), 3:475–76.

27. Charles Chauncy, *Seasonable Thoughts on the State of Religion in New England* (Boston: Rogers & Fowle, 1743), 239.

28. J. M. Bumsted, "Religion, Finance, and Democracy in Massachusetts: The Town of Norton as a Case Study," *Journal of American History* 57 (1971): 830; Goen, *Revivalism and Separatism,* 17–19. Cf. Lovejoy, *Religious Enthusiasm,* 179.

29. Edwards, *Great Awakening,* 232–33.

30. Edmund S. Morgan, *The Gentle Puritan: A Life of Ezra Stiles, 1727–1795* (New Haven: Yale Univ. Press, 1962), 33–34; Tracy, *Jonathan Edwards, Pastor,* 138–39; Goen, introduction to Edwards, *Great Awakening,* 34–35.

31. James Dow McCallum, *Eleazar Wheelock, Founder of Dartmouth College* (Hanover, N.H.: Dartmouth College Publications, 1939), 21–22; James Davenport to Stephen Williams, 9 February [1736], Gratz Collection, Historical Society of Pennsylvania, Philadelphia (hereafter HSP).

32. Richard Webster, *A History of the Presbyterian Church in America* (Philadelphia: Joseph M. Wilson, 1857), 536. See also Chauncy, *Seasonable*

Thoughts, 183–90, and William B. Sprague, ed., *Annals of the American Pulpit* (New York: Robert Carter & Brothers, 1858), 3:82–83.

33. Davenport to Wheelock, 9 July 1740, HSP.

34. Joseph Fish, *The Church of Christ, a Firm and Durable House* (New London: Timothy Green, 1767), 115–17; Trumbull, *A Complete History of Connecticut*, 2:157–60.

35. Richard Schechner, *Between Theater and Anthropology* (Philadelphia: Univ. of Pennsylvania Press, 1985), 10–12.

36. Morgan, *The Gentle Puritan*, 32–33; Christopher Jedrey, *The World of John Cleaveland: Family and Community in Eighteenth-Century New England* (New York: W. W. Norton, 1979), 21; Jared Ingersoll, "An Historical Account of Some Affairs Relating to the Church" (September 1741), Force Papers, series 7E, Library of Congress; Burr quoted in Webster, *History of the Presbyterian Church*, 538. Cf. Perry Miller, *Jonathan Edwards* (New York: William Sloane Associates, 1949), 169–70.

37. Jedrey, *The World of John Cleaveland*, 25–27; Ingersoll, "Historical Account" (28 November 1741, 30 December 1741, 14 February 1742), Library of Congress; Richard Warch, "The Shepherd's Tent: Education and Enthusiasm in the Great Awakening," *American Quarterly* 30 (1978): 183.

38. Charles Hoadley, ed., *The Public Records of the Colony of Connecticut* (Hartford: Case, Lockwood & Brain, 1874), 8:483; Ingersoll, "Historical Account" (20 May 1742), Library of Congress; Trumbull, *A Complete History of Connecticut*, 2:167–68; Goen, *Revivalism and Separatism*, 23.

39. Thomas Prince, "Some Accounts of the Revival of Religion in Boston," *Christian History for 1744*, 406–8; Dr. Cutler (minister of Boston's Church of England congregation) to the Secretary [of the S.P.G.], 30 June 1742, in William Stevens Perry, ed., *Papers Relating to the History of the Church in Massachusetts . . . 1676–1785* (N.p.: Privately printed, 1873), 362; Parkman's diary quoted in Tracy, *The Great Awakening*, 209.

40. Chauncy, *Seasonable Thoughts*, 196–99; Nathan Bowen's "Almanacs" in Bentley, *Diary*, 3:476–77; Mr. Brockwell to the Secretary [of the S.P.G.], 30 December 1742, in Perry, *Historical Collections*, 3:366.

41. Quoted in Sprague, *Annals of the American Pulpit*, 3:84–86.

42. Chauncy quoted in Warch, "Shepherd's Tent," 181–82; Nathaniel Gilman, "Diary," ed. William Kidder (M.A. thesis, Univ. of New Hampshire, 1972), 283. Typescript in the New Hampshire Historical Society, Concord.

43. Allen quoted in Warch, "Shepherd's Tent," 186–89; Harry S. Stout and Peter Onuf, "James Davenport and the Great Awakening in New London," *Journal of American History* 71 (1983): 575.

44. Ingersoll, "Historical Account," Library of Congress; Samuel Seabury to the Secretary [of the S.P.G.], 25 March 1743, in Hawks and Perry, eds., *Documentary History*, 189; Tracy, *The Great Awakening*, 248–49; Warch,

"Shepherd's Tent," 190–92; Stout and Onuf, "James Davenport," 575.

45. Joshua Hempstead, *Dairy of Joseph Hempstead of New London, Connecticut* (New London, Conn.: New London County Historical Society, 1901), 407.

46. Warch, "Shepherd's Tent," 194–96.

47. Davenport to Solomon Williams, 2 August 1744, in *Christian History for 1744*, 237–39.

48. Sprague, *Annals*, 3:88–91; Webster, *A History of the Presbyterian Church*, 542; Landsman, "Revivalism and Nativism," 158; Fish, *The Church of Christ*, 123–28; Davenport to Whitefield, 17 January 1757, quoted in Luke Tyerman, *The Life of the Rev. George Whitefield* (London: Hodder & Stoughton, 1876), 2:397n; Alan Heimert and Perry Miller, eds., *The Great Awakening: Documents Illustrating the Crisis and Its Consequences* (Indianapolis: Bobbs-Merrill, 1967), 389; James Davenport, *The Faithful Minister Encouraged . . .* (Philadelphia: James Chattin, 1756), 9.

49. Stephen A. Marini, *Radical Sects of Revolutionary New England* (Cambridge: Harvard Univ. Press, 1982), 19; Ahlstrom, *Religious History of the American People*, 290–92.

50. Goen, *Revivalism and Separatism*, 179; Fish, *The Church of Christ*, 140.

51. Cole, "The Spiritual Travels," 103. The Editor notes that Cole's phrase may have been derived from John Bunyan's spiritual autobiography, *Grace Abounding*.

52. Ibid., 103, 105.

53. Quoted in Goen, *Revivalism and Separatism*, 47–48, 82; quoted in Ola E. Winslow, *Meetinghouse Hill, 1630–1783* (New York: Macmillan, 1952), 378.

54. Goen, *Revivalism and Separatism*, 188–90; Peter Onuf, "New Lights in New London: A Group Portrait of the Separatists," *William and Mary Quarterly*, 3d ser. 37 (1980): 633–37; John W. Jeffries, "The Separation in the Canterbury Congregational Church: Religion, Family, and Politics in a Connecticut Town," *New England Quarterly* 52 (1979): 524–29, 541–42.

55. Quoted in Means, *A Sketch of the Strict Congregational Church of Enfield*, 41, 43. See also Francis Olcott Allen, ed., *The History of Enfield, Connecticut* (Lancaster, Pa.: Wickersham Printing Co., 1900), 2:1526–30, and Goen, *Revivalism and Separatism*, 85–86.

56. William G. McLoughlin, *New England Dissent, 1630–1833: The Baptists and the Separation of Church and State* (Cambridge: Harvard Univ. Press, 1971), 1:427–34, 437; Allen, *Enfield*, 2:1528–29, 1549; Henry F. Fletcher, *Studies in the History of Enfield, Connecticut* (Litchfield, Conn.: Enquirer Press, 1934), 7–8; James W. Greene, "The Meacham Family of Early Colonial Times," *New York Genealogical and Biographical Record* 65 (1934): 383.

57. Elizabeth Nordbeck, "Almost Awakened: The Great Revival in New Hampshire and Maine, 1727–1748," *Historical New Hampshire* 35 (1980):

47–48; Everett S. Stackpole and Lucien Thompson, *History of the Town of Durham, New Hampshire (Oyster River Plantation)* (1913; reprint, Somersworth, N.H.: New Hampshire Publishing Co., 1973), 1:184–85; Shipton, *Biographical Sketches*, 7:340.

58. Gilman, "Diary," 183, 241.

59. Ibid., 243, 253–55, 258.

60. Ibid., 274–79, 290.

61. Amos Everett Jewett and Emily Mabel Adams Jewett, *Rowley, Massachusetts: "Mr Ezechi Rogers Plantation," 1639–1850* (Rowley, Mass.: The Jewett Family of America, 1946), 144; Isaac Backus, *The Diary*, ed. William G. McLoughlin (Providence: Brown Univ. Press, 1979), 1:149.

62. Gilman, "Diary," 297–99.

63. Rogers quoted in Nordbeck, "Almost Awakened," 56.

64. Boston *Evening Post*, 30 July 1744, 1; Kidder, appendices to Gilman, "Diary," 392–94; Mr. Brockwell to the Secretary [of the S.P.G.], 1 August 1744, in Perry, *Historical Collections*, 3:387.

65. Samuel Chandler, "Diary" (20 August 1746), *New England Historical and Genealogical Register* 15 (1861): 23–24.

66. "A Record of the Transactions of the Annual Convocation of Ministers in the Province of N. Hampshire, begun July 28th, 1747," ed. Isaac W. Hammond, *Collections of the New Hampshire Historical Society* (Concord: For the Society, 1889), 9:7–8. Backus, *Diary*, 1:149.

67. Hannah Adams, *A Dictionary of All Religions and Religious Denominations* (Boston: James Eastburn & Co., 1817), 266; Ebenezer Parkman, "The Diary of Ebenezer Parkman, 1739–44" [31 December 1742], ed. Francis G. Walett, *Proceedings of the American Antiquarian Society* 72 (1962): 150.

68. Quoted in William G. McLoughlin, "Free Love, Immortalism, and Perfectionism in Cumberland, Rhode Island, 1748–1768," *Rhode Island History* 33 (1974): 74.

69. Isaac Backus, *A History of New England with Particular Reference to the Baptists* (1871; reprint New York: Arno Press, 1969), 2:11; Backus, *Diary*, 1:141.

70. Backus, *Diary*, 1:570 and n; and 2:703 and n; *Testimonies of the Life, Character, Revelations, and Doctrines of Our Ever Blessed Mother Ann Lee . . .* (Hancock, Mass.: J. Talcott & J. Deming, 1816), 128; Frances Caulkins, *History of New London, Conn.* (New London: H. D. Ulley, 1895), 457n.

71. Ebenezer Parkman, "The Diary of Ebenezer Parkman, 1754–55," ed. Francis G. Walett, *Proceedings of the American Antiquarian Society* 76 (1966): 188 [6 August 1754] and 161 [10 June 1755]; Backus, *Diary*, 1:293.

72. Shipton, *Biographical Sketches*, 8:249–51 (Prentice quoted 252); Samuel Abbott Green, *Groton Historical Series. A Collection of Papers Relating to the Town of Groton, Massachusetts* (Groton: Univ. Press at Cambridge, 1887–99),

1:27; *New England Historical and Genealogical Register* 6 (1852): 273.

73. Solomon Prentice, "Narrative of the Great Awakening," ed. Ross W. Beales, Jr., *Massachusetts Historical Society Proceedings* 83 (1971): 135.

74. Ibid., 136–41; Parkman, "Diary, 1739–44," 151–52.

75. Ebenezer Parkman, "The Diary of Ebenezer Parkman, 1745–46," ed. Francis G. Walett, *Proceedings of the American Antiquarian Society* 72 (1962): 208, 360, 402; Shipton, *Biographical Sketches*, 251.

76. Ezra Stiles, *Extracts from the Itineraries and Other Miscellanies*, ed. Franklin Bowditch Dexter (New Haven: Yale Univ. Press, 1916), 416; Parkman, "Diary, 1739–44," 161.

77. Backus, *History*, 2:462.

78. Ibid., 462; McLoughlin, *New England Dissent*, 738–39; Seth Chandler, *History of the Town of Shirley, Massachusetts . . .* (Shirley: Published by the author, 1883), 708.

79. J. M. Bumsted, "Presbyterianism in Eighteenth-Century Massachusetts: The Formation of a Church at Easton, 1752," *Journal of Presbyterian History* 46 (1968): 251–52; Stiles, *Itineraries*, 250; Parkman quoted in Shipton, *Biographical Sketches*, 8:256.

80. Goen, *Revivalism and Separatism*, 107, 187; Marini, *Radical Sects*, 25–28; Bumsted, "Norton," 830; Nathan O. Hatch, "New Lights and the Revolution in Rural New England," *Reviews in American History* 8 (1980): 323.

Chapter 6 A Prophetess in Manchester

1. Thomas Story, *The Life of Thomas Story*, revised and enlarged by William Alexander (York: William Alexander, 1831), 2:354; Hillel Schwartz, *The French Prophets: The History of a Millenarian Group in Eighteenth-Century England* (Berkeley and Los Angeles: Univ. of California Press, 1980), 217, 278, 289.

2. John Wesley, *The Journal*, ed. Nehemiah Curnock (1911; reprint, London: Epworth Press, 1938), 2:136, 226.

3. Anna White and Leila S. Taylor, *Shakerism: Its Meaning and Message* (1904; reprint, New York: AMS Press, 1971).

4. William J. Haskett, *Shakerism Unmasked, or the History of the Shakers* (Pittsfield, Mass.: By the author, 1828), 20; Thomas Brown, *An Account of the People Called Shakers* (1812; reprint, New York: AMS Press, 1971), 311–12.

5. *Testimonies of the Life, Character, Revelations, and Doctrines of Our Ever Blessed Mother Ann Lee, and the Elders with Her . . .* (Hancock, Mass.: J. Talcott & J. Deming, 1816) [hereafter *Testimonies 1816*]; "A Short Account of the Rise of Believers," Shaker Collection, V: B-60, Western Reserve Historical Society, Cleveland, Ohio [hereafter WRHS] (microfilm copy, Library of Congress). I am grateful to the late Theodore Johnson of the Sabbathday

Lake Shaker community for sharing the results of his own researches in Manchester with me.

6. John Jenkins, "Records and Recollections" (compiled 1821–22), typescript copy in the Friends' Reference Library, London; "Friends and the French Prophets," *The Journal of the Friends Historical Society* 22 (1925): 3; Hillel Schwartz, *The French Prophets in England: A Social History of a Millenarian Group in the Early Eighteenth Century* (Ann Arbor, Mich.: University Microfilms, 1974), 327n.

7. See Chapter 2 above. On the question of Quaker influence on the Shakers, see Lawrence Foster, *Religion and Sexuality: Three American Communal Experiments of the Nineteenth Century* (New York: Oxford Univ. Press, 1981), 24.

8. *Testimonies of the Life, Character, Revelations, and Doctrines of Mother Ann Lee and the Elders with Her*, 2d ed. (1888; reprint, New York: AMS Press, 1975), 50 [hereafter, *Testimonies 1888*].

9. George Whitefield, *Memoirs* (Salem, Mass.: Cushing & Appleton, 1801), 134–37; Robert Philip, *The Life and Times of the Reverend George Whitefield, M.A.* (New York: D. Appleton & Co., 1838), 427–32; *Dictionary of National Biography*, s.v. "Whitefield, George," by Alexander Gordon; Arnold Dallimore, *George Whitefield* (Westchester, Ill.: Cornerstone Books, 1980), 2:383–401.

10. Whitefield quoted in Stephen Marini, *Radical Sects in Revolutionary New England* (Cambridge: Harvard Univ. Press, 1982), 13.

11. John D. Walsh, "Elie Halevy and the Birth of Methodism," *Transactions of the Royal Historical Society*, 5th ser. 25 (1975): 7; Luke Tyerman, *The Life and Times of the Rev. John Wesley, M.A., Founder of the Methodists* (New York: Harper & Brothers, 1872), 2; John Wesley, *Journal*, 3:295, 520; J. Musgrave, *Origin of Methodism in Bolton* (Bolton: H. Bradbury, 1865), 4; *Short Sketches of the Work Carried on by the Ancient Protestant Episcopal Moravian Church . . . in Lancashire, Cheshire, the Midlands, and Scotland from 1740* (Leeds: Goodall & Suddick, 1888), 3–5; John Bennet, "The Life of John Bennet," Methodist Archives, John Rylands Library, Manchester.

12. John Wesley, *The Letters*, ed. John Telford (London: Epworth Press, 1931), 4:30; Charles Wesley, *The Journal* (1849; reprint, Grand Rapids: Baker Book House, 1980), 2:128–37.

13. Quoted in Frank Baker, *William Grimshaw, 1708–1763* (London: Epworth Press, 1963), 194.

14. Wesley, *Journal*, 5:9–18; Tyerman, *Life of Wesley*, 3:432–34; Baker, *Grimshaw*, 74; *Arminian Magazine* 3 (1780): 674–75 and 5 (1782): 126.

15. John Wesley, *Journal*, 4:540; *Arminian Magazine* 13 (1790): 42.

16. Ralph Mather to Henry Brooke, November 1775, Walton MSS, Dr.

Williams's Library, London. On Mather, see also Clarke Garrett, "Sweden-borg and the Mystical Enlightenment in Late Eighteenth-Century England," *Journal of the History of Ideas* 45 (1984): 77–81.

17. *Harrop's Manchester Mercury,* 5 May 1752, 4; 21 July 1752, 4; 28 July 1752, 4; 20 March 1753, 4; 27 March 1757, 4. Microfilm copy in the library of Sab-bathday Lake Shaker community.

18. Mather to Brooke, November 1775, Dr. Williams's Library; William Holland to unknown, n.d., MS 1076, John Rylands Library, Manchester; *Arminian Magazine* 6 (1783): 499 and 18 (1795): 74–75; John Byrom, *The Pri-vate Journal and Literary Remains,* published in *Chetham Society Remains* 44 (1857): 629–30.

19. Quoted in John F. C. Harrison, *The Second Coming: Popular Mil-lenarianism, 1780–1850* (New Brunswick, N.J.: Rutgers Univ. Press, 1979), 19; F. Ernest Stoeffler, *German Pietism during the Eighteenth Century* (Leiden: E. J. Brill, 1973), 169–70.

20. "A Short Account of the Rise of Believers," WRHS.

21. Mather to Brooke, 1 March 1778, Dr. Williams's Library; Musgrave, *Methodism in Bolton,* 15–20.

22. Brown, *An Account of the People Called Shakers,* 220; Frederick W. Evans, *Autobiography of a Shaker* (1869; reprint, New York: AMS Press, 1970), 60.

23. Garrett, "Swedenborg and the Mystical Enlightenment," 73, 78; James Dakeyne, *History of the Bolton New Church Society from 1781 to 1898* (Bolton: Speirs, 1888), 1.

24. Alfred P. Wadsworth and Julia De Lacy Mann, *The Cotton Trade and Industrial Lancashire, 1600–1780* (New York: Augustus M. Kelley, 1968), 241, 311; Francois Vigier, *Change and Apathy: Liverpool and Manchester during the Industrial Revolution* (Cambridge: M.I.T. Press, 1970), 86–113; P. Russell, Esq. ed., *England Displayed, Being a New, Complete, and Accurate Survey and Description of the Kingdom of England* (London: Adlard & Brown, 1769), 1:87; William Arthur Shaw, *Manchester Old and New* (London: Cassell & Com-pany, n.d.), 2:1.

25. *Testimonies 1816,* 66; "A Short Account of the Rise of Believers"; "Inci-dents of Father John Hocknell," VI: B-10, WRHS.

26. Haskett, *Shakerism Unmasked,* 15–16.

27. Edward Deming Andrews, *The People Called Shakers: A Search for the Perfect Society,* 2d ed. (New York: Dover Publications, 1963), 5–7.

28. *Testimonies 1816,* 50–57, 65.

29. Quoted in William E. A. Axon, *Lancashire Gleanings* (Manchester: Tubbs, Brook & Crystal, 1883), 86; Andrews, *The People Called Shakers,* 4; *Testimonies 1816,* 60–61.

30. *Virginia Gazette,* 9 November 1769, 1.

31. Jemima Blanchard, quoted in Robley Edward Whitson, ed., *The Shakers: Two Centuries of Spiritual Reflection* (New York: Paulist Press, 1983), 273; Valentine Rathbun, *Some Brief Hints of a Religious Scheme . . .* (Boston: Benjamin Edel, 1782), 7; Daniel Patterson, *The Shaker Spiritual* (Princeton: Princeton Univ. Press, 1979), 59.

32. Patterson, *The Shaker Spiritual,* 11, 60; Henry Nicholson, *The Falsehood of the New Prophets . . .* (London: Joseph Downing, 1708), 14; Kenneth Carroll, "Singing in the Spirit in Early Quakerism," *Quaker History* 73 (1984): 1–13.

33. *Testimonies concerning the Character and Ministry of Mother Ann Lee* (Albany: Packard and Van Benthuysen, 1827), 130, 170 [hereafter *Testimonies 1827*].

34. Haskett, *Shakerism Unmasked,* 20; *Testimonies 1816,* 45. It is interesting to note that the statement does not appear in later Shaker histories, which emphasize instead Ann Lee's complete obedience to the leadership of the Wardleys until her divine revelation of 1770.

35. *Testimonies 1816,* 6–7, 49, 61–63; *Testimonies 1888,* 5; Haskett, *Shakerism Unmasked,* 20.

36. James Hutton, "James Hutton's Second Account of the Moravian Work in England, Down to the Year 1747," MS 1076, John Rylands Library, Manchester.

37. Stoeffler, *German Pietism,* 215.

38. John Wesley, "Thoughts on a Single Life," in *The Works of the Reverend John Wesley, A.M.,* ed. John Emory (New York: T. Mason & G. Lane, 1839), 6:540–42.

39. Mary Pratt to Henry Brooke, 16 January 1792, Walton MSS, Dr. Williams's Library.

40. Francisco de Miranda, *The Diary of Francisco de Miranda: Tour of the United States, 1783–1784,* ed. William Spence Robertson (New York: Hispanic Society of America, 1928), 72.

41. *Testimonies 1888,* 220, 224, 238, 240.

42. *Testimonies 1888,* 166.

43. *Extract from an Unpublished Manuscript on Shaker History* (1850), 12 (microfilm reel 22, item 300, Shaker Collection, Library of Congress).

44. Testimony of Elizabeth Wood, VI: B-1, WRHS.

45. *Testimonies 1888,* 260–62; testimony of Abijah Wooster, VI: A-5, WRHS.

46. *Testimonies 1888,* 288.

47. Haskett, *Shakerism Unmasked,* 20–22.

48. *Testimonies 1816,* 66; *Testimonies 1888,* 50.

49. Haskett, *Shakerism Unmasked,* 24; James Whittaker to his parents,

Jonathan and Ann Whittaker, 20 February 1784 (microfilm reel 5, item 80, Shaker Collection, Library of Congress).

50. David Erdman, *Blake: Prophet against Empire,* 3d ed. (Princeton: Princeton Univ. Press, 1974), 14.

Chapter 7 The Woman in the Wilderness

1. The various primary and secondary accounts are in disagreement on practically every detail concerning the Shakers' first years in America. See *Testimonies of the Life, Character, Revelations, and Doctrines of our Ever Blessed Mother Ann Lee, and the Elders with Her . . .* (Hancock, Mass.: J. Talcott & J. Deming, 1816), 8–9 [hereafter *Testimonies 1816*]; *Testimonies of the Life, Character, Revelations, and Doctrines of Mother Ann Lee and the Elders with Her,* 2d ed. (1888; reprint, New York: AMS Press, 1975), 7–8 [hereafter *Testimonies 1888*]; *Testimonies concerning the Character and Ministry of Mother Ann Lee* (Albany: Packard & Van Benthuysen, 1827), 42 [hereafter *Testimonies 1827*]; Mary Hocknell's testimony in *A Review of Mary M. Dyer's Publication Entitled a Portraiture of Shakerism* (Concord: Jacob B. Moore, 1824), 62; Isaac Backus, *Diary,* ed. William G. McLoughlin (Providence: Brown Univ. Press, 1979), 2:1097; Thomas Brown, *An Account of the People Called Shakers* (1812; reprint, New York: AMS Press, 1971), 46, 315–16; William J. Haskett, *Shakerism Unmasked, or the History of the Shakers* (Pittsfield, Mass.: By the author, 1828), 26–29; Ezra Stiles, *The Literary Diary,* ed. F. B. Dexter (New York: Charles Scribner's Sons, 1901), 2:510; and Dorothy M. Filley, *Recapturing Wisdom's Valley: The Watervliet Shaker Heritage, 1775–1975* (Albany: Town of Colonie and Albany Institute of History and Art, 1975), 11. Cf. Edward Deming Andrews, *The People Called Shakers: A Search for the Perfect Society,* 2d ed. (New York: Dover Publications, 1963), 15–16.

2. Anna White and Leila S. Taylor, *Shakerism: Its Meaning and Message* (1904); reprint, New York: AMS Press, 1971), 82.

3. Filley, *Wisdom's Valley,* 11–12; Andrews, *The People Called Shakers,* 16–17; Richard Smith, *A Tour of Four Great Rivers,* ed. Francis W. Halsey (New York: Charles Scribner's Sons, 1906), 4, 16; Sung Bok Kim, "A New Look at the Great Landowners of Eighteenth-Century New York," *William and Mary Quarterly,* 3d ser. 27 (1970): 581–614; David M. Ellis et al., *A Short History of New York State* (Ithaca: Cornell Univ. Press, 1957), 75, 105–9; *Dictionary of American Biography,* s.v. "Van Renssalaer, Stephen."

4. Calvin Green, "Biographical Memoirs," 17 (microfilm reel 5, item 78, Shaker Collection, Library of Congress); *Testimonies 1816,* 12.

5. Revelation 12:1. The Shakers cited this passage specifically, saying the wilderness was "a place near Albany," when they talked to William Plumer

in 1782 (Plumer to Miss Coombs, 17 June 1782, Plumer Papers, Library of Congress).

6. James Thacher, *Military Journal of the American Revolution* ... (Hartford: Hurlbut, Williams & Company, 1862), 141–42. The entry is dated 28 July 1778. On James Thacher's later distinguished career as a physician and writer, see *Dictionary of American Biography*, s.v. "Thacher, James," and *National Cyclopaedia of American Biography*, 7:401–2.

7. Boston *Gazette*, 2 November 1778; William G. McLoughlin, *New England Dissent, 1630–1833: The Baptists and the Separation of Church and State* (Cambridge: Harvard Univ. Press, 1971), 1:614.

8. Richard Birdsall, *Berkshire County: A Cultural History* (New Haven: Yale Univ. Press, 1959), 17–22; Stephen A. Marini, *Radical Sects of Revolutionary New England* (Cambridge: Harvard Univ. Press, 1982), chap. 2.

9. Alfred B. Chace, "Columbia County in the Revolutionary Period," a special issue of *The Bulletin of the Columbia County Historical Society*, March 1933, unpaged; Thomas P. Hughes, *American Ancestry: Volume II (Local Series) Columbia County, State of New York–1887* (Albany: Joel Munsell's Sons, 1887), v–vi; Jackson Turner Main, *The Social Structure of Revolutionary America* (Princeton: Princeton Univ. Press, 1965), 13–15, 24.

10. Peter Werden to Isaac Backus, 29 August 1779, Backus Papers, Trask Library, Andover-Newton Seminary , Newton, Mass. [hereafter TLAN]. The letter is reprinted (with modernized spelling) in Isaac Backus, *A History of New England with Particular Reference to the Baptists*, 2d ed. (1871; reprint, New York: Arno Press, 1969), 2:279.

11. Marini, *Radical Sects*, 40–48; Backus, *Diary*, 2:1027, 1057, 1066, 1077.

12. *Testimonies 1827*, 106; Haskett, *Shakerism Unmasked*, 30; Andrews, *The People Called Shakers*, 18; Franklin Bowditch Dexter, *Biographical Sketches of the Graduates of Yale College* ... (New York: Henry Holt & Co., 1885), 3:341. In 1785, the Presbyterian church was reorganized on a congregational basis (*The Bulletin of the Columbia County Historical Society*, July 1944–April 1945, 3).

13. Quoted in Daryl Chase, "The Early Shakers: An Experiment in Religious Communism" (Ph.D. diss., Univ. of Chicago, 1936), 22.

14. *Testimonies 1827*, 157.

15. John Chauncy Pease, "An Historical Sketch of the Town of Enfield," in Francis Olcott Allen, ed., *The History of Enfield, Connecticut* (Lancaster, Pa.: Wickersham Printing Co., 1900), 1:13–20; James W. Greene, "The Meacham Family of Early Colonial Times," *New York Genealogical and Biographical Record* 65 (1934): 383; Oliver Williams Means, *A Sketch of the Strict Congregational Church of Enfield, Connecticut* (Hartford: Hartford Seminary Press, 1899), 28–33.

16. Calvin Green, "Biographical Account of the Life, Character, and

Ministry of Father Joseph Meacham," ed. Theodore E. Johnson, *Shaker Quarterly* 10 (1979): 22–24. According to Darryl Chase, ("The Early Shakers," 129n), Meacham's oldest son John was born in Claverack, N.Y. in 1770.

17. C. C. Goen, *Revivalism and Separatism in New England, 1740–1800: Strict Congregationalists and Separate Baptists in the Great Awakening* (1962; reprint, New York: Archon Books, 1969), 47, 174–78; McLoughlin, *New England Dissent*, 1:351–53; Hannah Adams, *A Dictionary of All Religions and Religious Denominations* (Boston: James Eastburn & Company, 1817), 266.

18. Green, "Biographical Account," 24–25; John Robinson's testimony (February 1830), Shaker Collection, VI: A-8, Western Reserve Historical Society [hereafter WRHS], Cleveland. Microfilm copy at the Library of Congress.

19. *Testimonies 1827*, 88, 108. Samuel Johnson's very detailed description of his ecstatic experiences before and after his conversion to Shakerism is reprinted in Robley Edward Whitson, ed., *The Shakers: Two Centuries of Spiritual Reflection* (New York: Paulist Press, 1983), 49–55.

20. *Testimonies 1827*, 106; Backus, *History of the Baptists*, 475; J.E.A. Smith, *The History of Pittsfield (Berkshire County), Massachusetts* (Springfield, Mass.: C. W. Bryan & Co., 1876), 1:178.

21. William Plumer to Miss Coombs, 19 February 1783, Plumer Papers, Library of Congress.

22. Haskett, *Shakerism Unmasked*, 31; Green, "Biographical Memoir," 25. The numerous Shaker testimonies are very sketchy on the first crucial encounter with the Shakers. See, for example, White and Taylor, *Shakerism: Its Meaning and Message*, 36–37.

23. Green, "Biographical Memoir," 26.

24. Haskett, *Shakerism Unmasked*, 31.

25. *Testimonies 1827*, 109–112, 88.

26. Testimony of Elizabeth Williams and Martha Deming, Shaker Collection, VI: A4 and VI: A2, WRHS.

27. Daniel W. Patterson, *The Shaker Spiritual* (Princeton: Princeton Univ. Press, 1979), 76; Brown, *An Account of the People Called Shakers*, 321.

28. Boston *Gazette*, 22 and 29 May 1780; William G. McLoughlin, "Olney Winsor's 'Memorandum' of the Phenomenal 'Dark Day' of May 19, 1780," *Rhode Island History* 26 (1967): 88–91; Angell Matthewson, "Reminiscences in the Form of a Series of Thirty-nine Letters to His Brother Jeffrey," Shaker MS 119, New York Public Library [hereafter NYPL]. I have corrected Matthewson's erratic if engaging spelling and punctuation.

29. Clifford Geertz, "Thick Description: Toward an Interpretive Theory of Culture," in *The Interpretation of Cultures: Selected Essays* (New York: Basic Books, 1973), 5–14; Geertz, "Religion as a Cultural System," in Michael Banton, ed., *Anthropological Approaches to the Study of Religion* (New York:

Frederick Praeger, 1966), 8–14; E. E. Evans-Pritchard, *Witchcraft, Oracles, and Magic among the Azande* (Oxford: Clarendon Press, 1937), 193–95; Robin Horton, "African Traditional Thought and Western Science," in Max Marwick, ed., *Witchcraft and Sorcery: Selected Readings* (Harmondsworth: Penguin Books, 1970), 366–67; Michael Polanyi, *Personal Knowledge: Towards a Post-Critical Philosophy*, 2d ed. (Chicago: Univ. of Chicago Press, 1962), 286–94.

30. Marini, *Radical Sects*, 47–48; Backus, *Diary*, 2:1048 and n; Asa Hunt to Isaac Backus, 31 May 1780, and Biel Ledoyt to Isaac Backus, 13 June 1780, Backus Papers, TLAN.

31. William Plumer to Miss Coombs, 19 February 1783, Plumer Papers, Library of Congress.

32. Holland, *History of Western Massachusetts*, 2:496–99; Smith, *The History of Pittsfield*, 1:178–82, 452–55; *History of Berkshire County* (New York: J. B. Beers & Co., 1885), 2:70, 286–95, 390–94; "History of Hancock," compiled by Anna May Smith, MS no. 13,377, Shaker Museum, Old Chatham, NY.

33. Thankful Goodrich, "Recollections," in Edward Deming Andrews Collection, SA 799.1, Winterthur Library, Wilmington.

34. Daniel Rathbun, *Letter . . . to James Whittacor [sic], Chief Elder of the Church Called Shakers* (Springfield, Mass: Printing Office, 1785), 113.

35. On Valentine Rathbun, see *History of Berkshire County*, 2:390–92; and Smith, *History of Pittsfield*, 452–55. On the value of Rathbun's pamphlet, cf. Andrews, *The People Called Shakers*, 27–28.

36. Marini, *Radical Sects*, 89.

37. Valentine Rathbun, *Some Brief Hints of a Religious Scheme Taught and Propagated by a Number of Europeans, Living in a Place Called Nisqueunia, in the State of New-York* (Boston: Benjamin Edel, 1782), 2–11.

38. Ibid., 6, 18.

39. Ibid.; John F. C. Harrison, *The Second Coming: Popular Millenarianism* (New Brunswick, N.J.: Rutgers Univ. Press, 1979), chap. 5; Clarke Garrett, *Respectable Folly: Millenarians and the French Revolution in France and England* (Baltimore: Johns Hopkins Press, 1975), chap. 4.

40. Ollive Miller, "A Brief Sketch of the Different Interviews Ollive Miller Enjoyed with Mother and the First Elders," Andrews Collection, SA 799.1, Winterthur.

41. Rathbun, *Some Hints*, 14, 19.

42. Testimony of Nathan Slosson, VI: A-6, WRHS.

43. *Testimonies 1816*, 70–72; New York Commission for Detecting and Defeating Conspiracies, *Minutes of the Commissioners for Detecting and Defeating Conspiracies in the State of New York. Albany County Sessions, 1780–81*, ed. Victor Hugo Paltsits (Albany: State of New York, 1910), 2:452–53; Hamilton Vaughan Bail, "Zadock Wright: That 'Devilish' Tory of Hartland," *Vermont History* 36 (Autumn 1968), 192–200.

44. *Minutes of the Commissioners*, 2:469–70, 506–7, 517–18, 553–55, 569–92; George Clinton, *Public Papers of George Clinton, First Governor of New York* (Albany: J. B. Lyon Co., 1902), 6:421; *Testimonies 1827*, 44, 89.

45. *Testimonies 1827*, 44; Haskett, *Shakerism Unmasked*, 39–41; Brown, *An Account of the People Called Shakers*, 318–19; testimony of Anna Cogswell, VI:A-4, WRHS. Cf. White and Taylor, *Shakerism: Its Meaning and Message*, 45–46.

46. *Minutes of the Commissioners*, 2:678, 723–24.

Chapter 8   Into New England

1. *Testimonies concerning the Character and Ministry of Mother Ann Lee* (Albany: Packard & Van Benthuysen, 1827), 169–70 [hereafter *Testimonies 1827*].

2. Elizabeth Wood's testimony, VI: B-1, Shaker Collection, Western Reserve Historical Society, Cleveland [hereafter WRHS], microfilm copy at the Library of Congress; Jeremy Belknap, "The Belknap Papers," *Collections of the Massachusetts Historical Society*, 5th ser. 2 (1877): 307.

3. John Chauncy Pease, "An Historical Sketch of the Town of Enfield," in Francis Olcott Allen, ed., *The History of Enfield, Connecticut* (Lancaster, Pa.: Wickersham Printing Co., 1900), 1:50.

4. Box 1, items 7 and 12, Shaker Collection, Library of Congress; Oliver William Means, *A Sketch of the Strict Congregational Church of Enfield, Connecticut* (Hartford: Hartford Seminary Press, 1899), 28–33, 43–46; "Shaker Death Records," *New England Historical and Genealogical Register* 115 (1961): 124–30.

5. Isaac Backus, *A History of New England with Particular Reference to the Baptists* (1871; reprint, New York: Arno Press, 1969), 2:297, 462; Thomas Hammond, "Sketches of Shadrach Ireland," and testimony of Deliverance and Beulah Cooper, VI: A-8, B-4, B-9, WRHS. See also Seth Chandler, *History of the Town of Shirley, Massachusetts, from its Early Settlement to A.D. 1882* (Shirley: Published by the author, 1883), 708–9.

6. Isaac Holden to Isaac Parker, copied by Parker in his letter to Isaac Backus, 28 June 1784, Backus Papers, Trask Library, Andover-Newton Seminary, Newton, Mass. [hereafter TLAN]. I have added punctuation and corrected the spelling. Backus summarizes Holden's account in *History of the Baptists*, 2:462. Although the sources of Holden's information were Abigail Lougee, Ireland's spiritual wife, and Abigail Cooper (both of whom became Shakers), the Shakers' printed histories all claim that Ireland died fearful and despairing.

7. Edward R. Horgan, *The Shaker Holy Land: A Community Portrait* (Harvard, Mass.: Harvard Common Press, 1982), 21–22; Angell Matthewson,

"Reminiscences in the Form of a Series of Thirty-nine Letters to His Brother Jeffrey," letter 3, Shaker Collection no. 119, Manuscripts and Archives Division, New York Public Library [hereafter NYPL]; testimony of Jemima Blanchard and Beulah Cooper, VI: B-9, WRHS.

8. "Further Testimonies of Shadrach Ireland," VI: A-11, WRHS.

9. Stephen A. Marini, *Radical Sects of Revolutionary New England* (Cambridge: Harvard Univ. Press, 1982), 90–95; *Testimonies of the Life, Character, Revelations, and Doctrines of our Ever Blessed Mother Ann Lee, and the Elders with Her...* (Hancock: J. Talcott & J. Deming, 1816), 90; [hereafter *Testimonies 1816*], Hammond, "Sketches of Shadrach Ireland," VI: A-8, WRHS; Backus, *History of the Baptists,* 464; William G. McLoughlin, *New England Dissent, 1630–1833: The Baptists and the Separation of Church and State* (Cambridge: Harvard Univ. Press, 1971), 2:713.

10. VI: A-8, WRHS.

11. *Testimonies of the Life, Character, Revelations, and Doctrines of Mother Ann Lee, and the Elders with Her...,* 2d ed. (1888; reprint, New York: AMS Press, 1975): 89–90 [hereafter *Testimonies 1888*]; testimony of Jemima Blanchard, VI: B-9, WRHS.

12. *Testimonies 1888,* 89–90; William Plumer to Lydia Coombs, 17 June 1782, Plumer Papers, Library of Congress. See also Amos Taylor, *A Narrative of the Strange Principles, Conduct, and Character of the Shakers* (Worcester, Mass.: Printed for the author, 1782), 15.

13. *New England Historical and Genealogical Register* 61 (1907): 341–44; Priscilla Brewer, "The Demographic Features of the Shaker Decline, 1787–1900," *Journal of Interdisciplinary History* 15 (1984): 35–36, 43; "Further Testimonies of Shadrach Ireland," VI: A-11, WRHS.

14. William Plumer to Lydia Coombs, 19 February 1783, Library of Congress.

15. Valentine Rathbun, *Some Hints of a Religious Scheme Taught and Propagated by a Number of Europeans...* (Boston: Benjamin Edel, 1782), 6.

16. Matthewson, "Reminiscences," letter 3, NYPL. In all quotations from Matthewson's "Reminiscences," I have corrected the wildly erratic spelling and added punctuation.

17. Jackson Turner Main, *The Social Structure of Revolutionary America* (Princeton: Princeton Univ. Press, 1965), 11–13; Backus, *History of the Baptists,* 2:468; McLoughlin, *New England Dissent,* 1:531–46.

18. Matthewson, "Reminiscences," letter 3, NYPL; testimony of Hannah Chauncy, VI: A-6, WRHS.

19. Quoted in Frederick Howes, *History of the Town of Ashfield* (N.p.: Published for the town, n.d.), 371; see also John H. Morgan, "The Baptist-Shaker Encounter in New England: A Study in Religious Confrontation in Eighteenth-Century America," *Shaker Quarterly* 13 (1973): 29.

20. Matthewson, "Reminiscences," letters 5 and 6, NYPL; *Testimonies 1816*, 106–8; testimony of Amos Buttrick, VI: B-11, WRHS.

21. Matthewson, "Reminiscences," letters 2 and 3, NYPL; testimony of Anne Matthewson, *Testimonies 1827*, 47.

22. *Testimonies 1816*, 128.

23. Elizabeth Wood's testimony, VI: B-1, WRHS; *Testimonies 1816*, 127–32.

24. *Testimonies 1816*, 135; Matthewson, "Reminiscences," letter 4, NYPL; Robley Edward Whitson, ed., *The Shakers: Two Centuries of Spiritual Reflection* (New York: Paulist Press, 1983), 181.

25. James Whittaker to [Josiah Talcott], 25 February 1782 (microfilm reel 5, item 80, Shaker Collection, Library of Congress). Edward Deming Andrews, *The People Called Shakers: The Search for the Perfect Society*, 2d ed. (New York: Dover Publications, 1963), 48, identifies the recipient of the letter as Josiah Talcott.

26. Matthewson, "Reminiscences," letter 7, NYPL; Taylor, *Narrative*, 15; Daniel Rathbun, *Letter . . . to James Whittacor, Chief Elder of the Church Called Shakers* (Springfield, Mass.: At the Printing-Office, 1785), 49; Isaac Backus, *The Diary*, ed. William G. McLoughlin (Providence: Brown Univ. Press, 1979), 2:1098.

27. *The Cooley Genealogy*, compiled by Vivien Bullock Keatley (Rutland, Vt.: Tuttle Publishing Company, 1941), 502.

28. Hamilton Child, comp., *Gazeteer: Grafton County, N.H., 1709–1886* (Syracuse: Syracuse Journal Company, 1886), 218, 234; Charles E. Clark, *The Eastern Frontier: The Settlement of Northern New England, 1610–1763* (Hanover, N.H.: University Press of New England, 1983), 354–55; James W. Greene, "The Meacham Family of Early Colonial Times," *New York Genealogical and Biographical Record* 65 (1934): 386–89.

29. Hamilton Vaughan Bail, "Zadock Wright: That 'Devilish' Tory of Hartland," *Vermont History* 36 (1968): 201–3; Anna White and Leila S. Taylor, *Shakerism: Its Meaning and Message* (1904; reprint, New York: AMS Press, 1971), 88–90.

30. Henry Blinn, "Historical Narrative of the Rise and Progress of the United Society of Shakers, Enfield, N.H." (1858), 27, xeroxed copy in the Shaker Archive, Sabbathday Lake, Maine; Wilson B. Roberts's information concerning the Pattee family, in Nellie Pierce Collection, ML 19, Box 3, Dartmouth College; Frederic Clarke Jewett, *History and Genealogy of the Jewetts of America* (Rowley, Mass.: Jewett Family of America, 1908), 1:80, 142–143; Robert F. W. Meader, "Another Lost Utopia," *Shaker Quarterly* 4 (1864): 123–24; David R. Proper, "More Notes on 'Lost Communities,'" *Shaker Quarterly* 6 (1966): 45–47.

31. Testimony of Joseph Stanley, Sarah Meacham, and Joshua Stevens, in Mary Marshall [Dyer], *A Portraiture of Shakerism* (1822; reprint, New York:

AMS Press, 1972), 135; Dan Charette, ed., "A Historical Narrative of the Rise and Progress of the United Society of Shakers in Enfield, N.H.," quoted in Marini, *Radical Sects,* 113; testimony of Jacob Heath and Jacob Hunt, in *Testimonies 1888,* 209–10; Blinn, *Historical Narrative,* 34–39.

32. Samuel Shepard to Isaac Backus, 28 May 1783, Backus Collection, TLAN; Lucius Harrison Thayer, *The Religious Condition of New Hampshire at the Beginning of the Nineteenth Century* (N.p., 1901), 16; *Free Baptist Cyclopaedia Historical and Biographical,* ed. G. A. Burgess and J. T. Ward (Chicago: Free Baptist Cyclopaedia Co., 1889), s.v. "New Hampshire" and "Lock, Edward"; Marini, *Radical Sects,* 66–67.

33. John Whitcher, "A Brief History of the Commencement & Progress of the United Society of Believers at Canterbury" (1845), 4–7, Shaker archives, Canterbury Shaker Village, N.H.; Calvin Green, "Biography of Elder Henry Clough," VI: B-25, WRHS.

34. I. D. Stewart, *The History of the Freewill Baptists* (Dover, N.H.: Freewill Baptist Printing Establishment, 1862), 1:67; James Otis Lyford, *History of the Town of Canterbury, New Hampshire, 1727–1912* (1912; reprint, Canterbury, N.H.: Canterbury Historical Society, 1973), 316–17, 352–53; Andrews, *The People Called Shakers,* 38; testimony of Alice Beck in Marshall, *Portraiture of Shakerism,* 142; Shepard to Backus, 28 May 1783, TLAN; Whitcher, "Brief History," Canterbury.

35. Belknap to Ebenezer Hazard, "The Belknap Papers," 327; William Plumer to Miss Coombs, 19 February 1783, Plumer Collection, Library of Congress.

36. Whitcher, "Brief History," 17–21, Canterbury; Plumer to Lydia Coombs, 19 February 1783, Library of Congress. See also the testimony of Alice Beck in Marshall, *A Portraiture of Shakerism,* 144–47.

37. Hugh McLellan, *History of Gorham, Me.,* completed and edited by Katharine B. Lewis (Portland: Smith & Sale, 1903), 200–203. See also Charles E. Waterman, "Shaker Communities of Maine," *Sprague's Journal of Maine History* 6 (1919): 139–46; and Marini, *Radical Sects,* 53.

38. Testimony of Elisha Pote, VI: A-1, WRHS.

39. Mildred Barker, "A History of 'Holy Land'–Alfred, Maine," *Shaker Quarterly* 3 (1963): 75–76; letter from Peter Coffin, quoted in Usher Parsons, *A Centennial History of Alfred, York County, Maine* (Philadelphia: Collins, 1872), 21, 23.

40. Quoted in Otis Sawyer, "Alfred, Me.," *The Manifesto* 15 (1885): 12. See also White and Taylor, *Shakerism: Its Meaning and Message,* 93–95.

41. Sawyer, "Alfred, Me.," 33.

42. Plumer to Lydia Coombs, 19 February 1783, Library of Congress; Isaac Backus, *Diary,* 2:1103 ["Travel Journal" for 28–29 June 1782].

43. Marini, *Radical Sects,* 100.

Chapter 9   Spiritual Wars and Sharp Testimonies

1. Thomas Brown, *An Account of the People Called Shakers* ... (1812; reprint, New York: AMS Press, 1971), 320; "Incidents Related by Jemima Blanchard," compiled by Roxlana Grosvenor, Shaker Collection, VI: B-9, Western Reserve Historical Society, Cleveland [hereafter WRHS].

2. Valentine Rathbun, *Some Brief Hints of a Religious Scheme Taught and Propagated by a Number of Europeans, Living in a Place Called Nisquenuia, in the State of New-York* (Boston: Benjamin Edes, 1782), 17.

3. Lawrence Foster, *Religion and Sexuality: Three American Communal Experiments of the Nineteenth Century* (New York: Oxford Univ. Press, 1981), 51–54.

4. *Testimonies of the Life, Character, Revelations, and Doctrines of Mother Ann Lee* ... , 2d ed. (1888; reprint, New York: AMS Press, 1975) 158, 252 [hereafter *Testimonies 1888*].

5. Richard Warch, "The Shepherd's Tent: Education and Enthusiasm in the Great Awakening," *American Quarterly* 30 (1978): 177–98. See Chapter 4 herein.

6. William Plumer to Lydia Coombs, 17 June 1782, Plumer Papers, Library of Congress; Daniel Rathbun, quoted in Mary Marshall [Dyer], *A Portraiture of Shakerism* ... (1822; reprint, New York: AMS Press, 1972), 48; Angell Matthewson, "Reminiscences in the Form of a Series of Thirty-nine Letters to His Brother Jeffrey," letters 4 and 22, no. 119, Shaker Collection, Manuscripts and Archives Division, New York Public Library [hereafter NYPL]; Josiah Watson's testimony in Marshall, *A Portraiture of Shakerism*, 138; Eunice Wild's testimony, compiled by Roxlana Grosvenor, VI: B-9, WRHS; Benjamin S. Youngs, "Early Journal," 58, MS 10,514, Emma B. King Library, Shaker Museum, Old Chatham, N.Y. See also Brown, *An Account*, 321; and Calvin Green, "Biographical Memoirs of the Life & Experiences" (microfilm reel 5, item 78, Shaker Collection, Library of Congress). In all quotations from Matthewson's "Reminiscences," I have corrected the spelling and added punctuation.

7. *Testimonies 1888*, 204.

8. Matthewson, "Reminiscences," letter 5, NYPL.

9. Rathbun, *Some Brief Hints*, 11; Brown, *An Account*, 321; Matthewson, "Reminiscences," letter 7, NYPL; testimony of Eunice Wild, VI: B-9, WRHS.

10. Plumer to Coombs, 23 February 1783, Library of Congress.

11. "Sketches from Beulah Cooper's Experience," compiled by Roxlana Grosvenor, VI: B-9, WRHS.

12. *Testimonies 1888*, 288; Reuben Rathbun, *Reasons for leaving the Shakers* (Pittsfield, Mass.: Chester Smith, 1800), 6.

13. Rathbun quoted in Marshall, *A Portraiture of Shakerism*, 66, 52–53;

Isaac Backus, *The Diary*, ed. William G. McLoughlin (Providence: Brown Univ. Press, 1979), 2:1148; testimony of Eunice Wilds, compiled by Roxlana Grosvenor, VI: B-9, WRHS; Joseph Meacham to [Calvin Harlow and Sarah Harrison], n.d., copied by Daniel Goodrich, Edward Deming Andrews Collection, SA 799.1, Winterthur Library, Wilmington.

14. *Testimonies 1888*, 124–25.

15. *Testimonies 1888*, 126–30; testimony of Alpheus Rude, VI: A-4, WRHS.

16. Daniel Rathbun, *Letter . . . to James Whittacor, Chief Elder of the Church Called Shakers* (Springfield, Mass.: at the Printing-Office), 17 and 45.

17. Brown, *An Account*, 291.

18. John Clarke Cooley, ed., *Rathbone Genealogy* (Syracuse: Press of the Courier Job Printing, 1898), 325–26, 352–53, 483–84; C. C. Goen, *Revivalism and Separatism in New England, 1740–1800: Strict Congregationalism in the Great Awakening* (1962; reprint, New York: Archon Books, 1969), 236–39.

19. Brown, *An Account*, 291 and n; Matthewson, "Reminiscences," letter 4, NYPL; testimony of Elizabeth Wood, VI: B-1, WRHS.

20. Backus, *Diary*, 2:1099; D. Rathbun in Marshall, *Portraiture*, 57.

21. *Testimonies 1888*, 140n.

22. Brown, *An Account*, 292.

23. François, Marquis de Barbé-Marbois, *Our Revolutionary Forefathers: The Letters of François, Marquis de Barbé-Marbois*, trans. Eugene Parker Chase (New York: Duffield & Company, 1929), 181; Isaac Backus, *A History of New-England with Particular Reference to the Baptists* (1871; reprint New York: Arno Press, 1969), 2:297; Jeremy Belknap to Ebenezer Hazard, 27 February 1784, "The Belknap Papers," *Collections of the Massachusetts Historical Society*, 5th ser. (Boston: Published by the Society, 1877), 2:307; *American Magazine, or Repository* 1 (February 1787), 165.

24. William J. Haskett, *Shakerism Unmasked, or the History of the Shakers* (Pittsfield, Mass.: By the author, 1828), 74.

25. Cotton Mather, *Diary 1709–1724, Collections of the Massachusetts Historical Society*, 7th ser. (Boston: Published by the Society), 68: 51; Mark Edward Lender and James Kirby Martin, *Drinking in America: A History* (New York: Free Press, 1982), 30–34; Jere R. Daniell, *Colonial New Hampshire: A History* (Millwood, N.Y.: KTO Press, 1981), 171; Matthew Patten, *The Diary of Matthew Patten of Bedford, N.H.* (Concord, N.H.: Rumford Printing Co., 1903), 417–18, 430–35, and passim; *Ames's Almanac, 1776*, contained in the diary of Daniel Rogers, New England Genealogical Historical Society, Boston.

26. Edward Deming Andrews, *The People Called Shakers: A Search for the Perfect Society*, 2d ed. (New York: Dover Publications, 1963), 305n., 53, 54; Anna White and Leila S. Taylor, *Shakerism: Its Meaning and Message* (1904; reprint, New York: AMS Press, 1971), 55.

27. James Whittaker to [Jonathan and Ann Whittaker], 20 February 1784 (microfilm reel 5, item 80, Shaker Collection, Library of Congress).

28. "Corrections and Additional Testimonies to Testimonies of . . . Ann Lee," VI: A-11, WRHS.

29. "Incidents Related by Jemima Blanchard," compiled by Roxlana Grosvenor, VI: B-9, WRHS; "Testimonies or Wise Sayings," VI: B-11, WRHS; Otis Sawyer, "Alfred, Me.," *The Manifesto*, 15 (1885): 34; testimony of Levit Clough in Marshall, *A Portraiture of Shakerism*, 96–97n.

30. Testimony of Elizabeth Wood, VI: B-1, WRHS.

31. Brown, *An Account*, 47, 170, 174. In 1816, two years after he had left the Shakers, Veeder repeated his allegations before a New York state legislative committee (Marshall, *Portraiture*, 253).

32. Marshall, *Portraiture of Shakerism*, 290.

33. "Testimonies or Wise Sayings . . . ," VI: B-11, WRHS; testimony of Elizabeth Wood, Andrews Collection, SA 799.1, Winterthur Library; William Lee quoted in *A Summary View of the Millennial Church* (1848; reprint, New York: AMS Press, 1973), 48; Whittaker quoted in *Testimonies 1888*, 267–68; White and Taylor, *Shakerism: Its Meaning and Message*, 63–65.

34. Haskett, *Shakerism Unmasked*, 50–53; Matthewson, "Reminiscences," letter 7, NYPL.

35. *Notable American Women, 1607–1950: A Biographical Dictionary* (Cambridge: Belknap Press of Harvard Univ. Press, 1971), s.v. "Wright, Lucy," by Edward Deming Andrews; Calvin Green, "Biographical Memoir of Mother Lucy Wright," VI: B-27, WRHS.

36. *Testimonies 1888*, 258; Reuben Rathbun, *Reasons for Leaving*, 6, 27–28; Brown, *An Account*, 290, 324; testimony of Jonathan Symonds in Mary Marshall [Dyer], *The Rise and Progress of the Serpent* . . . (Concord: N.H.: Printed for the author, 1847), 40.

37. *Testimonies 1888*, 267.

38. Matthewson, "Reminiscences," letter 8, NYPL.

39. Calvin Green, "Biography of Elder Henry Clough," VI: B-25, WRHS, confirms the statements in Freewill Baptist histories and Marshall's *Portraiture* that many at Canterbury left the Shakers in 1784.

40. Joel Munsell, *The Annals of Albany*, 2d ed. (Albany: Joel Munsell, 1869–71), 2:288.

41. Barbé-Marbois, *Our Revolutionary Forefathers*, 181. Barbé-Marbois and the marquis de Lafayette visited Niskeyuna shortly after Ann Lee's death.

Chapter 10   The Gathering into Order

1. François, Marquis de Barbé-Marbois to Mlle. d'Alleray, 14 September 1784, in Barbé-Marbois, *Our Revolutionary Forefathers: The Letters of François,*

Marquis de Barbé-Marbois, trans. and ed. Eugene Parker Chase (New York: Duffield & Co., 1929), 180–81.

2. Ibid., 183.

3. Calvin Green, "Biographical Memoirs of the Life & Experiences . . . " (microfilm reel 5, item 78, Shaker Collection, Library of Congress).

4. Quoted in Robley Edward Whitson, ed., *The Shakers: Two Centuries of Spiritual Reflection* (New York: Paulist Press, 1983), 269–71.

5. Angell Matthewson, "Reminiscences in the Form of a Series of Thirty-Nine Letters to His Brother Jeffrey," letter 8, Shaker Collection no. 119, Manuscripts and Archives Division, New York Public Library [hereafter NYPL]; Thomas Brown, *An Account of the People Called Shakers* (1812; reprint, New York: AMS Press, 1971), 331; Reuben Rathbun, *Reasons for Leaving the Shakers* (Pittsfield, Mass.: Chester Smith, 1800), 8.

6. *American Magazine, or Repository* 1 (February 1787): 163–64.

7. Calvin Green, "Biographical Account of the Life, Character & Ministry of Father Joseph Meacham . . . 1827," ed. Theodore E. Johnson, *Shaker Quarterly* 10 (1970): 27; Matthewson, "Reminiscences," letter 8, NYPL; R. Rathbun, *Reasons for Leaving the Shakers,* 7. In quoting Matthewson, I have corrected his spelling and punctuation.

8. Henry Van Schaack to James Whittaker, 20 November 1784, in Henry Van Schaack, *Memoirs* (Chicago: A. C. McClurg & Company, 1982), 113; James Whittaker to [Jonathan and Ann Whittaker], 20 February 1784, Shaker Collection, reel 5, item 80, Library of Congress; Rathbun quoted in Mary Marshall [Dyer], *A Portraiture of Shakerism* (1882; reprint, New York: AMS Press, 1972), 46.

9. James Whittaker to Joseph Meacham, 23 May 1786, Shaker Collection, IV A-77, Western Reserve Historical Society, Cleveland [hereafter WRHS] (microfilm copy in Library of Congress); Edward Deming Andrews, *The People Called Shakers: A Search for the Perfect Society,* 2d ed. (New York: Dover Publications, 1963), 52; William S. Haskett, *Shakerism Unmasked, or the History of the Shakers* (Pittsfield, Mass.: By the author, 1828), 94; Brown, *An Account,* 326.

10. Brown, *An Account,* 325–26; Haskett, *Shakerism Unmasked,* 93–94; Matthewson, "Reminiscences," letter 8, NYPL. See also Isaac Backus, *The Diary,* ed. William G. McLoughlin (Providence: Brown Univ. Press, 1979), 2:1075 and n; Andrews, *The People Called Shakers,* 51; and Morrell Baker's testimony, VI: A-6, WRHS.

11. *Testimonies of the Life, Character, Revelations, and Doctrines of Mother Ann Lee, and the Elders with Her . . .* (1888; reprint, New York: AMS Press, 1975), 286, 294 [hereafter *Testimonies 1888*].

12. Matthewson, "Reminiscences," letter 9, NYPL.

13. Stephen A. Marini, *Radical Sects of Revolutionary New England* (Cambridge: Harvard Univ. Press, 1982) 11–12.

14. Matthewson, "Reminiscences," letter 9, NYPL; Haskett, *Shakerism Unmasked,* 94; Mildred Barker, "A History of 'Holy Land'–Alfred, Maine," *Shaker Quarterly* 3 (1963): 86; Henry Blinn, "A Historical Narrative of the Rise and Progress of the United Society of Shakers, Enfield, New Hampshire" (1858), 46 [xeroxed copy in the Shaker Archives, Sabbathday Lake, Maine]; Marini, *Radical Sects,* 113–14.

15. *Testimonies 1888,* 294; testimony of John Robinson, VI: A-8, WRHS; Marini, *Radical Sects,* 114; R. Rathbun, *Reasons for Leaving the Shakers,* 7.

16. *Testimonies 1888,* 296–97; Green, "Meacham," 28; Matthewson, "Reminiscences," letters 9 and 10, NYPL; "History of the Church at Mt. Lebanon, N.Y.," *The Manifesto* 19 (1889): 148, 169–70.

17. Andrews, *The People Called Shakers,* 54.

18. Green, "Meacham," 27.

19. Testimony of John Robinson, VI: A-8, WRHS.

20. Matthewson, "Reminiscences," letter 10, NYPL.

21. Joseph Meacham to Lucy Wright [1796] (microfilm reel 19, Shaker Collection, Library of Congress).

22. Testimony of John Robinson, VI: A-8, WRHS.

23. "Millennial Laws, printed in Andrews, *The People Called Shakers,* 265; John McKelvie Whitworth, *God's Blueprints: A Sociological Study of Three Utopian Sects* (London: Routledge and Kegan Paul, 1975), 24; R. Rathbun, *Reasons for Leaving the Shakers,* 8; testimony of Daniel Goodrich in "Manuscripts Found among the Writings of Deacon Daniel Goodrich Sn^r," 2, Andrews Collection, Winterthur Library, Wilmington.

24. Green, "Biographical Memoirs," 12–17, Library of Congress.

25. Jonathan Clark's testimony in Goodrich, "Manuscripts," 65–67, Winterthur Library; Dorothy M. Filley, *Recapturing Wisdom's Valley: The Watervliet Shaker Heritage, 1775–1975,* ed. Mary L. Richmond (Albany: Town of Colonie and Albany Institute of History and Art, 1975), 14.

26. Andrews, *The People Called Shakers,* 56–57; Whitworth, *God's Blueprints,* 24–25; Matthewson, "Reminiscences," letter 12, NYPL; Green, "Meacham," 52–53; Lucy Wright, "Mother Lucy's Sayings Spoken at Different Times and under Various Circumstances," *Shaker Quarterly* 8 (1968): 103.

27. Andrews, *The People Called Shakers,* 57; Whitworth, *God's Blueprints,* 25–27.

28. Edward Deming Andrews, *The Community Industries of the Shakers* (1932; reprint, Philadelphia: Porcupine Press, 1972), 48–50, 67–68; "A Short Account of the Rise of Believers," V: B-60, WRHS; Edward Deming Andrews and Faith Andrews, *Work and Worship among the Shakers: Their Craftsman-*

ship and Economic Order (New York: Dover Publications, 1974), 44; Finney, *Wisdom's Valley*, 15; John Whitcher, "A Brief History of the Commencement & Progress of the United Society of Believers at Canterbury" [1845], Shaker Archives, Canterbury Shaker Village, Canterbury, N.H.

29. Julian Ursyn Niemcewicz, *Under Vine and Fig Tree: Travels through America in 1797–99, 1805 with Some Further Account of Life in New Jersey*, ed. and trans. Metchie J. E. Budka, vol. 14 of the Collections of the New Jersey Historical Society (Elizabeth, N.J.: Grassman Publishing Co., 1965), 179; William Bentley, *The Diary* (Salem, Mass.: Essex Institute, 1905), 2:149–51 (14 July 1795) and 173 (23 February 1796).

30. Testimony of John Robinson, VI: A-8, WRHS; Green, "Meacham," 63; Matthewson, "Reminiscences," letter 12, NYPL.

31. Copy of an undated letter from Joseph Meacham to the New Lebanon First Family in Goodrich, "Manuscripts," 37, Winterthur Library.

32. "Records Kept by the Church," Shaker Collection no. 7, NYPL; Blinn, "Historical Narrative," 37; Margaret Fuller Melcher, "Admiration Grew: The New Enfield Shakers," *Shaker Quarterly* 1 (1961): 92.

33. Goodrich, "Manuscripts," 1–6, Winterthur Library.

34. Whitcher, "Brief History, 23–32, 38, Canterbury; David Starbuck, ed., *Canterbury Shaker Village* (Durham, N.H.: Univ. of New Hampshire Press, 1981), 8–10; Rebecca Clark's testimony in Goodrich, "Manuscripts," 105–6, Winterthur Library.

35. Marini, *Radical Sects,* chap. 7; Whitworth, *God's Blueprints,* 213–14; Rosabeth Moss Kanter, *Commitment and Community: Communes and Utopias in Sociological Perspective* (Cambridge: Harvard Univ. Press, 1972), chap. 4.

36. Joseph Meacham, *A Concise Statement of the Principles of the Only True Church* . . . (Bennington, Vt.: Haswell & Russell, 1790), 15–16; Benjamin Waterhouse, "Dr. Benjamin Waterhouse's Journey to Saratoga Springs in the Summer of 1794," ed. Barbara Damon Simon, *Yale University Library Gazette* 40 (1965): 100.

37. VI: B-11, WRHS; Matthewson, "Reminiscences," letters 13 and 15, NYPL.

38. Quoted in Green, "Meacham," 100.

39. Daniel W. Patterson, *The Shaker Spiritual* (Princeton: Princeton Univ. Press, 1979), 107–16; Whitcher, "Brief History," 32, Canterbury.

40. William Loughton Smith, "Journal, 1790–91," *Massachusetts Historical Society Proceedings* 51 (1917): 49–51.

41. Waterhouse, "Journal," 102; Green, "Biographical Memoirs," 49, Library of Congress; Patterson, *The Shaker Spiritual,* 116–17.

42. "History of the Church at Mount Lebanon," 217.

43. Brown, *An Account,* 334; Haskett, *Shakerism Unmasked,* 106; Matthewson, "Reminiscences," letter 14, NYPL.

44. R. Rathbun, *Reasons for Leaving the Shakers,* 4, 6, 9, 13–15; Brown, *An Account,* 334; anonymous diary (Hancock), MS no. 10,514, Anna B. King Collection, Shaker Museum, Old Chatham, N.Y.

45. Goodrich, "Manuscripts," 5 and 17, Winterthur Library; Green, "Biographical Memoirs," 49, 76, Library of Congress.

46. Green, "Meacham," 61; testimony of Alice Beck in Marshall, *A Portraiture of Shakerism,* 51, 175.

47. Jethro Turner, "Memorandum" (microfilm reel 5, no. 83, Shaker Collection, Library of Congress); Mathewson, "Reminiscences," letter 15, NYPL.

48. Matthewson, "Reminiscences," letter 15, NYPL; Green, "Biographical Memoirs," 19–20, Library of Congress; Turner, "Memorandum," WRHS; Samuel Johnson, Jr., "Diary," MS no. 10,114, Shaker Museum, Old Chatham.

49. Green, "Biographical Memoirs," 42–47, Library of Congress; Isaac Youngs, "Memorandum," V: A-3, WRHS; "Records of the United Society of Believers for the Years 1788 to 1804 Inclusive," V: B-62A, WRHS; *Western Star* (Stockbridge, Mass.), 11 February 1796, printed in Flo Morse, *The Shakers and the World's People* (New York: Dodd, Mead & Co., 1980), 62; Whitcher, "Brief History," 42–45, Canterbury; Bentley, *The Diary,* 2:152; Patterson, *The Shaker Spiritual,* 116; Blinn, "Historical Narrative," 53–54, Sabbathday Lake; testimony of John Lyons, VI: A-3, WRHS.

50. Green, "Biographical Memoirs," 40–42, Library of Congress; testimony of Thankful Goodrich, VI: B-9, WRHS; Matthewson, "Reminiscences," letter 19, NYPL; "Records Kept by the Church," NYPL.

51. Meacham to Wright, [1796], Library of Congress.

52. Matthewson, "Reminiscences," letter 23, NYPL.

53. Marini, *Radical Sects,* 133; Andrews, *The People Called Shakers,* 67–69; Whitworth, *God's Blueprints,* 37.

54. Green, "Biographical Memoirs," 88, 101, Library of Congress; *A Summary View of the Millennial Church . . . ,* 2nd ed. (1848; reprint, New York: AMS Press, 1973), 258–71.

55. Green, "Biographical Memoirs," 83–85, 160, Library of Congress.

56. Andrews, *The People Called Shakers,* chap. 8; David R. Lamson, *Two Years' Experience among the Shakers . . .* (1848; reprint, New York: AMS Press, 1971).

Index

Fage, Durand, 41–42, 53, 57
Faithful Narrative of the Surprising Work of God, A (Edwards), 92
Farrington, John, 184, 215
Fatio de Duillier, Nicolas, 59
Fetter Lane Society. *See* Religious societies
Finland, 21
Finney, Charles G., 241
Fish, Rev. Joseph, 120, 128
Fitch, Samuel, 168, 175, 201–2; as missionary, 177, 185; at New Lebanon, 235
Fléchier, Bp. Esprit, 27
Foster, Lawrence, 197
Foundery. *See* Religious societies
Fox, George, 60
Francke, August, 36–37, 60, 62, 115, 130
Frankfort, 67
Franklin, Benjamin, 51
Freewill Baptists, 187–89, 190–94; and Shakers, 193–94
French and Indian War, 163
French Prophets, 54, 94, 151–52, 224, 239–40; in Bristol, 83, 85; and Community of True Inspiration, 73; on European continent, 61–63; later career, 140–41; in London, 42–54, 84; and Methodists and Moravians, 79, 85; new rituals, 49, 54–55, 63, 195; and Shakers, 141–42
Freud, Sigmund, 4
Furly, Benjamin, 59–60

Gazette (Albany), 213
Geertz, Clifford, 170
Gifts of the spirit, 117, 124, 134, 158, 215; and French Prophets, 45–46, 140; and Meacham, 222, 232; and New Lights, 128, 166; Saint Paul on, 8; and Shakers, 150, 153, 172, 180–83, 196, 212–17
—specific gifts: dancing, 133, 162; glossolalia, 2, 8, 149, 151, 159, 168, 189, 238; healing, 52, 199; nakedness, 197, 208–10; singing, 133, 150–51, 212; visions, 2, 7, 110, 187; visions and Great Awakening, 114–15, 131, 136; visions and Methodists, 81, 102–4, 144; visions and Shakers, 104, 158, 169, 174, 189; whirling, 151, 162, 191–92
Gilman, Rev. Nicholas, 124, 130–33, 191
Gleim, J. C., 72
Glossolalia. *See* Gifts of the spirit
Gloucester, Mass., 116. *See also* Essex County
Goen, C. C., 110, 128–29
Goodrich, Benjamin, 236
Goodrich, Daniel, 232
Goodrich, Elizur, 211
Goodrich, Hannah, 230
Goodrich family, 194
Gorham, Me., 191
Grace Abounding (Bunyan), 101, 263n.51
Grafton, Mass., 135–38, 178. *See also* Worcester County
Grafton County, N.H., 186
Gray, Elizabeth, 51, 57
Great Awakening, debates concerning, 106–7
Great Barrington, Mass., 202
Greece, 2
Green, Calvin, 215, 238; on Meacham, 165, 222; on New Lebanon, 168, 224–25, 233–35
Grim, John A., 4
Grimshaw, Rev. William, 91
Gross, Andreas, 67
Gruber, Eberhard, 69–71
Gruber, Johann Adam, 69–72, 173

Hall, David D., 106
Halle, 60–61, 64–66, 74; French Prophets in, 62, 64
Halle University, 14, 61, 107
Hamilton, Rev. William, 94
Hancock, Mass., 164–66, 229–30, 234
Harlow, Calvin, 168, 175, 180, 217, 229, 234; as missionary, 185; and Shaker succession, 221–22
Harlow, Isaac, 169, 176
Harris, Howell, 85
Hartland, Vt., 186
Harvard, Mass., 138, 178–81, 201–2, 236;

communalism in, 223, 227–29

Harvard College, 107, 123–24

Hasidism, 154

Haskett, William, 141, 148, 152–53, 168, 210

Haydon, John, 81

Hempstead, Joshua, 120, 125

Hessen-Kassel, 39

Hicks, Rev. William, 99

Hill, Christopher, 84

History of New England (Backus), 179, 205

Hocknell, John, 148, 159, 175, 218, 221; and Niskeyuna, 160, 177; spiritual gifts of, 158, 199

Hocknell, Mary, 209

Holden, Isaac, 273 n.6

Holland, William, 145

Hollis, Isaac, 79–80, 140–41

Hopkins, Samuel, 108

Horneck, Dr. Anthony, 36

Huckins, Hannah, 133

Huguenots: dispersal, 35, 38–45, 61–62; and popular religion, 17; and social class, 23

Huntingdon, Countess of, 105

Hutton, James, 77, 89–90, 154

Hysteria, 3–4, 136

Iconoclasm: and Camisards, 29–31; at New London, 124–25, 198; and Shakers, 198–200

Immortalism, 134–38, 178–79, 181–82, 213. *See also* Perfectionism

Ingersoll, Jared, 124

Ingham, Benjamin, 91

Inspired, German. *See* Community of True Inspiration

Ipswich, Mass., 116–17. *See also* Essex County

Ireland, Shadrach, 137–38, 178–79

Isaiah, 106, 210

Jacobites, 54, 96

Jeanne des Anges, 40

Jenkins, James, 86

Jesus, 7, 27

Jewett, James, 192

Jewett family, 186

Joel, 7–8, 19, 239

John, Saint (Second Epistle), 217

Johnson, Elizabeth, 167, 169

Johnson, Rev. Samuel, 164, 167–68, 175–76

Johnson, Samuel, Jr., 236

Jurieu, Mme. Hélène, 60, 65

Jurieu, Pierre, 18, 22, 33, 35, 60

Keimer, Mary, 51, 54, 57

Keimer, Samuel, 49–52, 54–55, 252 n.31

Keith, George, 60

Kelpius, Johannes, 13

Kentucky Revival, 238

Kidney, Jacob, 175

King, Anna Maria, 52

Kingswood, 85–88. *See also* Bristol

Knauth, Rev., 64

Knox, Ronald, 2

Kreiser, Robert, 23

Labadie, Jean de, 36

Lacy, John, 45, 48, 50, 173

Lafayette, Marquis de, 214, 238

Lancashire, popular religion in, 142–43, 153

Lanesborough, Mass., 164

Lausanne, 26, 39

Lavington, Mary, 84

Law, William, 89, 130

Lead, Jane, 14, 155

Lee, Ann, 135, 161–62, 170–71, 175–77, 202; as charismatic leader, 172, 185, 189–90, 207, 211–13; death of, 207–14, 217, 222; in England, 104, 148–59, 268 n.34; and Shadrach Ireland, 138; Meacham on, 231; and Methodists, 101, 104; nineteenth-century views on, 231, 238; on spirit possession, 196; and Whitefield, 143; Whittaker on, 218

Lee, Gen. Henry, 162

Lee, John, 149–50

Lee, Nancy (Ann), 218

Pote, Elisha, 191
Pott brothers, 66–67
Potter, John, 52–53
Prague, 71
Pratt, Joel, 185
Pratt, Mrs. Mary, 156
Prentice, Sarah Sartell, 135–38
Prentice, Rev. Solomon, 135–38, 171
Price, Caleb, 99–100
Prince, Rev. Thomas, 115, 125
Princeton College, 125
Prophetic tradition, 3, 195, 239; and
    Huguenots, 25, 154; and Ann Lee, 157;
    and New Testament, 7–8; and Old
    Testament, 6–7, 31, 39
Prophets, false, 39, 56, 69–70, 118
Psalms, 18–19, 25, 32, 64, 181

Quakers: in America, 107; in Bristol, 83;
    and French Prophets, 50; and mysti-
    cism, 37; and Pietism, 47; and popular
    religion, 47, 142; and Puritans, 14; and
    Shakers, 141–42, 160, 210; and spirit
    possession, 46; and women's role, 21,
    56

Randall, Benjamin, 187, 192
Ranters, 14, 83
Rathbun, Amos, 171
Rathbun, Daniel, 193, 196, 202–4; on
    Meacham, 198; on Whittaker, 218
Rathbun, Daniel, Jr., 203–4, 209
Rathbun, John, 203
Rathbun, Reuben, 196, 204, 211, 217–18;
    and celibacy, 200–201, 233–34; on
    Whittaker, 216, 221
Rathbun, Valentine, 171–74, 183, 196,
    205–6; and American Revolution, 167;
    on Shakers, 151, 171–72, 182; and spirit
    possession, 173
Rathbun, Valentine, Jr., 226
Rathbun family, 183, 203–4
Rehoboth, Mass., 183, 217
Religion and Sexuality (Foster), 197
"Religious affections," 109, 127, 131
Religious societies, 96, 107, 130, 144, 155;

in Church of England, 76, 78; and
    Methodists, 77–78, 90; and Moravians,
    78, 89
Revelation (of Saint John the Divine),
    20, 55–56, 162, 170–71, 182; and Ann
    Lee, 173, 186–88, 216–17; and Philadel-
    phia Society, 14; and Shaker com-
    munalism, 224
Revolution of 1688, 36–37
Richelieu, Cardinal, 15
Ring, Eliphus, 229
Roach, Rev. Richard, 48, 56–57
Robe, Rev. James, 95–96, 105, 131
Rock, Johann Friedrich, 69, 72
Rogers, Rev. Daniel, 116, 124, 131–32
Rogers, Rev. John, 131
Rogers, Rev. Nathaniel, 116, 124
Rome, 65
Rowland, Rev. John, 126
Ryan, Sarah, 120

Sabbathday Lake. *See* New Gloucester
Sacred theater, 3–5, 138, 216; and French
    Prophets, 44; and Methodists, 79; in
    New England revivals, 109, 113, 120,
    127–28, 172; and Shakers, 153, 169, 179,
    183, 200, 234, 238–39
Samuel, 7
Sartell, Capt. Nathaniel, 136
Savoy, Vt., 238
Schechner, Richard, 5
Schuchart, Anna Maria, 62
Schwartz, Hillel, 26, 57, 65
Schwarzenau, 70
Secession Church (Scotland), 92–94
Second Coming, 9, 149, 165, 168, 187;
    and Shakers, 189, 202, 215
Separatism, religious: in England, 38; in
    Germany, 36, 38, 64, 68; in New
    England, 124, 127, 133–37, 166, 183
Seven Years' War, 143
Shakerism Unmasked (Haskett), 210
Shamanism, 3–4, 195
Shelburne, Mass., 219
Shepard, Samuel, 188
Shepherd, James, 161, 211–12, 218

Shepherd's Tent, 124–25, 198
Shirley, Mass., 227, 229
Shrieve, Mrs., 80
Smith, Lucretia, 87
Smith, Nathaniel, 137
Southcott, Joanna, 173
Southold, L.I., 119, 123
Spener, Philipp, 14, 36, 66; *Pia Desideria*, 36–37
Spirit possession, 173, 213; defined, 2, 4–6, 10; Edwards on, 118; in Kentucky Revival, 238; in Maine, 193–94; and Shakers, 154, 191, 195–96
Spiritualism, 241
Staffordshire, 97
Standerin, Abraham, 149, 159, 161
Steed, Ann, 47
Stiles, Ezra, 137
Stockholm, 63
Stoner, Amos, 164
Stonington, Conn., 138, 183
Story, Thomas, 140
Strict Congregationalists, 127–29, 134, 164. *See also* Separatism
Suicide, and Conn. revivals, 110
Superville, Daniel de, 60
Swedenborg, Emmanuel, 146–47, 241

Talcott, Josiah, 184–85, 275n.25
Tennent, Gilbert, 105, 110, 112, 120
Tennent, William, Sr., 124
Testimonies . . . of Mother Ann Lee, 153, 156, 161, 212–13; on New England Shakers, 187, 196–97, 199, 202, 206; on Shaker origins, 149–50; on Whittaker, 200, 219
Thacher, Dr. James, 162
Théâtre sacré des Cévennes, 44, 66, 146n.10
Théot, Catherine, 173
Thirty Years' War, 13, 39, 61, 67
Townley, John, 148, 150, 158
Trance preaching, 20–22
Treaty of Utrecht, 63
Trinity, Holy, 216–17
Trumbull, Benjamin, 112

Turner, Gideon, 174
Turner, Jethro, 235–36
Turner, Victor, 1, 6, 95, 232

Universalists, 185
Upton, Mass., 178

Vallérargues, 19, 29–30
Van Renssalaer family, 160
Van Schaack, Henry, 218
Varton, John, 103–4
Veeder, Derrick, 209, 279n.31
Vienna, 63
Vincent, Isabeau, 19–21, 24, 39
Viney, Richard, 90
Virginia Gazette (Williamsburg), 152
Visions. *See* Gifts of the spirit
Vivarais, 25–28

Walsh, John D., 76
Wardley, James and Jane, 141, 148, 152–53, 157, 268n.34
War of the Spanish Succession, 63
Wars of Religion, French, 30
Washington, George, 161, 239
Watervliet, N.Y. *See* Niskeyuna
Watson, Josiah, 198
Way of Christ Discovered (Boehme), 145
Webster, Rev. Alexander, 94
Weekly History (Glasgow), 92
Werden, Peter, 164
Wesley, Charles, 76, 80, 84, 88, 90, 144
Wesley, John, 76, 80–83, 97–100, 140–41, 146; on celibacy, 155–56; conversion, 78; and Edwards, 92, 118; on Montanus, 9; and Moravians, 72, 77, 89–90, 102; as preacher, 82–83; on Scottish Awakening, 96; and spirit possession, 76, 80, 88–89
Wesley, Samuel, 79, 81
West Stockbridge, Mass., 167
Wetterau, 67, 70–72, 78
Wharton, Hannah, 77
Wheelock, Rev. Eleazar, 110, 116–17, 125
Whitcher, Benjamin, 190
Whitcher, John, 188, 190, 232

White, Eldress Anna, 141, 206
White, Rev. John, 116
Whitefield, George, 85–86, 105, 128, 130, 155, 241; in America, 110–12, 120; on conversion, 75, 77; on Edwards, 92; in Lancashire, 143; in Scotland, 92–93, 96; on spirit possession, 83
Whittaker, James, 148–49, 160–61, 173–77, 180, 196–97, 206; and celibacy, 158, 200; and communalism, 184–85, 207; leadership of, 208, 210–14, 216–21; and Meacham, 168, 172
Wight, Reuben, 168
Wightman, Valentine, 203
Wild, Eunice, 198, 201
Willard, Isaac, 178
William III, 26, 29
Williams, Rev. Solomon, 125
Williamstown, Mass., 229
Willison, Rev. John, 92
Wise, Rev. Jeremiah, 132
Witchcraft, 40, 178, 189
Withrow, Abraham, 56
Wittgenstein family, 67
Woman in the Wilderness. *See* Chapter of Perfection

Women, role of: and French Prophets, 54, 56; Meacham on, 223; and Quakers, 142; and Shakers, 229–30, 237; as trance preachers, 21
Wood, Aaron, 183, 199, 221
Wood, Daniel, 178–79
Wood, Elizabeth, 157, 177–78, 184, 204, 208
Wood, Jonathan, 182–83, 219
Wood family, 194
Woodbury, Richard, 130–33
Woodman, Elizabeth, 180
Wooster, Abijah, 157–58, 231
Worcester County, Mass., 127, 135–37
Wright, Lucy, 211, 219, 223–24, 226
Wright, Zadock, 175, 186, 229
Wurttemberg, 37
Wynantz, Francis, 77

Yale College, 107, 118, 121–24, 236
Yorkshire, 91
Youngs, Benjamin, 199
Yzenburg, 67, 70

Zinzendorf, Count Ludwig, 72, 80, 91–92